BLOOD HARMONY

ALSO BY BARRY MAZOR

Ralph Peer and the Making of Popular Roots Music

*Meeting Jimmie Rodgers: How America's Original Roots
Music Hero Changed the Pop Sounds of a Century*

The
EVERLY BROTHERS
Story

BLOOD
HARMONY

BARRY MAZOR

DA CAPO
New York   Boston

Da Capo
Hachette Book Group
1290 Avenue of the Americas, New York, NY 10104
grandcentralpublishing.com
@grandcentralpub

First Edition: July 2025

Da Capo is an imprint of Grand Central Publishing. The Da Capo name and
logo are registered trademarks of Hachette Book Group, Inc.

The publisher is not responsible for websites (or their content) that are not owned by
the publisher.

The Hachette Speakers Bureau provides a wide range of authors for speaking events. To
find out more, go to hachettespeakersbureau.com or email
HachetteSpeakers@hbgusa.com.

Da Capo books may be purchased in bulk for business, educational, or
promotional use. For information, please contact your local bookseller or the Hachette
Book Group Special Markets Department at special.markets@hbgusa.com.

Print book interior design by Amy Quinn.

Library of Congress Control Number: 2025934141

ISBNs: 9780306831737 (hardcover); 9780306831751 (ebook)

Printed in the United States of America

LSC-C

Printing 1, 2025

CONTENTS

INTRODUCTION: OF BLOOD AND HARMONY   vii

1 SOUTH BY MIDWEST: THE EVERLY FAMILY 1929–1952   1

2 GIVE ME A (COUNTRY) FUTURE 1953–1957   29

3 THE EVERLYS AND THE BRYANTS   57

4 WATCHING THEM ROLLING 1957–1959   69

5 THE HEIGHTS 1959–1961   95

6 HITTING THE WALL 1961–1962   127

7 THE TRYING TIME 1963–1967   153

8 RELEVANT AGAIN: COUNTRY ROCK 1968–1970   185

9 TO THE BREAKING POINT 1970–1973   221

10 DON 1973–1982   245

11 PHIL 1973–1982   269

12 REUNION 1983–1984   285

13 BACK AT IT 1984–1988   295

14 THE HOME STRETCH 1988–2000   319

15 ANOTHER CENTURY 2001–2021   335

ACKNOWLEDGMENTS   355
BIBLIOGRAPHY   359
NOTES   363
INDEX   385

INTRODUCTION

OF BLOOD AND HARMONY

THE MAIN DIFFERENCE BETWEEN THE FAMED AND THE REST OF US IS that so many people imagine they know them. Brothers Don and Phil Everly were performers for over sixty years, celebrated around the world, and over that time fixed ideas about who they were and vague impressions about their relationship took hold. Some of them were even true.

They made unique contributions to the popular music that much of the world has heard since, but they were products of the times they lived in, the places they came from, the parents who raised them, their ambitions and life choices and the sounds that struck them. What they'd create over those decades was deeply affected by the business they chose to work in, the collaborators they found there, and the demands of the audiences they attracted.

In the lives of Everlys Donald and Phillip, the names by which they often referred to each other, and the story of the performing act called the Everly Brothers, all of these elements were more complicated than they appeared, as were they themselves. Arriving sounding like young innocents, they were somehow expected to inhabit that image forever, in sound, and in how they related as brothers.

Those expectations could be brutal and were simply impossible to meet, but this was the hand they were dealt and worked hard to live with. They played it as best they could, to at least seem to be the pair their audiences responded to and cared about.

From their first entrance into public consciousness until the news of their deaths, Phil and Don would each be introduced as "a half" of the Everly Brothers. How is a sensitive, adult human being supposed to feel about *that*? And for how long?

In 1971, Don sighed, "Phil and I playing together doesn't make that The Everlys. 'The Everly Brothers' are something that's invented. When you're The Everly Brothers, you've gotta sing 'Bye Bye Love'; you've gotta sing 'Wake Up, Little Susie'; you've gotta sing 'Dreams.' You gotta sing all of them." Phil would remark, "If you're an Everly Brother, that's what you are. You aren't *yourself*."

Yet if it weren't for all that hit Everly Brothers music they did make in tandem, and the impact that it had, little of the rest would matter to us now, and I doubt you'd be reading this. The resonance of their music has been unstoppable.

The "blood harmony" explanation of why that's so can be very attractive—reducible to the idea that when their two sibling voices came together there was something virtually mystical that kicked in, where one plus one equaled more than two, simply because they *were* brothers with those related voices. That's not to be dismissed, but it doesn't consider the millions of family members on this earth who don't sound so great together, or whose voices don't blend at all—or that singing is about a lot more than exhibiting innate voices.

In practice, their resonant sound took work, care, and attention to get and keep the blend just right, a blend born of heredity, speech patterns in the home, and training to perform as they did from earliest childhood. Those made their shared sound instinctual, "organic," before most anyone had heard it. So, sure; it seemed like magic.

Country music, the principal music they were performing from childhood until stardom arrived, and the rhythm and blues they came to love, too, were both firmly and intentionally adult, relating stories of adult experience and perspectives. Don and Phil could not foresee—or avoid—being forever associated with hit 1950s songs of teenage angst and longing—one more card they were dealt.

While having massive pop hits is a problem most performers can only dream of being saddled with, music makers do wish each other the best of luck with what hits may come, because they'll be singing them forever. For the Everly Brothers, "forever" meant nearly a half century more after those hits first arrived. Some in their audience would commiserate with that and accept markedly more adult, fresh material from them. Others, not so much.

Nothing was handed to them. It's well known by now that they came from a musical family, that they were practically raised live on the radio, and that their father, Ike Everly, was an influential guitar wizard. But that upbringing took part in challenging times, from the late Depression and World War II through the very time that the live family radio that had sustained them was dying.

Ike and Margaret Everly and their kids "Little Donnie and Baby Phil" were known regionally, and found work performing here and there, but this was no equivalent of the Nelson family, for example, with Ozzie Nelson a nationally known swing bandleader and Harriet Hilliard singing in an Astaire-Rogers movie before the family act moved onto radio, then to TV. Ozzie and Harriet could introduce the excellent performances of their boy Ricky, the Everlys' friend, on prime-time national television. The Everly family, for all of their demonstrated talent, had never been nearly that successful or been heard so much.

The brothers Everly would be tenacious. They performed together through tremendous ups and frustratingly low downs from roughly 1945 to 2005, past a decade break about halfway through. There were times of great joy and satisfaction in their lives, and also more pain than those who only picture them as smiling young rock gods in ducktails perceive. Tensions and conflicts inevitably rose between them. They were very different individuals with sensibilities that could clash.

Phil, as quiet as he would sometimes be and as gentle as he appeared, a traditionalist by nature and a sharp observer, was relatively responsive to the thoughts and needs of those he'd encounter, deferential to them even—a reserved, considerate extrovert at heart, other-directed. He'd chat easily with those around him, happy with small talk, and he was slow to boil over. He was a lifelong collaborator with others. Almost everyone describes him as sweet. Famously, he was the harmony singer able to lock in on what Don was singing, to the microsecond. Creative, yes, but born to color within the lines.

Don, endlessly talkative in public, intense and at times explosive, a more adventurous explorer by nature and more accepting of the counterculture as that developed, was nonetheless especially happy painting at home alone, and writing solo, loyal mainly to a few close compadres. While generally polite as they were raised to be, he was markedly less solicitous of people. He would often head right to his hotel room after shows, alone—a volatile, charismatic introvert, inner-directed, not very fond of responsibilities, but the dominant lead singer in the duo.

Phil would say simply, "Our ways of life are quite different." The most amusing shorthand observation of those differences may have been "Phil was English; Don was Irish."

Since they'd become instantly recognizable pop stars, the "gentle" one lighter-haired, and the "intense" one darker, fan magazines and many of their most passionate fans saw them and fantasized about them as pin-up dating caricatures—Phil as the sweet, vulnerable, nonthreatening one with the big, agreeable smile whom they wanted to cuddle or mother; Don as the brooding, commanding bad boy who might do something to you, or for you, but you couldn't be sure just what.

For all that, Don and Phil did not experience much jealousy from young men, as singing idols from Sinatra to Presley did. For one thing, with their country-style, storytelling background, they rarely sang any sort of threatening, direct-to-girl come-on songs that boyfriends might get worked up about. When they offered something close to that, such as the forever touching "Let It Be Me," it was sung with that blood harmony working, by those "two halves as one voice," embodying one incorporeal, crooning "*Me.*" That seemed to stave off focus on either one as a nemesis. Young guys didn't resent the Everly Brothers; they more often wished they could be one.

Less often noted than their unquestionable influence on male rock and roll acts that followed is that with the especially tender vulnerability they projected with such confidence, and the songs that furthered that image, their hits were seen as perfect material for so many masterful women who followed—Linda Ronstadt, Connie Smith, Reba McEntire—or for female-male duets such as Bobbie Gentry and Glen Campbell, Betty Everett and Jerry Butler, Emmylou Harris and Gram Parsons, Carly Simon and James Taylor, Alison Krauss and Robert Plant, Norah Jones and Billie Joe Armstrong.

Their "nice, polite, family boys" image had a substantial degree of reality to it, and it stuck with them as they emerged as first-generation rock and roll stars, evidence that blatant rebellion and a sneer were not all that attracted that generation's pop audience. Yet they still shared the animus of the determinedly rigid parts of the adult press that considered their entire generation of rock performers menacing delinquents. And that bugged them.

In truth, many of the reductive characterizations commonly applied to Don and Phil as individuals could have been applied to the other one at different times—and were. Which was the talk-ative one or the more settled one, or the more inventive one—those varied. They both came to understand, gradually, that what they shared and what made them the men they'd become were factors as lasting and important as their dramatic differences. These were brothers, truly brothers, playing out American lives that would have a second act, and then a third.

Their longevity as performers meant that they were intensely challenged to find a viable, comfortable place for themselves through multiple shifts in pop music trends and tastes. They'd see music makers just a few years younger and notably influ-enced by them—the Beatles, Bob Dylan, the Beach Boys, Simon & Garfunkel—evolve drastically in musical approach and image, be credited for that, and achieve renewed acceptance, while their own perceived identities seemed frustratingly fixed and predetermined.

Over time, the perseverance paid off. They pushed on, while making some of the strongest and most fascinatingly varied, if less heard, music of their lives, and the size and nature of their musical contributions came to be better understood. It was not just catchy songs or nostalgia or sales figures that continued to attract perform-ers and audiences to what they'd contributed. It was the texture of their performances and the path their sensibilities would take that prefigured so much of what's come since—as preservers, creators, and reshapers of American music. They accomplished those things as a unit, together.

It's more than time for people of this century to clarify our picture of them, and it's possible. The Everlys came to prominence as mass media was burgeoning, youth-oriented television in particular, and since they were more than a little telegenic, there is a mass of sur-viving film that makes it possible to see the evolution of their style and level of enthusiasm for performing at every stop across their professional years. There is a massive trove of print interview and profile material as well, most long forgotten or not widely known in the first place. It's now history, important for getting this story told, as is the work of dedicated Everly Brothers enthusiasts who have kept files across the decades. New interviews with people who knew the Everlys at first hand, conducted for this telling, fill in some gaps.

Their music has been part of my life at every stage. When I was eight years old, in 1958, we didn't have much, and we were living in an ancient, tenement-like apartment building in that old coal mining town, Scranton, Pennsylvania. We didn't have a TV at the time, since the one we'd owned had conked out and we couldn't afford to have it fixed, but I'd been given an early transistor radio by my grandfather that became central in my young life. I recall hanging in the alley behind the place, listening to "Bird Dog" and laughing in appreciation, the way an eight-year-old could appreciate it. Because it was funny.

In 1970, at twenty, I had a college radio show in Washington, DC, that focused on American roots music, older and new, multiple flavors, electric and acoustic, a focus that puzzled some listeners then but would be a lot more commonplace and better understood later. The Everly Brothers' LP *Roots*, foundational in the emergence of country rock, and their freshly reissued original hit records, too, were vital in that playlist.

In 2009, here in Nashville, Phil Everly and I had a conversation about their use and interpretation of "T for Texas" on that *Roots* album and in so many live shows, for my book on the legacy of Jimmie Rodgers. His comments would be among the most quoted.

The Everly Brothers have long mattered to me. I'm very far from alone in that. This is my attempt to do them and their story overdue justice. It is, I think, quite a story.

—Barry Mazor
Nashville, Tennessee, 2025

Chapter One

SOUTH BY MIDWEST:
The Everly Family 1929–1952

KENTUCKY WAS THE OLD COUNTRY. FOR DON AND PHIL EVERLY, AS for so many others, it was first and foremost the place their immediate family had *left*, shared stories about, sang about, and sometimes, but only sometimes, would grow nostalgic about. It was a place that lived more in the brothers' imagination than in its occasionally visited reality, just as Ireland or Italy or Germany served for millions of second- and third-generation children of American immigrants who'd grown up here, not back there.

The actual state of Kentucky had as many social class, economic, and racial divisions as any other, maybe more than its share. For every rural or urban working-class Kentucky mining or farming family that resented the unpromising situation in which they found themselves, there was another aspiring to somehow join the upper crust with the mint juleps and Kentucky Derby Day hats—or could be persuaded to fantasize about it while remaining profoundly stuck in place.

The myopic, romanticized fantasy of the state as a place of untouched, bucolic charm, punctuated perhaps by cinematically vicious hillbilly feuds, had led folklorists and other old-school song catchers to crisscross its hills and hollers in search of the music they wanted—in fact, practically demanded—to be found there: white Anglo, centuries old, maybe even speaking in utterly imaginary "holdover Elizabethan." In any case, the music they pursued was supposed to be markedly different from the roaring sounds of the bustling urban centers and college towns the researchers tended to show up from. As music historian Charles Wolfe noted succinctly in his book *Kentucky Country* of the resulting irony, "Going into the age of mass media and commercialization in the 1920s, Kentucky had a popular reputation as the premier hunting ground for old ballads.... This attention had the effect of encouraging later commercial country music in Kentucky."

Getting up-to-date, proficient, and even commercially viable was a goal for Kentucky musicians who could now picture being all three. That impulse arose from experience in the make-it-yourself music culture that still thrived there in homes, dances, schools, and churches. In the 1920s and '30s, this was not an isolated world of never-ending backwoods hoedowns; it was the home of musical innovation and experimentation, with local sons and daughters creating sounds of their own time, while understanding that commercial success as musicians, if they were to pursue it, might have to come elsewhere.

That's the world Isaac Milford Everly Jr., born in 1908 in Muhlenberg County, Kentucky, near the Kentucky-Ohio border, and forever known as Ike, really came from—where music was a preoccupation and perhaps an opportunity to escape from working realities. It was coal mining country, far from the more well known and strife-torn mining center in Harlan County, three hundred miles farther west. It lies halfway between Nashville, Tennessee, to its southeast and Evansville, Indiana, to its northwest.

It's an area that would suffer the onslaught of destructive strip mining later, but was all about deep shaft mining, down in the dark, then—"dark as a dungeon," as local boy Merle Travis would put it. Ike's father, Isaac Milford Sr., had been a union organizer and sometime fiddler. He and wife Mary produced ten children—five boys, five girls—and struggled to feed them. By age thirteen, Ike began working in the same mine his father had worked, living and toiling in Brownie, a small mining camp settlement near Central City, Kentucky. It was the sort of no-win job where you had to load tons of coal and got paid for it only in scrip—"Brownie coins" useful only at the company store. He experienced cave-ins and underground fires, and he knew he wanted *out*.

"I never did like it," Ike would recall. "My daddy always told me, 'you should do something else; ain't nothing to this mining.'"

The "something else" would be picking guitar and singing, at first with his brother Charlie, who played and sang close higher harmony with him, appearing, unpaid, at local dances and church socials. Later on, everyone said Charlie had sounded much like Phil would. The music they'd play was not old-time, back-porch country balladry, but a more sophisticated, hotter, and modern combination of blues, ragtime, and pop—snappy things like "Five Foot Two, Eyes of Blue" or "Yes Sir, That's My Baby." Ike was a Jimmie Rodgers fan, but then, Jimmie's music was thought of as "hot vaudeville blues," too.

These were the Charleston years, and danceable numbers were in the air, as well as friskier, even more daring stuff from black songsters that interested whites would hear on records, stuff like Papa Charlie Jackson's "Shake That Thing." That spunky hit was adapted by the E.E. Hack String Band, a white Muhlenberg County band that included a horn player and also Ike's friends Slats Bethel on mandolin and Walter Cobb on banjo. Ike had to have been struck by the fact that they got to record it for the early Columbia Records label, as well as "West Kentucky Limited." You could go places with that kind of music.

Young Ike and musicians close to him, including his mining buddy Mose Rager, would be central among those taking the distinctive Muhlenberg County thumbpicking guitar attack places they'd not yet even imagined. Another local boy, their student and disciple Merle Travis, would bring the style to a wide audience—so much so that in the folk revival decades later they'd refer to it as "Travis picking." While the Maybelle Carter/Lesley Riddle "scratch" pick developing around the same time involved thumbing the melody on lower strings and frailing across the higher ones for rhythm, the Muhlenberg style reverses that—the thumb playing a bass line, the fingers handling often complicated melodies. What would flabbergast audiences watching Ike, Mose, and company is that besides that dexterous musical action, they could work in an infectious rhythm strum at the same time.

Ike was taught how to pick that way by his friend Kennedy Jones, whose mother, Alice DeArmond Jones, had brought the picking style to the area. Jones himself had introduced using celluloid thumb picks with it, which made the style more broadly accessible. It was the highly influential black country musician Arnold Shultz, a direct, credited influence on bluegrass founder Bill Monroe's chopping mandolin rhythms, who'd shown Jones how to interpolate those mind-boggling rhythm strums into the picking, by analogy with the transitional, passing chords New Orleans piano players used. He'd picked that up while down there. (Shultz, incidentally, was once hired by Ike's dad to teach an especially challenging guitar number to his sister Hattie.)

Performer and historian Deke Dickerson has noted an aspect of Muhlenberg-style performing that would filter through to Don and Phil Everly, and crucially so—the freewheeling *"mixture* of genre and styles—hillbilly, blues, pop, Dixieland, jazz, ragtime, big band, gospel—that gave it a sophisticated perch in the hierarchy of rural music." While in practice, neither Don nor Phil would spend their careers focused on Muhlenberg-style picking, they absorbed the adventurousness, honored their father—and would find their own innovations.

As a duo, Ike and Mose Rager put the style to work on the likes of "Tiger Rag," "Love Letters in the Sand," and a little later, "River, Stay 'Way from My Door"—none of them hillbilly songs. In 1929, Ike, Charlie, and a third Everly sibling and guitar ace, Leonard, formed a working trio, the first "Everly Brothers" act, and took off for Chicago to see if they could get anywhere. They briefly appeared on a small radio station, but accomplished not much more, and Ike returned to Brownie, feeling homesick.

There was a family myth, incidentally, that Charlie Everly was the secret composer of a song that became Glenn Miller's smash "In the Mood," but the claim doesn't stand up to scrutiny. The tune claimed had antecedents recorded before these Everlys came along, but the claim does indicate where their *aspirations* lay.

Each of the three brothers, family members would recall, wanted to be in charge, tensions that never were resolved, and the first formal "Everly Brothers" act didn't last. One point of contention was that Ike's brothers didn't see the importance of getting on radio and staying there, as he did. He joined a local five-piece country band, the Knox County Knockabouts, and in 1932 they landed a regular program on WGBF radio in Evansville, Indiana. Ike considered that his first real job in music.

Such family-oriented Midwestern radio shows wanted down-home rural music in the mix, and so he began to learn the repertoire of old-time country songs and breakdowns he needed to have ready, music that people would later associate with him and with his sons, too. By the time Don and Phil were in the picture, still very young, Ike had whole notebooks full of those crusty lyrics that they would learn—old songs like "A Picture from Life's Other Side" and "Little Rosewood Casket."

Ike had never had the money to own even a used car, but he didn't have to travel far to be aware of a girl back home in Brownie. Her name was Margaret Eva Embry. She came from a large mining family herself and had her own musical interests; she'd learned to play slap bass. Born in 1919, eleven years after Ike, she'd been right next door from his family her whole young life.

"I kind of watched her grow up," Ike would recall. "You know; I had my eye on her."

Even within that large family brood she received plenty of attention as a "cute" one, relished it, and would come to expect more of the same attention. Margaret was still a young teenager when Ike got interested.

"I was the girl next door and he'd carry my books home from school," she'd relate. "We would go to church and Ike would walk home with me. He'd been out of Kentucky...I thought he was a man of the world."

They were both particularly good-looking, with fine-chiseled features that lasted. Both stood out in a world of working-class folks who'd labored long hours in bad places for long years. Ike, everyone agreed, was gentle, funny, and attentive—when he could be found around. Margaret was exceptionally bright, seemingly unintimidated by anyone, and didn't mind letting them know where to get off if they crossed her. Musician Ike proposed to her from a distance—in a letter sent from the road. She was fifteen and he was twenty-six when they married on August 31, 1935—her age eyebrow-raising later, but not uncommon then and there.

Their neighborly proximity meant that young Margaret had a pretty good idea what she could be getting into with him. Her "man of the world" was, after all, a traveling professional performer who, like more than one of those, drank with his road buddies, sometimes too much, and ran into plenty of women along the way who'd respond to his looks, talent, and temperament.

Those were not things she ever talked about publicly, and when their relationship was inquired about, she'd present an exaggerated picture of uninterrupted marital bliss, but also of their genuine shared perseverance through travails ahead. On the rare occasions she'd refer to their issues even obliquely, she'd carefully control the spin: "We've had our stumbling blocks over the 36 years we've been together," she admitted to one British interviewer in 1971, "but they were stumbling blocks which became stepping stones in our lifetime." After Ike died, four years later, she'd confide more details to close friends about how his occasional straying and ongoing drinking continued into their marriage, until Ike acceded to her understandable demands that he cut out the former, and his health issues curtailed the latter.

This was a part of the actual domestic picture the Everly brothers grew up with. Ike and Margaret would stick with performing careers just so long, but would persevere in their marriage; Don and Phil would stick with music, and for the most part, each other, through career ups and downs, but would have four and three wives, respectively. Don would more often than not go on to choose self-defining, sharp-minded women as partners and wives; Phil, by contrast, tended to choose gentler and, at least on the surface, more amenable and compliant partners. As siblings so often do, they had different responses to upbringing in that same household. As for how aware the boys were of ongoing tensions between their parents and the cause, as they must have been, Don made a revealing, offhand interview comment in the mid-1980s: "Sons don't criticize in our family.... Fathers and sons should have more respect for each other." Mum was the word.

Margaret had her own perspective on how her upbringing prepared her for the life ahead: "Ike would bring his entertainment friends home for breakfast, and you'd have to cook, and I took it in stride, because I grew up that way. I was a middle child...so you become a buffer.... It's good for a lot of *other* people for you to keep at that—nothing falls apart." That self-perception leaves open the question of how much of a "buffer" she'd actually be later, as the rest of the family saw it.

On February 1, 1937, the Everlys greeted the birth of their first son, Isaac Donald—Don. Far from Kentucky being where he'd be raised, they all left Brownie just six weeks later for a dramatically different home in Chicago, the beginning of a formative seven-and-a-half-year urban period, with long-term effects for their sons, too—often skimmed over and underestimated.

It has been well chronicled how African Americans from the Deep South were arriving in that city in massive numbers, hoping for better lives, if only sometimes attaining them, and spawning the spirited Chicago blues, jazz, and broader black entertainment scene in the process. There were also, if less noted, a multitude of white migrants to the city, often rough-hewn, arriving from Appalachian Kentucky, Tennessee, North Carolina, and West Virginia, looking to land industrial jobs and better their own lives, too.

Many settled in Chicago's Uptown neighborhood, which had been affluent before the Depression but was now a run-down, cheap place to live. Locals referred to it disparagingly as "Hillbilly Heaven." Instructively, a *Chicago Tribune* reporter referred to these newcomers as having "descended on Chicago like a plague of locusts...[with] the lowest standard of living and moral code of all, the biggest capacity for liquor, and the most savage and vicious tactics when drunk, which is most of the time."

They were far from welcomed, but these newcomers created a growing market for country music, and Ike Everly was sure he could make the most of that, with his up-to-date style and familiarity with old country ballads when those were demanded. He'd been taken on by the touring country road show affiliated with the *National Barn Dance*, from the city's 50,000-watt WLS radio station, the very widely heard show featuring the likes of Gene Autry, Lulu Belle and Scotty, and the Hoosier Hot Shots.

The flavor of country music beamed from the *Barn Dance* was highly influential at the time and was heard throughout the Everlys' childhood in the Midwest. The station's manager, Glenn Snyder, called it "uptown hillbilly." Some of the artists were blunter, referring to it as "educated hillbilly." It's impossible to understand the Everly Brothers' real roots without a sense of this musical place and time—or what they were actually suggesting when they'd so often say, "We're country."

The *Barn Dance* audience was both rural and urban, many from immigrant families from Eastern and Central Europe and Scandinavia, many of them as at home with a polka party as with country music, and of Roman Catholic or other religious backgrounds than Southern evangelical. There was notably less gospel singing in the mix, and more freely expressed matter-of-fact material than on the rival *Grand Ole Opry*. That reflected the population the young Everlys lived among in Chicago.

Bringing modernizing pop sounds into country for broader audiences was the very basis of the music's post–World War II explosion in popularity, and it would become a basic element in the way the Everly Brothers perceived country music and what might be done with it. Unspoken at first, more consciously over time, they'd grasp it. *Country could be cool.*

Ike himself, it turned out, was never promoted to the *Barn Dance* cast proper, as he'd hoped, but he did appear on tour with comedian

Whitey Ford, the "Duke of Paducah," and with George Goebel, later a national TV star as "Lonesome George" Gobel, in the *Barn Dance*–connected live road shows.

It would be his appearances in the rowdy honky-tonks along Madison Street in the Chicago Loop that began to bring him attention, joints with names like the Domes Stables, the Club Flamingo, and the Southern Inn. In country, as in rhythm and blues, the small group with an electric guitar lead was now a loud and spreading musical setup, cheaper to hire than big bands, and pulling crowds just as well or better; club managers sought them out. But those colorful country bars in Chicago had not yet seen that newfangled electric instrument in action. As Ike would recall, "I had the first electric guitar on Madison Street." It had cost him thirty-five bucks—the equivalent of about $775 today.

As Margaret described, "He played two nights a week on Madison Street in the nightclubs, and you could hear him a block away; they'd open up the doors!" (They lived just that close, in what was an Italian section.) Ike often performed wearing a suit, with Margaret encouraging him to look sharp, which would become a continuing Everly family theme. He was more likely to be found playing electrified blues and rags in those dives than country music, but it was precisely in places like this that "hillbilly" evolved into harder-core honky-tonk, with its loud songs about drinking and cheating and slipping around. These were not locales for hymns or sentimental ballads of home and hearth. Ike was quite at home there.

By summer 1938, Baby Don was already showing signs of being musical. Just eighteen months old, he would respond with the answering "Haa-lo" in "Little Sir Echo." He was about to get virtually permanent musical company. On January 19, 1939, the second Everly son, Phillip, was born at Cook County Hospital. For years on end, promulgators of the "pure Kentucky roots" fantasy who wished Phil had been born in Brownie would report that he had been, to the point that he started to just go along with the story rather than correct them.

The Everlys' Chicago reality improved around the same time, when Ike landed a regular radio stand with the city's much-followed country music station, WJJD, a half-hour show at six o'clock in the morning, plus occasional appearances on the popular mid-morning *Sunshine Jubilee* program hosted by "country" Randy Blake. By 1940, he was paired with red-haired Thomas Greene, known professionally as "Red Green," a member of the Oklahoma Drifters family band. They soon had their own morning show, performing as the harmony-singing duo the Carolina Boys. (These alleged state origins were highly malleable.)

Margaret would recall, "Red was a very, very good singer, and they blended... Ike and Red Green would do like 'Barbara Allen' and 'Rocking Alone in an Old Rocking Chair,' so Don and Phil heard *all* that even when just cutting their teeth in the Forties." Red apparently became a boarder with Ike and Margaret at their apartment for a time, and would sometimes babysit little Don and Phil.

In 1942, of course, the overarching fact was that there was a war on, with recruits from all over America housed in Southern military bases and exposed to more country music than they'd heard before—live in bars, on local radio, or on the snazzy jukeboxes that were turning up everywhere. Segments of the *Opry* broadcasts were now heard nationally on the NBC network, and rebroadcast by Armed Forces Radio across Europe, too.

With so many Americans off in uniform, and so many from the South hanging in bars like those in Chicago, often alienated and homesick, there was a decided upturn in sentimental songs that spoke of people and places missed and longed for, whether that was Karl & Harty's "Kentucky" (they were on WJJD, like Ike), Gene Autry's "That Silver Haired Daddy of Mine," or Bing Crosby's "I'll

Be Seeing You" (in all the old familiar places). That sentimental trend would still have a hold on the Everly Brothers' memory and repertoire later.

Ike and Margaret were already beginning to see Don, age five, and Phil, age three, as potential performers. Ike was taking Don with him to some of his honky-tonk gigs. "I remember," Don told Kurt Loder, "he played this Greek-owned white club that catered to migrant workers from Kentucky, Tennessee... all those places. They had pool tables in the front and then the club in the back, with a little stage.... One time around Halloween I went down there with him, and we took along this little papier-mâché pumpkin I had, and he put a sign on it, and that was the kitty.... People would walk in off the street and just ask for whatever was on their mind, and Dad and the band would try to play it."

Don made his first recording at about that time: "I remember learning to sing 'Paper Doll,' the Mills Brothers song—this was during the war—and I remember my dad taking me down to one of those little record booths where you could make spoken letters to send home. He took me down there with his guitar, and we recorded that song."

The choice of that quite current pop song is revealing. The four Mills brothers—Donald, Harry, Herbert, and guitar-playing leader John Jr.—were among the most popular harmony singers of the time. "Paper Doll," their signature hit, had been written in 1915 but never recorded until it jumped out at Mills brother Harry when he saw it in a catalog because, he said, people go for songs with *stories*, and strong pictures in those stories. Perhaps it was fated that Don Everly would be attracted enough to that song to sing it; the Everly Brothers would put those country-like lyric attributes to work themselves, again and again.

They would hear other successful black pop vocal groups favored by Ike, too. Phil would recall, decades later, "I like to hear the Ink

Spots, because I listened to them with my dad when I was a child." That influential outfit's lead and bass vocal stylings on records such as "If I Didn't Care," "I Don't Want to Set the World on Fire," and "To Each His Own" set directions for the black vocal groups of Don and Phil's generation.

Pre-school, Margaret had both boys attending dance classes, and provided dance shoes that would eventually wind up in the Rock & Roll Hall of Fame's Everlys exhibit. Ike would take the boys with him when he performed out on Chicago's historic Maxwell Street—the famously busy, bustling shopping area where Chicago blues players often got noticed, playing to the crowds out on the street between the motley shopping stalls in front of mainly Jewish-owned stores.

Don would recall, "Dad was very aware of black blues and gospel, and he'd listen on the radio in Chicago. And I remember going down to Maxwell Street with him, with the little flea markets and people playing, passing the hat for money—all kinds of people playing." The kid noticed something out there on that street that would prove important. As he'd detail for *Guitar Player* magazine in 1990, "They were playing *tunings*, and all kinds of bottleneck sounds. Mostly old black blues, you know."

With his ragtime guitar pyrotechnics, Ike would get noticed, and he had his electric guitar and amplifier out there pretty early on, too. (The merchants would let electrified musicians run extension cords out from their shops. It was good for attracting business.) He began to let "Little Donnie" sing along with him out there, and have Baby Phil, too young to join in the singing, dance around a little. Don would eventually use varied guitar tunings as players on that street did, but, somewhat ironically, this member of the first rock-and-roll generation didn't emulate his dad's electric guitar playing but became renowned as an acoustic rhythm guitar whiz.

Despite her rural upbringing, Margaret, at twenty-three, was seeing to it that a certain level of urban sophistication would come to her two young kids early, which surprised people later on. "I'd dress them up real pretty," she'd recall. "We'd take them to the nicest restaurants, so they were used to doing that, going to a Chinese restaurant. They'd sit there and they had their meal like we did, and they acted like little people that knew what they were doing."

By 1943, with the boys reaching school age, Margaret and Ike made a joint decision that Chicago's tough Uptown neighborhood was not where they wanted their sons to grow up or go to school, and they relocated to Waterloo, Iowa, three hundred miles to the west, where Donnie and Phil attended first grade and kindergarten, respectively. Ike had been offered a job at KASL radio there, to sing with a country quartet called the Blackhoff Boys. If there's any doubt that Donnie was a well-urbanized little kid already, Margaret would relate that on their first night in town, staying at a hotel, he was in bed when he telephoned down for ice water from room service.

During that winter in Waterloo, Ike and the country band would rehearse in the Everlys' home, and now Don and Phil were encouraged to join in, at least during those rehearsals. Ike began using a Wilcox-Gay home disc recorder to record and test songs he was working on—numbers like Jimmie Rodgers's "T. B. Blues" and the instrumental "Cimmaron."

The Iowa location, farther into the Midwest, meant that the family could travel relatively easily to appearances throughout the region, especially in the summers, then return home so the boys could find some stability during the school year. That would be the family routine for years to come, but the location didn't last. "We wanted to raise the boys in a small town," Margaret recalled, "but Waterloo wasn't the right place. Ike talked to some people who had worked in Shenandoah at KMA, and they said if we'd go down there, we'd be sure and get a job."

Shenandoah, in southwest Iowa, with Omaha and Lincoln, Nebraska, the closest cities, and Kansas City to its south, was small but prosperous, the money mainly derived from successful seed nurseries that sold retail and wholesale seeds across the country. One of those concerns, founded by Earl May, a young man from nearby Nebraska, continues to this day, and May had some employees performing on a regional radio station. In 1924 he'd built a studio right in his Shenandoah company headquarters, and his KMA radio station became an ongoing operation a year later, many of its commercials hawking May seed products. In the two decades since then, the small 500-watt outlet had grown to 2,500 watts daytime, 1,000 at night, and given its location, it had reach. The programming was varied, even multiethnic, but serving local farmers was the main mission.

KMA radio was successful enough and competitive enough to build its own auditorium for live shows—incongruously in the style of a Middle Eastern mosque—and independent enough to resist joining the rising national networks. It reluctantly gave in and became an NBC affiliate in the late '30s.

Ike was hired by them as a staff musician at first, appearing in on-air outfits with names like the Utah Rangers and the Ozark Mountain Boys. With his sense of humor, "Cousin Ike," as they called him, became a regular on two long-running programs that called for it, *Stump Us*, a "stump the band" musical request show, and the *Country School*, pure hoary vaudeville in which all of the adult cast members played wiseass schoolkids, with snappy comic questions and answers.

When the whole family appeared on the station's Christmas show in 1946, nine-year-old Little Donnie, after being interviewed, sang "Santa Claus Is Coming to Town," all notes hit and with fairly swinging, if declarative, phrasing, and a clarinet playing behind him. Baby Phil, seven, is said to have rehearsed his number, "Silent Night," the night before, even in his sleep. His voice is already the higher of the two. And thus, two careers of performing—and of being interviewed—began. They would go on for some sixty years.

The money from KMA was not great; the Everlys lived in a trailer, then found a small house out on the countryside. Ike and Margaret supplemented the family income by working at May's seed house on the side, Margaret working at the candy counter part-time. Ike also played some live shows around the area. He needed help with rides to go back and forth from the station or to gigs, but by 1949 he had a daily fifteen-minute morning show of his own, and could finally acquire his first car, a used Ford. Stories of his early problems driving it were regular comic fodder around the station. The jokes only ceased when the Everlys rented a place back in town, closer to work.

Ike started to have Little Donnie make spot appearances on his show, with song and chatter, and he brought him along on full-cast station specials such as the *Cornbelt Jamboree*. Then KMA, which had had success with child performers before, gave young Don a weekly spot on an ongoing Saturday show, for which he was paid five bucks. The special attention probably felt like the best part.

"It was just a ten- or fifteen-minute show, part of another show, actually," he'd recall. "I had a little theme song: 'Free As a Little Bird As I Can Be.' Dad...was the instigator....He and a fellow on accordion and another on clarinet backed me up. I'd sing three or four songs, read a commercial, and go home." Neither that instrumental backup nor the songs were particularly "country."

It seems remarkable in retrospect, but this little regional farmers' station already had two other families appearing regularly that would have lasting musical fame. There was the Southern gospel-singing Blackwood Brothers quartet, who would become a dominant, massively popular group in their field, so adept that young Elvis Presley would say he'd have given anything to be taken on as a member. They'd go on to sell over fifty million records.

Secondly, and more specifically intriguing for Margaret and Ike, there was the large Haden Family act, with their youngest son the same age as Don. He'd been a solo yodeling vocalist in the group since he was two, and yes, that precocious toddler would grow up to be Charlie Haden, the great jazz bass player and father of the Haden Triplets blood-harmony trio—Petra, Tanya, and Rachel. The intriguing part: the Hadens got paid more because *everybody was performing.*

The Everlys proposed doing the same thing, and the *Ike Everly Family* show was born in late summer 1950, with Don and Phil as regulars along with Ike and Margaret. Everyone in and out of the immediate family agreed that she was not a performance-capable singer, certainly not a harmony singer, despite all the family practice on home recordings. Margaret didn't like the estimation, but she acceded to her role on the show as announcer and reader of commercials and audience mail. Their 1950 family pay reached the neighborhood of some $60 a week—the equivalent of a very nice $750 a week in today's dollars, and they would make more by doing live shows in small towns around the area from the back of a flat-bed truck.

The sheer frequency of the Everly Family show—a half hour at 6 a.m., six days a week, plus an extra half hour on Saturday afternoons—meant a lot of music needed to get made, in varying ways, to keep it all interesting for regular listeners. For two young boys, this was extraordinary training; they'd perform solos, duos, trios, and there was plenty of spontaneous or rehearsed patter to boot.

That flexibility and spontaneity of it all would remain a fond memory for both Don and Phil, and they would mention the ways of the show in early interviews and reports when they became famous, not for that broad musical range, but narrowed to just one—their blood-harmony duets. Since the format of the family show allowed neither guests nor backup musicians, and the audience was understood to be early-rising farmers, there was one other aspect of the show format the station required, and it would have consequences. It veered toward country music of varied flavors.

In the earliest going, Baby Phil was limited to telling jokes, unable to hold a tune consistently, but they were working on his singing as a family. Margaret would recall, "Don and Phil had some talent; it was a matter of developing it...Don would do a solo, then they'd do a duet. Then Phil would. So, it started like that."

There was a wide variety of station talent the boys could watch at work. Those surroundings, the preferences of their Midwestern friends and neighbors, and in particular the music Ike exposed them to would all be imprinted in their tastes and interests ever after. The music they were struck by, from World War II through the early postwar years, would be their true musical starting point.

Don and Phil were very specific in citing which of country music's brother acts of the day, a full generation older than they were, would be most influential for them—the *Grand Ole Opry*–starring Delmore Brothers, and the less widely recalled Bailes Brothers, York Brothers, and Milo Twins. Whether guiding the boys toward those suggests Ike was already envisioning a potential future for his sons as a working pair, we can't be sure. Maybe so.

Alton and Rabon Delmore bridged country styles from the days of Jimmie Rodgers to electrified, near-rockabilly at the turn of the 1950s. Their vocal harmony would often be tight; they could swap their blues-inflected vocal leads. They kept evolving their sound as styles changed, into the postwar country-boogie years, with numbers such as the charged-up standard "Freight Train Boogie" and the loping number-one hit of 1949, "Blues Stay Away from Me," later a regular part of the Everlys' live act. Alton lived long enough to say of the Everlys in his memoir, "If they had been on the scene when we were, you know what the label would have been? HILL-BILLY."

The four Bailes Brothers, from Charleston, West Virginia, were signed by the *Opry* in 1943, and with Shreveport's *Louisiana Hayride* later. They sang in a plaintive, declarative old-school style, and were much more gospel-focused than the Everlys would ever be. Their hard-edged "Dust on the Bible" would last, but for the young Don and Phil, the Baileses' secular heartbreak numbers made the strongest impression, most obviously "Oh So Many Years," which would be one of the numbers chosen for the Everlys' *Songs Our Daddy Taught Us* album.

The York Brothers and Milo Twins are not household names today, but both were reflecting country boogie's modernizing drive. George and Leslie York were Kentuckians with backgrounds as miners, a point of connection. They'd migrated to Detroit, where there was a hunger for country music from the many who'd headed up the "hillbilly highway" to work in the auto industry. Their 1939 small-label single "Hamtramck Mama," a suggestive country blues, was their most well-known recording; their '40s records had stinging electric guitar by Zeb Turner and tended to concern hot dates.

The Milo Twins, born Edwin and Edward Miolen in Tennessee, became nationally known when they were signed to the fledgling Capitol Records' "Americana" roots music line in 1948. The Milos recorded songs with such forward-looking themes as "Truck Drivers' Boogie," "Love in an Aereoplane," and the bayou-located "Swamp Woman Blues." On ballads, you can hear their own blood harmony at work, and some resemblance to the Everlys' sound to come.

Besides recommending records, Ike was showing young Don and Phil guitar moves, but it was Margaret who'd enforce practice time and, naturally, they didn't always appreciate that. They were kids, working on their instrumental capabilities, Don on guitar, Phil on mandolin. The radio station's quite professional monthly magazine, *The KMA Guide*, mentioned that Ike was having the boys, both left-handed as he was, learn to play from the right side, as a practical necessity: "Left-handed guitars and mandolins? There are no such things, so the two Everly boys...had to learn to play their string instruments right-handed....Donald has been playing guitar for sometime but made his first public appearance...in Council Bluffs—and before over 800 people!"

KMA would regularly lay acts off during the summer, because the farmer audience was out in their fields more of the day and listening less, so the Everlys had to find other things to do. In 1949, that gave them the chance to take the long trip back to visit family in Muhlenberg County. Ike very much wanted to show the boys what Brownie was like, since they'd never seen it. *The KMA Guide* reported how excited young Don was to get to see the place and grab a photo of it, which he told classmates he'd bring back for them to see, but "imagine his amazement when they reached Central City, drove to the spot where he was born, and THERE WAS NO HOUSE. Out of the large group of houses formerly owned by a coal mining company, only four remained standing. After the company had ceased operating the mine, the houses were sold and moved away. Poor Donnie...!"

Before long, there'd hardly be a trace of evidence that Brownie had ever existed at all. Something from that trip did last—Don and Phil's lifelong friendship with their uncle's Central City neighbor, Bill Harlan, just Don's age. He'd grow up to be a rockabilly recording artist himself and name his first son Phillip Don. With another local boy there, Tommy Payne, they formed an informal country band, the Green River Valley Boys, with Phil playing bass. A "summer off" for the Everly boys already meant just finding other people to play music with.

"At that point in time," Bill recalled for this author, "they were just trying to follow what their dad wished for them. When I first met them, they wanted to sing like the Delmore Brothers; that's the kind of stuff they were doing.... They were ten and twelve, and that's a pretty big difference then, but we were all thinking of going on and being *Grand Ole Opry* stars.... We were doing Hank Williams songs, and of course, Don and Phil were doing those Delmore Brothers. They were very important to me, and they referred to that time often as something that was meaningful to them."

A full half-hour *Ike Everly Family* show from 1950, preserved on audio transcript at the Everly Brothers Childhood Home museum now operating in Shenandoah, illustrates how far things had come along for Don at thirteen and Phil at eleven. After family chatter about laundry and such, Ike leads off with the upbeat traditional gospel "He Set Me Free" (an obvious predecessor to Hank Williams's "I Saw the Light"), with Ike on his guitar and vocal and the boys joining in on the chorus. There's an ad for a genuine vinyl toy pony, available by mail order, which Ike encourages listeners to report having heard about on their show. ("I wouldn't tolerate it if I didn't support it!" he says of claims made in these on-air offers.)

"Donnie boy" then sings "I'll Sail My Ship Alone," a hip country hit for Moon Mullican just a few months earlier, singing it with confidence, panache, and some carefully placed vibrato, with Ike on electric guitar. Margaret introduces Don and Phil duetting on "Teardrops Falling in the Snow," a recent weeper recorded by hillbilly queen Molly O'Day, and dedicates it to listeners who've written in. Their voices and their singing had clearly grown together, more squawky declarative and higher-pitched than they will sound five years later on records, but the basic duet elements are in place.

Ike banters with "Phillip," as he now calls him, about being in the safety patrol at school and having bawled out the son of the station's newsman for "crossing outside the yellow line," then Phil solos on "John Henry," which he's just learned, following the pattern of Merle Travis's recent version. They finish with Phil, Don, and "Mom" trading verses on the comical "Molasses, Molasses (It's Icky Sticky Goo)," described as "a cute song for all the folks making molasses this fall." It had to have been funny then, because it's still funny now. What's notable is that the repertoire has become overwhelmingly outright country—not heartwarming, retro, old-time material, but of the most current and up-to-date sort. It's what radio wants, and they're very ready to deliver.

By that point, Margaret had the whole family dressed constantly in matching black cowboy suits for on-air and public appearances that so many find charming and cute looking back, but which pre-adolescent Don and Phil couldn't stand at all. The suits just reinforced some schoolmates' perception of them as peculiar hillbillies who performed corny music—though many weren't even aware they worked pre-school-day mornings on the air. It wasn't just perceptions of their contemporaries that could be bothersome about this childhood job, however much they enjoyed it and sounded like they did. They'd basically been assigned to it and could not quit.

As Don would confess to music journalist Robert K. Oermann in 1990, "I don't think it's a natural state of being, being on stage.... You're taking your life in your hands. You can embarrass the hell out of yourself out there; I had a bit of that in Iowa with my father." He was apparently recalling the time he was standing on a chair to get closer to the studio mic while singing "Put My Little Shoes Away" and it folded beneath him. He somehow finished the song anyway. "There was always the radio job," he told Oermann, "and it separated me from my friends."

Evidently, that separation from nonperformers was still gnawing at him some forty years later, which suggests that the adult, famed Don who'd rather retreat to a hotel room than mix with "civilians" or media, and typically felt most at ease with some select group of similarly experienced performers, was as much forged by this sometimes separating upbringing as by his own temperament. He was this way, and he stayed this way.

The radio emphasis on country music added to that sense of disconnection, because what Shenandoah kids their age were listening to was current pop—Teresa Brewer, Tony Bennett, and soon Eddie Fisher. Don would recall checking those out because his peers were, but Hank Williams was his own definite favorite, as Lefty Frizzell was Phil's. They'd be thrilled to meet Lefty when he visited the station. However scary it all could be, or isolating, Don had nevertheless already formed a picture of a life for himself in music: "None of the other kids my age knew what they wanted to be when they grew up—but I did."

Don eventually made some complicated comments that were utterly reflective of being raised in the Midwest in this era, reaching his early teen years in country's "Age of Hanks," as in "Hanks" Williams, Thompson, Snow, Locklin, Cochran, and Garland. No doubt many latter-day country and rock fans have found his word choices puzzling:

"I wanted to follow Hank Williams," he noted. "Hank Williams *wasn't* country to me. Country was Roy Acuff." That "country" nails how Acuff sang old-school, declaiming *hillbilly* style, proudly and ever after. Hank was admired within country music of the time precisely for his ability to create songs that bridged the gap from country to much broader pop audiences—Tony Bennett having a smash pop hit with his "Cold Cold Heart," Jo Stafford with "Hey, Good Lookin'," Guy Mitchell with "I Can't Help It." Williams's role as a pioneer of roots-pop convergence was central to what the Everlys wanted to emulate. Don would add, "Hank Williams, to me, was the first real rock and roll star."

An important part of what would make the Everly Brothers singular when they hit was that the music from white America that moved them was almost exclusively country. Nobody has tried to make a case that they were influenced at all by the post-glee-club/barbershop pop of the swing era, the Pied Pipers and Modernaires sorts of 1940s vocal groups, or the Four Aces–Four Freshmen–Ames Brothers harmony groups that followed, as brothers Brian, Carl, and Dennis Wilson of the Beach Boys were, for example.

One early fifties pop duo *did* give the Everlys food for thought, though. "The Bell Sisters," Phil recalled, "had some interesting stuff... very modern things." The now largely forgotten, lively teenage siblings Cynthia and Kay Strother, who sang close harmony and recorded under their mother's maiden name, were discovered when they appeared on a Los Angeles TV talent show in 1951 singing "Bermuda," an exotic, pounding number Cynthia had written at age sixteen. Phil said, "We always thought 'Down in Bermuda' was really good, really unique, and very innovative." Recorded for RCA Victor, the song went top ten, and the sisters were soon on national TV with Bing Crosby and in multiple movie musicals—all intriguing possibilities for Don and Phil. In the years just before fame came, Phil would recall, "We did wind up being compared a little to the Bell Sisters and the Delmore Brothers."

As they became working performers, the brothers Everly were basically two shy early adolescents who, in Margaret's words, "kept a very low profile," avoided most parties, and signed on for just a few group activities—choir and the glee club for Phil; the Shenanigans, a school band (using the term loosely), for Don. There were stacks of games at home, the family would go on picnics and out hunting and fishing together. They could hold their own playing baseball, had some passing girlfriends their age, and fit in as best they could.

They were hard at work perfecting the close harmony they'd be famed for. They were not twins, of course, though they were increasingly being dressed in those unloved matching outfits, and

Margaret even had them celebrate their birthdays—several weeks apart on the calendar—together. As the older brother, Don was inevitably more annoyed by the forced pairing, and he'd admit that musically he was already attempting to dominate the duo. Shades of the previous generation Everly Brothers' tensions.

Don and Phil were emerging as temperamentally different from each other in daily life—though their performances very much emphasized their connectedness. In her 2011 PhD thesis "The Roots and Influences of the Everly Brothers," musicologist Paula Bishop pointed out a vocal commonplace Don and Phil would *not* exploit, even as the practice became more common in both country and R&B duets—the "he said" so then "he—or she—answered" alternating dialogue of theater-like character duets, a chance to perform good-natured clashing musically. Ironically perhaps, for mass audiences raised outside of down-home vocal traditions, that they were *not* singing that back-and-forth Broadway style would be exceptional—very old-time country.

Don borrowed Ike's electric guitar for use in that school band—playing shockingly loud there, as the others saw it. He won a safety-themed poster art contest for a painting based, amusingly enough, on Roy Acuff's grim, scolding song "Wreck on the Highway." Painting would be an important expressive hobby for him for years; a later family home would feature many of the paintings on the walls. Ike had drawn cartoons and painted for pleasure before him; Don's Christmas gift to Dad around that time was a new paint set. He already showed a strong interest in cooking as well, in particular the Italian food he'd loved at neighborhood restaurants in Chicago and couldn't get in Shenandoah.

Phil, meanwhile, would go to Sunday school and sing in the church choir, and was writing poetry and rudimentary songs by age nine. He tended to save money from their work diligently—and sometimes lent some to perpetually short Don, who only occasionally paid him back—a sort of "ant and grasshopper" situation.

The summer breaks, with Don and Phil out of school and radio work cut back, provided further chances for family appearances out of town. When they were home, both boys worked jobs detasseling corn. (This was Iowa, after all.) On one occasion, Don came home early from that job driving the boss's car and explained, "Well, he kicked me out—so I'll leave the girls alone."

The summer layoffs were challenging to the family's otherwise stable way of life, as they'd find themselves trekking from small-town outlet to small-town outlet looking for work, auditioning for county fairs, sleeping in parks and such. They even had a short stand on the other Shenandoah station, KFNF. The KMA ownership, like many in broadcasting, was now paying most attention to their growing TV outlet, and more and more stations the Everlys checked in with were turning to record-playing deejays rather than live shows. If things were thin in summer 1951, they would be thinner in 1952.

"Around '52 and '53 it was pretty rough," Ike would recall. "There were no bookings and the ones you got were on a percentage, so you didn't make any money anyway." They came to the reluctant decision that they'd have to leave Shenandoah.

Their answer, at least for a while, was found in Evansville, Indiana, where Ike had obtained that first professional work years before. It was a new version of the family show, on daily from 12:30 to 1 p.m., sponsored by Nunn-Better flour and advertised as "a new program of Old Fashioned and Homespun Music." The flour company would send them out to regional fairs to promote the brand in their booths, and they could occasionally visit family in Kentucky, who were now not so far away.

Don and Phil could look back at these Midwestern years and say, "Dad was blues; we were country." That distinction was true, though their "country" was a flexible variety with permeable borders. The country focus, as we've seen, wasn't so much a result of their family roots or even their geographical location, as so many commentators suggest, as it was a response to demands of the place where they'd truly grown up as performers—on country-hungry radio.

For the rest of their careers, it would be characteristic that they would raise their guitars up high for emphasis on a hard strum—an artifact of how you got those riffs heard better on AM mono radio. Like most everybody their age, they were beginning to hear other incoming and rapidly changing sounds arriving from outside those country confines. What music *they* played would soon demand some new sort of identification.

Chapter Two

GIVE ME A (COUNTRY) FUTURE
1953–1957

KNOXVILLE, TENNESSEE, SITS ABOUT 550 MILES SOUTH-SOUTHEAST OF Evansville. As of the summer of 1953, it was to be home for the Everly family, on and off the air, until events of 1955 changed their lives again—dramatically. Circumstances dictated that this would be the site of their last stand as a family radio act, and the time and place Don and Phil Everly began evolving into the gifted, immensely successful, and sometimes troubled entity known as the Everly Brothers.

Knoxville had a lively musical scene for a city its size. Its reputation as a talent incubator for country music developed in no small part because of the machinations of the shrewd and imaginative but prickly grocery-store magnate Cas Walker. A legend in the region, he promoted the stores on his *Farm and Home Hour* shows, broadcast on multiple local radio stations and on TV, too. Such stars-to-be as

Roy Acuff, Tennessee Ernie Ford, Carl Smith, Dolly Parton, Carl and Pearl Butler, Mother Maybelle and the Carter Sisters, Don Gibson, and Chet Atkins all worked in Knoxville for a time—before leaving for Nashville.

"We drove into Knoxville on a balmy day, and it was a beautiful place and I felt like I made the right decision," Margaret recalled. "We put everything on the rack of a Chevrolet, and we drove into Knoxville and went up to ask Cas Walker for a job, and he hired us. It was a miracle." That Chevy, a 1952 model, was the first new car the Everlys had ever owned. The four of them had saved up together to get it, and they owned and shared it jointly.

Although Ike had always been reluctant to have her sing, with plenty of justification, Margaret would now be contributing her voice and playing bass, besides doing commercials, for the same reason she'd become their announcer—more money. The four of them were to be paid ninety dollars a week for a substantial amount of work. There were two daily shows, early in the morning and at the boys' high school lunch break, and another on Wednesday nights, with occasional work on Walker's TV station as well, their first TV exposure. In this fading time for radio entertainers, that all sounded pretty good. As Phil put it, "We were mostly busy trying to stay alive and have enough to eat."

Don said, "I really did like Knoxville...I felt I'd found someplace really wonderful. I made a lot of friends in school very quickly." The comfort level in high school seems to have been more mixed than that sunny later assessment suggests. Don was sixteen to eighteen in those years, Phil fourteen to sixteen. They managed something approximating a conventional high school life while darting in and out of all those radio obligations—dances, drive-in movies, keeping up with the evolving pop sounds, and in Phil's case, playing multiple sports. But it wasn't all that easy.

In a 1986 *Playboy* feature on various brothers' relationships, Don would describe the situation more pointedly: "I couldn't go out late...because I had to be up at five A.M. for the radio show. Our dates could always stay out later than we could. Phil was on the track team and the basketball team and got better grades. I was an average student, because it didn't interest me. We had morning shows and noon shows, and there really wasn't much time for social life."

Phil recalled one aspect of that social life: "When we were on the radio in Knoxville...I was going with a girl whose brother was in Donald's class....She broke off with me because her brother had told her parents that Donald was real fast with the girls, and it was a bad idea for her to be going out with me. I was not old enough to have a reputation—so I got his."

This is not a particularly unusual story for two siblings in high school, a couple of years apart. Phil added, "When I started dating, I wouldn't want to hang out with Don. What kind of chances does a 14-year-old guy have getting a girl with a 16-year-old guy hanging around? I had no chance if Don was there. Zero." That an older brother might not want the younger one hanging around in the same circumstance will strike many as just as understandable.

Several decades later, a more worldly Phil would admit about the family, pointedly, "We were *all* theatrical, which means *you lie all the time.* I never took girls home. I went in the back seat like everybody else...but I didn't have any fun sex until I was old enough to afford it."

All indications are that their relationship in these years was pretty typical for high school brothers. Phil, with all of his athletic involvements, was beginning to fill out some. Margaret would recall a time when Ike took him to buy a new jacket, and looking into a three-way mirror, Phil complained, "Look, Dad, I don't have a neck. My neck is too full." And Ike replied, "Don't worry about that; Robert Mitchum don't have a neck, either." Don would find "No Neck" a good instant tease, but then Phil would call him "Ski Nose" in return.

If their lifelong stylistic differences were beginning to cement into place as adulthood neared, they were often perceived as a pair. They both wore conspicuously unconventional pegged pants, walked around with their collars turned up—and there was the hair, in those famous high-piled ducktail cuts. Nobody in town had seen anything like those in person before. Margaret had seen photos of the unorthodox style in magazine stories about young Hollywood actors, and while that look was still viewed with great suspicion by more conventional folks, she began cutting her boys' hair that way herself.

A year or two later, ducktails would be commonplace enough in town that they'd be thought of as trendsetters, but in the beginning, they were looked on with suspicion as probable "juvenile delinquents," despite the fact that they were not particularly rule breakers.

One of the girls Don dated at West High demands at least a footnote for history. Though he'd make clear the song's story had nothing to do with their relationship, he did date one Catherine Coe at the time, taking her to parties and football games. She could recall Don and Phil playing rock and roll at one of those parties—the first time she'd heard them play that. He was not her clown, but he would find use for that name "Cathy."

The Everly Family's on-air appearances in Knoxville were just an extension of what they'd been doing on radio all along—quartets, solos, duets at times, some hymns and old-school hillbilly numbers, and commercials for cough medicine and seeds. It was designed to be a country show, but frictions were developing.

Ike described the program's increasing built-in tensions in a first-person 1958 profile in *Country Jamboree* magazine, self-bylined "as told to Ben A. Green." His sons, he recalled, "got to playing tunes and singing songs that were difficult to follow on the electric guitar, and I was considered a pretty good country guitar player.... We'd sing hymns like 'I Saw the Light' and [other] Hank Williams songs and...what we thought was good. The boys would sing them, but they would go after other types of songs. Sometimes it didn't please the sponsor. Don or Phil would say, 'I'd like to play something with more of a beat to it.' Our sponsor called the boys 'bobbysoxers.'" That tag and attitude seems only to have increased Don and Phil's determination to sing what they liked and to look as they pleased.

That "music with more of a beat" was in the air. They were paying particular attention to black vocal groups that were presenting ballads in ways that were rhythmic, dramatic, and fresh, yet also cool and relatively understated—the Orioles with "Crying in the Chapel," Clyde McPhatter and the Drifters with "Money Honey," and especially the Clovers, whose vocals on "Lovey Dovey" and "Blue Velvet" put sweetness and close harmony right up front. "Rock and roll started while I was in high school," Phil recalled in 1971. "The Clovers and things like that started. It was so close to what we'd been doing that we picked it up."

Phil's involvement with the school choir would be brief. "They weren't singing anything like I sang," he remembered. "I'd always had trouble with music teachers. I was singing professionally and maybe the teachers resented it; I had a different attitude about what we were doing."

It seems that most of the brothers' classmates still had no idea or particularly cared about their ongoing performing work; they were known simply as a couple of pretty nice guys, despite their suspicious looks, and in Phil's case, for school fame as an athlete. The look and basketball met in an incident people in Knoxville still talk about.

The junior varsity Rebels team coach, Walter Ganz, kept riding Phil about the big hair, which would get wet from sweat and block his eyes during games. "The coach said we can't have it flopping around," recalled teammate Oliver Chavannes. No one's sure whether Ganz was joking or serious, but he warned Phil that he either had to get that hair cut or wear a hairnet—not a very macho way to be seen. Mocking the suggestion, Phil showed up at the next practice wearing said net. "He had the girls falling out of the stands," high school mate Gene Easterday recalled. "He'd be running down the court and he'd just stop and pull that hairnet out and stuff his hair back up in it when it'd come loose. He was just doing it to aggravate Coach Ganz."

All of this was happening at the very time the changes roiling popular music were accelerating. In 1953, Bill Haley and the Comets (known then as Haley's Comets) broke through to pop radio with the mildly rebellious "Crazy Man, Crazy." And the Everly brothers were regular listeners to the groundbreaking 50,000-watt Nashville R&B station WLAC, home of the famously white but musically hip deejays Hoss Allen, John R., and Gene Nobles.

Don would recall, "Between the Grand Ole Opry and WLAC in Nashville, you could listen to the best of both worlds. I hated it that you had to choose which field you were in because of the color of your skin." The brothers' lifelong buddy, rockabilly musician Bill Harlan, would add, "We *all* listened to WLAC."

At night, the historic R&B station was beaming records by such specific Everly influences as the Orioles, the Drifters, and the Clovers. In their various sizes and shapes, Big Mama Thornton, Big Joe Turner, Little Junior Parker, and Fats Domino were all getting airplay there, too, as were harder-core blues artists—Howlin' Wolf and Muddy Waters. Soon, there'd be Chuck Berry's "Maybellene." By 1954, in the South at least, breakthrough rock and roll artists were beginning to be heard.

When Bo Diddley's beat-defining, self-named single was released, the Everly boys picked up a copy at Knoxville's Dugout Doug's record store. It carried a sound that was nothing less than transforming for Don. As he noted in the introduction he'd write for George R. White's biography of Bo in 1995, "After hearing Bo Diddley for the first time in 1955, my idea of music was forever changed. He opened the door to rhythms and music that reached to the very soul of me. His original sound is evident in all forms of music—rock and roll, rhythm and blues and country."

Don and Phil's music had clearly evolved. As Phil would put it, "We were doing that strange brand of country and some other things we'd been listening to." The change had showed itself very quickly, and there was simply no way Cas Walker was going to assent to the trend.

Self-made, wealthy, and powerful, Walker was politically involved enough to be elected a councilman, then mayor. He was the subject of endless regional stories and legends as a master of stunts and hype that included burying a man alive in front of a store to attract press attention and throwing frying chickens off the roof to attract customer attention. He made it into *Life* magazine in a photo where he's attempting to punch out a fellow city councilman. He was just plain ornery, and not a man about to look kindly on rocking or rolling.

From the first, he hadn't liked the brothers' look. Ike remembered Walker's growing irritation with the direction of Don and Phil's music, as well: "The sponsor liked the 'real country' with the banjo. . . . We realized that the real country music sold groceries to the older people, while the beat-type music appealed more to the younger folks."

In mid-1954, the Everly Family was fired. Walker's explanation? "I told them that wiggle wouldn't sell groceries."

Don would stress how much they'd learned, working so hard and so often there, but also recalled, "I remember being really depressed." As for Walker, Don reckoned, "We worked about a year and a half for him, and he couldn't have picked a more inconvenient time to let us go." It was the year Don was to graduate from high school. Ike tagged this time the beginning of the end for the family act: "Rock and roll was just coming in, and I guess they started growing away from us, musically and otherwise.... We saw the writing on the wall. We didn't think we'd make it, and we thought they would, so we just kind of stepped out.... We knew it was time for them to be on their own."

A broader nail-in-the-coffin factor was that live performance radio was coming to a virtual end. When comedian Milton Berle's hour-long TV variety show had first aired in 1948, there were an estimated half million TV sets in all of the United States; when Elvis Presley performed his historic incendiary version of "Hound Dog" on the same show in 1956, that number had exploded to thirty million. It was not worth looking for one more local radio gig someplace.

There was, however, the glaring exception of the leading barn-dance variety show still on radio, the *Grand Ole Opry*, and with the country music business now centered in Nashville, it was more a target for aspiring country performers than ever, Don and Phil included.

The senior Everlys made some drastic changes just to stay afloat. They briefly moved the family to a cheap house in the country, with the boys temporarily changing schools, but they soon relocated to an apartment back in Knoxville where Ike served as the custodian and Margaret did some cleaning. Don and Phil returned to West High. Meanwhile, their parents both attended school, too—Margaret a business school, learning to be a beautician, and Ike a barber's college. As he recalled, "We thought this type of education would give us something to fall back on, a profession other than music."

The devastated teenagers scolded the mother who'd been the unstoppable force behind their continuing efforts: "It's *your fault*. You told us we'd make it someday...be rich."

In these fairly desperate times, the four Everlys would go to extremes to keep up appearances when visiting family in Kentucky, one more indication of both their accent on personal dignity and their particular attention to the surface look of things. The difference between looking your best and putting up a front can be slim.

Margaret recalled, "When we would go back home, nobody would ever mention that we were not doing well, that we hadn't come in a success....but we would go in looking like we had. Everybody would stop and dress....At the back of this service station was a restroom, so we'd take our good clothes, and we'd go in there, each one, and dress up....That's maybe pride; I guess maybe that's what I instilled in *them*." There was the dissembling theatricality Phil would refer to. Whether her sons felt pressured or humiliated to maintain appearances that way, whether either or both resented what was instilled, no one clarified out loud.

Don had been writing songs from time to time since childhood, noting that the first song he ever wrote was called "Lightning Bug Love": "That's how young I was." He'd been taking a more grown-up stab at songwriting the whole time they'd been in Knoxville, with country music the focus. That meant writing for adults, which the genre aimed at squarely, but that didn't daunt him. It might seem that the young ladies' man and lover of incoming rock would have been coming up with frisky songs along the lines of Lefty Frizzell's "If You've Got the Money I've Got the Time" and Hank Williams's "Move It On Over," but that was not the case.

It was Hank's sad ballads of hard times and heartbreak Don patterned his fledgling songs after. As he'd recall with amusement much later, "I was writing real tearjerker, cheatin' songs when

I was still in high school—16, 17 years old—and didn't have any experience whatsoever about this. But I was writing from material I knew." The family's new financial stress didn't change that. "I just stuck with my writing—which I was doing a lot of."

Both Margaret and Ike found work as hair stylists. Business was meager, but they wanted to hold on in town at least until Don graduated. Ike did some time working construction in Indiana, sending cash home monthly. None of them could see that everything was about to change.

Ike's old friend and de facto student Merle Travis, by now a very established star, had been talking about Ike's fingerpicking wizardry with an emerging, younger guitar whiz, Chet Atkins. Ike admired Chet's updated take on the complex picking style, which he'd been hearing on the radio, and they'd begun corresponding.

Atkins was just becoming a celebrity, but he was certainly not the powerful country music executive he would become. He was an admired master guitar picker, and he was running a small publishing firm in Nashville called Athens Music. It happened that Tennessean Chet had played fiddle on Knoxville radio himself during the war, and was now a regular on the *Opry*, initially as part of the Maybelle Carter and the Carter Sisters act.

When he returned to Knoxville to perform at the Tennessee Valley Fair, the hard-up Everlys didn't have the cash to get in, but Ike, spurred on by Margaret to go anyhow, brought his sons to meet him. Legendarily, their first conversation was through a chain-link fence, backstage, with Don and Phil and Dad very much stuck outside. Ike said, "Chet, I got two boys that I think are pretty good. Do you think you could do anything for them?"

Atkins would recall that first meeting in ways that say as much about mid-1950s country music-makers' hunger for respectability and perceived class, his own in particular, and Southerners' continuing feelings of cultural insecurity as it does about the Everlys:

"Don and Phil had been students in the music scene all their lives.... One thing, too, that interested me when I met those kids was that they were so *intelligent*. They used proper English, and they were raised mostly in Iowa...so they didn't have a Tennessee or Kentucky accent. I just thought they were a cut above, intellectually, and education-wise."

Atkins gave them his number in Nashville, saying that, sure, he'd listen to what Don was writing, and stayed in touch all through 1954 and 1955, sometimes making suggestions on ways to improve songs Don sent him to critique.

Don recalled their initial get-together in Nashville. "We...went over to his house, sat there in his den, sang him these songs [to record as demos].... And he told me, '*That* song—there.' It was a song I had written called 'Thou Shall Not Steal.'...He said, 'You need to put a bridge in there.' I went back to the motel where we were staying and rewrote it, brought it back and he said 'Thanks; that's good.' And we went back to Knoxville, where things were very bleak. And then a letter came."

That letter from Chet, dated July 28, 1954, marks the explosive news Don heard: "It looks like we will get a record on 'Thou Shalt Not Steal.' Kitty Wells likes it very much and says she will cut it in two or three weeks. I know you'll be glad to hear this...I hope to get some more records on the other songs, but it will take a little time to do that.... Also, we'll be trying to get you a record. Keep writing.... The two new songs you sent are fine."

Enclosed was a check for $600 from the publishing company.

Don, at sixteen, was a professional songwriter, and that check was a short-term family lifesaver. The song was a Bible-referencing, steel-guitar-driven admission of stealing a love directly from a best friend's arms, losing the friend, finding trouble—exactly the sort of song Ms. Wells, in the middle of her decade-plus reign as undisputed Queen of Country, was known for. It was also a good example of adult experiences described that Don had yet to encounter, although his parents had apparently warned him that habitually messing with other guy's girlfriends, as he had, might lead to issues. Released in October, the single went to number fourteen on the national country chart.

The fledgling country songwriter recalled, "We left Knoxville the day after I graduated from high school. I remember Mr. Love, the principal...calling me into his office and asking me if I was going to college. And I said 'No...I'm going to Nashville.'"

Margaret soon received a letter from Mrs. Chet Atkins informing her that her husband had just gotten recorded another Donald original, "Here We Are Again," and "got a real good record on it." This one was with very arguably the finest singer in the long history of country music's legendary Carter Family, Anita Carter. Don's song was a purely impure honky-tonk ballad on the reliable theme "I just can't bring myself to end our tumultuous illicit affair," recorded for RCA Victor, with Chet on electric guitar.

Margaret now decided, fairly presciently, that it was time to get themselves relocated to Music City and see what opportunities awaited there. She never would look for work as an on-air announcer or host, which might have pleased her. She quickly found a Nashville department store manager who'd been a neighbor back in Kentucky, and he hired her to cut hair; her pay was better instantly. And so, Don, Phil, and their mother moved into a rented apartment on Oakdell Avenue in Madison, Tennessee, a relatively inexpensive small town just north of East Nashville, within the city's Davidson County limits, where many of the best-known names in country music were residing. For a brief period, Ike kept on cutting hair in Knoxville, then continued doing it in Madison. Before long, he and Margaret both went off to Hammond, Indiana, where she cut more hair and he worked construction again, alongside Mose Rager.

The boys lived alone in Madison now. Phil entered the local high school, Peabody High. As the older brother with songs bought and paid for, Don began to throw his weight around, blatantly bossing his kid brother now that the parents were elsewhere.

In this rush to turn the page and seize the opportunity to make a more stable living, there were choices made, apparently without much discussion or questioning, that would have long-term consequences for Donald, for Phillip, and for this new entity known ever since as the Everly Brothers.

Phil seems simply to have accepted the change, going along with what was put before him, in keeping with his basic temperament. The more skeptical Don, on whose early writing success this decision was based, after all, had questions about the preordained paired setup and this new responsibility for taking the lead. In practice, though, they both followed their parents' wishes. It was about family survival. Sheer momentum decreed that the brothers were ripe to make it on their own, as Nashville country singers and writers, and that they'd do it as a duo of a highly practiced, tightly bound, inseparable sort. Phil would tell early biographer Roger White, "There were a lot of solo singers around, and I guess we thought we'd be a little different. I also remember my father taking a stick and breaking it. He then put two sticks together and said, 'You can't break that.'"

Twenty years later, it occurred to Don, or perhaps he just first expressed it then, that this was not necessarily the way things had to have gone. He would reflect, "Actually, Phil and I *could* have had solo careers. When you look back over the period of time, you think, 'Well, gee whiz. Did I really do what I wanted, or was it really just what my mother and father wanted?'"

Apparently never considered was working both together and separately as moods, opportunities, and inspiration arose. There must have been no serious conversation with Anita Carter, for example, about such matters. As she recorded Don's cheatin' song, she was recording solo, also with Mother Maybelle and the Carter Sisters (touring with newcomer Elvis Presley that year), and in a pop harmony girl group, 'Nita, Rita and Ruby. Varying setups weren't a problem for her.

That the Everlys received correspondence directly from Atkins's wife, Leona, suggests the modest size of the publishing operation he had going. He began talking them up to potentially useful, larger connections. Don recalled, "When we came to Nashville, we had our hair real long. We didn't sound like everybody else; we didn't look like everybody else. They would look at us like 'Well, what is *this* about?'... But people would see Chet talking to us and they'd think 'These are Chet's friends, so let's not chase them out of town *yet*.'"

One Music City operator that Atkins introduced them to was the ubiquitous Troy Martin, who worked as a go-between and scout for various music publishers, including Peer-Southern and Gene Autry's Golden West Melodies. People suggested more than once that he looked like a less shoe-banging version of Nikita Khrushchev, and they had a point. He was known to have a particularly close working relationship with Don Law, the great British-born head of country music A&R for Columbia Records, the man who'd recorded blues legend Robert Johnson and Western swing king Bob Wills. He had assembled, with talent-scouting help from Martin, a country roster at Columbia that included Lefty Frizzell, Carl Smith, Marty Robbins, Ray Price, and the young West Coast siblings the Collins Kids, who were already producing sharp, rhythmic rockabilly.

Martin was experienced enough to know that picking up and establishing the Everlys as songwriters would be a lot more valuable if they were successful recording artists at the same time. He took Don and Phil to audition for Don Law, whose girlfriend, both brothers reported later, thought they were cute, so they were signed. There was some expectation that they could appeal to a younger-than-usual country audience with the honky-tonk music they were offering. Martin quickly had a Columbia recording contract in hand for them and signed Don as a writer with Gene Autry's publishing unit.

On November 8, 1955, the Everly Brothers' first recording session took place at Nashville's Tulane Hotel. This makeshift sort of setup was still common in Nashville pre–Music Row explosion. Backing them was Carl Smith's band, including Sammy Pruett on guitar, Junior Huskey on bass, and Dale Potter on fiddle, as they sang and strummed their acoustic guitars—four Don Everly songs cut in all of twenty minutes. It played out so fast that they weren't entirely sure it had actually happened, with zero input from them on what it would sound like. Phil, nervous, sang sharp and knew it. He'd recall Don Law saying, "Well, maybe they won't think it's sharp; they'll think it's a new sound!" This long-anticipated event was an instant disappointment.

On the single released in February, "Keep A'Lovin' Me," backed with "The Sun Keeps Shining," both unremarkable waltzes, very little of why you'd want to have the Everly Brothers on your label can be detected. The lyrics are far from Don's most interesting of that early time, and the vocals are not as tightly tied as we'd all come to expect. Nerves, hurry, and minimal care seem to have ruled the day. They took a dub home from the session and played it and, heartbroken, knew instinctively it wasn't going to click. Phil would recall, "Elvis had just come out with 'Hound Dog,' and Don and I were doing a *waltz*. . . . But to get on country music records, we had to show them that song Don had written. . . . Stinko, boy! Really stinko."

Two other songs recorded, "If Her Love Isn't True" and "That's the Life I Have to Live," sounded more distinctive and smarter, but they weren't released at the time. When the first single tanked, the option on the Everlys' contract was not picked up. They discovered quickly that in some ways, their "weird outsider" status hadn't changed by recording a record.

In the December 1958 issue of the short-lived movie- and music-star magazine *Celebrity*, Don and Phil gave an account of their lives at this time in a feature entitled, pointedly, "The Other Kids Hated Us at First." It describes neighbors in Madison eyeing these strange-looking youngsters in faded denims and dark T-shirts, living alone, staying up half the night practicing music. They were known to buy Cokes and potato chips at a nearby grocer, and that was about all, for going out—or eating. Don explained what was really happening: "I really did think we'd starve. Mom and dad were living in Indiana, and they'd send us money pretty regular, but I guess we mismanaged. We never could make it last as long as we needed it."

It would be sixteen frustrating months before they'd see a recording studio again, but at least now they could be booked as a young country recording act, and Chet kept on looking for a situation that could work for them. Meanwhile, they'd be found, along with many aspiring country performers, in the alley behind the Ryman Auditorium, home of the *Opry*, looking for new connections. Don recalled, "Whoever would be passing back and forth, going in and out, we'd have our guitars, and they would say, 'They're the Everly Brothers, and they're singers.' . . . And we'd sing for them."

In 1956, Don was signed as a songwriter again, by Nashville's second-biggest publishing presence, Hill & Range, run by Austrian refugee brothers Jean and Julian Aberbach, who'd shortly become the publishers of Elvis Presley. There was a small advance very welcome at the time.

Eddie Crandall, who'd soon be managing Marty Robbins and was responsible for landing Buddy Holly his first Decca contract, volunteered to be the Everlys' manager. He'd had some success as a songwriter but was better known around town as the boyfriend of the late Hank Williams's ex-wife, Audrey. He pressed Don and Phil to maintain an acceptable "country" image, so when you see 1955 photos of them in corny jackets with big white checks, and their hair suddenly shorter, he had a hand in that. They got some local live and television appearances out of the relationship. On one of those TV shows, hosted by A&R man Joe Allison, an already quite successful Nashville songwriter was appearing, in her lesser-known role as a singer. Her name was Felice Bryant.

She'd recall, "All I noticed were these two gorgeous-looking kids in blue suits, waiting for their turn." Unaccustomed to singing solo, since when she performed it was usually along with her husband, Boudleaux, she was so nervous that she didn't even catch their performance. But she did recall those young brothers. They'd meet again.

Several more of Don's songs were placed at this time—and their trajectory was interesting. His ballads had shown real appeal as material for women—Kitty Wells, Anita Carter, and before long Wanda Jackson—within the limiting ways "heartbreak material for women" was understood in country then. But in 1956, Justin Tubb, the smooth, rhythmically adventurous son of that very different, great country vocalist Ernest, recorded Don's "It Takes a Lot o' Heart," followed by "The Life I Have to Live." They both show some drive, and the first likely reflects Don's recent *career* experience. Lovers may think all they need is "the will to succeed," but "it takes a lot o' heart... to make a love strong—and still you're not certain; it may not last long."

It's easy to see how the connection to Justin happened. By then, the Everlys were being additionally represented by his sister, Violet Elaine Tubb, another volunteer. She'd recorded one single with Ernest under the unlikely, never explained name "Scooter Bill Tubb," and was a regular on his weekly *Midnite Jamboree* broadcast. It was clear that, for all her very striking cowgirl looks—dark and a tad insolent—she wasn't going to have much of a perform-ing career. She had seen the Everlys on that same Joe Allison TV show, and then waited to meet them in the Ryman alley. For a time, she would be, in Don's words, his "girlfriend/manager... a year or so older—but a little more worldly. I was a very naïve young boy."

She introduced them to Ernest and to others around town that his very connected family knew. She took thousands of publicity cards they'd had made from their Hill & Range advance money but done little with and got them out to deejays, though none of that did much to forward them either. One label suggested they just wait two years until their voices "matured."

Work was scarce. Phil gave up on attending high school and fin-ished his diploma by correspondence course, to leave more time for work, wherever it might be found. Audition tapes were sent to mul-tiple labels; none of them got a positive response. Phil recalled, "We auditioned for every label in the United States, and we were turned down at least ten times." Among those, incidentally, was Cadence Records from New York, which had some interest in establishing a country side, but said no.

"Scooter Bill" was a friend of another Nashville girl, consider-ably more down-home, who'd sometimes be out there with her in the Ryman alley, a lively secretary, Mary Sue Ingraham. When Don met her, he quickly switched dating over to her, and "naïve and young" was apparently an apt description for both of them. It wasn't long before they found, in the 1950s way of putting it, "they had to get married." Underage locally to marry without parental consent, and not wanting to go into all of this with their parents, they eloped to Georgia and made it legal on November 22, 1956. Don informed Ike and Margaret about the marriage only after they got back home. "For a while, they were hurt," Phil noted, "but... pretty soon everything was just like it was before."

With money still hard to come by, Mary Sue, sometimes referred to as just Sue, moved into the Madison apartment with Don, and Phil stayed there, too; her secretarial pay helped. As publicity about the brothers picked up, Don and Sue would be portrayed in the "Sorry, girls, he's married" mode that a later generation associates with John Lennon. Reporters would ask Don plenty of questions about how to make young wedlock work—as if he knew.

Meanwhile, the Everlys were very much aware of the ongoing march of the R&B and fledgling rock and roll music they were taken with. Ray Charles had hits with "I've Got a Woman," "Leave My Woman Alone," and "Drown in My Own Tears"; Little Richard had shaken things up with "Tutti-Frutti," defining one direction rock would go. Chuck Berry had hits with "Maybellene" and "Roll Over Beethoven," introducing several others. These were substantial influences on them, from innovators whose music they would come not to copy, but to interpret their own way. Don's idol Bo Diddley's self-titled "Hambone" meets "Shave and a Haircut" rhythm single reached number one R&B in March 1955.

Don's writing began reflecting this other side of their interests, moving in the direction of the songs and sound that would make them famous. One of their demos would prove especially significant. The song was called "Give Me a Future." Lyrically, it seems to be another case where Don transposes their frustrating professional situation into a love song ("Say you'll be mine; give me a future"). The lyric is not the consequential aspect; Don's opening, driving guitar riff, a turn on the Bo Diddley beat, was a close model for the forever-influential opening of their breakthrough hit, coming in the spring of 1957 under new circumstances.

By all accounts, they were ready to pack it all in and look for construction work alongside Ike in Hammond. What could have been their last stop in Nashville was a visit to publisher Hal Smith. His friend, Kentuckian cowboy singer Dave Rich, signed by Chet as an

RCA rockabilly, had recommended Smith and the Everlys to each other. Smith clarified that he couldn't get them a new recording contract, but he'd put in a word with someone who could, Wesley Rose, head of the one publishing firm more powerful in Nashville than Hill & Range—Acuff-Rose. Scooter Bill had raised checking out the Everlys with Rose, as well.

Founded in 1942 by Roy Acuff and Wesley Rose's late, esteemed father, Fred Rose, when Acuff-Rose opened its doors Fred was already known as the composer of such standards as "Blue Eyes Crying in the Rain," "Deep Water," and "Waltz of the Wind." When he signed, managed, and cowrote songs with Hank Williams, he became a country music legend himself. He'd join Hank and Jimmie Rodgers as the three original inductees in the Country Music Hall of Fame, but he'd died young. Son Wesley was by no means as universally loved, which may have been inevitable given the large shoes he had to fill, and because he'd been an accountant before stepping up as the firm's head, very rarely a formula for being loved by working music makers. Tending to be set in his ways, Wesley was about to play a powerful role in Don and Phil's lives and unprecedented career.

When they auditioned for him, he was immediately taken with what he heard. As Rose recalled: "The Everly Brothers walked in, and I did a demo on them. It just so happened I was starting a country label for Archie Bleyer [of Cadence Records in New York]. . . . The kids were leaving town . . . so I called Archie and said 'I'd like to do a duet on your label . . .' He says 'Who?' I said 'The Everly Brothers.' He says 'No; I don't like them . . . I had demos sent up here.' And I said, 'Well, I'll make you a deal, Archie; I'll cut them, and after the session you tell me whether you want them on Cadence, or else I'll put them out here.' [Acuff-Rose was running its own label, Hickory, in Nashville.] So, he hung up, and an hour later he called me, and he says 'Look . . . I'll either take them or I won't. It's unfair to you that if they're good I get them and if they're bad [you do]. I'll take them.' And that's how the Everly Brothers got on Cadence Records."

They signed a three-year contract with Cadence on February 21, 1957. Wesley Rose became not just their working publisher, but their manager as well. The terms were pretty standard for the time, but no better than that.

Archie Bleyer had turned to Wesley to find and sign country acts because it was an area for possible label expansion he knew next to nothing about. As far back as the late 1920s, Bleyer had been a professional arranger of jazz-inflected stock band arrangements, an important step for the broad spread of swing-era jazz as pop. He went on to publish those arrangements and sidelined as a music magazine columnist answering musicians' questions about arranging. Some of his own compositions, such as "Business in F," published by Ralph Peer, were well known in their own right.

In the early 1940s he'd become a conductor of Broadway shows and musical director for the popular *Arthur Godfrey Time* show on CBS radio. When Godfrey became a major "just folks" presence on 1950s television, host of multiple shows, Bleyer went with him. Seemingly amiable but in truth increasingly tyrannical, Godfrey refused to let his regular on-air tenor Julius LaRosa expand his career beyond the show, a souring relationship that made national headlines. In 1952, Archie started up Cadence Records specifically to record LaRosa, which at once ended his relationship with Godfrey and launched the label. He had a sharp ear for making and marketing solid pop records. In 1954, Cadence signed both Andy Williams—who appealed to young pop audiences, and who'd first sung with his brothers in the Williams Brothers quartet—and the female Chordettes vocal pop group; Archie clearly liked harmony singers. He went on to marry Chordette Janet Ertel, which, as we'll see, would have resonance in Phil Everly's life a few years later.

Wesley Rose signed the Everlys as a young country duo, attractive, perhaps, to younger audiences, but definitely country, a new turn for Cadence. Their songs would be published by Acuff-Rose; among those the Everlys suggested might be candidates for early recording were "I Wonder If I Care as Much" and "Should We Tell Him," credited to both brothers as songwriters, but primarily Don's creations. They were recorded on March 1, 1957, at RCA Victor's temporary McGavock Street Nashville studio, rented from the Methodist Television, Radio and Film Commission. These would be the B-sides of the Everlys' first and third singles for the label.

Those Acuff-Rose demos, which surfaced years later, provide a picture of what Bleyer heard, and who the Everly Brothers about to find sudden stardom seemed to be. On the "I Wonder" demo, fused-as-one blood harmony is right there, though they sound as young as they are. Here, and on the release, Don unabashedly pronounces that key word "care" as "keer," which is more Appalachian than Midwestern. The brothers' performance accents would always be somewhat adjustable. The song's a country heartbreaker, with quite evident Hank Williams influence, agonizing self-examination included.

Put that all together, and you have brothers, probably Southern (or something), and the innocence in the sound suggests *young* love and tears. If you'd happened to hear this in the context of 1950s pop, you might hear the vulnerable male anticipation of 1960's "Will You Love Me Tomorrow."

The "Should We Tell Him" demo is upbeat, and Don's storytelling verses sound sly and waggish. Showing his growing experience, he works in both the narrator's and so-called friend's points of view in just a few lines. This one approaches rock and roll: the interloping best friend lives in one of country's haughty "mansions," but the woman is "my best girl." It's teenage drama—or comedy. On the released Cadence record, there's a repeating electric guitar riff between verses, apparently played by Chet Atkins. It anticipates and may have inspired the infectious one featured on the 1963 Phil Spector/Crystals hit "Then He Kissed Me." It was no waltz.

The Everlys and Wesley Rose were all thinking "country," and it would be another Acuff-Rose song they recorded in that first Cadence session that put the brothers on the map. Wesley had had it kicking around for some time and kept trying to get a succession of unimpressed country artists to cut it, among them Porter Wagoner, Brenda Lee, Gordon Terry, and the brothers-in-law pair Johnnie & Jack. The unloved song was "Bye Bye Love."

It had been written by Nashville's first full-time professional songwriting duo, Felice and Boudleaux Bryant, the year before. They'd knocked it off in the course of a short car ride to the site in Hendersonville, Tennessee, north of Nashville, where they were having a new house built. (*They* were already doing rather well.) It was raining, and as their son Del recalled, Boudleaux started singing the chorus to the rhythm of the windshield wipers. The song's verses are pretty much standard commercial country of the day, in sound and content. "She sure looks happy; I sure am blue" is the crux of it, if you take it literally. But in these hands in the studio that day, that "Bye-bye, love" chorus was practically a high school football cheer, with all of the winning enthusiasm Phil and Don bring to it. It also has the cold-blooded, triumphant tone that was the basis of rockabilly.

Honky-tonkers, faced with a lover who's gone and left them, cry in their beers a lot. Rockabillies generally respond with imperviousness or some sort of conquering, even violent, revenge. In this song, though the singer "feels like I could die" in the verses, the gleeful "but I don't care; so long, sweetheart" kiss-off would warm empathetic hearts all over. It would position the Everly Brothers, as the record broke out, in a place just shy of hard-edged rockabilly, but less jaded and angry about this whole love business and sounding pretty "country"—especially if you hadn't heard much of that.

It was, unbeknownst to most in the studio that day, the starting gunshot of a new roots-pop synthesis—with a future.

In the studio, the final, conclusive elements that would make it a breakout record were found. As Don would recall, "Archie Bleyer and Wesley Rose and Boudleaux were there, and they sort of sang the song to us, a rendition of it, and we learned it right away—just like that. They asked us what we thought of it, and we said, 'We can do it.' We knew we could. . . . I was probably more interested in doing my own material, but . . . it isn't the kind of thing you pipe up and say when you're twenty years old."

Backing Phil and Don on their rhythmic acoustic guitars, as they would be for many Cadence sessions to come, were go-to Nashville A-Team musicians Chet Atkins on electric guitar, the reliable and creative Ray Edenton on rhythm guitar, Floyd "Lightnin'" Chance on bass, and Buddy Harman on drums.

Boudleaux explained what happened next: "Although the boys were singing the song really well, there seemed to be something missing. We were having a break and Don started strumming something which made me listen . . . and I said 'That's it. Put it on as the introduction.'"

The strumming was the Bo Diddley–influenced opening Don had used on the "Give Me a Future" demo. With that added, Phil recalled, "that's when Archie was really keen on this and thought we could be something. Because that's pretty much the essence of what 'Bye Bye Love' is—the good thoughts and the intro."

That eight-second acoustic guitar opening, which would grab the attention of car-radio and jukebox listeners across the country and across the oceans, was, in Don's words, "all downstrokes." It's not simply the straight, driving Diddley beat some reduce it to; there's additional catchy, blues-derived spin on it that's Don's alone, and on top of that—literally up top of that—there's Ray Edenton's unobtrusive higher note in tandem with Don's riff, adding to what makes the sound so irresistible. That's called a "high third," created by restringing the extra rhythm guitar and replacing the usual wound G string with one an octave higher. Don would note, "All the guitar players in Nashville were trying to figure out how to do it."

Edenton himself would often employ it after that, as did many who managed to figure it out. He recalled hearing somebody play it around the start of World War II, and not since, almost certainly referring to several innovative records by Hank Penny's Radio Cowboys, "Sweet Talkin' Mama" in 1938 and "Peach Tree Shuffle" in 1941. The notable part: the hot fiddler on those records was a young, classically trained cat—Boudleaux Bryant. We are left to speculate whether the suggestion on adding the high-third guitar didn't come from Ray-and-Boud conversations.

The sound created in that studio moment would be central to defining the Everly Brothers as an ongoing outfit. It could be built on, and it would be, and it was not quite like anything anyone had heard before. Acts thought of then or since as "rockabilly" have generally mixed R&B-influenced vocals with country-style picking. The Everly Brothers, by contrast, would typically fuse R&B-influenced instrumentals with hillbilly-style vocals. That synthesis would have tremendous influence, but no one could have seen that coming at the time.

Phil recalled what he'd wanted out of the day, in those lean times: "A quick $64 to buy some hamburgers... I think we would've recorded anything." When Archie asked Don what he'd do if this song turned out to be a hit, he replied that he really needed a new guitar case and some strings. He hadn't been able to afford even those.

The session done and the record not due out for weeks, Don and Phil got themselves booked on a three-week *Grand Ole*

Opry–sponsored tent-show tour, with Bill Monroe headlining. It was done on the cheap. Phil recalled, "Most of the time you rolled at night.... You'd sleep in the car, or else in a real dive. I mean, we hit some really seedy places, places where you couldn't use the toilets.... And it was the biggest tour *we'd* ever been on." Given the locales and the year, it was also racially segregated for the most part.

Don wrote to Margaret from Daytona, Florida, "We played the pier, the casino here...last night. We've seen the Gulf of Mexico and today we went swimming in the Atlantic! Tired of traveling, though. We are making about $90 a week a piece." That was twice what the four of them had made together in Knoxville.

After a short stay back home, they were booked on a tour with Brenda Lee—younger, and definitely shorter, than they were, but the first big pop act out of Nashville of that generation. She was thirteen, and there's a photo of her beaming, looking up impressed, and probably more, at Don and Phil, but she was the one with hits—"Jambalaya," "Bigelow 6-200," and, just being released, "Dynamite." There would be interesting parallels in their future direction, crossing genre lines. She'd later be a good friend of the Bryants, and she definitely was entering the outright rockabilly world, yet she was still being booked as country, as they were.

"We were friends, and we did some shows together," she told this author. "And I appreciated their harmony; they were just so wonderful, and that they were fortunate enough to line up with Felice and Boudleaux—that's like something out of a storybook." Others on that tour, headed in a northern direction, were George Jones, Patsy Cline, and Mel Tillis, no less. This was hard-core, top-drawer country; no question about it—unless you were their label.

Don writing to Margaret again: "This next Sunday we go to Cleveland, Ohio. Archie...called us and told us to play the *pop* TV show there.... I can't tell too much how our record is doing; it's just beginning to break in this part of the country."

Momentary fears that a rushed-out version of the song by Webb Pierce might eclipse theirs faded quickly; with its rhythm-wrecking notes held in all the wrong places, it was just more evidence that the song had landed in the right hands. Felice would say, in retrospect, "I do not believe that anyone else could have made that song the giant the Everlys did." Boudleaux added, "They did it right."

Archie's instruction to Don and Phil to appear on the pop TV show was no fluke. He had been promoting them to top pop deejays, not just country stations. What that meant first dawned on the brothers in the course of that short tour. "We were in Buffalo," Phil recalled, "and the jock there had a recording that he played on the air of when he'd played the record at a sock hop, and everybody sang with it. He had 2000 kids singing that song! And so it started to register."

"Bye Bye Love" appeared on the *Billboard* charts in mid-May, and as more successful recording artists, they were now invited to appear on the *Friday Night Frolics* extension of the *Grand Ole Opry* on the famed Ryman stage, not in the alley. Don said, "The Opry was, to me, the top of the heap, the top of the mountain. It would fade in and out in Iowa; it was like listening to Never-Neverland, some place that you wanted to be." And Phil would recall, "We'd auditioned for the Grand Ole Opry the year before that, and we didn't fit!" Funny what a hit can do. Now they were there.

In his *Nashville Banner* country music column, Ben A. Green reported excitedly that their *Opry* debut, singing "Bye Bye Love," was a sensation—like nothing since Johnny Cash's debut a year before. "The tuneful duo swept the crowd off its feet within 10 minutes...an almost unprecedented event.... The crowd began to cheer with the opening words...[then] waves of cheers, screams from the high schoolers, bass roars from the men, and high soprano cries from the women coursed through the lofty-ceilinged auditorium.... Many were in tears.... Two great stars had been born. . . . Here are two who do not copy anybody but themselves."

Two weeks later, he would report, "The handsome Everly Brothers (Don and Phil) will become 'regulars' Saturday night on WSM's Grand Ole Opry. 'We achieve our lifelong ambition in becoming Opry members,' said Don, oldest of the modest pair. 'Our father and uncles had this goal, and they have told us the Opry represents the very top in music.'"

Well, one top. By early summer 1957, "Bye Bye Love" would be number one on the *Billboard* country chart for seven weeks. It was also number two on the pop chart, and, the brothers must have been amazed and delighted to see, number five as R&B. The record is said to have sold over a million copies—including some in Europe, where they started to be noticed as well.

The song and the way it was presented would go on to become a permanent part of the emerging first-generation rock and roll vocabulary. For Donald and Phillip Everly, all of this would be life changing. The October issue of *Country Song Roundup* informed its readers, "The Everly Brothers are Country all the way—they were born Country, raised Country, and sing a whole heap of Country Music."

Some others would start to tell their story differently.

Chapter Three

THE EVERLYS AND THE BRYANTS

FELICE BRYANT WOULD SAY, "WE NEEDED THE EVERLYS AND EVI-
dently the Everlys needed us, and we met.... I don't know who
made who, but I tell you, we all had a good time."

The celebrated combination might never have happened. Felice,
as we've seen, had crossed paths with them at that television studio without consequences; Boudleaux had heard about them and
thought nothing of it. "This barber in Madison," he'd recall, "I
used to go to him to get my hair cut. And he was telling me every
time... about his boys, and what great singers they were, what a
fabulous duet. But everybody's got a son or a daughter or a niece or
a nephew or somebody in the family that is the best singer you've
ever heard in your life, or the best songwriter or the best musician or something.... and I said 'Ike, I know they must be really
good... Could you take off a little more in the back there?' Nothing

happened; they were never around when I was there; we just didn't get together."

The Acuff-Rose relation with Cadence brought the celebrated songwriting couple into the picture, but even then, the pairing of the Everlys and their "Bye Bye Love" breakthrough number could easily have been missed. Johnnie & Jack had put "a hold" on it, to record it at some point, but did nothing with it. Porter Wagoner had even begun to record it, as he had two recent Boudleaux-penned hits, "Tryin' to Forget the Blues" and "Pay Day," which had lyric and sonic elements much like Everly Brothers records. Only a disagreement between producer Chet Atkins and Boudleaux about how to work the chorus prevented it from being Porter's next cut; they'd put it aside.

The Bryants had been writing with harmony singers in mind for years, but working with the Everlys opened new song possibilities. As Boudleaux put it, "After the Everlys came along, we were able to make a little more sophisticated...chord pattern structure. We started using C minors, and some progressions that we hadn't been able to use up to that point." Generously, Phil summed up how the evolving *hit* harmony sound was constructed: "Boudleaux designed that harmony; I just sang it."

The Bryants had had a string of hits since the turn of the 1950s—many full-on romantic, others comic novelties—with honky-tonkers like Little Jimmy Dickens, Carl Smith, and Moon Mullican, smoother country balladeers like Eddy Arnold and Red Foley, but also with Tony Bennett, Ruth Brown, and Sarah Vaughan. The trade magazine *Music Vendor* had dubbed them "the King and Queen of Songwriters."

Boudleaux, from rural Georgia, was thirty-seven when the Bryants met the Everlys; Felice, from urban Milwaukee, was thirty-two. He'd been given the exotic first name not because anybody in the family was French or Cajun, but after a man who'd saved the life of his lawyer father Daniel in World War I. She'd been born Matilda Genevieve Scaduto, her father an immigrant from Palermo, Sicily. When the two met on Valentine's Day 1945, it was a genuine "love at first sight" moment; indeed, she reported that she'd dreamed of meeting exactly this man when she was eight. (The power of dreaming would play a considerable role in their future.) When he suggested that she seemed like someone who should have a more musical name than Matilda, like Felice or something, she took the suggestion. They were married that September.

Boud, as she called him, was a sophisticated, classically trained violinist who'd played with the Atlanta Symphony, but taken a few jobs as a hoedown or Western swing fiddler on the side. He'd stayed a fiddler *and* a violinist. During World War II, he suffered from that bane of so many traveling musicians' lives, a drinking problem serious enough to keep him out of the military. He'd never shake that entirely, but now had it mostly under control. The Boudleaux that the Everlys would get to know well was introspective, with strong, unorthodox spiritual concerns. He was, for instance, a personal and financial supporter of the organization that promulgated the works of the reputed clairvoyant Edgar Cayce.

Felice had grown up singing Italian pop and folk songs, and taken with poetry early on, was writing some. She was also among those Midwestern listeners to the *National Barn Dance* shows. In virtually any interview she did once fame came, you can hear instant, original metaphors dropped by her as if that were an everyday way to speak. (She'd offhandedly describe the Everlys as working together "like a fine Swiss watch.")

In 1949, Boudleaux's very down-home song "Country Boy" was a hit for "little but loud" honky-tonk singer Little Jimmy Dickens, beginning an ongoing string of hits, some written by Boud alone, some together with Felice, all for Acuff-Rose publishing.

Their new home by Old Hickory Lake, just north of Nashville, became a hub for artists looking for hot songs. They'd come by, feast on Felice's spaghetti dinners (an exotic treat in the old, more provincial Nashville), and look over their song ledgers or listen to the Bryants perform suggested tunes. The Bryants' young sons Dane, ten, and Del, nine, were on hand, soaking it all up.

Don and Phil were among the earliest visitors. Well aware the Everlys were now a media sensation, Del recalls, "The first time they came out to the house, they were looking for more songs, a concept that I was very familiar with; people were *always* there.... We had just finished the house, [so] there were still sawhorses around...and Phil said, 'Wow, *sawhorses*. I run track,' and he put a bunch of those sawhorses in a circle in the yard and we ran and jumped those things. We were having a hard time with them, but he wasn't. He was invariably playing with us. These were nice people who treated us the right way—play with the kids, be considerate, good with Mom and Dad. They had a lot of respect.

"Almost every visit after that was very relaxed. I remember a time they'd already had a number of hits and they brought a big blow-up raft and took it down to the lake. And there were four women—young women, probably late teens—and they would do stuff like that, since we lived on the lake."

Naturally, Don and Phil were looking for a follow-up hit to "Bye Bye Love." Felice would recall Boudleaux beginning to find it: "I was upstairs; I hadn't gotten out of bed yet, and Boud was on the main floor...and I hear this 'Wake up, little Susie; wake up,' and I thought, 'That sounds great.' I'd better jump in there, because I wanted a piece of this. I added some lyrics because I thought Boud was getting a little too rough...for public consumption."

The original unedited lyric included the excised line "Susie open your eyes; you're in for a big surprise," which would certainly have been open to interpretation—intended or not. Felice's solution? "I put the bridge in...I put these two kids in a drive-in theater, bored out of their minds and they fall asleep. *Now* what are we going to tell everybody?" It would, of course, be a massive hit, bigger even than "Bye Bye," though in some towns, such as Boston, it was said, radio wouldn't play it.

The song was the first where the Everlys sang unabashedly about teen life. It was the sort of observational song the well-past-teenage Chuck Berry was specializing in with the likes of "School Days," released earlier that year. Don and Phil, however, were of the age and look that fit that kind of story, and it made a continuing difference. This growing, newly identified teenage demographic was proving reachable. As Peter Asher of Peter & Gordon would note, "Kids may have heard country music they liked, but they'd never heard country music they could *identify* with." Chuck Berry always referred to "Wake Up Little Susie" as the song by someone else he'd most wished he'd written.

The single explodes off the jukebox or car radio with those thrashing opening chords, and additional ones between phrases—Don with another new chugging beat. Boudleaux was now leaving space for these riffs in the very construction of Everlys songs. "Dad loved Don's writing and how creative he was, and he respected Don's playing," son Del noted.

Some commentators suggested that the "Wake Up Little Susie" opening riff must have been something Don picked up from Mississippi Delta blues somewhere, but nobody could ever identify precisely what they had in mind—because it was his own creation. That propulsive, downstroke guitar riff would prove to be one of the most seminal and leaned-on in rock history. If you see the Who's Pete Townshend doing his "windmill" on something like "I Can See for Miles," or take Keith Richards's slashing chords to set off "Jumpin' Jack Flash," or even the chords Bob Dylan employs between "It's Alright, Ma" verses, those and many more are ultimately derived from Don Everly's riff and how it was put to work.

Archie Bleyer had doubts about the number, apparently because of its content, so the musicians secretly worked on the session while he was out of town. When the sales reports started coming in, he was glad they'd brushed his questions aside.

With the new financial stability that hits on this level were bringing them, the Everly brothers could see to it that Ike and Margaret relocated back to Nashville, to a house they bought for them. Single Phil would move in with them, enabling Don and Sue to have their own place at last—nearby, but their own.

With the age and experience differences, the Bryants and Wesley Rose, too, were coming to function as bonus surrogate parents for the young brothers. Del Bryant, who would go on to know all four Everlys well for the rest of their lives, noted that his outgoing, down-to-earth mother Felice was closer to Phil, and his more introspective, spiritual father Boudleaux to Don. Not surprising, really.

Phil would later describe how the brothers' relationships with the Bryants deepened: "As much success as their music brought...the personal relationship was more beneficial. I would go to them for lovelorn advice." Don would note of Boud, "He was a very observant man and very deep....[He] would sit down and talk with us. A lot of his songs were written because he was getting inside our heads, trying to find out where we were going, what we wanted, what words were right." (Whether that comment was meant as a grateful compliment or an attempt to claim some credit for song ideas the Bryants came up with would remain in the eyes of Don's varied beholders.)

Boudleaux did have a growing sense of what Don and Phil could do. Two new A-sides he wrote, recorded in 1958, would introduce the sound most associated with the Everly Brothers in retrospect—the sound of gorgeous close-harmony love ballads.

Early rock and roll artists would record a good many "rock ballads," often with incessant, pounding piano triads behind them. These weren't like those; the brothers' country music background would be quite evident. The theme of the first—the tantalizing tangibility of a desired one in dreams—had a long sturdy history in American music. It was particularly hot in the '50s for being romantic and suggesting getting physical, but not *that* physical. In just the two years before, the Louvin Brothers had finally found commercial success with "When I Stop Dreaming," and Faron Young had a hit with Don Gibson's "Sweet Dreams."

Phil and Archie Bleyer, who would hear "All I Have to Do Is Dream" on a demo sung by Boud, saw a hit coming with this one from the first. The versatile musicians who played on the Cadence records turned immediately to it just after they'd backed the Everlys' versions of outright rockers "Rip It Up" and "Be-Bop-a-Lula." Don admitted, "I was worried about us pulling a ballad off, but it was a good song. There's one thing that I want to mention—that tremolo at the front...one of the first times that had ever been used, which became a standard thing...Chet had built that himself. He was the one who was always there for us."

"Dream" was another number-one hit, and stayed there for weeks, once again, as pop, country, and R&B. Phil saw it as a career-changer: "The biggest compliment we got was that it generated people [coming] into stores. It was also a ballad, so we weren't just a beat act. We had *agility*." It was also the point where their reputation and reception in Great Britain began burgeoning; this single would top the charts there even longer.

It is interesting, from today's perspective, that while "Wake Up Little Susie" raised eyebrows in conservative cultural quarters just by suggesting two kids fell asleep at a movie, there was little kickback about this new one, probably because of the romanticism of the melody and vocals. The narrator of this song wants "all" of an envisioned girl's "charms" in the night, and dreams she's there so vividly that her "lips of wine" taste and feel palpable, probably very damply palpable. And then, "Gee, whiz"—there it goes, dreaming his life away. It wasn't Cyndi Lauper's "She Bop" or the Who's "Pictures of Lily," but you have to figure a lot of teenagers recognized this experience. Meanwhile, Boudleaux's putting that "Gee, whiz" teen talk in there was unprecedented pop genius.

The second of those change-of-pace ballads, "Devoted to You," was a declaration of serious constancy applicable to couples of any age, with a rhythm so basic it echoed "Twinkle, Twinkle, Little Star's" children's doggerel. The striking, quiet harmony made it resemble something from Renaissance church singing. The record sounds as beautiful as it does because Don, unlike many others, is able to get at and hold its vocal lead, and Phil's extraordinary ability to follow right along in that tight configuration is very evident. The song has defied many who've covered the Everlys' original ever since.

Phil noted, "Boudleaux designed that piece for me to use more fifths, to get that madrigal sound. . . . I didn't know 'fifth' from a hole in the ground." The signature, typical Everlys harmonies were in thirds—three notes up in the chord at hand. The fifths introduced in "Devoted to You" would be more associated with some aspiring young vocalists well aware of these records—the Beatles. Doing either sort well is tricky. Felice would describe the Everlys' vocal sound with one of her off-the-cuff metaphors: "There was an innocence about it; it was so fresh it was like slicing a spring tomato."

That would not be the word anyone applied to the Everlys' next, comical hit, penned by Boudleaux, recorded the same day as "Devoted to You," and at least as well loved and remembered— "Bird Dog." Novelty records were massively popular at the time and wide-ranging in their beeps, whistles, and nonsense babble.

They appealed to all ages—arguably to young kids in particular. In 1957–1959, your average preteen, teenager, tolerant parent, or senior citizen could well have been spotted cracking up to the likes of "The Purple People Eater," "Witch Doctor," "Beep Beep," "Splish Splash," "The Chipmunk Song," and "Yakety Yak." Don and Phil added another.

Boudleaux recalled, "I was sitting around the house one morning and . . . I remembered what my father used to call people that he thought were a little bit mischievous, slick, or rascally, yet likeable; he'd say 'Oh, he's a *bird*.' And the thought came, 'if he were such a rascal, he's a dog, too. Bird-dog.' . . . My head lit up. What a title."

This was apparently the record Archie Bleyer favored over recording Buddy Holly's "Not Fade Away," which Holly had submitted with the Everlys' love of the Bo Diddley beat in mind. Don delivers another catchy guitar riff, and the record went to number two. The B-side was "Devoted to You," and that reached the top ten, too.

"Bird Dog" was another "by teens for teens" song, as the rattled-off line "he even made the teacher let him sit next to my baby" clarifies. The next single, "Problems," written by both of the Bryants, was decidedly that, too, but perhaps starting to be too predictable in mood. When the record, released in October 1958, reached only number twenty, Phil said, "I felt like we had failed, somehow. . . . We all had this sense of people looking at us with that open eye: 'Maybe you're losing it.'" That was the new level of pressure Phil and Don were subject to, or at least perceived.

It was time for another change-up. And they all saw where it might come from.

The commercial folk explosion was a few years short of its full scope in 1958, but the Kingston Trio's smash success with their upbeat, if emotionally aloof, "Tom Dooley" got the music industry's attention. Not so coincidentally, between 1958 and 1960, US television offered no less than forty prime-time Western series, and plenty, such as *Rawhide, Have Gun—Will Travel, The Rebel, Bat Masterson*, and *The Life and Legend of Wyatt Earp*, featured theme songs that worked their way into the national consciousness.

Country music had been relatively uninterested in narrative ballads for some time, viewing them as part of the past, not its shiny pop future, but since country had just about given up on the Everly Brothers as a country act, that was beside the point. Pop was liking the potential of this "commercial folk" blip. The Bryants' "Take a Message to Mary" would be created in that context.

Felice and Boudleaux's older son, Dane, told music journalist Michel Kosser, "Mom wrote it while she was vacuum cleaning. There was a rock stuck in the vacuum cleaner. She wrote the whole song [to that beat], then called Dad on the phone. Boud wrote the lyrics down immediately, to save them before she could forget how they went." He wasn't that impressed, Felice recalled, laughing, "He says, 'That's not for them. That's not their style.' Automatically, he became an expert on what their style was!"

Felice's original lyrics would have placed it as one more teenage heartbreak number—sung by a contemporary young man in jail, not wanting Mary to know he was there. It would surely have been considered a "juvenile delinquent" song delivered that way. Bleyer doubted that it was strong enough, and Boudleaux tinkered with it, adding the opening that relocated it as the words "of a frontier lad" and "please don't mention the stagecoach." As history, the story was fine. (The same sort of trick would be applied to the Bobby Fuller Four version of Sonny Curtis's "I Fought the Law" a few years later, with the "zip gun" changed to a "six-gun," safely in yesteryear.)

Felice would always express amazement at how the record's sound got that way: "Archie Bleyer, who knew nothing about my vacuum cleaner, said to Boud, 'You know, I hear a chink, chink in this 'Take a Message.' . . . Somebody bring me a Coke bottle . . . and get me a screwdriver.... Hit this Coke bottle and that'll take care of what I think I hear.' And that's what you hear on the Everlys' record."

This would be, like "Bird Dog"/"Devoted to You," another single with two Bryant-written sides to it, the second also partly jail-located, "Poor Jenny," and they didn't object to delinquency rearing its head on that. The Jenny in question is misidentified by the papers as "the leader of a teenage gang" after being hit in the head at a party, and *she* winds up in jail. (Don and Phil must have related to her being taken for a young hoodlum when she's not.) The comical 1950s side-note is that in the single sold in England, that fight happens at one in the morning; in the American version, it's pushed back to 10 p.m. so she's not out so late—juvenile reputation-saving time. Apparently, they talk about you more for being out late than for being arrested in a violent brawl.

"Message" peaked at number sixteen and "Jenny" at twenty-two on the Hot 100 *Billboard* pop chart of the day. These songs, for all of their rootsy storytelling aspects, still got no country airplay. Two years after "Bye Bye Love" was number one country, a shift in how the Everly Brothers act was perceived was well underway.

Phil and Don would record more songs by the Bryants, some of them well loved, but none would have quite the impact these first 1950s hits did. There was room, those records established, for Everlys variations on old-school country, rock and roll, relatively unthreatening rockabilly, and a genial version of what we might as well call roots pop. Donald and Phillip would be singing those foundational Everly Brothers songs for the rest of their lives.

In her dissertation on the Everlys' hits-era music and its sources, musicologist Paula Bishop would note: "The Everly Brothers strove to emphasize the vocal aspects of their approach while still acknowledging the need for a dynamic rhythmic profile.... [They] resisted formulas and were willing to explore new ideas. The thoroughgoing parallel harmony...benefitted from the structural variety."

By the end of 1958, with millions of records sold, Don and Phil were still just twenty-one and nineteen. For all of their differences, neither was really inclined to leave behind any of those musical flavors they handled so well. Could they be roots-music-connected, rock-and-roll wild, and vocally and personally gentle all at the same time?

There was also a more personal question: How could they live, and live harmoniously with each other, with a demanding, conflicting public profile like that?

Chapter Four

WATCHING THEM ROLLING
1957–1959

Hits on the order the Everly Brothers had achieved are bound to change lives, and they did. The boys who'd been hanging out in the alley and considering chucking their musical careers were now touring relentlessly. One feature on them counted 134 personal appearances in the second half of 1957 alone.

Through '58, they'd appear in all-star rock lineups, including the one at the historic Alan Freed Paramount Theater show in New York City, but also joined Hank Williams's widow, Audrey, at the annual Hank memorial program in Montgomery, Alabama, where they were touted as among the elite of country music.

In July 1957 the cover of the trade paper *Cash Box* presented a full-length photo of the two of them with the caption "From out of nowhere come the Everly Brothers, who have a smash on their very first...record, 'Bye Bye Love.'... The Everly Brothers are now not only zooming in the Country field, having just been signed by the Grand Ole Opry, but they have become a major factor in the Pop field."

They were reportedly making some $2,000 per appearance—the equivalent of ten times that today, although announced numbers can sometimes be exaggerated for effect. Phil would detail, "We got to be, next to Presley, the highest paid act on the road. . . . 'Bye Bye Love' sold about a million and a half, and 'Wake Up Little Susie,' in the United States, a little over 2 million, which was a very large record at the time." Sales overseas were climbing, too.

By their contract, 4 percent on two million records sold comes to over $80,000 in 1958 dollars, the equivalent of some $836,000 today, just on "Wake Up Little Susie"—and Don would receive the songwriter's royalty for the same number of "Maybe Tomorrow" B-sides sold along with it. When Phil said, "We were doing pretty well," he wasn't kidding. *Modern Screen* would note, "They are very conscious of insurance, investments, stocks."

Their first investment was more tangible—their first car, an Olds 98, shared, but all theirs, not their parents', too. Don noted in wonder that for teens from their starting station in life, this was "unheard of." They sped to the Chicago area where Ike was working construction, and as Don recalled, "We picked Dad up and we said, 'You don't have to do this anymore. Come on back to Nashville.'" A few months later, Phil, who would always love cars, stepped up to a sporty black MG and was working on supercharging it.

They bought Ike and Margaret a modern house in the rural Oak Hill section, not far from downtown Nashville. Phil had his own room there, which he proceeded to paint solid black, causing many who'd hear about it to wonder if he'd suddenly gone all morbid and "goth" before his time. It seems that he did it just to have a room different from everybody else's, and maybe one slightly intimidating to parents living under the same roof. The hard-traveling brothers were back home in Music City less and less now, anyhow. While Don and Sue could finally afford to be on their own, she had to choose either to stay home alone or join him on road trips, which was unappealing to her homebody nature and rarely her choice.

And there was celebrity itself, which would define public perception of the brothers, and of Don and Phil individually, in ways that would stick, even as the picture of who they were was evolving. In these earliest years of success, Don and Phil were generally portrayed as "100 percent country," even by themselves. But when Tom Sellers, reporter for the *Montgomery Advertiser*, asked Phil during that Hank Williams memorial weekend whether they were singing "Western" or rock and roll, he smiled, shrugged his shoulders, and replied, "Who knows *what* it is?"

Early country coverage of Don and Phil, found mainly in the pulp, song-lyric-focused magazines aimed at country fans, began promulgating the "Southern boys, both born in Kentucky" myth as soon as "Bye Bye Love" hit, emphasizing what nice, polite, well-raised boys they were, and avoiding any hint of them transgressing in any way.

An elaborate feature published in *Country and Western Jamboree* lionized how Margaret and Ike had raised them. "Their parents mattered most" is the angle emphasized, and how their handlers and the Nashville production crew had made this all happen. They hadn't talked to the boys themselves at all. *Folk and Country Songs* magazine enthused, "Complete with guitars and a love for music, The Everly Brothers...lead the way in the world-famous Country music field; it's going to be pretty difficult to beat this bundle of Southern joy.... Both soft-spoken and somewhat shy.... No matter where they appear, the rafters really ring as this 'long-tall brother combination' make with those sweet Country sounds."

Songs and Stars noticed that, sure, they were country, yet *different*: "Many of the oldtimers are still shaking their heads in wonder over the phenomenal overnight success of these two 'rebels' from Central City, Kentucky."

As soon as "Wake Up Little Susie" hit, Phil and Don began to be presented as rockers in broader-circulation publications, for better and worse. Don lamented that to the day's often-hostile mainstream press, rock and roll wasn't the least bit respectable: "They really wondered if you were outside stealing hubcaps between shows.... The guys who were in charge at newspapers...hated it. They all hated *us*.... If your hair was a little longer and you dressed a little different, they threw you out of town."

There's no better example of the complicated ways that hostility played out for the Everlys in particular than in the special "Revolution in Records" issue of *Look* magazine of April 15, 1958. The large-format magazine was a direct competitor of *Life* magazine, heavy on photos, and another circulation powerhouse. That cover story, by Richard Schickel, later a well-respected film critic and historian, provided a remarkable display of dismissiveness and myopia when it came to any flavor of post-swing music and its audience.

He notes that with kids having a lot of spending money these days, the music business is suddenly all directed at that huge new audience, "whose tastes are youthful, to state it kindly." He doesn't stay kindly for long, quoting admiringly rock's description by musicologist Sigmund Spaeth as "a reversion to savagery." For an added blatantly racist touch, if that one wasn't clear enough, he notes that the music comes from areas of the South where blacks and whites are evenly mixed, causing country and R&B to "integrate"—disdainful quotation marks included. The kids, see, have only turned away from swing because "they can't dance to it." Archie Bleyer, of all people, suggests they'll likely turn to jazz of the "Brubeck or Dixieland variety," and "discover the virtues of...Perry Como and Doris Day" once they get through college.

One page later, on a separate but related focus feature, there's a large photo of Don and Phil leaving a Nashville radio show, met by autograph-seeking fans as Ike and Margaret look on from either side. They're praised for hitting it big "without going for Presley-like suggestiveness," and because "they even contend they are not truly rock 'n' rollers," playing country and pop "in an attempt to widen their appeal." One other observation provided about their "not-all-that-rock" music: "They remain innocently unaware of musical subtleties."

Thank you very much, *Look* magazine. That nice, nonsuggestive Phil is shown awakened in bed by puppy dogs, and having a soda with some local Nashville teens who appear to have been gathered for the photo shoot. Don is shown at home in an eye-lock with wife "Susie," called that, no doubt, because they think the recent hit record was about her. The Everly Brothers abided this sort of "rock and rollers...but not all that nasty" handling, imagined to be praise, for quite a while. "Our line was 'Yes sir; no sir,'" Phil would recall.

Donald and Phillip, it need hardly be noted, were both photogenic, though even their looks could be reported on condescendingly. Entertainment columnist Dick Kleiner noted for papers across the country, "They fit the bill of particulars for sensations in '57. They have good looks of the peculiar smoldering type so sought after these days." He apparently found them peculiarly smoldering.

The never-ending photography of the two of them, as often as not showing them practically stapled to each other, they're so close together, certainly had powerful impact on how audiences perceived these brothers they'd heard on the radio and couldn't distinguish. At least as impactful were their very regular appearances on TV. Mid-century modern, the Everlys came to popular attention just as it became possible for every stage of their performance capabilities and style to be seen by millions. Some of these prime-time broadcasts would reach more people in minutes than they could perform for live in years.

It's unsurprising that their first national exposure came on *The Julius LaRosa Show* in June 1957, as "Bye Bye Love" was exploding. He was, of course, on the same Cadence label they were and close to Archie. LaRosa hangs right behind them as he introduces them, hands on shoulders, coaxing smiles out of them as they reveal their ages. "I think Pat Boone is old enough to be their grandfather," he quips, and suggests they're nervous. In fact, they pop right up and jump into the sharp guitar opening. They're dressed in identical white suits, play identical guitars, and thanks to the miserable TV audio fidelity of the time, telling who's singing what as they vocalize is still nearly impossible, though Don, looking right into the camera at the home audience, gets close-ups on the solo parts, as he pretty much always would. And so began their television prominence. It wasn't always gratifying.

"The acts were treated *terribly*," Don would recall. "I remember the *Arthur Murray Dance Party* had us on television and everyone connected with the show said, 'We don't like this music, but we have to have it on the show.'" It could be chilly out there.

Ed Sullivan wasn't saying "And now...for all you *youngsters*" just yet, but the sense that any rock and roll act booked was there to please viewers, not him, was made clear enough. Their first appearance on his legendary show was just three days after the LaRosa broadcast, but Ed was absent that night; Hollywood musical star Dan Dailey introduced them. The second number they performed, "Hey Doll Baby," a countrified reworking of a Clovers doo-wop single, would only be released on record six months later, as an album track, but there was the unmistakable sound of females screaming as they sang it.

The most life-affecting event of that evening, it would turn out later, was that Sullivan had arranged to bring out a young blonde movie and TV actress who'd been voted "The World's Most Photogenic Girl" by *Popular Photography* magazine. A lot of people thought it was a good choice. Her name was Venetia Stevenson, and Don Everly, at the very least, registered that unusual name as interesting. Later, he would definitely recall encountering her.

Sullivan himself was on hand for their second appearance in October, and the producers apparently thought they were doing them a favor by adding awkward orchestral backup to Don's slashing riffs on "Little Susie." Production values—the bane of rock on TV.

A few months later the Sullivan show pushed that further, as Phil and Don, in slick matching Continental-cut jackets, performed their current single, Ray Charles's "This Little Girl of Mine," without guitars, standing and clapping out the beat in unison—and well. They looked unusually uncomfortable, though, with the modified soul beat they were clapping made lumbering by the less-than-compatible show orchestra.

As for those jackets, there was the money to upgrade the clothes they were seen in, and they'd jumped at the chance. Later that year, Don told two young reporters, "We both wear the same style when doing shows. . . . We bought almost 900 dollars worth of custom-made suits the day before yesterday and today at Phil's Men's Shop on Third Avenue, here in New York." They would rarely be seen looking anything but elegant, and only as trendy as elegance allowed. Care concerning how you presented yourself was an established Everly family legacy.

The growing fan reaction they evoked is conspicuous on the very popular *Perry Como Show* in December 1957. Affable Perry clearly plain likes them and how they sound. Their appearance, performing "Bye Bye" and "Susie," is marked by extended and repeated screams from the audience. Perry says, "That's nice singing, fellahs. That's nice squealin', too!" Orchestral backup is piled on once again, and for "Bye Bye Love" they're called on to dance—*American Bandstand*–style rock-and-roll jitterbugging, along with some girls who are adept at it. So are they.

They were less than thrilled to find themselves described in roundups of the teenage lust scene in terms similar to those of less musically talented faves of the moment such as Fabian, Frankie Avalon, and George Burns and Gracie Allen's son, Ronnie—all being pushed by the established music business so uncomfortable with rock and roll that they'd promoted tame ersatz Elvises. Phil would insist, "The last thing I want to be is a teenage idol and we never *have* been.... We didn't have that sex symbol image. Sure; we heard screams...but we [didn't] set out to fool audiences with cleverly worked-out tricks."

He seems to be referring to, for example, the famous Presley pelvis action, but in fact the brothers sympathized and understood the position *he* was in. Phil would say, "Elvis, above all, had to take an awful lot of rudeness and he—like the rest of us—had to be unfailingly courteous to people." The Everlys always gave him credit for opening doors, but they were not great fans. Don commented, "Elvis didn't have the kind of voice I liked, nor a sound I like. I was listening to Ray Charles, Brownie McGee & Sonny Terry, and Bo Diddley." By late '58, though, *16 Magazine* would report, "The Everlys think, as a singer, he's *improving.*"

No doubt with encouragement from manager Wesley Rose, they cooperated with the growing slew of teen fan magazines—only a few interested in anybody's music per se, instead featuring them as if they were auditioning as potential dates for teen readers. The articles filled in some blanks, accurately or otherwise, and established some early perceptions about who those two guys seen on TV were in life.

Given later chapters in the Everlys' story, it's fairly amusing that Don is generally portrayed as the calmer, more settled, more conservative brother—an Oldsmobile, not an MG. Since he was the married one, most wanted to play up his idealized domestic life; others chose not even to mention it and may not have been aware that he was married. For example, *Cool and Hep Cats* reported of the Everlys' alleged dating habits, "They are much too busy flying around the country filling engagements...but when they get home to Tennessee, Phil still dates the same gals he knew when he went to school. In fact, during school days, the boys double-dated, but now that they have their own cars..." Sentence left uncompleted, with all those cool and hep things Don must have been doing unleashed from Phil implied.

A domesticated Don was portrayed in *16* saying, "You know my idea of a nice evening at home? Just sit and watch TV and eat; we call it snacking around." Those were very different times: the same article describes the Everlys as fans of "especially odd" exotic foods—spaghetti, cheesecake, and Chinese. *Screen Stars* reported that "Don...recently completed a beautiful Chinese Modern home on four acres of land way up on the top of a quiet hill. There is plenty of room for children, since he and his wife want a large family. He attributes most of his current success and happiness to his wife, Sue."

In the months after Don and Mary Sue married in late March 1957, she was staying in that "high on a hill" home most all of the time, and she'd given birth in October to the infant she'd been carrying, a girl they'd only had time to name Mary. Sadly, the newborn died the same day, as Don rushed home from the road. Talk of making room for a large family must have been in part a way to look forward. They would have a daughter together two years later, Venetia Ember Everly, born in Nashville in May 1959, given the unusual name of that photogenic actress Don had met on *The Ed Sullivan Show*. (This would call for explanations later.)

Phil, meanwhile, was consistently questioned about his teenage dating habits and what he was looking for in a girl (always "girl," never "woman"), and portrayed as a naïve young guy just like ones readers knew, which seemed to be the point. "I like a good show and afterwards I like to stop off at a drive-in for a hamburger and a malted," he told 16. And there were multiple articles bylined by him, "as told to" sorts of things, where he's portrayed as a hapless dating underachiever, a loveable sad sack, in stories with titles like "The Night I Got Took" and "I'm Lonely" (*Modern Screen*), "The Kiss I Missed" (*Teen World*), and "Don't Rush Me into Marriage" (*TV & Screen Life*). It's not clear who'd been pushing him in that direction, but he says, "I've got to admit that I really don't understand girls, and I need more time to learn."

Endless touring was well underway. The Everlys had started playing big venues as soon as "Bye Bye Love" hit, places like Chicago's Civic Opera House, where fellow Nashvillian Brenda Lee was on the bill with them again, since she was an emerging rock star now, too, but no longer the likes of George Jones or Bill Monroe. That September, they joined the city-to-city bus rides of the Biggest Show of Stars for '57 rock and roll tour, with Fats Domino, LaVern Baker, the Drifters, Frankie Lymon, Paul Anka, and some important new friends, the Crickets, featuring Buddy Holly. Jerry Lee Lewis and Bill Haley and the Comets soon joined in, as well. History was being made.

The four-man Crickets lineup of Buddy Holly, Jerry "J.I." Allison, Joe B. Mauldin, and Niki Sullivan had recorded their breakthrough "That'll Be the Day" single just a few days before the Everlys' "Bye Bye Love" session, but it wasn't released until late May, and only since become a hit. The two charting outfits first met face-to-face at the Forum in Montreal on September 15, 1957, sharing a dressing room for their first stop together on that monthlong Show of Stars tour. Buddy Holly had been born just four and a half months before Don, Jerry "J.I." Allison just seven months after Phil. It was almost preordained that the Everlys would find a special bond with Buddy and band.

Some thirty thousand were in that audience. Don recalled first seeing the Crickets: "They were all down in the basement of this big arena, wearing these gray suits.... They had grown up together, so *they* were like brothers; they even had a kind of Texas language we didn't understand." Phil said of the quick connection they made, "All around the country there were people in the *same* straits as us—country, but so aware of what was going on in music that country couldn't contain them. Buddy Holly and Jerry Allison were doing the same thing down in Texas." Their relationship bloomed from the first, Buddy and Phil, with similar ambitions and compatible ideas about how to attain them, becoming particularly close.

That said, smart music makers are almost always attracted to what others are doing that they can't do themselves. The Crickets admired the Everlys' vocal harmonies, not featured in their band; the Everlys were struck by the practically unheard-of aspect of Holly and company—their setup as a cohesive outfit with electric guitar-bass-drums that wrote original songs, recorded them, and played them live.

Phil once described relations among the tour-bus-bound, first-generation rock and roll stars as "like a college fraternity." Given the climate, with frequent media hostility and shared pressures, that was entirely understandable. Still, there were differences among those legends-to-be. Most of the performers on those early tours were solo acts or traveled that way. Some, such as Chuck Berry and Fats Domino, were somewhat older, and even with the camaraderie on those racially integrated adventures it would be starry-eyed and silly to pretend that the 1950s racial divide never induced any awkward, wary separation between the black and white performers.

The high point of the thirty-day Show of Stars tour was the cele-brated week of all-star Alan Freed shows at the Paramount, around Christmastime. In some ways, Holly and company were the new kids in rock town, and certainly in the big city. The tour program had them in down-home white T-shirts, which may have looked cool to later generations, but didn't register that way at a time when tailored suits or tuxes were de rigueur for successful male music stars. The fashion-conscious Everlys noticed the unflattering gray business suits they'd brought along, and Don escorted the Crick-ets to that hip Manhattan men's store where the brothers got their stage wear. When Buddy and band appeared on *The Ed Sullivan Show* that week, the unstylish business suits had been replaced. It was reportedly the Everlys who suggested Buddy get himself some slicker-looking eyeglasses, too.

Dick Clark was a powerful TV host who quite evidently appre-ciated featuring Phil and Don. They were on his prime-time, ratings-seeking *The Dick Clark Beech-Nut Show* out of New York repeatedly, and introduced "All I Have to Do Is Dream" to TV on that show in April 1958. Also friendly toward them—Patti Page, who was hosting a competitor to *Your Hit Parade* called *The Big Record.* "What a beginning!" she enthused on a February 1958 episode. "Here are the boys who've rocked the nation's juke-boxes." They rip into "Wake Up" on a soda shop set—but there's still that big-band horn augmentation. Network TV just can't let Broadway-inflected production values go—yet.

While rehearsing for a Perry Como broadcast in September 1958, they encountered a six-year-old boy backstage, unable to walk without crutches—a fan whose show-business father had arranged for him to meet them. His name was Preston Bealle, and with the empathy for kids they felt, Phil especially, they interrupted the show rehearsal to sing him their new song "Problems" person-ally. He'd remain their friend for the rest of their lives, was able to eschew the crutches in five years, and would later become a serious collector of Everly memorabilia.

They were now regularly facing screams and fan frenzy, mainly female-led, heading in and out of most any performance, marking Phil and Don's full emergence as pop stars, which among other things, entails becoming famous objects of desire. There are reports of incidents where gangs of girls jumped on Don and ripped off his clothes, which happened often enough that they kept extra sets of stage wear with them just to be safe.

A peculiarity the Everlys lived with was that teen magazines ran contests where winners received "dates" with both brothers. Eventually there was that album called *A Date with the Everly Brothers*, too. If any of those generated any audience fantasies of threesomes, as they certainly could have, nobody was talking about it.

The closest thing to male protest about the Everlys' musical direction were remarks by a British reviewer in *New Musical Express* who lamented that "All I Have to Do Is Dream" was softer than he'd expected: "That almost vicious guitar work that has been the distinguishing feature of these two boys has gone.... The sharp attack and punch of their first two hits has been replaced by smooth-flowing harmonizing." Shades of "nothing but hard rock for me" macho that would metastasize in parts of rock culture up the road.

There was a number-one pop hit in April 1958 inspired by encounters with Don, though few have been aware of it, then or since—Ricky Nelson's "Poor Little Fool." It was written by a Newport Beach, California, girl, seventeen-year-old Sharon Sheeley, who'd been pursuing encounters with Elvis, Eddie Cochran, and Ricky, too, along with her sister, and their mother didn't mind them receiving idols in their home. Ricky brought the Everly Brothers along one time; she then visited them whenever they played in Los Angeles.

On one occasion, she, her sister, and the Everlys were threatened by "hoods" who'd followed them home after they had a few drinks at a hotel bar; Phil honked the car horn loudly, to no avail. Don, she recalled, pulled out a gun and they fled. She went on to date Don several times until, as she noted in her memoir, "Phil took me aside, and said 'You're too nice a girl to be involved with my brother Donald, Sharon.' He felt compelled to tell me about Don's marriage."

Heartbroken, Sheeley wrote her first hit song, "Poor Little Fool," and Rick Nelson carried it from there. She would go on to cowrite a number of memorable songs with Jackie DeShannon, including Irma Thomas's great pop song "Break-A-Way," and with Eddie Cochran's brother Bob, "Somethin' Else," for Eddie, who became her boyfriend. She'd remain close to Phil and would stay in the Everlys' circle. No hard feelings, apparently.

The musical capabilities of the brothers Everly were growing markedly. For the first time, Phil's songwriting began to approach Don's in terms of sheer output. Acuff-Rose demo recordings, released much later, included upbeat pop love songs ("Sally Sunshine") and teen problem stories—"You Can Bet," "I Can't Recall," and a strong one that should be better known, "Wishing Won't Make It So." Phil took some inspiration about how to focus on songwriting more seriously, crafting his creations more carefully, when they were touring with Chuck Berry and espied him backstage with pencil and paper, working and reworking new lyrics between stage appearances. Phil reached a songwriting milestone later in the year when Pat Boone recorded his sad, melodic ballad "Gee, but It's Lonely," which reached number thirty-one on the pop Hot 100 chart.

In January 1958, Cadence released the first Everly Brothers album, *The Everly Brothers* (catchy title), often referred to by the "'They're off and rolling,' says Archie" slogan Bleyer put on the cover. They're pictured looking back at us from a motorcycle, with a guitar on Don's back, as they're speeding away, self-promoting Archie on a second bike, rolling by their side. The "Bye Bye" and "Susie" hits are on there, the less-promoted Everly-written ballads mainly heard on jukeboxes, and their notable takes on Gene Vincent's "Be-Bop-a-Lula," Ray Charles's "Leave My Woman Alone," and the previously unissued "Hey Doll Baby" from the Clovers.

Their versions of songs from such varied sources would always have their own vocal and instrumental stamp and arrangements on them, and you'll not hear stories of the originating artists peeved that they did them. More often, they were pleased. While albums were not the heart of rock sales at the time, this offered a broader picture of what Don and Phil could do.

Despite their virtual disappearance from country radio, their *Grand Ole Opry* appearances continued. They were cheered performing both their version of Roy Orbison's "Claudette" and "All I Have to Do Is Dream" on one appearance, performed with more pounding rock piano triplets than usual and with Chet Atkins on hand adding more guitar filigree than on the record. Their recent adventures in New York and the Paramount Freed shows are mentioned—supportively, not mockingly, as New York references on the *Opry* typically were. The rock-star screaming is evident at the Ryman now, too.

As for "Claudette," it had been paired with "Dream" as the faster B-side to the hit ballad. It was really the first breakthrough as a songwriter for Roy Orbison, written as a salute to his wife. He'd pitched it to Don and Phil while opening a show for them in Indiana, singing them this one song he had ready; they'd had him write down the lyric on a cardboard box. Wesley signed Roy with Acuff-Rose as his publisher, and from there the major phase of Orbison's career was launched, often in quite parallel directions to the Everlys'.

The 1958 Biggest Show of Stars tour, which featured the Everlys along with Sam Cooke, Jackie Wilson, Paul Anka, and Clyde McPhatter, stopped in over ninety towns, none for more than two nights, with the performers just sitting up nights in what amounted to a school bus, taking zigzag routes without much sense and with long distances between stops.

"Paul Anka and Frankie Lymon used to sleep up in the luggage racks," Phil would recall, "and LaVern Baker stretched out across the aisle with suitcases in between the seats. Now, LaVern was as sweet as anybody could be. She'd sew buttons on for us and things—but nobody would ever wake LaVern if she was sleeping, because she got...a little cranky."

These were—black and white—all rock and roll kids, musicians on the road. Poker games, pranks, horsing around, drinks all around were in store, or if you were Frankie Lymon, shooting heroin. Nonetheless, there were elevating private moments. The Everlys walked into a dressing room one evening and found Sam Cooke and Clyde McPhatter, two of the most original, artful, and moving vocalists of the era, singing together. "It was," Phil would say, "the most spectacular thing, the two of them changing off... about the best I ever heard." On occasion, he'd find the same pair singing country songs.

In late February of '58, the Everlys and Crickets played a six-day tour in Florida together, with Jerry Lee Lewis also on the bill. Phil and Don discovered that the young high school boys who were supposed to be their pickup band on February 20 simply, in Phil's words, "could not play," and so for that one time, Buddy Holly and band stepped up as the Everly Brothers' backup, as their single "Peggy Sue" was just leaving the top ten and Jerry Lee's "Great Balls of Fire" was heading into it.

Phil recalled, "Buddy opened the second half, then Jerry Lee came out, and Don and I closed it. Buddy was blowing it apart; he had it to fever pitch. . . . Then Jerry Lee came on and rock and rolled it up one way and down the other. Without Buddy behind us, Don and I would have had trouble handling it, but he was playing with us. I've never had such a good time on stage, because we just had the *power*."

Phil and Buddy had drawn closer as friends. Neither, frankly, were the courtly innocents their more ethereal balladry suggested to many they were. Phil recounted years later, "Buddy Holly put me to bed with a girl—and he laughed." Sometimes Buddy would have problems holding his liquor. As Phil recalled, "We were sitting around one evening and I had managed to score. . . . This girl was quite pretty, Buddy was drinking. He got into a few words with her about friendship and he said, 'If I asked him, Phil would tell you to leave if you irritated me, because we're friends. *Wouldn't* you Phil?' I said: 'Well, you know, if she was bothering you . . .' 'Well,' he said, 'she's bothering me.' He called me on it, damn him. . . . I had to tell her to leave, because we were friends. He did it just to see if I would."

The astute brothers Everly habitually kept an eye on their ongoing musical and commercial situation. It was at this point, with the commercial folk revival rising and their place on contemporary country charts having fallen, that they began creating their much-loved concept album *Songs Our Daddy Taught Us*. Don vaguely recalled that they decided to do the project because they were thinking about leaving the Cadence label and didn't want any singles left behind to compete with whatever came next. The timing doesn't seem quite right for that, though. Wesley Rose started to look for a next recording home for them in 1959, a year before the Cadence contract was up. They began recording the *Songs* project in August 1958—and they remained on Cadence Records the full three years.

A possible, unspoken business motivation was that artists on Cadence heard talk going around about the label's possible sale to some odd, unexpected hands—to Studebaker-Packard, the firm cobbled together in the latter days of those two once-mighty car manufacturers. The firm was contemplating setting up an entertainment division and acquiring Cadence and Imperial Records, home of Fats Domino and Ricky Nelson, as a start. Those talks fell through, and *Billboard* reported, gleefully, that Ricky "will not, after all, be required to join the UAW," the auto workers' union. It's possible that Don, Phil, and Wesley were concerned they might wind up in inexperienced hands, with less say in what they could do, and with production disrupted.

What seems most likely is that they were aware that there'd been no old-school country records from them, material that was as much a part of their musical DNA as the other genres they'd been recording. It wasn't more so, as many like to see it, or viewed by them as a "purer" and better musical variety, but it was no less a part of who they were either. They did it because they wanted to, and now they could. The current pop interest in folk ballads likely helped them get a yes on the project, which didn't require complicated production and would be inexpensive to do. They got the go-ahead.

The *Songs Our Daddy Taught Us* concept was to record songs Ike had had them check out. Any comparison to the recorded source material ought to put to rest the notion that these were throwback interpretations and the album a retro excursion. They're Everly Brothers recordings—blood harmony, shared lyric interpretation, and acoustic guitar accompaniment included—and with untrammeled beauty that has been moving listeners ever since. (The all-acoustic aspect was apparently only decided on while the sessions were in progress. Outtakes of the "Down in the Willow Garden" murder ballad surfaced with Don, unusually, on electric guitar.)

The entire twelve-song set was recorded in just three sessions in August 1958 at RCA's Studio B in Nashville, with only

Lightnin' Chance, their regular studio bass player, joining them on the stripped-down recordings. Don said, "It was a natural...as good a thing as we'd ever done. It was true and it was from the heart and that's exactly where we were in those days....I still love the whole thing, that whole album, I love 'Silver Haired Daddy,' all that...sentimental stuff."

The comparatively recent songs in the lineup included Gene Autry's 1931 hit "Silver Haired Daddy of Mine," "Rockin' Alone in an Old Rockin' Chair," written by Bob Miller in 1932 and popularized by Eddy Arnold in 1947, "Oh So Many Years," a smoother rendition of the Bailes Brothers' 1947 record, and a take on the York Brothers' 1950 "Long Time Gone," quite close to the original. With Cadence's careful production, the guitars ring and the voices have a presence that on the older records they could not; the record buyer is brought as close to sitting there in the room with Don and Phil, listening along, as was possible.

Other selections were hoary enough to be considered "folk"— "Barbara Allen," "Roving Gambler," "Who's Gonna Shoe Your Pretty Little Feet," "Down in the Willow Garden"—the sort of songs the commercial folk boom was reviving. In the Everlys' hands they're performed charmingly and involvingly, without the sing-along distancing or irony commonplace in the era's commercial "frat house" folk.

Not that they weren't well aware of the incongruities of trying to match these songs and their young audience. By about the twelfth take on "Willow Garden," the brothers and Lightnin' broke the tension with some revealing joking. Don, apparently pondering the lyric that they've been singing over and over for the first time, with both a knifing and a poisoning in it, wonders, "It hardly makes sense...I killed her *twice*? Now, friends—we bring you a killing song. In two easy lessons you can slay your pregnant girlfriend. Well...that's what the story's about!" And Phil adds a final folk-album-style explanatory intro, not to be included on the actual record: "Music to kill by, for all you teenagers."

The recordings that would have the most lasting impact for the Everlys themselves were both from the pen of Karl Davis, of the Karl & Harty duo that had introduced the songs in the 1930s and were working the same Chicago radio station as Ike during the war. There was "I'm Here to Get My Baby Out of Jail," which Cadence released as a single a few years later. The second, which was strongly associated with Don and Phil ever after, was the nostalgic, even spiritual, ballad "Kentucky," which fuses memory of the old home place with visions of heaven. The Blue Sky Boys, brothers Earl and Bill Bolick, more melodic than Karl & Harty ever were, had also recorded both songs, and their 1947 version of "Kentucky" certainly seems to have influenced Don and Phil's take.

That single song may have done as much to unite the ideas "Everly Brothers" and "old Kentucky" as anything, and there are ironies in that. Back in the actual Kentucky, Karl & Harty had formed a rather jazzy, modern hillbilly outfit, the Kentucky Krazy Kats, and the song still maintains swing rhythm traces. The tune and even some of the words were their modification of the Carter Family's "You Are My Flower," which Maybelle and Sara had dashed off while working on Texas–Mexico border radio. The fairly hilarious part: "You Are My Flower" was Maybelle's modification of "La Paloma," the Basque Spanish tune around since about 1860, as played by area Mexican musicians. So there's the Appalachian mountain purity people think they hear.

The "Kentucky" song did effectively crystallize what most commercial country music has always been about at its core— displacement to the city (or later, suburbia) by someone whose *family*, at least, had once been rural. As Don said of the Kentuckian diaspora, "Even if you were born in Chicago, it meant you were working there; it didn't mean that you were from there...you were *from* Kentucky."

Novelist, music journalist, and poet laureate of Kentucky Silas House suggests: "I think the rest of America thinks Kentucky is the best of America, or the worst—no middle ground. If you're from a place that's sometimes vilified, it makes you prouder to be from there, so families who have left carry Kentucky with them. You take your food ways, your vernacular, your value system, and it's still very much a Kentucky household. For a musician, there's some gravitas in saying you're from there—although, it can really mess with your sense of identity, because you've grown up somewhere else, but held to Kentucky standards by fans."

In the UK, albums in general were still nonstarters, too expensive for many and for most all of the younger audience, so there, *Songs Our Daddy Taught Us* was broken into three separate extended-play records—EPs. Cadence didn't put much money and effort into promoting the album in the US, and it didn't chart, but it lasted. Some twenty years later, Archie Bleyer would note: "I still get mail in regard to the old Cadence records, and *Songs Our Daddy Taught Us* . . . that's the strongest mail-puller to date."

It is not hard to see why. Don and Phil deliver up the old songs with special beauty and connection, and with the continuing movement of segments of the American population from the countryside to the towns, south to north and east to west, many people can relate to its longing for the old-homeplace sentiments, whether as shared experience or as metaphor. Indeed, as performed live through the years, the album's material proved strong enough to speak to those across oceans and with different native tongues.

Why did they never follow up with a volume two? The closest thing to an answer available is what they did instead—a succession of varying styles of music that were all parts of who they were, too. The Everlys moved on.

Over that same summer, Buddy Holly and band sometimes joined Don and Phil in Nashville for their downtime on Felice and

Boudleaux Bryant's boat. Then, back in Texas, Holly woodshedded with his old writing partner Bob Montgomery and penned two new songs with the Everlys in mind—"Love's Made a Fool of You," in the Bo Diddley–beat mode, with a Latin rhythmic tinge, and the gentle, yearning "Wishing," designed for Everlys harmony. Wesley Rose apparently finessed his response to Buddy's demos by suggesting they couldn't risk recording songs Holly might hit with himself. In truth, he remained uninterested in songs not published by Acuff-Rose. The Everlys never got around to them.

Buddy and Phil, relatively business-minded as musicians go, were both looking at possibilities beyond writing songs and performing—producing and perhaps managing other artists, in case that "What will you do when rock and roll dies?" question turned out to need an answer. They'd been running new songs by each other for comment since they first met. Phil said, "I heard almost everything of Buddy's in the prior stages . . . I remember when he showed me 'Maybe Baby' in a dressing room; just fantastic." Buddy was talking about building a recording studio of his own in Lubbock.

In September, the two of them got together in New York, writing a song each for both sides of a single they produced for young singer Lou Giordano. The Holly-penned song, "Stay Close to Me," is a love ballad; Buddy is recognizable on guitar. The flip side, "Don't Cha Know," is an upbeat Latin-like rhythm number written by Phil, with what sounds like a female vocal chorus repeating or answering each line's ending. The answering "girls" were in fact Buddy and Phil working falsetto. Giordano would have a long and storied career as a producer and engineer, and a very short one as a potential teen idol.

"New York was great then," Phil would recall. "I remember walking through Times Square with Chuck Berry, and him buying us our first cheesecake at Lindy's." This was the time when several often-seen photos of Phil with newlyweds Buddy and María Elena Holly, or J.I. and his wife Peggy Sue (of hit song fame), were captured, out on the town. Spanish music—and restaurants—were in vogue, and Phil, Buddy, and María Elena were all taken with a flamenco guitarist at Café Madrid, on Fourteenth Street in Greenwich Village, enough so that Buddy asked the performer to give him lessons on how to play like that. At another Spanish restaurant nearby, El Chico, the Hollys were photographed with Phil and his date, Virginia Hebel. Phil, still just nineteen, had quietly been dating Virginia for about a year.

A few weeks later, Buddy recorded a Felice and Boudleaux Bryant song that Phil and Don had passed on but suggested might be right for him. As Boudleaux recalled, "I believe...they told him that he ought to come out and listen to some of our songs. I met him out at Acuff-Rose, and I showed him a few songs, among them 'Raining in My Heart,' and he fell in love with that one right off the stick....And he did it on his next session." It was the elaborate string session that also produced "True Love Ways" and "It Doesn't Matter Anymore."

Buddy ran by Phil what became known as the "apartment tapes" songs, homemade demos of such lasting originals as "Crying, Waiting, Hoping," "Peggy Sue Got Married," and "Learning the Game," looking for some encouragement that maybe those could be hits, which he needed badly. Phil found them "sensational," and recalled Buddy asking why he couldn't get a hit record, "he was so low."

As he told Kurt Loder, "The last time I was really with Buddy was at the Park Sheraton in New York; that was the hot hotel where all the rock & rollers used to stay. Eddie Cochran was in town, and we were all up at his room there. Buddy was having a drink, and he asked me to make sure he got home that night, and I did." Don would lament, "The last time I saw Buddy Holly, he'd been financially screwed; he didn't have any money, and he was on his last tour."

In January 1959, with the Everlys' strong sales in Great Britain and parts of the European continent in mind, Archie decided it was time to introduce Don and Phil there in person, on a Cadence artists mini-tour that included Andy Williams and the Chordettes. Phil was by this time tentatively dating, among others, Jackie, daughter of Chordette Janet Ertel, Archie's stepdaughter.

Newspapers announced their approach with great fanfare, though contractual complications meant they couldn't perform in live shows. The whole gang stopped in towns in eight countries in ten days—England, Belgium, Holland, Denmark, Sweden, Germany, Luxembourg, and France—took questions at press conferences and on the London TV program *Cool for Cats*, and performed on Dutch television. These were places that would become some of the most frequent stops on Don and Phil's international tours, homes of immensely loyal fans.

On that Dutch *Archie Bleyer Show*, Phil and Don, in black jackets, slowly snapped their fingers alongside Archie at the piano, while Andy Williams crooned. Then they looked right into the camera and showed the Dutch what singing "All I Have to Do Is Dream" *looked* like—lip-synched. They introduced themselves as guys from Brownie, Kentucky, now living in Nashville, and in a short film, Phil, Don, Sue, and their dog are shown heading into the living room of Don and wife's new house. The brothers perform "Long Time Gone" in shirtsleeves, guitars in hands, a good representation of its performance at the time.

Back home in February, the call came. J.I. and Joe Mauldin had split off from the Crickets because they'd preferred to stay based in Lubbock, but Buddy and some substitutes (Waylon Jennings and Tommy Allsup) had joined the Winter Dance Party tour in the upper Midwest, along with Ritchie Valens and J. P. "the Big

Bopper" Richardson. As the world would soon know, the plane carrying Buddy, Ritchie, and J. P. crashed on February 3, killing all three.

Don was too shaken to attend the funeral, set for Saturday, February 7, in Lubbock: "I didn't go. I wouldn't go," he'd recall. "It just freaked me right out when Buddy died. I took to my bed. Quit riding planes for a while, too." Phil and mother Margaret Everly flew to Texas together on a chartered plane; Margaret checked in to a local hotel while Phil, set to be one of the pallbearers along with Jerry Allison, stayed with the Holley (Buddy's real surname) family themselves. At the service, Phil was not a pallbearer after all, because, he said, "I didn't want to see him put down in the earth." He sat with the Holley family and María Elena, and joined Allison, Mauldin, Niki Sullivan, and Sonny Curtis in singing the hymn "Beyond the Sunset."

Holly and the Crickets, like the Everlys, would attract some pretty smart followers. In retrospect, the creative power and pithiness that would be shown in the songs written by Buddy and J.I., their Lubbock friend Sonny Curtis, and by Don, Phil, and the Bryants made them all, along with Chuck Berry, the first rockers especially beloved by those who value lyrics with observational sharpness and riveting storytelling. All, not so incidentally, had been fans and practitioners of country music, where those observational tools were already central.

A few months after the funeral, in July 1959, Allison and Curtis both took part in the Nashville session for the Everlys' "('Til) I Kissed You"/"Oh, What a Feeling" single, right along with A-Teamers Chet Atkins and Floyd Cramer. The record would snap Don and Phil back into the top ten on the pop charts. And J.I.'s steady, pounding-yet-rolling tom-tom on the Don Everly–penned "('Til) I Kissed You" played no small part in its appeal. It marked the beginning of a continuing and important working relationship between the Everlys, Allison, and Sonny Curtis, who was now formally in the Crickets, too.

Over more than fifty years ahead, J.I. and Sonny would continue to be close and valued friends of Phil and Don, as session backup, significant songwriters for them, and appearing with them on some of the most remembered and influential tours of the Everly Brothers' career. They were relationships that stuck. Phil and Don had made contact with new audiences, forged important friendships like those along the way, and were going to ride higher still.

They'd certainly come a long way "from Brownie"—or Shenandoah. They had a long way to go.

Chapter Five

THE HEIGHTS
1959–1961

PEOPLE ALWAYS ASKED TWO QUESTIONS, NO MATTER HOW MANY TIMES they'd been answered: No, Don and Phil were not twins. Some may have just glanced at the endless pinup pics of the pair and decided they looked just alike. With dual profile photos, you might think that—if you didn't look too closely. Their eyes and their glances never looked that much alike at all. Then again, with the sheer number of ersatz, unrelated "brothers" and "sisters" acts in show business, some would always ask whether they were really brothers at all, or only like the Doobie Brothers or Righteous Brothers. To miss, by sight and sound, that they were so obviously siblings would take cynicism or sensory deprivation.

By 1959, the public was beginning to understand them as two differentiated personalities—not necessarily accurate pictures, but distinct. Strong-willed Don versus clash-avoiding Phil is a binary that typified much of the Everly Brothers story, and some of that was on public view. At *Motion Picture* magazine, Barbara Henderson had parallel, teasing "as told to" pieces, "You Just Can't Teach Phil Nuthin," according to Don, and "Since When Are You a Teacher?" as Phil's rejoinder.

"Most people say Don takes after Mom and I take after Dad," Phil is quoted as saying, and that was certainly true. "Mom is the most determined woman you ever met. She's got enough drive for all of us, and once she makes up her mind it's made up for good. Our dad is just the opposite. He's the world's most easy-goin' man. He's a real...country humorist type...the knee-slappin' variety.... Instead of makin' a big incident he'll step back to avoid an argument." That picture of Ike was a reasonably good description of Phil, too, if with a tad less knee-slapping.

The press's "responsible, polite Don" versus "adventurous, reckless Phil" dichotomy would hardly be the lasting impression of the two of them. At this point, Don says in his reply, "People are always comparing the two of us, and saying I'm the serious one and he's the clown....But he's got guts and he's an individual...sometimes too much for his own good." And Phil adds, "I think the responsibility of havin' a younger brother gets to be just too much for him....Sometimes you'd think he learned his manners at a boy's finishing school."

At twenty, Phil was still being portrayed as a happy-yet-unlucky girl chaser, much like the Dobie Gillis sitcom character on the air that year, and he didn't discourage that picture. In one article he mentions how he lost five girls on the same night; why they all felt like leaving—that he doesn't detail. Phil, of course, now had much, much more money than TV's girl-crazy son of a grocer. He added a Porsche and a Jaguar to the MG he already had, and apparently liked to push them to their limits. An August 1959 wirephoto shows him and a buddy in court in Nashville after being arrested for drag racing. They were acquitted.

Don and Mary Sue, by contrast, are regularly portrayed as domesticated young lovebirds peering deep into each other's eyes and laughing a lot, comfortably at home. An often reprinted photo from the New York *Daily News* showed the two of them cracking up, seated at a table in a soda shop, while Phil and his date of the moment dance by the jukebox in the background. Whatever Don was or was not actually doing out on the road, things were evidently going along well. Their daughter, Venetia Ember Everly, was born on May 16, 1959.

The Everly Brothers' musical identity continued to evolve as well. While they were not showing up on the country music charts anymore, "('Til) I Kissed You" was the exception that did. *Grand Ole Opry* appearances had become rare, though, since they were out of town so often.

Don would recall of this time, "I didn't mind being called country too much; I like being called rock and roll, but when they called me rockabilly, well, in the South to be called a hillbilly is an insult...so I got really insulted...I used to hate the term." He'd become more accepting of the word, but it's self-evident that people wondered, and continued to wonder, exactly how to label what the Everly Brothers were doing. What must have been especially irking was the sort of lingering "adult" review that marked them as superior to their fellow rock-and-roll cofounders for not "really" being one of them.

Derek Johnson, in Britain's *New Musical Express*, noted, "The boys success in this country lends weight to the theory that country-and-western music, with its roots deeply bedded in the authentic folk origins of the Middle-West, is gaining in popularity here, at the expense of the basic crudeness of rock 'n roll."

Setting aside the misunderstanding of country's complex commercial and regional origins (in a supposedly knowing article that also praises them for writing the Roy Orbison–penned "Claudette" and locates the *Grand Ole Opry* in Kentucky), what's striking is that country music is understood to be gentlemanly, so *non-crude*, which would have been news to the honky-tonkers, let alone the rockabillies—country as essentially about a mild evening at the club with a decorous crooner. And that was supposed to be praise.

Over the rest of their lives, Don and Phil would provide varying answers to the never-ending questions about their musical identity—we're country, we're rock and roll, we're *entertainers*—all of which were true, but the answers would reflect their current mood, or the answer they thought the interviewer wanted to hear. It was *not* yet clear that they were carving out a special, formidable place on the rock-country spectrum, one that would eventually demand new labels from "country rock" to "roots pop" and "Americana," but there were early, milestone indicators.

In the wake of the smash "Tom Dooley" hit, a good many country artists with their careers in decline rambled into the growing hootenanny-industrial complex with varying degrees of success—Merle Travis, Eddy Arnold, bluegrass giants Bill Monroe and Flatt and Scruggs, the Carter Family, and Johnny Cash, who asked on the *Town Hall Party* TV show whether rockabilly kids might maybe sit still for a story song. Don and Phil, still riding high, had no pressing need for desperate moves, but the "Take a Message to Mary"/"Poor Jenny" single provided prophetic opportunities.

On April 26, 1959, Roy Rogers and Dale Evans acted as guest hosts of *The Dinah Shore Chevy Show*, Nashvillian Shore's long-running, immensely popular NBC variety program, for a special episode they simply called "Country Style." Joining cowpokes Roy and Dale on the opening boogie number "String Along, Sing Along," which described the rise of country music in upbeat folk sing-along terms, were the Kingston Trio, Ernest Tubb, Minnie Pearl, the Everly Brothers, pop singer Betty Johnson, comedian George Gobel, and Johnny Cash, all together, strumming along and taking verses. This was a fresh, relatively inclusive (if ethnically and racially exclusive) vision of roots-pop convergence, and Don and Phil had just the song for it.

Later in the show, in a signifier bonanza, they introduced "Take a Message to Mary," not in their sleek matching suits, but in shirtsleeves with dark vests and string ties—reminiscent of the coming New Lost City Ramblers' "authentic folk" look, yet TV Western-like, too. They're first seen on a wanted poster as the Dalton Brothers. (*Wanted! The Outlaws*, anybody?)

This broad amalgamation as an attractive way to present the music was not a one-off. A few weeks later the city of Portland, marking its place in the state of Oregon's centennial exposition, hosted a huge Fourth of July country music show. The context was presenting American roots-music connections to history, in a pageant that included Conestoga wagon parades to recall Oregon Trail treks. It put the Everlys and the post–Buddy Holly Crickets on the same bill as Hank Thompson, Hank Snow, Merle Travis, and Grandpa Jones.

That "('Til) I Kissed You," with "Oh, What a Feeling" as the B-side ballad, not only managed to reach number eight in the Everlys' return to the *Billboard* country chart and number four pop but was another notable milestone. Both songs were written by Don, and that's the first A-side hit written by either brother. Don would admit that his inspiration for the song was one of his brief road encounters—in Australia at the beginning of the year. "I wrote [it] about a girl I met [on that trip]," he told Kurt Loder in 1986. "Her name was Lilian, and she was very, very inspirational. I was married, but...I wrote the song about her on the way home." Nobody knew.

The two sides were recorded on July 7 at the RCA Nashville studio, at the session that brought in Jerry Allison on prominent "Peggy Sue"–style drums, and Sonny Curtis joining Chet Atkins on guitar. The strong drum sound presented a challenge for the new engineer that RCA's Studio B had just hired, the celebrated Bill Porter, who would make significant contributions to the Everlys' recordings. He was working with a new console that introduced then-innovative "peak limiters," and they were getting track-wrecking sound distortion, which proved tough to eliminate. Archie Bleyer was incensed. This particular technical problem was worked out, but there would be increasing episodes where what Archie Bleyer demanded, Wesley Rose preferred, the engineers needed, and the Everly Brothers wanted to create musically would clash.

This was the final year of the Everly Brothers contract with Cadence, which increased tensions. Wesley was quietly looking into other label possibilities for them now; substantial dollars were on the table and egos were roaming through the house. Chet Atkins recalled, "There got to be a lot of jealousy between Archie Bleyer, the producer, and Wesley Rose, the publisher. Archie wouldn't want to do Wesley's songs every time," as Wesley thought he had the right to demand. "It was no fun to work any more, because they weren't getting along, and this was infectious to the musicians.... We got inhibited."

A serious clash came later in the year over whether, where, and how to do one of the signature recordings and songs of Don and Phil's career, "Let It Be Me." There's no better example of the Everly Brothers' blood-harmony alchemy and vocal finesse meshing their two voices into one poignant point of view on the record, or in hundreds of live performances of the song. "Let It Be Me," in the wake of the "Devoted to You" ballad, begs to get some of that intense devotion back. From the opening words, "I bless the day I found you," there is an exceptional sense of what this combined "I" is feeling and wanting.

The song was not published by Acuff-Rose. In its original 1955 form, the tune had been written and sung as "Je t'appartiens" by the popular French singer Gilbert Bécaud, with words by Pierre Dela-noë. The original lyrics are kinkier; the singer is eagerly submitting to being his love's docile slave. The song made its way across the ocean, with the more romantic lyrics we know, as written by veteran ballad composer Manny Curtis, and recorded in 1957 by the rarely remembered Jill Corey, a coal miner's daughter who sang on 1950s TV shows. Her single was less regular rhythmically than the Everlys' would be, and sung with some odd, overly careful diction.

Chet Atkins recorded the tune as a delicate instrumental for his 1959 *Chet Atkins in Hollywood* album; Don apparently first heard the song that way. "It was one of the great songs of my lifetime," he told Colin Escott. "I said to Chet, 'I love that melody. Is there a lyric?' He said, 'Yes, and it's a great one.' I went to Archie and told him I wanted to do it with strings." Chet's instrumental had a thick orchestral introduction similar to the one they would employ, though Archie would claim the Everlys' arrangement for himself, and he was, after all, a veteran of that sort of arranging.

The December 15, 1959, "Let It Be Me" session would be the Everlys' first held outside of Nashville, at Bell Sound Studios in Midtown Manhattan, a favored site for much rock and roll recording. With the exception of J.I. Allison on drums, the musicians were all new to the Everlys—and included a lush string section conducted by Archie. Guitarists Howard Collins, Barry Galbraith, and Mundell Lowe were all known for jazz work, as was bass player Lloyd Trotman, but he'd become relied upon for New York rock and R&B sessions, too.

To Jerry Allison, it felt like justification. Not long before, he'd been excluded from playing on Buddy Holly's last, New York session, the one with orchestral backing. "Joe B. and I were there for those sessions," Allison told this author, "but we didn't get to play on those. I always enjoyed the fact that when the Everly Brothers cut 'Let It Be Me,' I went to New York to play on *that*—another string session."

Wesley Rose didn't enjoy the whole setup. Don recalled, "He just sat there pouting like a kid." The song would remain a central one for the rest of the Everly Brothers' career.

The other melodic song recorded that day was the Don Everly original "Since You Broke My Heart." The backing track had been brought north from Nashville, with Chet and, apparently, Sonny Curtis on the guitars, and Allison on prominent, pounding drums. The vocal, beginning with that intriguing "They say...the blues went out of style," was then added there in New York—a sign of production methods just coming *into* style.

Both Don and Phil were clearly reaching maturity and accomplished artistry as songwriters. Phil continued to place songs elsewhere—the gentle rockabilly numbers "Darling Talk to Me" with Johnny Rivers and "All Right, Be That Way" with Jesse Lee Turner, for two. Over the next three months, "When Will I Be Loved," "Cathy's Clown," and "So Sad" would be major hits, permanent repertoire A-sides that were all Everly originals.

The Bryants were proud to see their virtual protégés coming along like that. The flow of new songs from them was in no danger of stopping—for the moment. In the same period, Don and Phil would record such first-rate Bryants songs as "Like Strangers," "Sleepless Nights," and "Love Hurts," regularly anthologized and covered classics, though none were chartbusters then. "Sleepless Nights" and "Love Hurts," for all their later fame, were never pulled out as singles.

Meanwhile, all of this quality recording played out under increasingly fraught circumstances.

The quiet poking around for a potentially larger and better recording deal had begun. Phil and Don were clearly in the position that recording stars and sports stars are when they've proved to be big moneymakers on first contracts; they and their management look for bigger, longer deals. Archie was pushing for more outright pop in their mix as much as Wesley stressed, even now, that they should stay close to Nashville country. It was about power over them more than about the music, and it was getting to be an uncomfortable squeeze.

The brothers were working in a much larger arena now, with international potential, and they wanted more payback as they grasped that. Paul Anka alerted them that they were really bigger than they understood and should be getting much more, implying strongly that manager Wesley wasn't filling in a lot of details he should be. But then, they hadn't asked him all that many questions. He sometimes acted more like a controlling father than as their manager-publisher.

"Wesley was like their surrogate parent, in a strange way," Del Bryant would recall. "When they got motorcycles, he'd said 'I'm taking the cycles away; they're too dangerous.' Like they'd 'misbehaved'! He was pulling their strings." That paternalism affected business decisions, too.

"We wanted a guarantee," Phil told interviewer Joe Smith, "and I had an idea. I told Wesley that if he could get us half of Hickory [Records], we'd sign with Hickory, which wouldn't have been a bad deal." Hickory, recall, was the Nashville label owned and operated by Acuff-Rose themselves. A half-ownership stake *could* have been seen as assuring Don and Phil's commitment to producing for Acuff-Rose, and whether Wesley relented on using writers from outside or not, the Bryants and the Everlys themselves would certainly be contributing more under an arrangement like that. In practice, Wesley seemed reluctant to consider any opportunity but a potential new one on the horizon with the emerging Warner Bros. record label, recently established by the celebrated movie studio, but still somewhat shaky.

"There was a little bit of managerial handling of us in that transition period," Phil would recall. "RCA was also interested, but we didn't have the nerve, and didn't know enough, even after three years, to do this on our own—and that we should have had our own lawyer, not Wesley's.... There could have been other things... but we came from nowhere and didn't think enough about what was best for us.... [Don and I] were equally naïve about it, which put us in synch. We were too busy to talk about it, really more concerned with trying to cut a hit."

If the Everlys were trying to avoid leaving leftover singles at Cadence, they may have been underestimating a new song from Phil that they knocked out on February 18, 1960, the same day as Boudleaux's "Like Strangers." It was "When Will I Be Loved," inspired by Phil's long-brewing yet never quite locked-in relationship with Jackie Ertel. He suspected that the song got the go-ahead because the label was just running out the contract. Those would indeed prove to be the last sides they recorded for Cadence, but that one would be the most celebrated song Phil would write alone, and it went top-ten pop when released in May. By then the Everlys had gone on to their next label, and the record would compete, not at all badly, against their blockbuster first single there, "Cathy's Clown."

Trade papers began mentioning rumors that they might be headed to Warner Bros. Records.

Inside Warners, though, things weren't so clear. Just two years old, the label was losing money and Jack Warner, the famed studio chief, was ready to shut it down when the label's head, Jim Conkling, told him there was a chance to sign the rock-star Everlys. Don and Phil were excited to work for a firm that could, just maybe, put them in the movies, too. It would take an unprecedented million-dollar, ten-year contract to bring them there. Longtime Warner Records executive Stan Cornyn recalled Jack Warner resisting the idea, then allowing it to happen, by securing dollars from outside record distributors, and only after Conkling's "45 days of phone calls, [with] lawyers getting paid for 300 hours."

Cash Box reported Jim Conkling enthusing, "The Everly Brothers are the strongest group attraction in the record business today. Thanks to their unique talent, astute choice of material and smart management, they have risen in three years to the top position in their field.... We believe their wide appeal to record fans of all ages and tastes can be increased through our joint efforts." The unnamed "smart" management, Wesley Rose, concurs; the Everlys themselves are not interviewed. Such was music industry reporting in 1960.

Those million-dollar terms were unheard of and headline-grabbing, but they've been frequently misunderstood. The payments were split into ten $100,000 pieces, and not as simple paydays, but as annual advances against royalties. Don and Phil wouldn't see any more than that from sales until they recouped that amount in profits each year. That was not an issue at first, with things going so well, but it also explains why so many singles were released, thrown at the wall to see if they'd stick, when things got thinner later.

On the bright side, and at least as important to Phil and Don, they were theoretically handed nearly complete artistic control over what they would write, produce, and record.

Archie Bleyer was out of the picture, along with his very specific tastes and ways of working, as of the signing date, February 15, 1960. No specific producer is credited on their earliest Warner Bros. recordings, though Chet Atkins was still on hand, and according to engineer Bill Porter, both Wesley and Warners' Jim Conkling tried supervising the first new sessions. In practical working ways, not much had changed yet. The Bryant songs "Nashville Blues" and "Sleepless Nights" were recorded in the same RCA Studio B where "When Will I Be Loved" and "Like Strangers" had been a few weeks earlier, for Cadence—and with familiar Music Row personnel.

With the large, probably label-fate-determining bet made on them, the Everlys were well aware that they needed to come up with something that could be a massive, expectation-confirming hit, to prove themselves yet again. Don recalled, "We were looking for a record. We'd just gone to Warner Brothers, and everybody said, 'You're never gonna make it without Archie.' . . . We were waiting to find that right hit song. Boudleaux was writing, and as great as he is, I didn't hear anything whatever with that magic . . . I was writing something and got to thinking about the 'Grand Canyon Suite.'"

This was not a piece of music that would have crossed the mind of all that many in the 1960 rock and roll business, but Don was recalling the semiclassical 1930 piece by Ferde Grofé, which has a bouncy, clicking section, "On the Trail," meant to represent mules trekking in the canyon. Don may well have seen the short 1958 Walt Disney *Grand Canyon* film that made use of it. In any case, it was in his head now. "That walking thing with the drums and stuff," he called it. In addition: "My father was telling me a story about how when he was a boy he had a girl named Mary, and everywhere he went all his friends would say, 'Mary had a little lamb.'" And he recalled that high school girlfriend of his own named Cathy. Put it all together and there it was.

Since this would be both the biggest record of the brothers' career together, selling over two million copies out of the gate, multiple millions more over time, and its authorship was later a bone of contention, what they had to say about its creation is noteworthy.

As Phil would describe, "Don called me and said he'd started writing a song and could I come over. He'd written the chorus of 'Cathy's Clown' and had the melody for the verses. I just put together the verses and it was finished." And Don recalled, "Phil came over and we hashed it out and we went into the studio." That was how it was regularly described, for decades—mainly Don's creation, with that additional input from Phil, although "put together" and "hashed out" are at best vague descriptions of what he contributed. The song was credited to both of them. "We wrote 'Cathy's Clown' one night, and recorded it the next," Don noted in 1972. "We knew it was going to be a hit."

Recording it required ingenuity. Don recalled, "It was astounding—great musicians, great engineer, great studio, and Chet sitting there to put in the most wonderful touches." They asked engineer Bill Porter if he could get the drum to sound like the Grand Canyon Suite percussion; Porter thought the live drummer's pattern was not quite "jerky" enough to match the suite's bounce. His solution was to apply a tape loop, which RCA had recently acquired, to Buddy Harman's drums, live, making it sound as we know it. This may explain what Dick Clark meant when, as he introduced Don and Phil's performance on his prime-time show, he called it a record with "a sound all its own—a little unusual, a little *strange*, but very, very successful."

It was the strange, open sound of the future—and it hit home with people worldwide. The story and the song have two distinct halves—the clip-clop chorus, with the singer's rejection of Cathy while admitting "dying" each time someone calls him her "clown," then a total change of rhythm and tone in the verse, which is virtually an interior monologue about what fuels the rejection—how a man must "stand tall," with Don soloing.

That's some sophisticated song construction. It anticipates songs Lennon and McCartney would be writing half a decade later, "We

Can Work It Out" for example, and in fact, though still obscure themselves, those two were quite struck by the song and were performing it as soon as it was released.

A flood of astonishingly strong, memorable releases buttressed the sense that the Everlys had arrived on top of everything. Warners rushed out *It's Everly Time*, their first album on the new label, just two weeks after "Cathy's Clown" was locked, bearing every track they'd recorded for them save that single.

The opening cut was another standard-to-be from Don, not released as a single until late summer, the searing ballad "So Sad." If Phil's "When Will I Be Loved" was discreetly personal in its origin, this one was too, only more so. Written "in a flash" in that house on a hill Don and Sue shared with their new baby, it admitted, obliquely, that their marriage was in trouble. Nothing in the two songs demands taking either as singer-songwriter's confessionals, and with both sung by the two of them, of course, listeners are directed away from connecting the stories to one or the other brother. Being "half of a whole" can be an excellent disguise.

"So Sad" is as often pointed to as Don's finest song as "When Will I Be Loved" is singled out as Phil's; both would certainly be among their most recorded by other performers. In May, Cadence released that last-minute classic of Phil's as a single, too, and the two records raced each other up the charts. By July, both were in the top twenty and each placed higher still. Don and Phil simply promoted both records. Also in July: Cadence released their final album of new-to-LP Everlys material, *The Fabulous Style of the Everly Brothers*, and since that included "Let It Be Me," "All I Have to Do Is Dream," "Take a Message to Mary," and "When Will I Be Loved," it was an equally strong long-play entry, and both labels' albums did well.

By that point, the Everly Brothers, who'd prove such an inspiration to 1960s British Invasion performers, had invaded Great Britain themselves, arriving there on April 1 with manager Wesley Rose and, as their band, the Crickets—J.I. Allison, Joe B. Mauldin, and Sonny Curtis—admired, trusted friends with a following around the world, who'd picked themselves up after Buddy Holly's death and moved ahead.

They'd since had records out on Buddy's "Love's Made a Fool of You" and the first recording of Sonny's standard-to-be, "I Fought the Law." The band's identity was announced live at shows, to the surprise of audiences, since it was not advertised. As Jerry Allison explained, "We like to work with Don and Phil, and when we were offered a return trip to Britain as their accompanying group, we jumped at the chance. . . . The plan for the tour envisioned one American act, not two. If people had seen the Crickets billed to appear, then they'd have rightly expected us to do an act of our own, but that wouldn't have been right; this was Phil and Don's tour."

Sonny Curtis recalls their reception in the UK "going down like a storm. . . . The adulation of fans was terrific. I had never personally been exposed to that sort of thing before and was a bit awed by it. Those shows drew big audiences. It was obvious, in public, that Don and Phil were stars, but when we were alone with them, they were just a couple of good ol' boys."

As a tight, forward-looking rock and roll unit—extraordinary harmony singers up front, an ace electric guitarist and rhythm section, including one of the most celebrated drummers of their generation, behind—they would appear in over twenty towns and cities in England, Scotland, and Wales. The impression made was large and lasting.

In Liverpool, as Phil would still recall vividly over fifty years later, "We were doing 'Dream,' maybe a couple of years after it was a hit, and the audience sang it with us. They wouldn't quit applauding, so there was kind of an encore, and then the audience was singing it by themselves—a theaterful of people singing 'Dream'—and they did a really good job!" A young local guitar player, George Harrison, caught that tumultuous show; the buddies he was generally playing with, John Lennon and Paul McCartney, were traveling at the time, on vacation. The three of them were in a loosely tacked-together group of guitar players with shifting band names—and no permanent rhythm section. That this Everlys-Crickets outfit, made up entirely of musicians beloved by all three of them, was a self-contained, harmonious unit playing original songs they knew and loved made an impression.

In Manchester, Graham Nash and Allan Clarke, two eighteen-year-old local boys who'd been singing together since they were in their school choir at age six, had recently been flabbergasted by a record they heard at a school dance. Graham set the scene for this author: "We see a friend of ours across the dance floor—she was my girlfriend for a while—and we start to walk across and say hello, and halfway across, 'Bye Bye Love' by the Everly Brothers comes on, really loud, and it stops us in our tracks. . . . One of the things that was different, from the opening notes, was that chunky guitar, different from anybody else's."

They were struck by the blood harmony sound, too, of course, and when the Everlys and band arrived in Manchester, they not only attended the Free Trade Hall show, but they waited outside Don and Phil's hotel hoping to meet them—and they did. "We told them that we sang," Nash continued, "and we loved the way that *they* sang, and that one day we wanted to go down to London and make a record. . . . And they encouraged us and said, 'If you've got the energy and you've got the passion, you'll probably make it.' It was that kind of conversation—for a half hour. They made us feel human. . . . They inspired me to get more into music. One of the things we talked about that night was writing songs."

A broader national impression of the Everlys and band was set by their appearance on variety show *Val Parnell's Startime*, hosted by

British entertainer Alma Cogan, which aired in two parts on April 7 and 14. At this time, when the brothers were already at a peak, this was among the most galvanizing television performances in their careers—a document for the permanent record.

Singing close-in around one mic, as they often did, with their dark suits and matching guitars, they provided a memorable visual image. This was how their indivisible harmony looked as it happened, whether in full-tilt rock-band mode met by screams on "Bird Dog," "('Til) I Kissed You," and "Cathy's Clown," or hushing the place on "All I Have to Do Is Dream," which was treated more like a duo plus backup. When rocking as a unit with the Crickets, this was a striking picture of what much of the world would be bopping to four or five years later.

We can wonder if all five of them ever considered making this an ongoing performing and recording unit, a band that would have included four talented songwriters. Sonny Curtis answered that one: "We never considered such a thing, at least in my presence. I don't think Don and Phil were up for it, and it is something we never discussed. . . . Also, the Crickets were trying to reemerge as a group ourselves, after Holly's death."

Veteran British music journalist, author, and radio host Spencer Leigh researched and reported on Don and Phil's offstage activities while in England in 1960 and later; it's certainly a place where they would both come to feel very much at home after repeated tours and stays. It's not surprising that they came to love British tea and tailoring. Leigh has also named names of several of Phil's overnight involvements along the way—BBC photographer Lucinda Lambton, and a sixteen-year-old, Carol Drakely, whose enraged mother came back looking for him but was kept away from a direct confrontation by Wesley.

"Everlymania," while never dubbed that, gripped the UK record business and music scene enough that between 1957 and 1962 dozens of Everlys soundalike outfits got to record singles there, though few of the records were widely distributed. Only a few were outright covers of Everlys hits. Mainly duos by brothers and others, they tried to get into the mode. The best known included the Brooks Brothers, the Most Brothers (future producer Mickie Most was one of those), and Billy Fury, whose record "Colette" was among the more convincing imitations. They demonstrate mainly that it's not that easy to sound like Phil and Don. Decades later, Jasmine Records could put together a compilation called *The Brit-Everlys' Sound* with thirty-seven tracks by several dozen aspiring imitators.

The mania wasn't limited to the UK. By 1960, two Jakarta-born brothers, Ruud and Riem de Wolff, were performing Everlys covers in Holland and Germany in virtually impersonator style, performing as the Blue Diamonds, and referred to as "the Dutch-Indonesian Everly Brothers" for years ahead.

Another death provided the only sad and sour note during Don and Phil's British excursion. On April 16, the night they were playing in Sheffield, Eddie Cochran, close to both the Everlys and the Crickets, was involved in a car crash while traveling from Bristol to London after a show; he died from his injuries on April 17. Gene Vincent and Eddie's fiancée, the Everlys' friend Sharon Sheeley, were injured in the crash. The loss of Eddie and Buddy would leave Don and Phil forever wary about tour travel—but they rarely stopped touring anyhow. From England, this tour proceeded right on to dates in France and Australia and found crowds as enthusiastic as in the UK.

The Everlys returned home intent on seeing what they could do with the new artistic freedom and empowerment the Warner Bros. contract provided. The situation presented its own conundrum: the label had intrinsic power, Wesley did all he could to keep or enlarge his, and Don and Phil had that new leeway and added responsibility for their choices. (Wesley gave some interviews in which he said that "we" had that leeway, not the brothers alone.) The stakes were high, clashes inevitable.

Well into 1962, Phil and Don continued to record in Nashville for the most part, and would tell reporters they would always record there, even as Warners' Los Angeles home base beckoned as the place for them to be. Over the summer of 1960, they became fascinated by fast-evolving studio technology, turning to it especially on songs by others they wanted to customize—Little Richard's "Lucille," Mel Tillis's "Stick with Me Baby," and "Temptation," the dramatic pop number introduced by Bing Crosby in 1933 and revisited by Mario Lanza in 1951, a showy song for big voices. These more complex Everly outings would be recorded in exploratory sessions, sometimes fraught, where there might be thirty takes to get at that elusive specialness the brothers were searching for.

Phil explained, "We were still working to solidify some long-term—*something*. We kept trying to do innovations, because the basic element of rock and roll was change. That's how we got into the song 'Temptation'; Donald said he wanted to do it and I said it sounded like a good idea to me. . . . We had eight different guitars doing the same riff, [as] with 'Lucille.' The two of them were pretty much the same riff. . . . That's eight electric guitar players that sound like one guitar [with] Jimmy Day on steel, and that's why that's strange! . . . That large guitar approach was Donald's idea, which had never really been explored."

Steel guitar on a Little Richard song was original in itself, and all of this was before Phil Spector focused on his big "Wall of Sound" productions, before the Beach Boys and Beatles and so many others would be interested in trying things like this in the studio. Years before.

Engineer Bill Porter was typically the one who had to work to make the Everlys' production ideas real, and he'd say, "The biggest problem I had with them was they sang pretty loud, and my philosophy of recording was not to minimize the dynamic range; to enhance it as much as I possibly could without saturating any tape. It was always a problem with them, because they wanted the band up around them, too. When Don started producing some of the Warner Brothers sessions...he *challenged* you. I guarantee you; he really did....He basically had me trying to do things that were three or four years ahead of their time—what you'd do with multi-track recording."

Revealingly, when people talk about the era's all-too-frequent record industry practice of "covering" records by black R&B artists with blander versions by white pop performers, intent on snatching sales from the original, it never includes this "Lucille" record. With that big beat and guitar difference, and the Everlys' ever-identifiable vocals, it's never described in those terms. Indeed, Little Richard Penniman, like Chuck Berry, Bo Diddley, and Ray Charles, would always speak of these two interpreters of their songs, and these two individuals, in very positive terms. Ray Charles would cover "Bye Bye Love" himself. Twangin' guitar star Duane Eddy, later a close friend of Phil's, would recall asking Chuck Berry who he was listening to most, and getting the answer "Kitty Wells and the Everly Brothers. I'm country at heart."

That salability of Phil's writing was underscored by the placement of his jangly, jubilant, and very pop earworm "(Girls, Girls, Girls) Made to Love" with fourteen-year-old Eddie Hodges, who'd sung "Gary, Indiana" in the Broadway production of *The Music Man*. The Everlys' own version would be the opening track on their second Warners LP, the one with that slightly disconcerting title, *A Date with the Everly Brothers*. It was to be the highest-selling album of their lifetimes.

The album included the first of two Everly versions of Boudleaux Bryant's "Love Hurts." It was Roy Orbison's version of the often-to-be-revisited song that hit, though, not theirs, which was never released as a single. Writing together, the Bryants came up with "Always It's You," and the plaint "So How Come (No One Loves Me)," later to be performed by the Beatles on BBC radio. On July 27, Don and Phil recorded another of the Bryants' timely and trenchant teenage life observations, this one about the growing, comforting centrality of popular media in a teen's life, "Radio and TV" ("They do a lot for me").

No one would hear it for four long years, good as it was. Fallout from conflicts that came to a head in the following weeks made that so.

Don and Phil were determined to record "Temptation," electric guitar orchestra and all, no matter what Wesley Rose thought about it. Don said the arrangement had come to him in a dream. Perhaps so, but this idea of a large, near-operatic rock sound was itself becoming timely, even trendy. In New York, an evolving version of the Drifters vocal group was recorded with lavish Broadway-inspired production on numbers like "This Magic Moment" and "Save the Last Dance for Me." In Nashville, Bill Porter had engineered another prodigious voice song with Mario Lanza connections, in the very same room as "Temptation"—Elvis Presley's hit "It's Now or Never."

None of this seems to have registered with Wesley, who opposed the whole idea as being *too* pop. Nothing country in it at all; no lovely harmony. Which was true, and also not at all what they were after in the rhythmically creative and dramatic mini-aria. "Wesley made it as difficult as possible," Don commented. "That's when the shit hit the fan. . . . He hated 'Temptation.' I loved it. If he'd owned the publishing, he'd have loved it, too."

Their manager-publisher's insistence that he, more than anyone, knew what they should and should not perform, and even who they were, had become a serious issue for Don and Phil both, no matter how much of a protective father figure he'd been. In fact, they'd produce three different versions of the number, determined to find a way for it to be a single.

Against their wishes and behind their backs, Wesley persuaded Warners to demote "Temptation" to a future B-side, turning instead to the maudlin teenage plane-crash epic "Ebony Eyes," written by the generally masterful John D. Loudermilk. Loudermilk signed with Acuff-Rose, he'd note, *because* he wanted to get songs to the Everlys. Wesley no doubt recalled the success of the late 1959 song by Nashville's Jean Dinning and her husband, published by Acuff-Rose—"Teen Angel." There would be those who loved "Ebony Eyes," others who'd forever go out of their way to avoid it—Don and Phil themselves among them. Teen death-trip songs were becoming so prevalent that Boudleaux Bryant wrote a number satirizing the trend, a country hit for Bob Luman, "Let's Think About *Living*."

If teen death pop could be thumbs-up to Rose, but lavish production pop was a no, and they could now, after all, record some songs Acuff-Rose hadn't published even while other numbers from outside were automatically rejected, then what, we might wonder, was Wesley Rose actually thinking? In making "Temptation" a B-side, he was negating the expressed wishes of the most lucrative act he had, two young stars barely past twenty who'd relied on his guidance. So what did he *want*?

"Power," Del Bryant says. "Control." No one was closer to Rose in those years than the Bryant family. On occasion, the kids Del and Dane would stay with Wes and wife Margaret Rose when Boud and Felice had to be out of town. Mrs. Rose and Felice bowled together; there were Acuff-Rose picnics and parties and softball games.

"As the music exploded across the South, and then around the world," Del observed, "Wesley became maniacal. The big cigars came on, and he was like a little Napoleon....He started to revise the history of his father Fred, like 'I recorded Hank Williams.' There was also some real Rose brothers rivalry, and the boys loved Lester." (Wesley's brother Lester was now operating as Don and Phil's road manager.)

The immediate consequence of the troubling conflict with Wesley is that in late September 1960 the Everlys got out of town and away from him, to escape toward something both he and they had anticipated when they signed with Warner Bros.—a shot at making it in the movies. Before taking that leap in earnest, they'd get down one more lasting, much-loved hit—"Walk Right Back," written by their buddy Sonny Curtis.

After the tour with Phil and Don in 1960, Sonny had been drafted into the peacetime Cold War army for a two-year term. He was in basic training at Fort Ord, near Monterey, California, when he got his hands on a beat-up old guitar in the barracks dayroom. "I had the lick before I went to the army, and I was just trying to write a song to go with it," he recalled.

Later, on a three-day pass, he went down to Los Angeles to visit Jerry Allison and was surprised to find Don there, the brothers having arrived in town to begin their stab at movie stardom. "We were sitting with him in his motel room and J.I. said, 'Sonny, sing Don that song you wrote.'" Don loved what he'd heard. "He immediately called Phil and said 'Get down here and listen to this.' They worked out that wonderful harmony, and they said if I'd write another verse, they'd record it." He headed to Fort Gordon, Georgia, for occupational training, then: "I sent them the second verse, and I got a letter from J.I. that said, 'The Everlys recorded your song *yesterday*.' I was a bit confused, but happy." And that's why the Everlys' hit didn't include the second verse he'd sing himself, and Perry Como would later record, about eyes "changed to shades of cloudy gray." And they never would add it in.

Getting into movies had looked attractive to the Everlys for some time. Elvis had already had *Love Me Tender*, and Ricky Nelson *Rio Bravo*, both Westerns, and they'd generally responded that they were waiting for some big Western duo roles themselves. Everything offered to them had been musicals about rock and roll stars—likely of the plotless, "rockers in a show" sort that others in Alan Freed movie lineups had agreed to do—grade-C drive-in fare, and dead ends for film careers. The news now broke that the Everly Brothers were cutting out all live appearances for months, to screen-test at Warner Bros. and enroll in the studio's in-house acting school.

"We had to start thinking about the future," Don told Bob Thomas of the Associated Press. "All we were thinking about was how to get back into the Top 10....We had to plan what we would do if the hits stopped coming." After a brief stop back in Nashville for the November 1960 recording date where the most compelling version of "Temptation" was recorded, along with "Ebony Eyes," they visited their families, then hurried right back to Hollywood. They would not record again for a full six months.

The move west marked the formal end of their association with the *Grand Ole Opry*. Phil would note, "We had to pay a percentage of our earnings to them, and we didn't use them. You were supposed to appear there one Saturday out of every four, and sometimes that was impossible."

The fan press saw the oncoming acting-school recording hiatus as a golden opportunity to fabricate melodrama, playing their proto-clickbait "your beloved boys are in great danger" card for their teen readers; *16 Magazine* screamed of "The Tragedy of Don & Phil Everly." (The boys, you see, had "embarked on a completely new way of life....Like two little children thrown adrift on a surging sea without a compass." And the public is allegedly demanding to know "Are they planning to have separate careers?

Has Phil 'Gone Hollywood?' Is Don flirting with Hollywood starlets and about to divorce his wife, Sue?") Actually, they were getting a little closer with those last questions. A common theme was "Are the Everlys Really Splitting Up?" Phil assured *Screen Stars* magazine that they "shiver at the very thought" of recording separately or breaking up: "Are you kidding? That we would *never* do."

The time was not without real, unfabricated drama. Wesley's ongoing attempts to keep them off-balance and under control included working to deepen any slight discord between them, as destructive as that could be. Del Bryant commented, "Wesley didn't really *get* everything. One thing that really bothered Phil, and probably did some damage to him, was Wesley saying 'Phil, you'd better not argue with Don. If you upset him, he'll just get another harmony singer.' There was that feeling that the lead singer is the star, but that *wasn't* the Everly Brothers. Don wasn't the star; the Everly Brothers were the star. But Wesley did pull that stuff."

Phil and Don both had had about enough of him, and now they were learning some operational facts they hadn't really understood. As Phil recalled, "Jim Conkling at Warners, a real gentleman, gave us more of a viewpoint. . . . He was the one who told us that it didn't really matter if Wes was there or not, as long as *we* were happy. That was a major surprise, because Wes had us under the impression that the company wanted his input." That would soon yield fallout.

"We went to acting school at Warners in '60," Phil continued, "but every day we were off the road cost money, so it was really a kind of investment. We were doing well enough to do it. We spent three months . . . with apartments that cost them a fortune, going to acting school all day and partying all night. We had a very good time."

No surprise that the "partying" involved wine, women, and occasionally even song. Phil was dating fifteen-year-old magician's assistant turned actress Mimsy Farmer, who'd soon be cast as early sixties TV's idea of a "bad girl" fairly regularly, one of a number of open, reported-on relationships. He laughed later that he'd pretty well decided to relocate to Los Angeles more permanently—and soon: "I said, 'That's it; I ain't *ever* going to leave this place!'" His brother, out there away from Sue, was having similar thoughts.

They were both serious about trying to make the acting work, piling into the obligatory acting tomes by Stanislavski, and attending surprisingly intense classes at Warners' acting school. The teacher-coach there was a singular fellow who had, for better and worse, singular influence.

His name was Paton Price. A Texan, he was known as a sort of actor's guru, a teacher who would dispense ideas about values to consider and ways to live, not just acting techniques. Phil would call him "a life teacher." Highly flexible as an actor-director, he'd appeared with John Gielgud on Broadway but was equally at home directing *Partridge Family* episodes. Politically, he was focused and single-minded. He'd been a conscientious objector during World War II, an outspoken member of the War Resisters League, and in 1943 had been one of six like-minded prisoners at Lewisburg Federal Penitentiary who conducted one hunger strike to resist mail censorship and another to fight racial segregation of the prisoners. (The Vietnam War–era Chicago Seven's David Dellinger was another of that six.)

Price's Hollywood students often came away determined to stick up for themselves in an entertainment system not particularly friendly toward anyone who did, emerging with more self-confidence and sometimes with commitments in wider spheres than show business. Tom and Dick Smothers, who'd become friends and to some degree stage-patter models for Phil and Don, were among their fellow students at the time; the Smothers Brothers would go on to fight censorship at CBS. Price's student Jean Seberg, best remembered today for her role in Jean-Luc Godard's *Breathless*, became an active backer of the Black Panthers and other radical activist groups, and the subject of continuous, serious harassment by J. Edgar Hoover's FBI.

And then there was Dean Reed, an Everlys classmate who at the time was appearing in guest roles in TV situation comedies and singing some mild rockabilly, a slightly country Frankie Avalon in the making. He would become a lifelong friend of Phil's, which would be more than a little trying, because this seemingly innocuous Coloradoan would emerge as a buddy of legendary Chilean singer-activist Victor Jara, then go on as a full-tilt Stalinist living and working in East Germany, starring in Eastern bloc singing-cowboy movies and variety shows.

For many, not just in the arts but in many walks of life, knowing what you want, let alone how to get it, and arriving at self-awareness and even maturity come slowly, slowly, then in leaps. By twenty-four and twenty-two, Don and Phil Everly had spent years sticking to their more-or-less inflexibly assigned roles, and doing as they were told. Paton Price's teachings appear to have played a serious part in swaying them to take more thoughtful, individual grips on their own lives, and to take more charge of themselves—and they sounded like it. "Yes sir; no sir" was over.

In a penetrating article in the July 1961 *TV-Radio Mirror* magazine, Martin Cohen interviewed them after they'd been taking Price's classes for a while; a photo shows them working with him. Their comments reflect it. Phil says, "We have separate lives now." And Don pipes in, "If a producer comes up with a movie for Phil alone, that's it. I'm not going to stand in his way, and he won't stand in mine." Are they willing to split up to make pictures? "That's what we *expect*," Phil replies. "I can't imagine a picture script that would have two good parts for Don and me."

Cohen describes them in terms miles away from the "just polite, down-home country boys" narratives of just three years before, sounding more like a *Playboy* magazine profile: "Fashionably dressed, smiling and relaxed, they discussed books they'd read. They argued about Freudian theories and the sense of progressive jazz. Don says he'll never work in nightclubs if it means he has to dance, and Phil cracks, 'You have too many inhibitions.' Don snaps back, 'Just because you walk around with a copy of Freud under your arm doesn't mean you can analyze me!' Phil answers, 'You're obviously in need of medical care.' And then they both laugh out loud.

"'Don and I *often* argue,' Phil says. 'We've disagreed on a single point for days or months. But, in the end, we find that we want the same things. We want success—but not if we have to sacrifice integrity and performance.... It's a funny thing that's happened to us. It's like *starting all over.*'"

They would soon realize that the much-desired Hollywood career wasn't going to happen. The abrupt end of their movie-career pursuit story has often been told: The Everlys are called in for the long-expected Warner Bros. screen test, Western-style, and naturally, with Don in the dark, menacing-guy cowboy suit and Phil in the white one. Don comes to a cabin window and through it, they sing "Take a Message to Mary" together. What there is of dialogue is laughable, and after many, many takes, Phil answers Don's last line, "I'll be seeing you," with "Not in the *movies.*" The test was destroyed, and Don and Phil moseyed away.

While they were Hollywood-occupied, the "Lucille"/"So Sad" and "When Will I Be Loved"/"Like Strangers" singles were selling over a million each, and "Cathy's Clown" reached four million copies sold. The second Warners LP, *A Date with the Everly Brothers*, was a strong seller like the first; it included "Cathy's Clown," so it could hardly miss. Disc jockeys on both sides of the Atlantic were discovering that they preferred the B-side of that "Ebony Eyes" single, "Walk Right Back," which would reach number seven on the pop charts, beating out that Wesley-inflicted A-side by one slot.

Behind the scenes, they had indeed started some things over, as best they could. In August 1961, Wesley noted in *Billboard* that Don and Phil had informed him back in January that they'd no longer be "abiding" by their personal management contract with him, which had been set to run through May 1962. This presumably followed Jim Conkling's clarification of Rose's relationship with the label, and personal advice from Paton Price. Wesley said he'd heard nothing more from them at all until early April, when they sent a formal letter quietly dismissing him outright as their manager-publicist. They were going about their business without him, and now he was demanding 10 percent of everything they made in 1960, plus damages.

A financial settlement was reached by November, and Wesley Rose was out as the Everlys' manager. However, Acuff-Rose remained their publisher, and there he had leverage. He made it impossible for that July 1960 recording of the Bryants' "Radio and TV" to be released, and it became clear that he had effective veto power over use of any Acuff-Rose songs, old or new—whether from the Bryants or, unbelievably, Phil and Don's own. Felice believed Wesley had been using the threat of denying the songs simply as leverage to tighten control over the Everlys and Bryants, but it went this far, and all Acuff-Rose songs were taken out of bounds for the Everly Brothers, damaging everybody.

The movie careers that didn't happen and the denial of Acuff-Rose songs were not the only problems arising. Don and wife Mary Sue separated formally on August 15, 1960, as "So Sad," the song their situation inspired, reached number seven on the pop charts. In May, the divorce suit began. *Photoplay* magazine reported, "Mrs. Don Everly sues for divorce, claims Don loves another woman." The actual divorce suit was otherwise focused, and to whatever degree accurate—rather than just dramatized for legal effect, as was then common—it offered a disturbing picture of Don.

The UPI national wire service reported, "Isaac Donald Everly, 24...was accused Monday of choking and kicking his wife. Mrs. Mary Sue Ingraham Everly, 23...made the charges and asked for $1500 monthly alimony, $250 child support...[and that] Everly be constrained from disposing of community assets." (He'd apparently intended to buy an $85,000 yacht. The man liked boats.) The divorce was finalized by January 1962. It has been repeated in multiple places that Don finally told Mary Sue that he was leaving, and snapped, "You're just not Hollywood, babe." He wouldn't have shared that line himself, so it must have been a story she shared with others, if it had come from either of them at all.

Sue was granted custody of baby Venetia Ember, and Don had visitation rights—which he would not pursue. For a few months, Margaret looked after her granddaughter while Sue, who retained possession of that house just across the street and up the hill, recovered. Don and Mary Sue had married young, under pressured 1950s circumstances, and never gotten past wanting different things. In 1962, her Tubb family connections came into play again, as she married Ernest Tubb's nephew, the noted Nashville singer-songwriter Glenn Douglas Tubb, known simply as Glenn. He was the cowriter of the memorable Johnny Cash song "Home of the Blues" and the unusual country hit "Skip a Rope" for Henson Cargill, which decried spousal abuse and racism. They were married for forty-six years, until her death in 2008 at age seventy.

All of this turmoil on top of the years of relentless touring had taken a physical toll on Don and Phil both. They were exhausted. They were not inclined to follow the lead of many in country music at the time and swallow variously colored and speckled uppers and downers. But Phil's long-pursued intended, Jackie Ertel, and her stepdad, Archie Bleyer, both recommended a New York doctor who had vitamin supplements they'd tried, as many other sophisticates had, even the president of the United States, John F. Kennedy.

The Everly Brothers would go to see him. His name was Dr. Max Jacobson. People called him "Dr. Feelgood."

Chapter Six

HITTING THE WALL
1961–1962

THE EVERLY BROTHERS WERE NOW RESIDENTS OF LOS ANGELES. PHIL was still single, but he was sometimes photographed on dates with his latest, British actress Maura McGiveney, who was appearing in episodic television and the new B-movie feature *Twist Around the Clock*. Practically speaking, Don was now returning to the single life—if not for long. In truth, they'd relocated for the Hollywood lifestyle, not the work; throughout 1961 all but one of their recording sessions were still back in Nashville.

Their high-flying lives and interest in getting their look just right were noted in *Cash Box*, as "Walk Right Back" sat at number twelve on its pop chart. A photo shows them boarding a TWA flight for "a one-day visit to New York, where they were fitted for specially designed suits they plan to wear on a forthcoming guest shot on the Tennessee Ernie Ford TV'er."

That network *Ford Show* appearance must have seemed a welcome respite from the ongoing crosscurrents. Tennessee Ernie was utterly compatible with their down-home-to-Hollywood trajectory, multi-genre musical tastes, and show business adaptability—the whole layout of their wheelhouse. He introduced them enthusiastically, gave them time and instrumental backup appropriate for "Lucille" and "Walk Right Back," and joined in re-creating the "three on one guitar" vaudeville stunt they'd learned from Ike. Ernie fits right into a "Bird Dog" finish. It's one of their more lovable televised performances.

Yet that one-day round trip to New York to buy suits may very well have masked another Manhattan errand of about this time—appointments with Dr. Jacobson. (They would never be precise about exactly when those started—but it was about then.)

Jacobson's sophisticated patient list included Van Cliburn, Zero Mostel, Edward G. Robinson, Lee Remick, Tennessee Williams, Chita Rivera, Lee Marvin, Salvador Dalí, and, via the same Archie Bleyer connection, Andy Williams. Dr. Jacobson had helped relieve Archie of a bad case of tinnitus—ringing in the ears—which explains his enthusiastic recommendation when he saw Phil so pressured that he'd been "hysterical" in a visit to his house one night. Don would later report walking into the office one time and finding singer Eddie Fisher in the waiting room.

None of these patients understood themselves to be going there for illicit drugs. Jacobson was configuring various vitamin and pharmaceutical "cocktail" injections, however unconventional, intended to deal with exhaustion and stress. Vitamin B_{12} injections for similar problems were well known. This *seemed*, at least, to be akin to those.

For Phil and Don, the principal drug he administered and prescribed was what became known commercially as Ritalin—the stimulant methylphenidate, later widely prescribed (many agree, overprescribed) for childhood attention deficit hyperactivity disorder, ADHD. It had just become available in 1955 but was still experimental, with its potential long-term effects on adults not well understood. It acts on the body much like amphetamines do, including inducing substantial weight loss, though it's not precisely the same thing. Overdosing can lead to "euphoria, delirium, confusion, toxic psychosis and hallucinations [and] extreme anger with threats of aggressive behavior."

Phil explained the thinking behind the treatments: "With me, the idea was just to use it as a guide to make myself better able to handle my own pressures. [Jacobson] would change the metabolism of your chemical make-up, but it wasn't good for you, because you had no permanent control of it and you were depending on some outside influence....I could see from what it was doing to Donald that it was dangerous to mess with. At the time...it was better than the other options."

Don recalled for Kurt Loder his considerably darker experience and the doctor he'd come to call "a dangerous Svengali-type" character: "People didn't understand drugs that well then. They didn't know what they were messing with. It wasn't against the law: I saw a picture of my doctor with the president, you know? But it got out of hand....It was a real disaster for a lot of people, and it was a disaster for me. Ritalin made you feel energized. You could stay up for days. It just got me strung out. I got so far out there, I didn't know what I was doing." As he elaborated for author Roger White, "At the beginning, you don't realize what's happening...I got to a point where I couldn't go onstage without it...I had the drug on prescription and injected myself."

The Everlys were calling on Jacobson and taking his cocktails in 1961 until that autumn, and Don was showing more effects than Phil—particularly visible, otherwise unexplained weight loss. In those same months, he began dating the photogenic actress he'd earlier espied and chosen his daughter's name after, Venetia Stevenson, having crossed paths with her again at a young Hollywood-set party. The fan and scandal magazines were reporting on the budding relationship even before Don and Mary Sue's pending divorce was finalized.

Venetia was twenty-two in 1960, the glamorous and sophisticated Hollywood-raised daughter of British actress Anna Lee and film director Richard Stevenson, who had directed *Jane Eyre* and would go on to direct Disney's *Mary Poppins* and *The Love Bug*. She was an in-demand model by age fourteen and had appeared in multiple prime-time television episodes and several feature films. She told anyone who asked that she'd never really liked acting at all. To many, she was best known for her much-chronicled personal life: she'd been married to musical movie star Russ Tamblyn for about a year, ending in spring 1957, dated Elvis Presley, and served as an accommodating beard publicity date for her gay friends Tab Hunter and Anthony Perkins, who were actually a couple themselves. Then she met Don.

The fan magazines described them alternatively as about to marry soon or as very cautious, both being recently divorced, and in Venetia's case, "bitter and caustic" and dubious about ever marrying again. Neither of them wanted to talk to gossip columnists about any of this. *Photoplay*, undeterred, asked the question in September 1961, "Is Venetia the kind of woman Don wants, or is there still so much 'boy from the country' left in him that he is more affected by Venetia's physical beauty than her intellect?" This wasn't some emotion-packed question for him now, but years later, it would be.

The more immediate, pressing life and career issue for both Everly brothers was being cut off from the Bryants' songs and their own. New recording sessions were scheduled for spring 1961 regardless, and their own creative itches were no less strong than they'd been since changing labels. They saw two ways forward, and they took both.

In keeping with their never-flagging interest in exploring one corner or another of their broad musical comfort zone, they proceeded to record two albums' worth of material dominated by traditional, pre-rock pop, sometimes even nineteenth-century Tin Pan Alley pop—which they had handled all the way back to childhood radio, though that was unsuspected by their rock and roll and country fans. The second way forward was the creation of their own label, distributed by Warners—Calliope Records. This was both a business move and a musical autonomy extension, liberated as they were from Wesley and Archie, not just some vanity project, as "personal" label imprints often are.

There were current models. Frank Sinatra had set up Reprise Records to control his own recording content and offer creative freedom to other performing friends such as Bing Crosby, Dean Martin, and Rosemary Clooney. Sam Cooke had founded SAR Records to expand his reach as a producer of otherwise struggling black performers such as Billy Preston, Bobby Womack, and Mel Carter. Similar to Sam's situation, the Everly Brothers, by terms of their Warners contract, couldn't appear on the "side" label themselves. This was the sort of enterprise the far-seeing Buddy Holly had suggested could be a way to evolve their careers. *Billboard* would note that "Calliope" was both the name of Greek mythology's beautifully voiced mother of Orpheus, and a loud steam-whistle organ at circuses. Whether classical beauty or steam blasts were more relevant remained to be seen.

Their own Music Row recording stands continued, with a three-day session beginning on Memorial Day that included such added guitar luminaries as Hank Garland, Harold Bradley, and Sammy Pruett. Tracks that worked were rare; there is a removed, careless "let's just get through this" quality to most of the material, and obvious unsuccessful attempts to distract from the tossed-off sound with layers of arrangements and production.

The outlier numbers that worked were also the least fooled with—slower ballads such as "When I Grow Too Old to Dream," a 1935 predecessor to their own "dream" songs; a take on "Hi-Lili, Hi-Lo" from the Hollywood picture *Lili*; and their version of the 1932 standard "Don't Blame Me," with a delicate guitar intro by Hank Garland. The latter became the single, with the B-side a rocked-up version of the Merle Travis–Harold Hensley country number "Muskrat," which daddy Ike performed, too. The single squeaked into the top twenty.

Such ancient chestnuts as "Grandfather's Clock," "My Gal Sal," and "Bully of the Town" are taken up, then buried in production. The resulting album, *Both Sides of an Evening*, would be marketed as if side one were for dancing and side two for dreaming, but the consensus was that much of it was more likely to provoke dozing, and the sales failure confirmed it.

Phil would admit to Andrew Sandoval, "We knew the songs; we just couldn't *find* the songs. I don't know what the hell we were thinking.... We had to get an album out, so we fooled around with that stuff." Don would comment, "By then, our life was under pretty much of a strain and pressure and a lot of things were happening to us." It's fair to wonder if the "things happening to us" included early effects on their judgment of the Jacobson cocktails.

What the fussy, over-cluttered production was intended to do is more understandable if heard alongside the experimenting they were bringing to their Calliope label records at the same time, which, to the surprise of many in the music business, worked for at least some of the public. They're an often fascinating, if relatively obscure, side trip for the Everlys' music. Mainly instrumentals, they reflect especially Don's ongoing fascination with sounds and studio possibilities—far from the aspirations of the kid who just wanted to write like Hank Williams.

"Music's always been really important, and songs too," he commented to Sandoval, "but the *way* you do them is really important." The fellow who sometimes wondered if he might have been a distinctive, expressive solo artist, when given this new authority chooses to explore—and perhaps the phrase is "retreat into"—his most *impersonal* music by far.

Calliope, and a second Everly business entity, E.B. Enterprises, were set up a few blocks from Warner Bros., on Barham Boulevard in Hollywood. The brothers were clearly identified as founding and running Calliope in the trade papers, but when the first single was issued, *Billboard* played ball and noted, "Sides are recorded by Adrian Kimberly as instrumental, plus voice used as instruments." This unknown "Kimberly" fellow was Don; this was the first of a number of pseudonyms the brothers would use in attempts to work around the Wesley Rose–imposed ban on taking writing or arranging credits without his approval.

That first side, released in May and aimed, in *Billboard*'s words, "directly at the June graduation market," was a thick, peculiar but popular marching-band take on what was indeed a graduation ceremony must in the United States, "Pomp and Circumstance (The Graduation Song)." It was on the US pop chart for five weeks and reached number thirty-four midsummer. The B-side featured a chattering teen chorus and horns on "Black Mountain Stomp," a popped-up version of the country "Black Mountain Rag."

But nothing was simply straight-ahead sailing for Don and Phil at this time; this was no hit in the UK. The tune, known there as "Land of Hope and Glory," is a virtually sacred second national anthem, and the estate of its composer, Sir Edward Elgar, successfully sued to have the record banned in "most of the world."

By the summer of 1961, the Everlys had to deal with much more immediate life issues. "I'd got to draftable age," Phil recalled, "and Donald was going through a divorce, which in those days made you eligible for the draft again." That was looming now—and they'd also been rushed right back into the studio under pressure after giving up on the movies, with no manager to schedule supporting live dates. They found one.

"We went with Jack Rael," Phil recalled. "Jack was an old-time manager, and he got us a lot more money soon as he came on... doubled it." Once a band-leading sax player, Rael had managed Patti Page since the end of World War II, and he'd manage Don and Phil for the decade ahead, restarting their touring, staying out of the way of the music they made, and avoiding making himself a center of attention for the public.

"Don and Phil... were inactive; they came to me and said they wanted to get *back* into the business," Rael noted. "I made most of the decisions, but I would never take anything without first discussing it with Don and Phil.... When they finally put their act together," by which he means a more set, nightclub-style act, "I'd listen to it and make suggestions.... They basically called their own shots when it came to recording."

Their return to live performance came in August, with a week of shows at the Steel Pier in Atlantic City, headlining along with Ricky Nelson. Backing them, and also appearing, were Dickie Doo and the Don'ts, a Dick Clark–backed pop outfit that had a series of hit novelty records and used revolving members for live shows. That band's current bass player, Philadelphia-raised Joey Paige, would go on to be a significant Everlys friend in the near future. Joey would recall the New York audition with them, after Jack Rael explained the band needs: "There was a thirteen-piece band there, and in walk these beautiful guys that I'd admired, watching them on TV...."

Don and Phil asked us to stay after the band left...and we jammed the blues. This was heaven—and I knew we had the gig."

The pseudonymous shenanigans continued as Don, writing as "Jack Pegasus," and Phil, writing as "Ellen Carrol," wrote both sides of a Calliope single they produced for Larry Barnes, a young Kentucky farm kid who afterward recorded for RCA and other labels.

Their own next recording decision, though a dubious call, proved Warners were sticking by their promise of freedom to choose material. The Everlys chose to do another album similar to *Both Sides*, no exciting new song sources having emerged. The results for *Instant Party* were not much different. "Love Makes the World Go 'Round" sounded just like the previous album's "Hi-Lili, Hi-Lo," no accident, since it had substituted for the latter in *Carnival*, the Broadway show based on the movie "Hi-Lili" came from. There was a fairly funny bit of obscure nonsense, "When It's Night-Time in Italy It's Wednesday over Here," a 1923 Tin Pan Alley novelty, and they did do a perfectly fine job with Cole Porter's harmony duet "True Love," which had been introduced by Bing Crosby and Grace Kelly. Golden moldy "The Sheik of Araby" and a rock-and-soul take on "I'm Gonna Move to the Outskirts of Town" were only released later. No single would be culled from the set.

Around this time, Phil was dating Sharon Sheeley's songwriting partner Jackie DeShannon, not yet nearly as famous as she would be. "A sweet girl, a talented singer and songwriter," Phil called her. "I enjoy dating her. Nothing serious between us." He was still seen out occasionally with Mimsy Farmer, and that other Jackie, Ms. Ertel, was perpetually in the background.

The brothers' touring resumed with a trip to the Pacific in late September, with stops in the Philippines, where their following was still growing, then in Australia, for a show at Melbourne's Festival Hall, backed again by the Dickie Doo group. Immediately after that, Phil Everly received his notice that he was to appear in Nashville for an army physical, as he'd sensed would be coming.

Another decision was made, just at this moment when they meant to be ramping up their performing career again. Two years of summer and weekends service in the peacetime army—the choice Elvis Presley, Johnny Cash, and Steve Lawrence had made, for examples the Everlys were well aware of—would not be theirs. They'd suggest to the UK's *New Musical Express* that they'd noted increasing pro-American feelings on that Pacific tour, with the Kennedy administration at work and that young president's call for volunteerism. And they'd thought of an uncle, wounded in the Pacific in World War II as a marine, still lying in a veterans' hospital disabled for life. They'd choose the Marine Corps Reserve.

Phil would claim Don talked him into it: "We were there for six months and then we had to do a month a year for eight years. It seemed to go on forever." He'd sometimes tell people that Don had been attracted to the marines by their alleged "shiny helmets," which didn't exist, but it plainly was a more seriously considered choice than that. "It's going to teach us more self-discipline than we've got now, give us a better outlook on life, and be much better for our careers," an optimistic Phil suggested to a New York reporter.

They'd only recently been talking about willingness to work separately in Hollywood; they were now emphasizing sticking together while in uniform and beyond. As volunteers, not draftees, they could head to boot camp together. The place was the Marine Corps Recruit Depot, near San Diego. They suggested to several reporters that following orders in the marines should be no problem, since everyone in television appearances had been telling them "stand here, now over there" for years. Don brushed off the many questions he was getting about Venetia but suggested it would be unfair to lock anything down with her until boot camp was over.

They had just a few weeks between signing up in October and reporting for training around Thanksgiving. A single version of "Muskrat" followed "Don't Blame Me" to the bottom of the top twenty—but both sides got that far, at least, and the brothers performed "Don't Blame Me" on *The Ed Sullivan Show* on October 29—another stop back in New York. They looked uncharacteristically pale and nervous in the performance, perhaps even high.

In an interview with freelancer George J. Jaffe just before that peculiar appearance, Don and Phil offered some frank comments about their state of mind. Phil admitted, "Both of us can use a period of mental security.... That's why [we] are so anxiously looking forward to Marine life.... Neither of us has really had an extended period of relaxation, freedom from career pressures.... It'll be a ball having some time to ourselves, to unwind." To which Don added, "Show people forget there are other worlds outside of ours; I think the six or seven months...in the Marines will help us get back in touch with fellows our own age."

How lost and anxious the two of them had been feeling is certainly underscored by that unique characterization of marines boot camp as a great place for relative relaxation and time to free themselves from pressure. It should be noted that the US military was not then testing for Ritalin use during physicals and may not even have noticed anything especially unusual about their behavior. That's ironic, because in the present day the military routinely rules out people from service who'd been prescribed Ritalin even as children, a contested point being challenged.

Phil and Don recorded the last of the songs for the *Instant Party* album plus two more significant ones at a last, pre-marines session in Nashville, mid-November. Fortunately, it turned out, they'd befriended producer Lou Adler out in Los Angeles, and he'd picked up a new song of interest that *his* buddy, publisher Don Kirshner, had on hand from his growing stable of Brill Building pop writers—an especially good connection to make considering the song drought. They went to New York to check it out—back in Jacobson's city once again. The song was a good one for them, a one-off collaboration of Carole King, not with her husband, Gerry Goffin, as usual, but with Howard Greenfield, who was typically writing with Neil Sedaka. This was "Crying in the Rain."

The amusing B-side of the "Crying" single was surely a salute to Wesley Rose, "I'm Not Angry," a sharp, jangling litany of ill wishes, which they wrote under the pseudonym "Jimmy Howard." ("I hope your phone will never ring...I hope your TV's always bad...but I'm not angry, I'm just sad.")

The success of the "Walk Right Back" and new "Crying in the Rain" singles, and Don and Phil's continuing rock and roll presence heading into 1962, belies the often repeated and fundamentally untrue meme that suggests that rock and roll just faded away with the death of Buddy Holly, jailing of Chuck Berry, spiritual calling of Little Richard, and marginalizing of Jerry Lee Lewis, quietly awaiting resurrection by the British. But then, so did the ongoing success of the girl groups that the Beatles would cover, the rising Beach Boys, Roy Orbison's new success, and the rise of Motown. The Everlys were carrying evolving, first-generation American rock forward—still.

The service-approved press photos of Donald and Phillip Everly taken on November 25, 1961, the day they arrived at boot camp, reveal a startling change in Don. His famous sharp-featured, dark-eyed face, which the world had generally responded to as just as photogenic as Venetia's, or Elvis's, has become pale and gaunt; his cheekbones and chin have become pinpoints. He's not well. Phil isn't noticeably changed. The requisite marine buzz cuts, removing most of their hair, further emphasized that emaciated look.

They did not enter basic alone. Fellow musician and singer Joey Paige, by then a close friend, was also facing the draft, and he volunteered at the same time; their marine months together would further cement their relationship. There as well was Marshall Leib, who'd been one of Phil Spector's Teddy Bears and would later be in the Everlys' touring band, too.

Their marine reserve experiences would essentially be like those of most everyone in the peacetime marines—drilling, marching, learning the fundamentals of small and larger arms, plus exercises with live ammo flying by. Phil reportedly spent more time socializing with the guys, playing poker and so on; he remained a PFC—private first class—as did Joey and Marshall. Unexpectedly, the typically responsibility- and discipline-avoiding Don quickly became a platoon leader. More predictably, he was likely to wander off alone to find some privacy.

Just before Christmas 1961, the "Crying in the Rain"/"I'm Not Angry" single was released, and it would be a major hit—reaching number six on the *Billboard* charts in the weeks that followed. Brooklyn-raised Carole King had already been a fan before she had anything to do with them directly. She recalled in her memoir, "The first time I heard 'Crying in the Rain' on the radio I was... immediately transported back in time to relive my excitement at seeing the Everly Brothers at an Alan Freed show. I recalled the hours spent in my room singing the third part to the Everlys' distinctive dual harmonies.... Later I learned that I wasn't unique in that regard.... Suddenly I was crying...hearing the Everly Brothers' recording of my song...with millions of other people in the greater New York listening area."

As basic training concluded, what had been percolating and toyed with in magazines became a fact: Donald Everly and Venetia Stevenson were wed in the chapel at the San Diego base on February 4, 1962, with Don and best man Phil both in dress uniform.

Five days later, during a short-leave honeymoon, the Everly Brothers appeared on a special episode of *The Ed Sullivan Show* staged at the Fontainebleau Hotel in Miami Beach, performing "Crying in the Rain" in full marine dress and the "high and tight" butch haircuts. They were welcomed to the stage with the "Marines' Hymn." Ed comments to Don, "They say you've put on twenty pounds; you look great." Don agrees that's correct. He certainly looks better than he had on the show in October. Ed suggests they sing for "Colonel Glenn," with John Glenn about to be launched into earth orbit two days later.

Don and Phil would always recall with fondness their time at San Diego boot camp and the weeks that followed stationed at nearby Camp Pendleton—not least because the rigors of training, the exercise, the food regimens all contributed to improving the condition both were in, as they'd hoped. They would also have to serve a month for years to come, somehow fitting that in amid everything else that would ensue.

When their company finished infantry training at Pendleton in March 1962, the Everlys performed for their fellow marines, bringing in other entertainers to join the private show, including rockers Dorsey and Johnny Burnette. They never would be called up to active duty, even as the American miliary commitment in Vietnam increased year by year. There were some eleven thousand military "advisors" in place there as early as late 1962.

Don would reflect about this time a year later. "I got so confused and seemed to have so many things to do at once—boom! Being in the Marines helped us physically, but mentally, I suppose we felt our career slipping away, so when we came out, we had to catch up."

Ann Marshall, who'd become a card-carrying Everly Brothers fan club member in 1957 after seeing them on *Bandstand* and, as she recalls, her "eyes wobbled," was a witness to the continuing presence of the Ritalin cocktails in their lives through this freshly pressured "catching up" time. They were both self-administering now.

"Phil used to shoot it in his hip," she recalls of the "vitamin shots." "Don was more intravenous."

The witty, Hollywood-raised daughter of old-school movie star Herbert Marshall, Ann had been introduced to Phil by their mutual friend Lou Adler and they briefly were a couple. In May 1962, gossip columns even reported, inaccurately, that they were engaged. Her entanglement with the Everlys would have multiple chapters over the years, and as we'll see, most involved Don, not Phil, but this one didn't last. The same papers reported that relationship was over a month later. That summer, finally, it could be said, Phil was engaged to Jackie Ertel, his actual wife-to-be. "And that was the end of me," Ann would laugh.

The Everlys were rushed back into the studio less than a month after their release from service. A sign of things to come, the session was not on Music Row, but at United Recording in Hollywood with, among others, Glen Campbell and Buddy Holly's friend Tommy Allsup on guitars, and Leon Russell on piano. They would be spending a lot more time in those environs.

The song recorded was practically regional, and possibly personally meaningful—"Little Hollywood Girl," which warns said girl, rather darkly in some of the multiple takes recorded, that her dream of making it in the movies is going nowhere. The lyrics were by Gerry Goffin and the music by Jack Keller, rather than Goffin's better-known writing partner, his wife Carole King. All three were now working for Don Kirshner's publishing company. The success of "Crying in the Rain" had clearly impressed Don, Phil, and the publisher. Those very writers were in the process—as so many from the New York pop music business were—of relocating to Los Angeles themselves.

The Everlys were back in the more usual Nashville setting a few days later, however, recording Roger Miller's typically clever and rhythmically surprising "Burma Shave," and another tune from

Goffin and Keller, the jaunty "How Can I Meet Her?" That one became the upbeat B-side of their next single, "That's Old Fashioned," a horn-driven pop song that presents them as guys who just like to hold hands with their girls at the movies. "Old Fashioned" did reach number nine on the pop chart and, interestingly enough, number four on the adult "easy listening" chart—which was pretty much what Warners was after with it.

The most forward looking *and* fraught recording adventure of this time was Don's near-obsessive attempt to get the eerie song "Nancy's Minuet" into some version both brothers felt seemed "right." It's unlikely they ever thought it could be commercial, and it was never released at the time, but it would be included on a 1977 album of unreleased Warners tracks. Don was taken with Henry Mancini's chilling "Experiment in Terror" theme music written for the now obscure Blake Edwards movie of the same name. There would be seemingly endless takes on this evolving original in multiple sessions—in both Nashville and Hollywood. Don's lyric, which also evolved, is sung by a character completely under the spell of this temptress Nancy, a helpless puppet on a string—a not-unlikely theme from a guy who's maybe just begun to perceive that he's drug-addicted.

In those sessions, what started as something close to the Calliope marching-band rhythms evolved toward darker, slower versions and eventually to clanging mid-'60s album rock. They try different instruments—a harpsichord, a trombone, a saxophone, fuzz guitar—changing keys, changing harmony. Some of the attempts might have appealed to ears later in the decade, when people went for the musical dramatics of the somewhat similarly toned "MacArthur Park."

Don and Phil Everly were working in the more complex, slow-constructing studio style associated with rock heavyweights later, and that's impressive. The sheer obsessiveness, however, also reveals that, once again, things were not quite right with Don. He would later admit as much: "I was drugged out by then. That's why I couldn't get it together. It was a bitter time for me."

It was in this context that Don sought out Boudleaux Bryant. Even in this period when the brothers could not engage with him professionally, he was still an empathetic mentor, and also a man who'd dealt with his own alcohol issues. Del Bryant, then a teenager, recalls, "Don came over once, and I was at home. He was going through some stuff, and was kind of down, and Dad was sitting there with his arm around him. Dad took a long walk around the edge of the big yard with him. Then they came back, and Don went to leave, and Dad called us in and said, 'Wow, Don broke down and said "Boudleaux, I'm a druggie" and started crying.' Those were the exact words. Dad was shaken by it and felt so sorry. I'm sure Dad tried to bolster him."

Warner Bros., meanwhile, was releasing the first, self-titled album by a new and commercially substantial act in May 1962— *Peter, Paul and Mary*. There would be immediate hit singles from that one ("If I Had a Hammer" and "Lemon Tree"), which heralded commercial folk's major commercial phase. As the trend unfolded, Archie Bleyer reordered the *Songs Our Daddy Taught Us* album tracks and sold it as a "new" album, *Folk Songs by the Everly Brothers*. Disc jockey Hugh Cherry provided new liner notes explaining that, yes, the recordings are within this new pop idea of "folk," since they share "a Folk-Country feel that will please both the purist and the listener who delights in a good song, no matter what its origin." "I'm Here to Get My Baby Out of Jail," perhaps reminding people of "Take a Message to Mary," was released as a "new" single and managed to chart at number seventy-six.

One thing the folk craze did do was sell a substantial new round of acoustic guitars, and plenty of growing youngsters had seen the Everlys playing theirs on TV. The matching pair they'd regularly played both on records and appearances were big, relatively loud Gibson J-200 models, with their added trademark two-sided pickguards designed by visually conscious Don. Gibson now proposed selling a model named for the brothers, and for that they took a thinner, lighter, and less expensive J-185, added the identifying pickguards, and sold them as the Gibson Everly Brothers guitar for a decade, reissuing them with multiple color schemes, under several different names. The earliest models remained quite desirable to collectors—though they weren't really designed for fancy folk or country picking, but for Don-style slamming rhythm guitar. The pickguards tended to limit the sound clarity.

At a June session in Nashville, Don strained to hit the high notes on two Goffin-King songs, "What About Me" and "Nice Guy"; neither were considered releasable at the time. There'd been no new good-to-go album material from Don and Phil for seven months, so the orange-covered *Golden Hits of the Everly Brothers* LP was cobbled together from released singles and issued in August.

With Phil and Don's rising appreciation for the contemporary material the Goffin-King-Keller gang could provide, their own relocation to Los Angeles, and the recording industry increasingly centered in Hollywood, it was practically inevitable that production of Everly Brothers records shifted west. The July and September 1962 sessions at United Recording on Sunset Boulevard are among the more intriguing in the Everlys' recording story.

In July, Carole King was herself the pivotal session leader and conductor of a set of musicians that included Glen Campbell, Tommy Allsup, and an eight-piece string section. They first turned to the Goffin-Keller ballad "Don't Ask Me to Be Friends," quite unusual in that Phil sings lead and takes the solos, and Don is barely heard behind him when there's harmony—and it works. That one becomes the slow side of their next single.

Carole then serves them up a Goffin-King song that many have no idea the Everlys were first to record, "Chains," which would be a number-six R&B hit for the Cookies girl group a few months later and recorded by the Beatles the following February. It might have been an Everly Brothers hit, but everything seems a little off in the two takes extant. The first drags, unlikely to have been the fault of the rhythm section on hand—jazz legend Red Callender on bass and rock giant Earl Palmer on drums. The other take, someone's bad idea, adds clanking chain sounds, and that only succeeds in making it all the more awkward.

They may well have intended to revisit "Chains" the next day, but it didn't happen. Increasingly erratic, Don left early and was unavailable to record, an ominous sign. That left Phil, Carole King, and Glen Campbell in the studio, and they decided to make use of the time, recording two novelty numbers as "the Keestone Family Singers." "Melodrama" is a bouncy Goffin-King joke about the machinations of the Dudley Do-Right cartoon's evil Snidely Whiplash mistreating "the nicest girl in the whole wide world," but stopped by Dudley, all in two minutes flat. The other number was the banjo-driven, partly French "Cornbread and Chitlings," written by country rock piano player Glen D. Hardin, with Phil, Glen Campbell, and Carole quite identifiable on solo verses. Phil made these a rarely heard Calliope single, the last on the Everlys' little label.

The Everly Brothers went back on tour that summer, to the West and upper Midwest, then back to the Steel Pier and a stand at the short-lived Bronx, New York, amusement park Freedomland. The backup was by Joey Paige, Marshall Leib, and drummer Chuck Blackwell, who'd been recommended by Leon Russell. When Don and Phil returned to Hollywood in need of a single, there were epic sessions trying to work up "No One Can Make My Sunshine

Smile," a very suitable ballad from Goffin and Keller, and the poppy Goffin-King song "I Can't Say Goodbye to You." Endless in-studio searches for rhythms and arrangements were becoming a pattern, in the "Say Goodbye" case, nothing was deemed releasable even after thirty-six takes. The next single would be "Don't Ask Me to Be Friends" backed with "No One Can Make My Sunshine Smile"; it didn't rise higher than number forty-eight pop but again scored higher—number sixteen—as adult pop/MOR.

At this point, Don and Phil's friend Sonny Curtis was among the backup musicians at work. He recalls, "For whatever reason, they didn't seem to get along very well during that period, and some of the sessions were a bit strange. They seemed to be pulling against each other; whatever one wanted, the other wanted just the opposite. I always tried to stay out of their way."

Phil reflected later, "What we needed was to take a long vacation, to get off the merry-go-round. There were too many people making too much money off us, keeping us going. Things were too confused. We should have taken a long rest, but in those days, we couldn't. The tensions between Don and I...well, we're just a family....You could just as easily say that the tension between us existed from day one, from birth."

A return to Europe beginning with a multicity tour in the UK was set for a few weeks later. There was one more unique stop in October before the projected trip—in Omaha, Nebraska, to record vocals for what would become *Christmas with the Everly Brothers and the Boystown Choir*. Plenty of Everlys fans are grateful that album exists come holiday time, but the results were mixed at best. Don and Phil recorded their vocals separately from the thirty-three-voice choir at the famed home for neglected and orphaned boys, and away from its huge pipe organ. It doesn't always gel. The chorus tends to overwhelm their vocals, and some tracks feature the chorus alone. Nevertheless, it's the Everly Brothers singing traditional

Christmas carols—"Adeste Fideles," "Silent Night," a Don solo with the chorus on "What Child Is This?," and a Phil solo on "O Little Town of Bethlehem." The album was released by November.

Don Peake joined the backup band on guitar at this point, recruited by Marshall Leib, who couldn't make the scheduled trip himself. They got in some rehearsal and were set to fly to London for the tour, scheduled to run from October 15 into November, with Joey Paige on bass and Chuck Blackwell on drums backing Phil and Don.

When the time to take off for England came, a troubled Don didn't appear at the airport for the flight out, nor for a second one later in the day. In London, Joey Paige recalls, "the press had a field day asking why Don wasn't on the same flight." They were told that he'd been delayed when his car broke down heading to the airport. He showed up the next day, along with Venetia, who was in an early stage of pregnancy.

After checking into the swanky Savoy Hotel, the whole group headed to the Prince of Wales Theatre near Leicester Square for a run-through rehearsal. It didn't last long. They'd only begun the first number, "Crying in the Rain," when Don dropped his guitar and rushed to his wife's arms, crying indeed. The band sat there stunned, and Phil sent them back to the hotel.

Back at the Savoy, Donald Everly attempted to kill himself by sleeping-pill overdose. He was rushed to Charing Cross Hospital, then released six hours later; it's presumed they'd pumped his stomach while he was there. Phil would recall, ruefully, years later, "I was in the hotel room with him at the time, but deep down inside I just refused to believe that he was really trying to kill himself. Donald had not been well for a while, and we were semi-cognizant of his situation. It was just the most dreadful period I could imagine."

That night, Don again attempted to end his own life. He was rushed, unconscious, to Middlesex Hospital where police watched as he was tended to in the emergency room. Venetia told some of the press that she thought he was suffering from food poisoning; Bobby Weiss, from Warner Bros., reported someone on the duo's staff was saying he was suffering from "complete nervous and physical exhaustion" from overwork. Hospital officials said nothing.

It was the glibly cynical (if accurate) *Express* reporter Logan Gourlay who quoted someone unnamed on the duo's staff, probably Weiss, saying "he may have taken some drugs to quiet himself down." The *Express* added the often-reprinted photo of Don looking as shattered and awful as he ever would, sitting in a car beside his visibly distressed wife. Middlesex arranged for them to be driven straight to a TWA flight home from Heathrow, where Don simply told reporters, "I wanna go home. I don't feel good." It was the morning of the day the first show was scheduled. Chronicler Roger White quoted him as saying later, "I was so high it didn't matter whether I went on living or not."

Manager Jack Rael met Don and Venetia at Idlewild Airport in New York and got Don into a waiting ambulance. An Associated Press photo was captioned, "The singer returned to New York from London where he was treated in hospitals for an overdose of sleeping pills, twice in 24 hours." He was initially treated at Manhattan's Gracie Square psychiatric hospital. While he was there, Venetia stayed with Phil's onetime date Ann Marshall, who'd moved to New York for work as a model.

The story, if sometimes distorted, was out. Don would be in and out of multiple hospitals for the following six months, where nobody, it should be understood, including Don himself, recognized that he was experiencing effects of prescription drug addiction. He was treated, inappropriately, as a mental patient. Over those months ahead, a psychiatrist helped, but it would take at least three years for him to get the chemicals fully out of his system—the background to his life well into the mid-1960s. In the short term, they subjected Don to electroshock therapy. He'd say later, "It didn't do me any good. It was a pretty primitive treatment at the time; once they gave it to you, you couldn't remember how long you'd been there. It knocked me back for a long time. I thought I'd never write again."

Back in London, Phil and band were confronted with what to do next. This was a highly charged, intimidating situation. They were contractually committed to a series of shows—sellouts in advance. And, as Joey Paige would recall, "Phil had never sung on stage without his brother on a major tour like this one. I encouraged him to seriously consider going on without Don.... On opening night he was a bundle of nerves—but he pulled it off."

Reporter Andy Gray of the *New Musical Express*, the *NME*, described that first show, at the East Ham Granada Theatre: "After the Everly Trio...played three instrumentals, Phil appeared in a black suit, looking very worried. He got a terrific ovation, which he accepted with a timid smile. He said how sorry he was that Don wasn't there...but said he'd do his best.... To start with, it wasn't too good.... When Phil sang solo he sometimes was out of tune and was too quiet.... Then Joey Paige from the backing trio joined him vocally and it sounded like the Everlys. After that, Phil went on improving.... I saw Phil backstage just after his act. He was still trembling."

The set had been all of fifteen minutes long. Phil admitted to Gray, "I've never been so scared. I was trying to sing by myself... but after harmonizing for so long it was almost impossible." A scheduled television appearance was canceled, but the tour proceeded, through some twenty towns and cities. The English audiences tended to be supportive, and Phil increased the set length along the way.

On the other hand, a reporter in London's *Stage & Television Today* offered up some not-untypical British press snark for Phil daring to present unmasked, honest emotion: "He...played good guitar and sang most efficiently under the circumstances, but what really nauseated was his frequent sickly sentimental references to his brother." Yes, sans byline, they really printed that. None of "that sort of thing" around here, mate. It's not "efficient."

It was October 1962 and the world at large was really not especially focused on musical performances. The Cuban missile crisis standoff between the USA and the USSR was at hand, and there was that palpable worldwide fear that everything, not just stage shows, could be finishing in nuclear blasts. Phil told the *NME* on October 26, speaking of himself and Joey, "We are, first, reserves for the U.S. Marine Corps and if President Kennedy calls, then we'll have to go—even if it happens right in the middle of the show tonight." That call didn't come, but Phil did phone Venetia, who reported that Don was out of the hospital and doing better, but would not be rejoining the tour.

Less than two years after Phil and Don spoke so confidently of taking more charge of their own lives, they seemed less in command of anything than ever before. In November, Phil suggested that Don was "fully recovered" (not precisely the case), that they weren't splitting up, and that they'd spent time together in New York: "We did a lot of things together and I went out with some of my own friends; it has been something of a rest for me."

At Christmas, Don and Phil visited their parents back in Nashville. There are no reports on how that went. And then, two months after the fateful tour ended, in what must have been a relief on multiple levels, Phil and Jackie Ertel finally married, on January 12, 1963, in a private ceremony in New York City. It was on oddly short notice, considering their years of engagement and near-engagement. Don managed to serve as best man; Venetia was there, too, as were a number of celebrities—but not Ike and

Margaret Everly. It all had come together, they said, too fast for them to attend.

The wedding was held just twenty-four hours after England's Parlophone label released an appealing, harmonious, quite Everlys-like single called "Please Please Me," by an outfit with a name taken to be odd at the time—the Beatles.

Chapter Seven

THE TRYING TIME
1963–1967

IN 1963, AT THE START OF THE ERA MOST OFTEN RECALLED AS THE SIX-ties, the Everly Brothers were still making new music that audiences responded to but, no question, a page had been turned in their careers, and they knew it. "If you look at the industry," Phil would say, "you have to last five years to be known, really. That five-year period is... 'the hot period.' And [then] you can bubble occasionally, but... that initial thing is really *over*."

They would have lesser if notable hits and some glorious new records, but they'd never have a top-ten hit in America again. Performers who would dominate pop music in the oncoming era had the ability to switch gears and sounds and images as the zeitgeist evolved, fast as it would—because their audiences assented to it. Some, of course, would always want the Beatles to stay forever clean, smiling mop-tops, Dylan the protesting "voice of a generation" (which he'd point out he wasn't even in), the Rolling Stones a maracas-shaking blues band.

With their broad musical comfort zone, Don and Phil were generally ready to move from one genre to another or mix them up. The open questions now were where to land and what their audiences would accept. For many, they'd always be the fresh-faced pin-ups with harmonious songs of 1950s youth, no matter how they matured and how many decades they'd spend addressing who the heck they really were now.

It had to be an especially painful reality that they would so often be treated as standard-bearers, even artifacts, of that 1957–1962 period while watching acts who'd been directly and proudly influenced by them rise and rule. The irony was, the Everlys had gotten such an early start that many of those hot new performers were the same age, or no more than three or four years younger. The newcomers weren't really from such a different generation—but their audiences were.

As early as 1957 two middle-class kids from Forest Hills, Queens, New York, Paul Simon and Art Garfunkel (both sixteen), recording as Tom & Jerry, had appeared on *American Bandstand* and seen their small-label single "Hey, Schoolgirl," unabashedly inspired by the Everlys' sound, sell one hundred thousand copies and take them to the pop charts. Other "Tommy Graph and Jerry Landis" singles, such as "Our Song," leaned even more explicitly on Don and Phil harmonies. Together and separately, under varied pseudonyms, they'd be writing and recording related rock and roll right through 1962. Solo, "Artie Garr" had "Dream Alone," the sort of Everly-aware "dream" ballad you do when not in a harmony duo, and "Landis" had "Anna Belle," which sounded as if a hiccupping Buddy Holly had recorded an Everly-penned number. In 1963, Paul and Art were a few months from being signed by Columbia Records. They would be Everly Brothers boosters, and eventually friends, over decades to come.

In Minnesota, another teenager, born just two years after Phil, was a dedicated Little Richard, Buddy Holly, and Everly Brothers fan, and played piano for Holly-successor Bobby Vee, all in the late 1950s, before metamorphizing into Bob Dylan. After steeping himself in American blues, country, and Anglo balladry, he'd have a strong role in transforming much about how popular music would be approached. On his very first album, his craggy young turn on the old blues song "Highway 51" was built around the "Wake Up Little Susie" guitar riff, and the liner notes acknowledged it.

He expanded on that in a 1984 talk with Robert Hilburn: "It was the early folk music, done in a rock way...the kind of music I played. I did 'Highway 51' like an Everly Brothers tune because that was the only way I could relate to that stuff." Dylan would turn to Don's riff again, as the propelling guitar line in his incantatory "It's Alright Ma (I'm Only Bleeding)." Not many noticed. He would go on to perform Everlys songs in performance and on record, and eventually offer them songs he'd written. In 1963, he was rising to a level of stardom within the more traditional and sometimes political folk music world, a scene Don and Phil were not yet familiar with. They'd get there.

Out on the West Coast, several sets of brothers were well aware of the Everlys. Up north, in El Cerrito, circa 1959, Tom Fogerty, just two years younger than Phil, and younger brother John were leading local rock-and-roll bands playing songs by Bo Diddley and Little Richard and Buddy Holly—a familiar set of favorites—but were also attending the annual Berkeley Folk Music Festival, where they heard blues artists like Lightnin' Hopkins, and catching country music on California TV—notably, Johnny Cash. John Fogerty would recall riding in a '56 Chevy Bel Air with Tom when something new came on the radio, the "When Will I Be Loved" guitar riff: "We just looked at each other with that I-just-died-and-went-to-heaven look." John would perform it for years. *Musician* magazine found it fitting to publish a conversation between John and Don in 1986 so they could compare notes—if not their respective brotherly frictions.

No one would claim that the Fogerty brothers' best-known band, Creedence Clearwater Revival, sounded like the Everlys, though there are marked similarities between their version of "Susie Q" and Don and Phil's. But as they worked up the gumbo that made them international stars and one of the greatest of American bands, the Everly Brothers had demonstrated for them that the range of American roots music they'd digested could be merged with a rock sensibility, plus some imagination, and be heard.

Much closer to the Everlys' Los Angeles home base were the Wilson brothers and company, the Beach Boys. There was blood harmony at work in that family, too, certainly, but the performers they'd modeled their harmony on were swing-era pop vocal groups and later outfits derived from them, the Four Freshmen and Four Preps in particular. Country harmony tradition had played no real part there, but they had incorporated Kingston Trio–style commercial folk, doo-wop vocal sounds, and Chuck Berry into their mix.

Brian Wilson and Al Jardine, the band cofounders, were three years younger than Phil, Wilson cousin Mike Love a year older, and the other Beach Boys younger still. They'd taken to using guitars, and if you were looking for models of rocking brotherly harmony along with those, you were bound to follow the Everly Brothers carefully, and they did. Mike Love and Brian didn't agree on much, even in high school, but they agreed on harmonizing on songs by the Everlys. "The thing that brought us together was music," Love would recall. "We used to love singing those harmonies. Brian and I would sing Everly Brothers songs." In 1965, when the Beach Boys did their loose album of favorites, ersatz "party" style, one song choice would be "Devoted to You," and they'd eventually record with the Everlys. In 1963, they were easily the biggest guitar-wielding harmony vocal band in America.

In downtown New York, meanwhile, John Cale, a sophisticated, classically trained musician with occasional taste for simpler rock and roll sounds, and his partner in the avant-garde musical outfit the Dream Syndicate, country-music admirer Tony Conrad, were hired to play on cheap cover records for jukeboxes by the semi-sleazy Pickwick label, where they'd be paired with a songwriter named Lou Reed. Cale told author Will Hermes that, as unlikely as it might seem for the proto–Velvet Underground lineup, they were "besotted" by the Everly Brothers harmonies and "played similarly to the way [they] used to sing.... They sang...so perfectly in tune that you could actually hear each voice." It was a model for what they were working to do *instrumentally.*

Over in England, young men, such as the Hollies founders Allan Clarke and Graham Nash, would soon be singing explicitly Everlys-inspired harmony vocals, whether in bands or in Don-and-Phil-like duos, such as Peter & Gordon. Less obviously, yet another pair of sometimes clashing brothers, Ray and Dave Davies, would call hearing the Everlys "crucial" for them, and recall their older sisters singing Phil's high parts with their boyfriends taking Don's leads. "Later," Ray noted, "my brother and I tried to sing the parts, and after a while we would start to blend.... It gave us the sense that for once we both had the same energy...united in what we were doing." Less commonly then, Dave would stress the importance of the *content* of the Everlys' hit songs: "I learned about life— how people interact, what boys and girls do together.... It's not just the notes, it's the *life* that comes with it."

There was no question, of course, who had become the dominant force in British pop—with their arrival in the United States still a year off—John, Paul, George, and Ringo. Little Richard would tell the story of being pressed by their manager, Brian Epstein, when he played Liverpool in 1962, to take their demo tape to some US label. His reaction? "The Beatles sounded like four Everly Brothers to me.

I said, 'There's no sense in having four Everly Brothers, when there already are two.'"

The Everlys first heard a little about these Beatles boys as their earliest singles were released. The Everlys' friend Don Wayne, soon to be their road manager for a decade, was working with producer Jim Lee's small Monogram label, which had their artist Chris Montez touring in England behind his hit, "Let's Dance." The Beatles were lower on that bill, and Lee thought it might be a great idea for the Everlys to record their song "Please Please Me," which no one had heard in the States. Don and Phil rebuffed that, saying these were new kids who deserved their own chance, and they had no intention of stepping on theirs with a cover. It's quite possible that that story got back to the Beatles, and it could only have added to their admiration for the Everlys.

Decades later, Paul McCartney would sum up that early, central admiration: "The biggest influence on John and me was the Everly Brothers. To this day, I just think they're the greatest. And they were different.... We idolized them. We wanted to *be* them." When they heard "All I Have to Do Is Dream," he'd note, "it just blew us away." Each new Everlys single release would become part of the fledgling Beatles stage set. "When John and I first started to write songs, I was Phil, and he was Don." The admiration was just as strong from George Harrison, who'd caught that 1960 show and was singing material of theirs, too.

More importantly, the way they'd digest the Everlys and Bryants' song structures, and the Everly guitar riffs and harmonies, would be one of the central qualities that marked *them* as crucially different—in a Britain that was not broadly familiar with the long-standing country-duo tradition the Everlys came from. Yes, they'd heard more country music in Liverpool than most, brought in by ship workers and sailors, and there were limited country elements in the amateur skiffle craze they'd joined as the Quarrymen. But when following Lennon and McCartney's life-changing February 1962 audition in Manchester the local BBC radio producer Peter Pilbeam described them for the network as "an unusual group, not as rocky as most, more country and western with a tendency to play music," the pair's lauded aspects were their most Everly-like. The description applied to Don and Phil in 1957.

In a 1964 Beatles group interview with humorist Jean Shepherd for *Playboy*, McCartney proved to be well aware of one aspect of his heroes' plight: "The Everly Brothers... went into the Army at the height of their fame, and the Army seems to do something to singers.... They may not be as popular when they come out of the Army. It may also make people forget them, and consequently they may have a harder job getting back on top when they get out."

Returning to the studio in Nashville, Phil and Don tried looking for a love song reminiscent of their earlier hits, if in a fresh setting. They turned to the ballad "So It Always Will Be," by Arthur Altman, composer of the standard "All or Nothing at All." The released version became the A-side of a single that didn't even crack the Top 100 in the United States but would reach, in a pattern that extended over the next few years, number twenty-three in the UK. The flip side was a version of Don's studio obsession, "Nancy's Minuet." Despite its silent reception, that was and remains a fascinating song, ahead of its time in its baroque rock sensibility.

They also tried returning to teenage-problems songs, including a pretty inane one offered by their friends Jackie DeShannon and Sharon Sheeley, the too obvious and derivative "Baby Bye-Oh." Nothing came of it; in fact, they cracked up trying to record it, probably a short-lived sign of health and calm.

Don's six months in and out of hospitals with harsh, inappropriate treatments reached into April 1963, and some of his clashes reported in the first half of the year have to be understood in that context. On May 5, Venetia gave birth to the first of their three children, daughter Stacy (Anastasia Dawn Everly). Delighted with the new baby, Don is seen in photos playing with her when she's a toddler. His activities remained relatively limited, but there was now talk about a UK tour to make up for what had fallen apart on the last attempt. There were also discussions between the brothers about what in the world they ought to try next.

Don would say, "We're pretty independent about our music.... When we stopped having pop hits...some people wondered why we didn't go country—but I couldn't imagine tailoring our music to some preconceived formula like that." Ironically, the first in a set of three varied, high-quality albums they were about to record, albums that rank among the most consistently strong and lasting they ever made, would be entirely devoted to their own special take on contemporary country. It was recorded in Hollywood in just two days, as summer 1963 arrived.

Country was exciting again. This was the year of Buck Owens's "Act Naturally," Bobby Bare's "Detroit City," Johnny Cash's "Ring of Fire," George Hamilton IV's "Abilene," Bill Anderson's "Still," and Flatt and Scruggs's bluegrass hit "The Ballad of Jed Clampett." The Owens and Bare records were prime examples of how twangy, rock-influenced electric guitar was now a serious element in country music. Bobby Bare and Waylon Jennings were being marketed as "folk country," as they picked up material from the commercial folk revival and RCA Victor hoped they could reach into that market.

The brothers' fresh, vital album that emerged in that context was *The Everly Brothers Sing Great Country Hits*. It bears three songs by Don Gibson, the hero of all of the most forward-looking songwriters in Nashville; two songs that were hits for the tenor Hank Locklin; Hank Williams's "I'm So Lonesome I Could Cry" (an uncontested, blatant breach across the Acuff-Rose song barrier); and a harmonious take on "Silver Threads and Golden Needles," which had recently been a roots-pop hit for the Springfields (Dusty and company) in England. There was also a dark, memorable lament about the plight of a performer who fails to make it in Nashville, "This Is the Last Song I'm Ever Going to Sing," written by Sonny Curtis and J.I. Allison.

The album was recorded not on Music Row, but at Radio Recorders in Los Angeles, with the West Coast equivalents of the Nashville A-Team, masterful players of rock and country such as Glen Campbell, Leon Russell, Billy Strange, and Hal Blaine—certified members of the Hollywood "Wrecking Crew." Don and Phil would be working with them plenty now. Together with Don and Phil, they would arrive at a fresh "country rock" sound about half a decade before anybody was using that term.

Phil and Don sing Gibson's "Oh Lonesome Me," "Just One Time," and "Sweet Dreams" more in unison than usual, with Hal Blaine on insistent drumming, and those studio guitar aces filigreeing details. The patented, searing Don-and-Phil ballad harmony comes to the fore on Ted Daffan's "Born to Lose," the Hank Locklin ballads "Send Me the Pillow You Dream On" and "Please Help Me, I'm Falling," perfect for them, and on a "Lonely Street" that rivals Patsy Cline's. Country radio never even considered any of these as possibilities; Warners then had limited sway in that direction and pop radio wasn't interested either. It's a groundbreaking album that should be heard and can easily be appreciated now.

With this exceptional music-making going on, it would be reasonable to imagine that things were copasetic between Don and Phil—but not so. During those very sessions, columnist Dorothy Kilgallen reported, "The Everly Brothers are tiffing rather loudly," and a trade report detailed that further: "The Everly Brothers' act is near collapse. The boys have been feuding for some time, but it became a matter of public discussion when Phil tried to belt brother Don during a Warner Bros. recording session. Other people got between the boys before blood was shed."

If the details were accurate, it's a reminder that Phil, slower to percolate, could boil over once riled far enough. No blood harmony there, more like near bloodshed. This may not have been the only unfortunate altercation. That summer, the Don-Venetia marriage also evidenced serious tensions.

At home, Don and wife were living with the same lingering, sometimes rough aftereffects of his addiction and electroshock therapy. She now reported that he'd hit and kicked her, and she charged him with mental cruelty. Venetia was awarded temporary alimony and child support, with Stacy all of three months old. Just a few months later, though, they reconciled, with years more together and two more children arriving along the way.

In mid-September, Jackie, Venetia, and baby Stacy all accompanied Don and Phil on a memorable European tour, flying first to London, where reporters greeted them with question after question about their opinions of the scene-dominating Beatles, who'd had two big hits in England by then, but none yet in the United States. Both the Everlys and the Beatles were featured on the BBC radio *Saturday Club* anniversary show in October, but the Beatles' segment had been prerecorded, so no meeting occurred. Don and Phil compared Los Angeles surfer haircuts to the Fab Four's, and performed "Walk Right Back" and "Wake Up Little Susie." The Beatles offering was a brand new one—"She Loves You."

New Musical Express found a reenergized Don laughing and talkative. ("In comparison now, Phil is the quiet one.") He informs them, "I have a new motto....No one can pay me enough to be unhappy. I insist on something new for me—one full, free day a week...of my own, for sharing with my wife and baby." They prerecorded several TV appearances before leaving for Germany, where they recorded four sides in phonetically learned German.

This tour, the band consisted of Don Peake on lead guitar, Joey Paige on bass, and on drums, a newcomer recruited by Joey who'd have a long, storied, and eventually tragic road ahead—Jim Gordon, just seventeen and not even out of high school. He had to register for the draft while out on the road. He'd already written an Everlys B-side called "I'm Afraid." Before starting the long UK itinerary, this lineup played the famed Olympia theater in Paris, along with that hotter Warner Bros. act, Peter, Paul and Mary, and there were shows at the Beatles' old haunt in Hamburg, the Star-Club.

The main tour, reminiscent of bus tours of the late fifties, wended through some thirty auditoriums and movie theaters in England, Scotland, and Wales, as arranged by the notorious tough-guy promoter Don Arden. It featured a lineup still talked about—the Everlys on top, with their old hero Bo Diddley next, and momentarily popular young British pop singer Julie Grant. Lower on the bill were two little-known bands to note for different reasons. The local horn band the Flintstones had as lead vocalist one Terry Slater, who would go on to have a substantial role in the Everlys story, as their regular bass player, songwriting provider, collaborator, and friend, for decades to come.

And then there were some cheeky kids who'd gotten together in London intent on being a blues band. They had exactly one record to their name anyone had heard at all, their take on Chuck Berry's "Come On." These were the Rolling Stones, on their first tour ever. Arden would boast that he landed them for forty pounds a night. When attendance at the first few dates disappointed him, he added Little Richard to the bill. This was not, needless to say, a setup in which promoting the Everlys' new country album felt appropriate—and they didn't, to its sales detriment.

Jim Gordon described their band's music, and the atmosphere: "It was really soft, but really fast. The Everlys figure the faster you play the more exciting it is. They were weird to work with, as they fought like crazy.... They'd get in fights, and they would stop the bus and have it out."

The Stones' Keith Richards could recall singing duets with his aunt on "When Will I Be Loved" well before meeting them. "When I think of that tour," he'd reminisce, "I just think I had a very, very compressed education...I'd watch from the wings or climb the rafters, even stand right out front, and watch and see how they worked." Watching Don, he got his first intimation that American roots musicians used multiple guitar tunings. He'd recall, "Don... always used open tuning. Don is *the* killer rhythm man. He was the one who turned me on to [the downstroke windmill slamming]... all of that. It's the weirdest thing...because it's country shit, basically. That was why the Everly Brothers stuff was so *hard*—because it was all acoustic."

Mick Jagger would fondly recall playing *with* the Everlys in the course of the tour. "We all used to bowl along to the Evs' dressing room and sort of join forces, just for kicks. Can you imagine... singing numbers like 'La Bamba' and going mad with tambourines and maracas....It really was fantastic....The Evs really are artistes; [what] strikes you is their professionalism—and that Don is the more talkative of the two."

In a BBC 4 documentary broadcast in 2015, a seventy-eight-year-old Don would contribute to a discussion of whether people working with Little Richard back then understood that he was gay (bisexual, in fact), remarking, "Oh, he was. He's gay as can be. He invited *me* in, but I said, 'No thank you; that's not for me.' Things were going on man; we were kids." That can serve as a probably unnecessary indication that not everyone who found the brothers Everly attractive specimens would have to have been straight women with pinup collections.

Both Ringo Starr and Paul McCartney were in the audience for the London show at the Hammersmith Odeon on November 3; Paul ran into Jim Gordon at an after-hours club and complimented him on his drumming.

At tour's end, Phil and Joey stayed on a few days to record some tracks sung by Joey solo. One thing was becoming clear: despite the brief attendance gap starting the tour, the British remained especially conscious of the Everlys and more commercially supportive of them, and would stay that way right through the trying years just ahead. That loyalty was true of parts of Europe (the Netherlands and Germany, notably) and Australia, too, even when their presence diminished back home.

Don and Phil couldn't help but notice how much the pop sounds, looks, and atmospherics were changing, months before those trends arrived in the States. Phil was very interested to see, for example, that the Stones did *not* wear cute matching clothes onstage. The Everlys' gentle yet muscular approach had been presented amid pretty hard rockers for the time, and they didn't want to be the tame ones. Two and a half weeks after the tour ended, John F. Kennedy was assassinated in Dallas. In early February, the Beatles—with their cute matching suits intact—landed in New York and appeared on *The Ed Sullivan Show.*

When Don and Phil returned to recording in Hollywood in January, quite a squad of guitar players was on hand—Sonny Curtis, Glen Campbell, and Don Peake, and Ricky Nelson's celebrated young backup buddy, James Burton. Both Jerry Allison and Jim Gordon were available on drums—assembled for several exhausting sessions, one of them with horns, as Don's version of a "wall of sound" was applied to four new songs he'd written under his own name.

None were released immediately, but they did seem to indicate that Wesley's self-written song prohibition could be cracking. A strong one of the four, "The Drop Out," is a rarity for the time—an empathetic portrayal of a kid who has to drop out of school, not for lack of ambition but because he needs the money from a supermarket job to get by. Clearly, Don had not forgotten their lean years.

In April, he'd tell a reporter from *New Musical Express*, wistfully perhaps, "My brother Phil is in New York, seeing music publishers and writers about songs. Material is getting harder to find; so many writers are also recording artists—like the Beatles." In practice, as the Beatles' songwriting capabilities emerged and evolved, the Everlys' admiration for them grew right along with that. They also admired the way the agreeably cheeky Liverpudlians mocked the press, rather than being polite as they'd had to be earlier. And they'd soon begin to make rock music for adults that was taken seriously—a day the brothers had long been waiting for.

Don also revealed some significant news about possible returning song sources in that *NME* interview: "Boudleaux Bryant, a very good friend of ours, is writing some new songs. Phil and I will be seeing him in Nashville next week....[He] has a tremendous list of songs we'll be working out with him." It was all smiles when Phil and Don, Wesley Rose, and Boudleaux got back together, which some might find odd, considering the role Rose had played in slashing the Everlys' prospects. But the memory of the first role Wesley had played—getting them started toward stardom—somehow lingered.

The reconciliation didn't lead to an instant return of Bryants-Everlys hits. None of the first batch of new Bryants songs recorded—the ballad "Don't Forget to Cry," the British Invasion–like "You're the One I Love," and the novelty "Honolulu"—had the sorts of musical hooks and utterly current, audience-nailing content that had made for smash singles five to seven years earlier. It just wasn't quite as before.

The Bryants' biographers Bobbie and Bill C. Malone have suggested that after all that hit money had come in, Boud and Felice had begun to take it easier, take vacations, and write less. Boudleaux admitted to songwriter Layng Martine Jr. that writing songs "is a young man's game." The urgency had passed for them—and the landscape had changed in ways that they were not precisely in tune with.

For a time, that "not quite with it" feel held for Don and Phil, too. "It was a different period of our career," Phil would note. "We moved into the middle Sixties and late Sixties and times were changing and sounds were changing, and you're weighted down a little bit. We were able to survive the English Invasion, but many did not."

Reconciling with Acuff-Rose did enable them to rerecord back in Nashville their biggest early hits for a more encompassing Warner Bros. hits collection. This was useful, even necessary, because Archie Bleyer was in the process of selling Cadence to Andy Williams outright, finishing off that life chapter in the wake of his label's biggest album smash, Vaughn Meader's instantly dated JFK-satirizing comedy record *The First Family*. Andy intended to put the entire label catalog on ice, just to get his own early records out of sight, so the original Everlys records went into deep freeze. The Warner versions, on the album *The Very Best of the Everly Brothers*, are much like the originals, but in stereo. They don't always quite recapture the original magic, but they would be the main versions a generation of new fans would hear, with the originals unavailable for more than a decade.

The Everlys recorded in Nashville at Fred Foster's Monument Records studio through 1964, generally with Wesley on hand. The first memorable record to emerge from that was "The Ferris Wheel," written by Ronald and Dewayne Blackwell—the latter of those two brothers also the composer of major hits, from "Mr. Blue" (the Fleetwoods and Bobby Vinton) to "Friends in Low Places" (Garth Brooks). "The Ferris Wheel" is dark and edgy, sounding like the James Bond themes or the Johnny Rivers "Secret Agent Man" song of the time. As the next Everly Brothers single, which they'd promote on a summer US tour, it charted only as high as number seventy-two in the States, but number twenty-two in Great Britain, that pattern repeating.

When a reporter from the UK's *Record Mirror* suggested to Don that they hadn't been charting higher simply because there hadn't been very strong material, he agreed: "I think there's a lot in that... I figure it must have been our material that let us down. *We* haven't changed." That September they'd record—wryly, it seems—a song by John D. Loudermilk, "It's Been a Long Dry Spell." The subject was desperately missing a woman ("starving to death for your sweet love"); the unmissable subtext was starving for a hit.

That same recording session provided proof that the Everly Brothers were far from finished, and it was their own songwriting together that provided it. "Gone, Gone, Gone," with those slashing opening chords so identified with them—electric this time—was the hardest rocker they'd done to that point. Like "Bye Bye Love," it's a gleeful tune about a breakup, only it's about leaving the girl, not the other way around. As a single, it peaked at number thirty-one in the United States, a recent high for them.

Their natural affinity for the small screen was still at work. It can be hard to decide whether key appearances helped reinvigorate them or simply captured them at moments of renewed strength—a cause or an effect. Appearances picked up again, as some of their closest West Coast friends began working for what was arguably American television's most knowingly conceived and adeptly executed prime-time rock and roll show, ABC's *Shindig!*

This series actually focused on presentation of the music, without excuse or mainstream show-business schtick, or the sort of bland "acceptable to adults" hosts other shows, including its competitor, NBC's *Hullabaloo*, turned to for safety. The format suggested that the whole decade-long rock and roll catalog belonged to the day's working rockers, and that anyone might join in on a number, no matter when they'd showed up themselves.

Sometimes predecessor music was included, too. *Shindig!* could say yes to Howlin' Wolf joining a Rolling Stones appearance or featuring a Rosetta Tharpe number. The regular cast members and invited guests were from across rock demographics—American and Anglo, notably multiracial, and inclusive of female newcomers, too. For those then coming of age, it was not to be missed.

The show's creators and producers included the host, Los Angeles deejay Jimmy O'Neill, and his wife, the Everlys' old friend Sharon Sheeley, plus British producer Jack Good, who'd previously had a similar music-centric program in the UK, *Oh Boy!*—Buddy Holly reference intended. Sheeley and Jackie DeShannon had only recently placed and recorded Phil's song "Wild Boy" with the young Minnesota rock band the Castaways. The friendly relationship continued.

Other Everly friends who'd be *Shindig!* regulars included Leon Russell, Glen Campbell, James Burton, Chuck Blackwell, Glen D. Hardin, and Larry Knechtel—all recent players on Everly records or in their live band. The terrific regular cast vocalists included the Righteous Brothers, Darlene Love and the Blossoms, a pre-fame Billy Preston, and Bobby Sherman, at this point a pop rockabilly, not the teen idol he'd be later. With all of these Los Angeles connections it's not surprising that the Everlys were featured multiple times, or that they were so at home on the show.

They were the headliners along with Sam Cooke on the September 16, 1964, series premiere, joining an unusually history-aware, full-cast opening rave-up on Rosetta Tharpe's gospel "Up Above My Head," then singing the new "You're the One I Love" Bryants song, and joining Sam in the closer, an especially hard-rocking version of "Lucille." A few weeks later they introduced the audience to an inspired version of "Gone, Gone, Gone" with a flank of wildly enthusiastic dancers stomping and clapping behind them, in one of their strongest TV appearances ever. Over the course of the next year, they'd exchange hits with Gerry and the Pacemakers and return some of their early hits to prime time—as music, not nostalgia. In 1965, they joined the Rolling Stones, the Kinks, the Byrds, and Peter & Gordon on the second season opener, belting Little Richard's "The Girl Can't Help It," and later joined Roy Orbison on Ray Charles's "What'd I Say."

They also introduced their lasting 1965 original, "The Price of Love." It did not break the Hot 100 in America, but was a hit single in the UK (number twenty-one), as was their take on Mickey & Sylvia's "Love Is Strange," which would not chart in the States at all. That those two fine singles, as strong as a number that hit earlier, were not better responded to in this country may seem puzzling, even astounding. But we hear them, in retrospect, as so engaging and important after their justified inclusion in collections of all-time Everly hits, box sets, "Warner Bros. years" compilations and such, and with the songs having been taken up by latter-day roots rockers. ("Gone" by Fairport Convention, for example, "The Price" by Buddy Miller.)

Don would bemoan the lukewarm "Price of Love" reception: "People hear the R&B backing and think we're trying to copy the Rolling Stones. They should listen to some of our earlier albums; we were doing R&B backings before the Stones were ever heard of!" A footnote to the "Price of Love" session: on that same day they recorded the chugging "Follow Me," the only song to be credited to Don and Boudleaux Bryant as collaborators.

Throughout 1964 and 1965, they'd be asked why they stuck with so many of their old hits on tour instead of highlighting the newer singles, since the new ones were actually more recognizable to the younger '60s audience. But a majority of the crowds who'd come out for their shows were in their mid- to late twenties, as they were, and there to hear the oldies. In the face of those shows, they then were asked if, with all the demand to sing their old hits, they could ever have any new ones.

Don addressed this audience-demand dilemma head-on: "I expect you're sick of hearing recording artists say they've reached the point where they don't need hit records any more," he suggested to *NME*'s John Wells. "It's true for us—except when it comes to personal satisfaction. We want to prove to *ourselves* we can still make hits, and we owe it to the fans who have been so loyal." They were glad and determined to press right ahead: "There's too much pleasure to be had from entertaining people, and there's always something new going on. We've been delighted by the advent of English groups onto the American scene. . . . They've brought new excitement into the business."

Pressed, Don would also find it necessary to make clear that career pressures weren't likely to get to him again, psychologically: "Once you have a complete breakdown, as I did, you build up an immunity. . . . I used to overwork, worry a lot, and take the whole business too seriously. Not any more. I can honestly say I've never felt better in my life."

Through the summer of 1964, they toured Canada and the upper Midwest, by now another regular stomping ground for them— across Iowa, Wisconsin, and Minnesota, in particular—with one change in the band. At Sonny Curtis's suggestion, they brought on Terry Slater as their bass player. They took that suggestion immediately, impressed that during the 1963 tour, Terry had been so little starstruck that he'd barely spoken to them at all. So Phil had invited him and his wife to dinner at Trader Vic's in London. "Phil said, 'Do you have any dreams?'" Terry would recall. "And I said, 'Yeah, I want to go to America.' And he said, 'You got it.'" Phil sponsored Terry's immigration to the USA.

This was also the point where Don Wayne signed on to be their road manager for just two weeks, then stayed on for close to ten years, finding the travel to his liking, the brothers and their bands compatible, and making both day-to-day tour arrangements and sometimes assuaging feelings all in his ballpark.

"I was like a third brother," he suggests. "I used to call them 'the push-me-pull-you boys," which fans of *Doctor Dolittle* will understand. "When they were booked for shows too close together or had too many bookings... that's when they would get a little edgy. If I had to live with *my* brothers twenty-four hours a day and not see my family, I'd be the same. I did hear them arguing at times; we'd be together, and one would say something they probably regretted later, and they'd get into some type of fisticuffs. It was sad."

At the end of that year, Don and Phil turned to projects that again engaged more of their varied sides, including two albums that surveyed contemporary, harder rock and R&B, released as *Rock 'n Soul* in March 1965, and *Beat 'n Soul* the following December, separated by the summer's *Gone, Gone, Gone* LP, culled from recent singles and "return to Acuff-Rose" Bryants songs.

Those December 1964 *Rock 'n Soul* sessions were conducted back in Nashville, with veteran A&R and promotion man Jimmy Hilliard producing. Many of the songs Don and Phil chose to rock out on were hits from friends they'd known well—Buddy Holly, Chuck Berry, Little Richard, Ray Charles—and some from rock and rollers outside their circle—Elvis Presley, Charlie Rich, and Dale Hawkins. That said, not one of the album's dozen tracks was a carbon copy of the original hit. With Boudleaux Bryant's "Love Hurts" available to them again, they even reengaged with that one, in a harder, more rocking version. It was still not a single.

The song choices were contemporary in more than updated instrumentation and production. The Beatles, for example, were reintroducing material from essentially these same first-generation rock sources to younger audiences, so in an ironic way, the selections were very 1964–1965, too. Martha and the Vandellas' classic "Dancing in the Street," released only five months before, gets the most surprising and effective take in the Everlys' set, with a boom-chuck rhythm, and Don and Phil singing "Can't forget the Music City" instead of "the Motor City," a new sound added to their mix.

"That'll Be the Day" gets a thumping, slowed-down treatment. "Maybellene," the first Chuck Berry song they'd recorded, is revealing, in that it adds a heavier beat than Chuck (or Marty Robbins) had applied, yet the song's essentially country roots are all the more apparent in their hands.

Their touring itinerary was becoming predetermined, based on previous successes and the record company's needs. In 1965, the Everlys headed back for their seventh European tour, with Sonny Curtis, Marshall Leib, and Jim Gordon as the relatively underused band, and some TV and recording to get done while there. Future Everly Brothers International Fan Club leader Martial Bekkers caught one of these shows and was astounded by how much louder they now sounded than on their old hit records.

Sonny Curtis would recall the whole trip with some amusement: "That was a promotional tour paid for by Warner Brothers, for the Everlys to record songs in foreign languages. We weren't needed a lot, which was great for us, but not so much for Don and Phil. They had to work very hard learning the phonetics of German and Italian and recording the songs. Warners paid the band $150 a week each—good money in those days—and a lot of our expenses. It was one of the best vacations I ever had."

Phil would recall this excursion fondly, too: "We had the best time in Paris. It was when the original discotheques were just happening, and beer was five dollars a bottle. We drank Warner Brothers out of a fortune. And I met a young French girl." (No details from then-married Phil on how *that* went.)

Jackie went along with Phil for part of the ensuing summer tour through the upper Midwest and nearby Canada. In Appleton,

Wisconsin, a long-favored location, Don had revealing comments for the local paper: "Sometimes...I'm scared, like I never sang before.... Show business is a precarious thing. There's nothing you can point to and say you did it. It's almost like being a court jester—not like having a factory and really *making* things." This from a fellow with millions of records sold, dozens of songs written, the most recent ones very good. None of that seems to have made him any more secure. Phil makes a long face and chimes in, "He's been on the road too long." That may have been truth disguised as jest.

An excellent two-sided single was released, "Love Is Strange" backed with "Man with Money," a fascinating original, absolutely contemporary in sound and perspective, sounding at times like a Mamas & the Papas track, with lyrics on the order of the Kinks' social observation songs. The song would be noticed, recorded by the Who, for instance.

Written, like "Gone, Gone, Gone," by Don and Phil together, it's a more pointed and dramatic elaboration of the financial pressure presented in "The Drop Out." This time, the man in question has a woman who thinks "money makes a man...and I'm a poor boy." So he robs a neighborhood store. The beat is incessant, until it breaks into the quietly suspenseful part where Don considers, then moves to the robbery solution. It's one of those non-hit Everly Brothers recordings people ought to hear. The more often recalled "Love Is Strange" recording presented them with the question of what to do with the original's "Mickey?" "Yes, Sylvia" byplay. It becomes "Hey, Donald?" "What, Phil?" "How do you call your baby home?" ... "Like this..." and on it goes.

The quality single was an advance indication of the high level the whole new *Beat 'n Soul* set would achieve. "Man with Money" was the only original on that impressive album—one, like the country LP, that's among their strongest and most consistent. They recorded it back home out west, working with the adroit Wrecking

Crew gang for a change in rock sound, which they got, and turned out at a pace that would have surprised even "three sides a session" Music Row. These were all R&B and early soul songs everyone knew; it was a matter of making them Everly Brothers records.

Unsurprisingly, the soul ballad renditions—the Impressions' brand-new "People Get Ready," Chuck Willis's "What Am I Living For," and Ivory Joe Hunter's "I Almost Lost My Mind"—are especially sweet and stirring—and pure Everly Brothers in performance. The blood-harmony principal is strong; the voices are blended so far that a conventional lead would not be easily identified. Doc Pomus's "Lonely Avenue," a hit for Ray Charles, gets a surprising twist, as they transform it from a halting ballad to an energetic pop "beat song." There's also a funky take on Rufus Thomas's "Walking the Dog," with a striking rock guitar solo, most likely by ace chameleon Glen Campbell. And they transform Little Walter's "My Babe" into folk rock.

Released in September; it didn't climb higher than number 141 on the *Billboard* album chart, but the brothers themselves were rightfully proud of the quality achieved. Don would say of this succession of records, "That was our *best* period. I like those albums.... We were just out of vogue here [in the States]."

That fall, they were headlining another British tour, promoted by Brain Epstein no less, and costarring Cilla Black. While they were in London, they happened to note a scheduled TV performance by those kids who'd met them at their hotel in 1960 and were now leading the hit-making Hollies; it would have surprising consequences the following year.

Venetia, meanwhile, was pregnant again, and Don was getting "a daily transatlantic report" on that. Home in Hollywood, Don and Phil returned to the studio while waiting for the baby to arrive. "We have two or three weeks allotted for that purpose," the expectant father noted. "The recordings, we mean." The sessions produced a few stabs at a single; Don's new ballad, "It's All Over," prettily sung, is the strongest, and also an outlier, with Phil singing lead, and though not well known then, it would be picked up by several bands from a generation not yet born, close to fifty years later.

Don and Venetia's new daughter (Don's third), Erin Invicta Everly, arrived on November 8, 1965. It was a relatively tranquil time in both brothers' home lives. Both Jackie and Venetia seem to have been content with fairly conventional "wife tending the home" roles, and their husbands agreed to limit the months a year spent away on the road. They'd get home more, and when they got there, they tended to stay there.

"We seldom go to night clubs or anywhere," Phil told the Ottawa *Journal*. "I don't think I could tell you where the good clubs are or even what they are." His longstanding interest in collectibles and antiques is noted, and apparently Jackie went for them, too: "Phil lives in a true millionaire's home.... Some of his prized possessions are a four-poster Elizabethan bed with the story of Adam and Eve carved on it, and one of the first nickelodeons ever made.... Every light in the house is covered with genuine Tiffany shades." In some ways that's a very au courant style they're describing; it's also an indication of Phil's preservationist, nostalgic taste, increasingly accompanied by conservative political views.

The Everly Brothers fan clubs, very active on both sides of the Atlantic, sometimes sent out letters to fans written, or at least signed off on, by Phil or Don. There was an unusual new one from Jackie: "Fans have asked me what it's like to be the wife of Phil Everly. All I can say is, fabulous...Phil's a great joker, so if you don't like to be teased, stay away from him. He can also be quite moody, especially if he's had a hard day working...Don is a perfect brother-in-law...much quieter than Phil, and maybe even moodier....One thing about Don, he'll tell you his opinion of matters.

Don and Venetia have a beautiful house out in the San Fernando Valley. They have acres of land to assure Stacy and Erin plenty of room to run around in private. Both girls are just dolls." She may or may not have known yet, but she was pregnant herself, due in November.

Don noted, "Venetia is a great cook, and she has done all the interior decorating in our house," two areas that will virtually always loom large for him. That his politics were headed in a different direction from his brother's was underscored by an encounter he had at Mama Leone's Italian restaurant in New York, where Robert Kennedy, whom he much admired, was dining at the same time. Kennedy shook his hand and told him how he'd always been an Everlys fan and admired their music. Untypically, Don was reported to be rendered speechless.

In the United States, the midsixties is rarely viewed as an Everly Brothers comeback period, but elsewhere, a case could be made. Phil said, "Even when the British Invasion happened, we still...had two Top Tens, English, with 'Love Is Strange' and 'Price of Love.'... a very *large* resurgence, compared to the thinner times. Warners... recouped all the money." The Everlys even updated their look to contemporary Swinging London (or Paris) haircuts and clothes; late-'50s pompadours looked comical to people by this point.

It wasn't just the UK that remained especially supportive. Canada and the upper Midwest region of the United States remained so; Holland and Germany always provided audiences. "In the Philippines," Phil recalled later, still amazed, "they had an Everly Brothers show that ran for over ten years there, every Saturday; they took 'Devoted to You' and changed the lyrics and used it in church services!" These were places central to their story in 1966. "You know, it's strange," bass player Terry Slater commented that summer, after a dramatic and unforgettable world tour. "The Everlys draw more crowds and better reactions in other countries than they do in the States. In a gig in Canada, they were mobbed not only by teenagers but by grown men and women. One forty-five-year-old woman even fainted."

They were booked for stops in Asia right through March—Manila, Hong Kong, wartime Saigon, Bangkok, Taipei, and Tokyo. During the week in Manila, where they were wined and dined as major visiting celebrities by media and officialdom alike, they drew the largest crowds of their entire careers, selling out the enclosed twenty-five-thousand-seat Araneta Coliseum for eight shows. Slater recalled, "It was just a thrill to go out there every single night and to see that amount of people. And the response was so beautiful!"

Road manager Don Wayne points to less obvious, behind-the-scenes issues that had to be dealt with. "There was a lot of tension between the countries. It was dangerous. We were under armed guard in that coliseum complex, and we couldn't go out and meet people from there—just for safety. The scariest part of that tour was when we landed at Saigon's Tan Son Nhut Air Base on the DC-3 we flew in. We had an extra piece of luggage, and so the military swarmed around us and got us out of the area; they were checking all the buildings that we were going to be in for bombs and explosives." They stuck to the airmen's club at the air base.

American forces in Vietnam were nearing the two hundred thousand mark and bombing of the North was about to begin. Not many acts were appearing, besides the large, more official Bob Hope shows, but Phil and Don chose to perform there—at a fundraiser for the air base orphanage for kids left parentless by the war. These were Marine Corps Reserve brothers, after all, not indifferent or particularly skeptical about military defense, but what they saw made a stark impression. As Phil put it, "Politics didn't come into it at all.... It was about a hundred and twenty degrees on stage.... The floor was wringing wet with sweat...and we sang

Margaret and Ike, Don and Phil
Everly, circa 1946.
*Everly Brothers International
Archive*

KMA radio, Shenandoah, Iowa: Ike, Don, and Phil with Eddie Comer, clarinet, and Jerry
Fronek, accordion. As much pop as country.
Everly Brothers International Archive

Phil and Don with Lefty Frizzell, 1952. Hated the cowboy suits, loved Lefty.
Courtesy of Willie Nelson & Friends Museum, Nashville, Tennessee

The country Cass Walker Show, WROL radio, Knoxville, Tennessee, 1954: Everly Family with Margaret on bass.

Tennessee Archive of Moving Image and Sound

Cast members of the Grand Ole Opry, Ryman Auditorium.
Grand Ole Opry archives

In the recording studio with Wesley Rose and Boudleaux Bryant.
Courtesy of the Country Music Hall of Fame® and Museum

Rocking on *The Ed Sullivan Show*, 1957.
CBS Photo Archive/Getty Images

New pop stars, new fans.
Screen Stars, December 1958

On Alan Freed's TV show.
TV-Radio Mirror, November 1958

With Buddy Holly at New York City hotel, 1958.
Keith Russell Collection

BBC TV, 1960. Harmony vocals with Crickets backing—the rock band future.
© *Harry Hammond/Victoria and Albert Museum, London*

In the marines, 1962. Shorn.
Everly Brothers International Archive

UK tour, 1963, with hero Bo Diddley and pop star Julie Grant.
© *Harry Hammond/Victoria and Albert Museum, London*

Arrival in Germany, 1963: Phil and wife Jackie, Don and wife Venetia and infant Stacy.
Everly Brothers International Archive

Starring on premiere of *Shindig!*, with Sam Cooke.
ABC Photo Archives/Getty Images

Country rock: ovation at the Bitter End club, New York City, 1969.
Getty Images/Michael Ochs Archives

On *Johnny Cash Presents the Everly Brothers*, primetime 1970.
ABC Photo Archives/Getty Images

With Phil's wife Patricia Mickey and Chet Atkins, Nashville. 1972.
Nashville Banner Archives, Special Collections, Nashville Public Library

Warren Zevon and Phil on tour.
Courtesy of Crystal Zevon

Knotts Berry Farm, July 1973. The breakup show.
Lynda Harpe

Reunited after ten years.
DavidMcGough.com

The dramatic Royal Albert Hall reunion show, September 1983.
Lynn Goldsmith/Getty Images

Don, son Edan, and (*left to right*) daughters Erin, Stacy, and Venetia Ember, with Phil and sons Jason (*top*) and Chris, 1984.

With Duane Eddy and John Prine, Central City, Kentucky, Homecoming, 1989.
Barbara McIntyre

The Everly Brothers band, 1988: Phil Cranham, Phil, Albert Lee, Don, Hank DeVito.
Pat Borowicz/Everly Brothers International Archive

With Simon & Garfunkel, New Jersey, 2003.
Michael Brito/Alamy Stock Photo

everything we knew. All I got out of it was the view that no war is worth one leg."

"That night," Don detailed, "we sat on the roof of this house and watched them napalming stuff outside the city. We played a lot of hospitals in the Philippines, too, full of Vietnam casualties. That's when it began to dawn on me that something was dreadfully wrong with that war. I became very political in my mind...but there didn't seem to be much I could do about it. We were working nine, ten months out of the year; we were really out of touch with what was going on in the world."

The popular culture was changing as fast as political responses. This was the full-tilt sixties now, the emerging album-rock era, the very time when those slightly younger rockers the Everlys had influenced were in peak form and having tremendous influence. The formerly "sweet, mop-top" Beatles were producing *Revolver*; the "blues band" Stones *Aftermath*, the "folkie" Simon & Garfunkel *Parsley, Sage, Rosemary and Thyme*, the "surfing" Beach Boys *Pet Sounds*, and "protest singer" Dylan *Blonde on Blonde*. They all had hit singles through those dramatic changes, competing for attention with the massively popular Motown and Stax-Volt soul stars.

That was the context for one of the more unexpected, outlier Everlys projects, which took the exploration of things they might at least try a step further, into "if you can't beat them, join them." It would be an album that engaged directly with British Invasion sounds—the instrumentation, riffs, production style, and, naturally, Everly-influenced vocal harmonies—their *Two Yanks in England* project.

Warners producer Dick Glasser had suggested they try recording an album in London with new songs found there. Those would be, it turned out, primarily from the Hollies—hitmakers in Great Britain and Europe now, and about to break through in the United States with their new single "Bus Stop." They'd wanted to be "the

Everly Brothers of Manchester," but neither Graham Nash nor Allan Clarke had actually been in touch with Don and Phil since they'd met in 1960.

Nash recalls how the reconnection happened in October 1965: "The *London Palladium* show is kind of like the *Ed Sullivan Show* of England—Sunday night and eight o'clock, pretty important. Pete Seeger was the headliner, and the Hollies were supporting him. At the sound check, the phone rings backstage and our tour manager answers the phone and goes, 'Yeah, yeah; hold on a second' and hands me the phone and I say, 'So who is it?' and he says, 'I don't know; he says his name's Phil Everly.' I go, 'Get out of here!'

"So I pick up the phone and, of course, I recognized his voice immediately. He says, 'We're in town and we want to know if the Hollies have any songs that they haven't recorded yet. I said, 'Well, yeah, we do. What should we do about this?' And he said, 'Can you come to the hotel where we're staying [London's May Fair].' And so, we went down and the first question I asked Don Everly was '*Now* would you show me how you do those opening chords for "Bye Bye Love"?'"

Graham and Allan proceeded to play the Everlys some of their latest songs, some only recently recorded, and others barely written down. "I've never heard so many good songs all at once," Phil would tell a British reporter. Very soon after the spring 1966 Asian tour and several weeks in Ireland and Germany, sessions with the Hollies began in earnest, at London's Pye Studios, with Glasser producing.

Graham, Allan, and Tony Hicks, a third band vocalist-player, were collaborating as songwriters under the pseudonym "L. Ransford." Phil and Don initially recorded a half dozen of their songs in London, with Nash and Hicks on hand demonstrating the songs and playing. Session men and future Led Zeppelin bandmates Jimmy Page and John Paul Jones as well as keyboard player Reg

Dwight (better known later as Elton John) also appeared on these recordings. They'd take up several more Hollies originals back in Hollywood, as well as Manfred Mann's UK hit "Pretty Flamingo" and Spencer Davis's "Somebody Help Me."

On Everlys versions of Hollies' originals such as "Have You Ever Loved Somebody" or "Don't Run and Hide," Don, singing lead, takes the vocal harmonies lower than Allan Clarke centers them. The rhythm section, and at times the electric guitar, too, are more prone to tick-tock, rim-slapping sounds than on typical Everlys records, and in the case of the Hollies' songs finished with Hollywood's Wrecking Crew, the knife-sharp guitar riffs are just as "British." Clearly Glen Campbell and James Burton had those Invasion sounds down; they'd invented some of them in the first place.

For the first time ever, two of the numbers were released on a single credited to "Don Everly Brother" on one side ("Fifi the Flea") and "Phil Everly Brother" on the other ("Like Everytime Before"), both sung solo. Don's is as delicate as songs about brokenhearted fleas can go. Phil's offers an early preview of the sort of Eastern-inflected sound Graham would bring to "Marrakesh Express" soon after, on joining Crosby, Stills & Nash. He'd apparently given Don a preview of that still unrecorded song, too.

For all of the justified interest in it later, the album proved to be yet another dead end for the Everlys from a commercial standpoint. The Hollies believed the collaboration made a significant difference in how seriously *they* were taken, after years of label resistance to their own compositions. "It was the greatest honor bestowed on us," Clarke would say. "When the Evs accepted so many of our songs...it was probably the greatest confidence booster of our career." Better gigs, and the hit in America followed.

For Phil and Don, nothing much had changed; they recorded some oldies again, numbers like "Blueberry Hill" and "Sea of Heartbreak" that appeared on an LP with the disingenuous title *The Hit*

Sound of the Everly Brothers. (The hits referred to were other people's.) On a tour stop in Detroit that August, Don and Phil were in the audience for a Motown gang show at the Roostertail club. The Four Tops' Levi Stubbs summoned them onto the stage, and that's how they came to appear singing backup, along with the Supremes and Marvin Gaye, on "I Can't Help Myself," released on the *Four Tops Live!* album later that year—a different kind of harmony.

Just a few weeks later, on September 9, Phil and Jackie's son, Phillip Jason, to be known as Jason, was born in New York City. He'd be the first of the next-generation Everlys to take up music himself, but that, of course, was years away.

In 1967, Phil and Don were up against formidable musical headwinds. The midsixties music-making style they were still comfortable with, edgy yet connected to long-accepted notions of pop—hooky, single oriented, suitable for some current dance—was losing its hold. In rock at least, it was giving way to the heyday of album-spanning psychedelia, which the Everlys, particularly Phil, were not ideally suited for, in their own eyes or those of fans. Finding material that would suit them but be up-to-date was becoming challenging.

Occasional attempts by the Everlys to get all incense-and-sergeant-peppermints could result in awkward, unintended embarrassments. Songwriting buddy Terry Slater felt relatively at home with such material, and along with Phil, wrote the song recorded in April 1967 as "Mary Jane," which Phil had originally titled "Mary Jo" because he thought that was the year's nickname for weed. "That's how out of it I was," he'd admit. The record goes, "I've found the key to tomorrow . . . I've got my Mary Jane." As a single, backed with Slater's very Summer of Love life recommendation, "Talking to the Flowers," it went nowhere.

It may be unimaginable that the Everly Brothers could have been accepted or understood as part of the dark kickback reaction to all the "flower power and love" soundtracks at work, the line that runs from the Stones, through the Doors, to the Velvet Underground and punk, no matter how much the Stones and Velvets admired the Everlys. In fact, though, they dared to record two pretty strong songs along those lines and seemed neither uncomfortable nor self-conscious doing them.

One of the originals on the *Two Yanks* album was "The Collector," written by Sonny Curtis working with Don, based on the skillful John Fowles bestseller and William Wyler's Terence Stamp film adaptation, concerning a butterfly-collecting psychotic who holds a beautiful girl captive for his "collection." The song is as menacingly creepy as it's meant to be, all the more so for being beautifully sung. And then there was "Even If I Hold It in My Hand," also known as "Hard Luck Story," written by Carlyle Hughey and William Smith, which Phil and Don recorded in two versions, neither of which would be released for thirty years. It ends with the despondent narrator putting a gun to his head. This was not "Wake Up Little Susie."

With audiences shrinking, the venues they played were often smaller, if interestingly diverse. "I think about our worst year was '67," Phil would comment. "It was costing us as much on the road as we were making, and I said 'Hey, I might as well stay home.'"

There was a sign of light at the end of this tunnel, though, a song that would strike a chord, find some audience traction, become part of their permanent set, and point toward a direction that would carry them into a rebirth of relevancy. The song was "Bowling Green."

The Everly Brothers hadn't done a new number extolling or pining for the partly real, partly imaginary Kentucky in many years. This one began with an infectious guitar riff Phil had come up with; Terry worked up the melody from there. On the demo records, for the intro, they whistle the tune in tandem. Slater and Jackie Ertel, standing in for her husband, were credited with the words and music in the end; Phil apparently wanted to avoid antagonizing his brother by highlighting a major songwriting cowrite with anyone else. Phil and Terry would collaborate on many songs to come.

"A man in Kentucky, sure is lucky," that one goes—and it would find enough airplay to reach the Top 40 in the United States—and number one in Canada. The Bluegrass State is portrayed as a place to retreat to, an oasis, a place that's kind, where "folks let you think your own mind," and, incidentally, the "girls wear dresses cut country tight." Don and Phil would always sing it with gusto. Over the course of the next four decades, it would go on to be recorded by Glen Campbell, the Gosdin Brothers, Jesse Winchester, Neko Case, and Railroad Earth, among others; it has remained familiar.

In the years immediately ahead, in the face of national tumult and disruption, there would arise a whole new demand for songs and sounds that evinced that sort of "back to the country" escape. The Everly Brothers were exceptionally well equipped to provide them.

Chapter Eight

RELEVANT AGAIN:
Country Rock 1968–1970

A SHIFT IN THE AMERICAN MOOD SHARP ENOUGH TO CHANGE THE tone of an era's popular music has at times followed specific dramatic events—the 1929 stock market crash, the entry into World War II and its end, the attack of September 11, 2001. One of those shifts played out in 1968, as punishing events piled up.

The year began with the Tet Offensive, which clarified for millions that the Vietnam War was futile, no matter how against it or for it you were. Four years after his landslide win, Lyndon Johnson gave up running for president again. The assassination of Martin Luther King, traumatic in itself, was followed by rioting and burning by the frustrated and hopeless in dozens of US cities. Those spring '68 eruptions were followed by the assassination of Don's hero Robert F. Kennedy. Things were no less calm in Europe, where political uprisings from Paris to Prague ensued as well.

Extravagant, baroque, and inflated 1967-style rock albums hardly seemed appropriate for the disquieted mood of that moment; for many, they quickly became white elephants in a tottering, overcrowded china shop. There was so little artiness left to add that artists began to subtract. For many, the conflict sparked escape-velocity nostalgia.

The time was ripe for comebacks by the first rock and roll generation, Phil and Don very much included. Through 1968–1970, Elvis Presley, Chuck Berry, Little Richard, Jerry Lee Lewis, Rick Nelson, Johnny Cash, and Fats Domino all found renewed visibility and rising traction, and so would the Everly Brothers. None of these gents (all male, you'll notice) could seem as transgressive as they'd been or were portrayed on the first go-round; they were thirty- or even fortysomethings by this point, if still rocking and gifted—comforting reminders of receding youth, not rebels.

As we've seen, the Everlys had worked, even struggled, to maintain relevancy all along, and they had mixed feelings at best about this whole "rock and roll revival" business. Phil would comment, "I'm sure the 'Rock Revival' is not going to affect *us* much. . . . Anyway, it won't have any influence on our music. I don't think any movements have yet."

Given their efforts to work in British Invasion pop, the part about "movements" is debatable, but in any case, Phil and Don returned to describing themselves most often as essentially "country." They always tended to see themselves that way, at least in part, if with flexible ideas about what "country" included.

In late November '67, they appeared on a Dinah Shore–hosted *Nashville Sound* prime-time TV special, where they performed "Love of the Common People," a country single that they'd just recorded; it did well in some places, particularly in Canada. Their inclusion might have seemed like a throwback to Nashville television appearances of a decade before, but then, Ray Charles and Johnny Mercer were guests as well; Dinah was featuring an expansive view of the sound of her hometown.

The Everlys appreciated that, and the changing music scene. A more engaged, even respectful rock press was beginning to emerge, with the history of pop culture—rock, country, movies, and TV included—being taken more seriously. And people about their age were increasingly in charge of music-business decision-making. They were often honored as veterans who'd made historic contributions and might again.

"When we started," Don said, "young performers like us were regarded as . . . hoodlums, a necessary evil. Those who ran the business belonged to an older generation; they didn't understand the music they were selling. It was a big drag. Now we can work with people who are sympathetic. We're not regarded as hoodlums any longer!"

As there'd already been early indications, the age-old romantic dream of taking off for the peaceful, calming countryside, to get back in harmony with nature, beckoned for many seductively. For some, that changed lives; for many more, the relatable metaphors and evocative sounds were enough. White middle-class collegians who were mocking what they took country music to be months before were reconsidering. What so many people, across social lines, wanted music to do for them was suddenly straightforward: get back, get away—just get me *out of here*.

One of the first responses, much better known since than it was at the time, were the sessions Dylan, in seclusion with the practiced R&B/country outfit about to emerge as the Band, was engaging in through 1967. They were playing with ancient ballads and modern country, constructing new songs, many of which would last, evoking an imaginary space where the distant and more recent past fused with darker concerns of the moment.

Bob, always the Everlys fan, had been filmed singing "When Will I Be Loved" in a Glasgow hotel room just months before, and one of the new "basement tapes" songs, "All You Have to Do Is Dream," certainly references the Everlys' hit—or responds to it. (Dylan would harmonize on the Bryants' "Dream" itself, with George Harrison, in 1970.) It nevertheless shocked many of his fans at the time when his next "official" album, *John Wesley Harding*, released in the last week of 1967 and recorded in Nashville, proved to be not an attempt to one-up the elaborate psychedelic albums of that year but a stripped-down record, some of which had Music Row–style country backing, oozing steel guitar and all. In the following months, "basement" songs offered to other artists began to appear—on Ian & Sylvia's *Nashville* LP, the Band's *Music from Big Pink*, and the Byrds' *Sweetheart of the Rodeo*, the latter including the anthemic country-rock call to lay back and hang tight, "Strap yourself to a tree with roots; you ain't going nowhere."

For many, the *Sweetheart* album was also their first sighting of a singer who would go on to reintroduce songs of the Everlys, Bryants songs recorded by the Everlys in particular—Gram Parsons. He'd already crossed paths with Don in their travels around the Los Angeles roots scene, as Don's endorsement on the back cover of the February 1968 album by the International Submarine Band, Gram's previous country-rock group, made clear.

"This record is really refreshing," Don is quoted as saying. "It is a unique experiment done well. There are thousands of soulful young musicians around, but most of them completely ignore country music. What the International Submarine Band is doing could and should change that." Parsons would appear on an Everlys record, look for ways to emulate their harmonizing, and take up their music more directly, with further encouragement from Don.

The Everlys themselves, of course, had recorded an album's worth of country songs approached with a sixties pop sensibility as early as the 1963 *Sing Great Country Hits* album. There was now a chance that the bewilderment that greeted that might lessen, because they were not alone. They may not have realized it yet, but everything they'd ever done could now be seen as *adding up* to something, something that mattered.

Occasionally, they'd be booked into folk-circuit clubs, just as those were evolving into homes for singer-songwriters and roots rock. In the summer of 1967, they appeared at Washington DC's Cellar Door and discovered they were staying at the same upscale hotel, the Hay-Adams, as Joan Baez, who'd just given a free concert on the Washington Monument grounds to thousands, having been barred from appearing at the Daughters of the American Revolution's DAR Constitution Hall.

They'd not been particularly attuned to the folk-music/political-activist scene, but they hit it off with Baez right away. "She sat down in her...suite with Phil and Don Everly," the *Miami Herald* reported, "looking like a couple of raddled angels in their $25 dollar Jay Sebring trims [i.e., expensive Hollywood haircuts] to sing Everly Brothers hits. She likes to harmonize with the boys. They think she is a groovy chick. She never talks politics with the Everly Brothers." She might have found Don compatible if she had.

In August, appearing on Mike Douglas's Philadelphia-based daytime talk and variety show, the brothers were apparently surprised by the now rare appearance of Ike and Margaret, flown in by the producers for the occasion. A joint interview about the early Everly Family act and shows ensued, a snippet from one of the old radio-show tapes played, then all four joined in a live performance of "I Saw the Light." This seems to have been their first joint broadcast appearance since Knoxville in 1954; the parents were to stay more visible again in the time just ahead.

Later in the year, Don and Phil were spending time at the Troubadour club, back in Los Angeles, where they would catch the Dillards and spend the better part of a night singing hymns a cappella with Rodney and Doug Dillard—double brotherly harmony. That band, moving gently away from more traditional bluegrass, was working up their celebrated *Wheatstraw Suite* concept album, released in March 1968, demonstrating that, for younger, rock-attuned audiences, country theme albums could be extended beyond the familiar "salute to Hank Williams" or Christmas varieties.

When the Everlys debuted at the Troubadour themselves, David Crosby and Stephen Stills, John Hartford, Chris Hillman and Michael Clarke, and singer-songwriter John Stewart were among those in the audience excited to catch them—leading lights of the soon-emerging country rock scene. Rock still took Phil and Don to larger venues occasionally. As part of a post–Monterey Pop "Festival of Music" they played the eleven-thousand-seat San Francisco Cow Palace and the seventeen-thousand-seat Hollywood Bowl on successive November nights, in an all-star lineup that included the Who, the Association, and the Animals. That's, in a row, a folk club, an arena, an amphitheater, and then in December—the San Francisco Playboy Club.

As far as recording went, the Everlys and Warners were still flailing; their 1967 albums went nowhere. The summer's *The Everly Brothers Sing* album (another LP title that sounds like no one bothered with it much) was a motley, undistinguished mix of more contemporary material. It had "Bowling Green" going for it, but also numbers trying too hard to be with-it ("Mary Jane" and "Talking to the Flowers") and a funereal take on, of all things, "A Whiter Shade of Pale." From the 1966 *Two Yanks* sessions through summer 1968, they'd record exactly one song that they'd written together, and one Phil collaboration with Terry Slater, a writing drought.

Their time was taken up with endless small-venue appearances, which could go on for months, with quiet time at home, and, for Phil, remaining weeks of the annual marine reserve training. (Don had been granted an honorable discharge in the wake of his physical issues.) Show reviewers sometimes lamented that they were just going through the motions in performances. "We were running back and forth, and in the confusion... it was most difficult to get something done," Phil would tell Roger White. "What we should have been doing was writing our own songs and singing them, but you can't do that unless you can function together."

He is alluding there, obliquely, to renewed tensions between the two of them, rising again over what sorts of places they should be playing ("adult" supper clubs? The Fillmore?) and what this whole Everly Brothers act ought to be looking and sounding like *now*. At thirty-one and twenty-nine respectively, the basic differences of temperament between them were all the more evident as lifestyle, performance style, and even political differences—Don looser, more in tune with the counterculture, Phil wanting to stick to the elegantly, familiarly tried and true. Warner Bros. executive Joe Smith would recall an incident where their singing during a recording session suddenly just stopped: "Phillip had knocked Donald down. Something had happened in the harmony, and he turned and just plowed him under."

The episode was strikingly similar to the reported studio dustup of 1963, and it's telling that a vocal-harmony issue sparked it. Don's more improvisational, more declarative singing style he now employed so often was always tough for Phil to follow, but Don stuck right with it, challenging existentially the blood-harmony basis of their sound—and of their act as a duo. They both knew what the audience demanded from them. Whether sticking with that while returns diminished was their only, inescapable option became a gnawing question.

The Everlys' ten-year contract with Warner Bros. Records was eight years on. From the label's perspective, after their repeated failures to sell well, something new had to be tried—but was still worth the effort. Through all that time, Warner-Reprise had made but a very limited mark outside of their still marketable swing-era crooners circle—Frank Sinatra and Dean Martin, and their kids Nancy Sinatra and the Dino, Desi & Billy pop band. Warners' Petula Clark and Peter, Paul and Mary, of course, also had some hits. Things began to change when the label, and all of Jack Warner's controlling share of Warner Bros., was sold to a smaller production company, Seven Arts, and became Warner Bros.-Seven Arts in 1967. That conglomerate then bought the fabled, dynamic Atlantic/Atco label as well. Besides Atlantic's great soul artists, everyone from the Kinks to Buffalo Springfield, the Young Rascals, Jimi Hendrix, and, soon, the Grateful Dead were now Everly "label cousins."

Making Warner and Reprise more contemporary, in some distinctive and workable way, was an urgent new focus. Executives Mo Ostin and Joe Smith (the same man who'd later interview Phil at some length) identified someone who might make that happen, a new addition to their A&R staff, a twenty-seven-year-old who'd been pitching quality demos to them that he'd produced, Lenny Waronker.

Lenny was virtually record-business-raised and had habits of mind and taste that would serve the Everly Brothers particularly well. His father, Si Waronker, had run the studio orchestra for 20th Century Fox for years, then founded Liberty Records in 1955, initially as a home for film-score records and novelties like the Chipmunks singles, but soon adding such rockers as Eddie Cochran, Johnny Burnette, Bobby Vee, and the Ventures. Si Waronker had always emphasized pairing distinctive, self-defining artists with exactly the right song to bring out those special traits—as had strong "artist and repertoire" executives since Ralph Peer defined the job at the turn of the 1930s. At Warners, Lenny produced such surprising song and artist combinations as the Mojo Men's airy version of "Sit Down, I Think I Love You" and the Harpers Bizarre version of "The 59th Street Bridge Song."

Lenny shared his father's tendencies. The film-score-composing Newman brothers, Alfred and Lionel, had worked and recorded with Si, which is how their nephew Randy Newman got to be Lenny's buddy from childhood on, and Lenny brought Randy Newman along with him to Warners, at first as a session piano player. What led Lenny toward the Everlys was his work with the Beau Brummels, the San Francisco band best known for their 1965 hit "Laugh, Laugh," when they were still dressed and named to suggest that they were British. By 1968 they were down to a duo, songwriter and deft guitarist Ron Elliott and singer Sal Valentino. Lenny produced their praised 1967 album *Triangle* and their following, surprising album, *Bradley's Barn*, recorded in Nashville in the spring of 1968 with country musicians backing them—even as the Byrds were recording *Sweetheart*.

Finding a way forward for Don and Phil was now put in Waronker's hands. What did he have in mind for them? "Looking for survival, more than anything else," he'd say. "And trying to do something that was cool." The backup musicians employed were still from the regular Wrecking Crew mix—James Burton, Glen Campbell, Leon Russell, Hal Blaine, and so on, in varied configurations, sometimes abetted by Everly buddies Terry Slater, J.I. Allison, and Sonny Curtis.

That was still the case with the February 1968 recording of the memorable song "Lord of the Manor," as Waronker became their official producer. With its references to the upstairs maid and the suffering gardener who knows she's in the "real soft hands" of that lord, it all seems pretty British. Released only as a B-side months later, tastefully overdubbed with orchestral sounds, an ongoing Waronker production specialty, "Lord of the Manor" became "kind of an underground thing for us," as Don would note, and there were those who loved it. While credited to Terry, the idea was in fact actually Anglophile Phil's, and both brothers had worked it up before bringing it in to record. It would become clearer later that the Everlys were keeping their names off some songs in this period, crediting Terry or their wives or using pseudonyms, to skirt the Acuff-Rose publishing contract once again as they contemplated taking their publishing elsewhere.

While the Beau Brummels worked on their Nashville session, Waronker had that band's Ron Elliott join in on guitar as Phil and Don recorded John D. Loudermilk's poppy "It's My Time," then a movingly wistful ballad written by Ron that would be added to any future compilation of the Everlys' best ever—"Empty Boxes." With Elliott's delicate, masterful acoustic guitar and gentle harmony singing by Don and Phil, the track was a model for how to realize something organically of this time, yet unmistakably Everly Brothers. With real pain expressed regarding fleeting romance, it was right in the brothers' emotional lane—and no kids' stuff.

"It was a song I played for them," Ron recalled, modestly, for this author, "and, well, they *recorded* it, so they must have liked it." In fact, they thought the world of it. Don would say, "The song was sensitive, emotional and wonderful." In the liner notes for *The New Album*, a compilation of overlooked sides released almost a decade later, Phil said, "If you only have time to listen to one song in this album, listen to 'Empty Boxes.' It's pure Everly Brothers—one guitar and two voices. It's my favorite." It would be for many others.

Soon after, they recorded a modernized, surprising turn on the twangy 1956 Ray Price waltz "You Done Me Wrong," which Ray had written with George Jones, and which would find its place as a track on *Roots*, their next, long-gestating album, one of the most influential and esteemed of their career. The cut may not have been thought of as part of any larger whole at the time;

sessions specifically for the LP would only begin months later, and this track alone was arranged by Perry Botkin Jr., best known for string-dominated hits such as "Nadia's Theme" and the theme from the soap opera *The Young and the Restless*. With its surprising arrangement, including sprightly brass and poppy glockenspiel sounds, it fit right in with a project that would disassemble and reassemble Don and Phil's varied excursions along the country/ pop borderline, help spark country rock, and predict the Americana field of decades later.

The piecemeal recording approach over the five months ahead left time for the realization that there was, once again, viable, identifiable material exactly right for Don and Phil—that fit them, fit together, and fit the times. Officially, Ron Elliott was the overall arranger of the tracks assembled, with Lenny Waronker and an astute Englishman who'd recently joined Warners as a talent scout, Andy Wickham, assembling the pieces, with the Everlys' cooperation.

Some would recall Wickham as a straightlaced Brit with multi-label experience, but when Warner-Reprise executive Mo Ostin met him at the 1967 Monterey Pop Festival and hired him at age twenty-one, he was quite ready, and apparently often stoned enough, for a role as the "company freak," as the new West Coast publication *Rolling Stone* noted several major labels were employing. He would be their long-haired ambassador to the whole fast-growing Laurel Canyon singer-songwriter scene, and responsible before long for signing Joni Mitchell, Van Morrison, Gram Parsons, and then Emmylou Harris, helping to transform Warners into a celebrated album rock label, for roots rock in particular.

These were highly creative minds that Phil and Don were working with, but their own preset touring schedule meant the project would take months to bloom. That endless travel, taking up to seven months out of the year, inevitably affected their home lives, too. Don would send little daughter Stacy letters from the road with long stories and illustrations; by the following year, when she was five, he'd report she was already literate and had some French and Spanish.

He also admitted that both he and Phil were so bored with touring that they often spent much of their time on the road asleep, only getting up late in the afternoon to head for work. They'd mention to a number of reporters that they no longer found much reason to rehearse their locked-in set. In a change of pace from the usual "we're country; we've always been country" self-description, Don told one inquiring writer, "We started singing beat music and we're *still* singing it."

Don, Venetia, and family were ensconced in Hancock Park, California, and Phil and family lived less than ten miles away; there were family picnics and the like, together at times. They seemed to be very close in this period. Don would tell an interested reporter that his own tastes continued to get more sophisticated, since Venetia had become "a fan of Julia Child" and gone to a French cooking school. Domesticity still reigned there, when he managed to be home. Don and Venetia's third child and only son, Edan Donald Everly, would be born in late August. Don got back from another tour stint a few days after the birth.

Things were different for Phil. On that food front, he would suggest a lingering preference for cornbread, ham, and beans—on the run. A sit-down dinner at home may already have become less than appetizing for him. That ever-increasing travel schedule and the obligatory weeks of marine service had driven a wedge between him and Jackie; they very quietly separated around this time. As with their engagement, the process of disconnection would take a long time to complete.

Phil and Don's private views on the counterculture continued to diverge, though not publicly. There was an unusual television appearance when they were asked by a Vancouver CBC teen show to comment on the drug references in so many songs of the psychedelia period. Others taking part included the guru Maharishi Mahesh Yogi, Pat Boone, Richard Pryor, Frank Sinatra Jr., Dr. Timothy Leary, and Ray Charles—quite a group. Don, without comment on his personal history, would testify, "I'm not trying to preach or change the world, but...I don't believe in drugs." Phil added, with no mention of the "Mary Jane"/"Talking to the Flowers" single they'd recently had out themselves, "You can sing something today and it will be misconstrued; one of the main reasons is the publicity that psychedelic has gotten, with the magazines and articles....People look for it in the lyrics of a song."

There was a deepening clash between the country-related material the Everly Brothers were slowly amassing in the studio and what they were performing on the road, where they touched on their new rural material only in passing. In fairness, the live-show audiences tended to demand the oldies, and they gave those to them, sometimes, they'd admit, disengaged and flying on autopilot. They'd be away from home and the studio for another two and a half months.

Through April and May 1968 they toured through Germany and taped television and radio in the UK. They often played for US armed forces in Europe, at officers' clubs in Wiesbaden, for example. A gig that July put them in the dark, mod tuxedos that would become emblematic stage wear for them—two weeks at New York's Latin Quarter nightclub, with multiple sets of just thirty minutes. By this late point in its history, the club was heavier on scantily clad showgirls and lighter on the topline stars and high-end clientele. The place would close a year later when the showgirls went on strike.

Along with the tuxes, Don, Phil, and band were doing more and more joking and banter between numbers, often in the form of caustic monologues from Donald. It was all relatively slick, with an old-school, showbiz-joke-machine approach that was generally expected in nightclubs from New York to Las Vegas.

They likely had been impressed by the brotherly banter and song act of their old acting school buddies Tom and Dick Smothers, whose TV show they'd appear on twice during the year—the first airing in July, where they'd be alongside such guests of the oncoming "country rock" tide as Bobbie Gentry and John Hartford. The Smothers Brothers had risen from a change-of-pace coffeehouse folk act to hosting their own highly successful, then increasingly controversial prime-time TV variety show. Dick worked as the straight man who lambasted comic Tom for mistakes, and tongue-tied Tom would eventually answer back and win the argument before they finished with a song.

The comedy setup the Everlys used produced a less good-natured tone: Don would lay into Phil, and Phil just took it, endlessly, with shrugs and winces. It could come off as harsh. While before long, Don would complain in song of such nightclub appearances, he seemed particularly comfortable in that setting. It was Phil who said he preferred supper clubs to rock halls with psychedelic light shows—a point of difference and ongoing tension. They had apparently worked up the material themselves; for all of the act's hard teasing of Phil, there's no reason to imagine he didn't play a part in the writing. The nightclub mood and approach had the effect of disassociating the brothers even further from the familiar lyrics they'd sung hundreds of times, limiting their emotional connection with the audience—the very things that had served them best before. In this mode, doing repeated short shows in the course of a week or more might have taxed them physically—but not much emotionally. Some who valued their music most would take note of the trend—and did not approve.

The reviewer from *Cash Box*, commenting on the Latin Quarter shows, said, "Don is at times too glib for his own good. As pleasant as he is, he often gets trapped in finding a *finis* to his casual talk." *Billboard* noted the familiarity of the musical sets and the limiting context: "Time hasn't changed the Everly Brothers...with essentially the same repertoire that made them high school heroes of the age group which is now crowding 30.... The butter and egg men [i.e., the big-spender tourists] who patronize the Latin Quarter found the performance right in their groove."

To appeal to audiences under thirty in 1968, you needed to be as anti-showbiz glitz as you could manage, or at least, avoid those antiquating ways. The change in fashion—and that's what it was—was as stark as when the mass audience turned to sweater-clad crooners like Bing Crosby and left John McCormack–style declarative, operatic tenors behind. In volatile 1968, Don and Phil, notwithstanding their varied venue appearances, remained unconvinced that they could appeal strongly to the huge younger audience who'd never think of heading to the Latin Quarter for a good time.

The most revealing artifact of these pre-scripted nightclub-style shows is a full performance recorded for national television broadcast in Australia, at the Chequers club in Sydney during three weeks of performances that summer. The audience sits at supper-club tables. Don and Phil, with their now more rounded faces and post-Beatles haircuts, are in those tuxes, and they're backed by Terry Slater on bass, Milwaukee's Sammy McCue with electric guitar solos, acceding to current rock trends, and Tulsa's Jimmy Karstein on drums.

Don is often singing leads in his current "yay-yay, *yeah!*" scat-and-improvise style, with Phil following very closely, by necessity. With the majority of the songs speeded up, the brothers' stage moves seem planned and choreographed. Their take on "Susie Q" begins with "Na, na-na, na-nah" from the Cannibal & the Headhunters/

Wilson Pickett "Land of 1000 Dances" update. "Wake Up Little Susie" is reordered to open from "Oo-la-la" and is introduced, jokingly, as "one of our prewar songs" for any Vietnam soldiers in the audience on leave.

One change that seems inexcusable is a deliberate comic demolishing of their own touching "So Sad," with Terry Slater, presented as a silent, dim-witted cross between Stan Laurel and TV's Gomer Pyle, demonstrably waiting for his chance to get in his bass-line break. Some may find the shtick funny, but the song is rendered emotionally meaningless in the process. Don completes the odd mood, asking, "Did everybody follow the words? That song goes by very quickly and Phil has a habit of mumbling when he sings. That's a 'story song,' as we say in the biz." Self-satire? Audience mocking? Or insider glib, as if he were Bob Hope? "The *biz*?"

The monologues from Don involve enough ribbing of Phil that we can wonder if it didn't become irritating for him, after night after night of the same—even if he'd taken part in setting up the material. "I'm the eldest of the Everly Brothers," Don informs the crowd. "I'm the intelligent one; that's how you can tell us apart."

Local reaction to the cabaret-style shows Down Under was decidedly mixed. The reviewer for the *Go Set* rock paper was merciless and specific, dismissing the performance as "slick insincerity . . . with stereotyped rehashes of their golden oldies (what else could they have done?) Don and Phil came off as something of faded, carefully preserved curios of a past era. . . . Their self-conscious patter, their guitar-swinging, hip-wobbling mannerisms . . . everything they did on stage."

There were, in fact, other things, new things, they could have been doing. Back home in Los Angeles in September, they'd appear at the Rose Bowl in what was billed as "An American Music Show," alongside Big Brother & the Holding Company with Janis Joplin, Country Joe & the Fish, Junior Wells with Buddy Guy, the Byrds, and the Mothers of Invention. Don probably liked the vibe more than Phil. That was no supper-club situation.

Before the trip to Australia, they'd begun sessions clearly designed to create a renewing, redefining concept album, a project that would make their own claim to resurging relevancy, as Elvis's TV special would at the end of the year for him. Much of its recording was squeezed into just one week, then finished up after the tour. "We decided to do one all-out assault" is how Warners' Joe Smith put it.

"What would happen," Lenny Waronker wondered, "if we put those voices in a certain musical frame?" "Basically," he noted, "I wanted their *Roots* album to make a solid statement. . . . I really idolized them both, [but] it was a difficult time for them; they weren't absolutely together musically . . . Don was more interested in change; he wanted to experiment more with the newer music, where Phil is more traditional in taste."

On the LP cover, when that arrived, Andy Wickham was explicit about the "frame" the new Warner Bros. gang and the Everlys had arrived at: "This work is an attempt to explore the roots, explain the aesthetic, chart the progression and capture the incomparable beauty of the brothers Everly." In short, the project was meant to clarify who they were, what they do, and how that still mattered.

The shape and order of the week's sessions are revealing, as they worked through genres destined to be included. For roots rock, they began with two more songs from Ron Elliott. "Turn Around" appeared on the Beau Brummels' *Bradley's Barn* album as well, with a similar tinkling guitar riff by Ron, but with a snarly vocal from Sal Valentino quite different from the smooth, tight harmony Don and Phil bring to it. "Ventura Boulevard," written by Ron and Sal together and previously unheard, is a slow, gentle ballad that describes a sweet ride down that long local thoroughfare. The opening line, "Everyone thinks I've been gone too long; I only went for a ride," had to be striking to Everly fans just returning to the fold.

The next day, attention turned to some outright, contemporary country, in no way retro—Merle Haggard's "Sing Me Back Home" and the Glen Campbell hit "Less of Me." The moving ballad from Merle, of a death-row prisoner in his last minutes serenaded by a singer friend, had been a hit single only a few months earlier, and no one else had recorded it or likely considered it duet material. Don and Phil's version is paced by a relentless muffled drumbeat and rising church organ behind them. They sing it together, with the once-typical Don solo verse in the middle, and with great reverence. "Less of Me" is paced by dobro from James Burton and, in retrospect, comes off as country rock. The now very busy star Glen Campbell was not in on these sessions, though he likely heard about them as they unfolded; he'd have a similar duet take of this older hit of his on the duo album with Bobbie Gentry, released just weeks before *Roots* was.

The following sessions were devoted to songs viewed today as Americana standards, by both style and content. Connecting back into history, a complicated one, "Shady Grove," has strong ties to both Appalachian mountain balladry and square dancing (many first heard it sung by Kentucky folk singer Jean Ritchie) and to the more ancient British narrative song "Matty Groves." In truth, the song is apparently a twentieth-century product that simply sounds older, with the title chorus referring variously to a girl or a place. The upbeat *Roots* version has new narrative verses, almost certainly from Phil and Don with credits obfuscated, and offers pure country-rock escapism—away from "the maze of city streets" down a road "that leads to cool green fields" where, as in "Bowling Green," a really desirable "little miss" awaits.

It's not well known, but Don, Phil, and company then spent hours trying to work up a version of Robbie Robertson's "The

Weight," which had been recorded in January but wasn't released as the first Band single until a few weeks after this session, in August. Clearly the radio advance on the record must have reached some music makers who quickly saw its strength. Jackie DeShannon recorded it, too, two days before the Everlys took a stab at it, and her single version would do better commercially than the newcomer Band's original. The Everlys' attempt never got far, though a rough vocal rehearsal is included in Bear Family's *Chained to a Memory* Everlys set.

The last session before the scheduled travel break tackled country—brand-new and very old. Merle Haggard's "Mama Tried" was released as a single by Merle just as Don and Phil recorded it, that same *week*, and it would be a number one for him. They'd perform it from here on out. It uses the same signature guitar opening as Haggard's record (via James Burton on dobro, in this version), and a slightly faster pace, but the chorus becomes a two-voice shout, with Phil more dominant than usual. It was very effective.

Just a few weeks later, Merle was getting to work on one of his own historical reclamation projects, his landmark modernized interpretation of Jimmie Rodgers songs, *Same Train, A Different Time*, with scene-setting historic commentary between tracks. It would be another instance of satisfying the audience hunger for cultural reconnection, putting the music in context and engaging with it. The Everlys were also turning to the perennially useful Jimmie Rodgers repertoire in their own way.

Recorded the same day as "Mama Tried" was Jimmie's forty-year-old hit "T for Texas," the first of his blue yodels. Don and Phil reconstruct it radically. After a wah-wah pedal introduction, they attack the chorus with untypically ragged, out-of-synch shouts; Phil continues the "T for Texas" chorus in the background as Don moves on to the verses. It all turns on a dime into a loping, clip-clop cowboy song with more expected sweet Everlys harmony, switches back to the frantic wah-wah rock, and repeats the mood switch all over again—roots rock from a rooted source.

Phil spoke to what the recording and its originator meant to them as this author discussed it with him directly in September 2009: "With where we came from, and my dad, Merle Travis, and Mose Rager there, these were the songs we sang all our lives—and on the radio as kids, with our parents. It's a shame, in a way, that people think of Jimmie Rodgers as the root of just *one* thing, when he was a root for so many things. And then, people will talk about how rock 'n' roll is just a black thing, but…there's so much of *that* country in it."

It was not surprising that a song they'd sung in their childhood radio broadcasts would be brought up here; their relation to those memories would become part of the album's fabric. "T for Texas" would become the number Phil and Don used as a bravura show closer for years—together, and also on their own.

After the Australian tour hiatus, last-minute material would be recorded and assembled for *Roots* that would make it one of the Everlys' most recalled and honored albums over time, and an entrance ramp to new possibilities, immediately. The album title suggested that the continuity between the day's more mature Everlys and the Everlys of a decade or two before especially mattered now. The track that demonstrated that most explicitly was their revisiting of the 1957 B-side "I Wonder If I Care as Much." When Don first asked that question, writing the song at age twenty, it was one more song he'd written in the country heartbreak mode, a genre exercise, and the performance was focused more on getting that perfect brotherly harmony sound than on what the lyrics suggested. In this new take, they harmonize beautifully, but their vocals are slower, contemplative, as if just arriving at the lyric's thoughts as they're sung. Delicate acoustic and electric guitars play a circular riff that seems to dig back through time, the totality highlighting just how changed by experience they are. You could wonder, hearing this just then, if they were weighing whether they cared about their whole *career* as much as they did before.

The last newly recorded songs added were the contemporary and quite pop "Illinois," from Waronker's buddy Randy Newman, which salutes both the rural and urban in that state, and "Living Too Close to the Ground," a solo ballad from Don that calls for widening our perspectives. But the bulk of the late work on the project, which gave it its particular flavor, was production.

More orchestration was added, tastefully, and a 1952 Shenandoah Everly Family radio show recording was weaved around multiple tracks, at a time when not many were necessarily aware of that background at all. They would be now. A clip of the "Kentucky" recording from *Songs Our Daddy Taught Us* was reused in the finale, tying together three Everly eras, while doing as much to lock in the semi-fictional Kentucky origin story and the family act's genuine significance as anything had before. Amusingly but revealingly, on the LP's back cover, in thanking Ike and Margaret for providing the 1952 Iowa radio tape, Andy Wickham misidentifies it as having come from a Brownie, Kentucky, home recording.

At some point along the production stretch, marketers at Warners somehow lost faith in the landmark project, perhaps because it produced no big hit single. Promotion proved surprisingly meager, though "progressive rock" format radio stations, critics in the new rock press, and plenty of fascinated musicians took particular note. The thinking behind the album worked for those who paid attention, which, over time, would be a lot more people.

In *Rolling Stone*, Ed Ward found it "a showcase for the superb talent of the Everlys as they are today...a warm, sentimental album that is nostalgic and contemporary at the same time... right fine." Noted folklorist Ed Kahn, not typically a commenter on rock, wrote, "The Everlys...have a strong awareness of their own background and how it relates to their early hits.... Their public often tries to deny them the right to grow and change. On this album [they] are telling us through recording where they come from musically as well as where they are now."

Don sighed, "There was a resurgence in country music; the businessmen at Warners understood that. They said, 'Well, maybe we can make something.' So there was a little bit done, but the album did not sell as well as leftover singles we had been putting out had. It was a turntable hit." A "turntable" hit was one that caught the attention of those radio hosts, music critics, and venues' show bookers—rather than record buyers.

That did have some immediate effect. If they weren't chartbusters again, the Everly Brothers had come to represent continuity in American music across time, and that mattered, for them and for others. They were seen as relatable music makers comfortable with current trends and stars, but with working ties to traditional ideas of family and home—for many, an attractive combination again. The Band's *Music from Big Pink* showed those gents posing with their "next of kin," startling as that was in this same rock context. No one marketed country rockers as "They're kind of young, they rock, and they don't hate their parents," but they might have.

With this freshly reinforced image, the Everlys would find more demand in the folk-adjacent side of the roots music world, and they begin to accept the invitation. That the borders between commercial folk, soft singer-songwriter rock, modernizing country, and electric roots rock had become porous, nebulous even, certainly helped. Asked the perennial "What do you call what you play?" question at this time, Phil responded, "We're still basically a country rock group. That's what they called us at the beginning, and that's what we are now."

In reviewing their stand at the storied hungry i club in San Francisco, with comedian David Steinberg opening, the *Examiner*'s

Phillip Elwood pinned their returning appeal: "Their country leanings make them increasingly popular among the younger hip set who are leaning strongly in that direction, especially since Dylan's hit LP earlier this year." Apparently Don and Phil were utterly unfamiliar to some of that young set on hand. "I don't know who they are, but they sing pretty good—*kind* of rock and roll, I guess," one was overheard commenting. They'd been around long enough to be taken as fresh all over again. This was indeed the beginning of a comeback—by their audiences.

Phil commented, "It's finally a real audience.... They don't care about...baloney. Now they only ask, 'Is it good; do I like it?'" Don was on the same page on that. "The days of screaming crowds are over. It's more satisfying to appeal to adult crowds; I never enjoyed the screaming bit."

A few weeks later, in early 1969, still on tour with comedian Steinberg, they had a much-covered and -publicized show at the Bitter End in Greenwich Village, which was famed for having held weekly folk hootenannies. *Billboard* would report that the banter in the Bitter End stand, evolved somewhat for a crowd different from that at the Latin Quarter, "seemed to fit the intimate coffeehouse...better....Even their usual oldies set was well-taken, with increasing interest today on rock's early days." Don noted after a straightforward, sweet rendering of "All I Have to Do Is Dream" that "people have asked why we look into each other's eyes, so I thought I'd clear that up: Some of the words to that last song are written on Phil's forehead." The downtown crowd applauded.

Cash Box noticed the Smothers Brothers parallel and wondered if at this rate they might soon be able to "dispense with the songs altogether." *Billboard* added, "Their...single, 'Lord of the Manor,' which has been receiving underground play, was a good up-to-date folk-style number." ("Underground" now suggested "right for freeform-playlist FM radio shows.") The *New York Times* noted that besides those old hits, "they also sing some smooth versions of progressive folk songs. . . . The Everlys are cool, polished and effective." It had to be a refreshing response.

Graham Nash and Leonard Cohen were among those who headed from a Joni Mitchell show uptown right to the Bitter End to catch the must-see Everlys; Simon & Garfunkel and Johnny Winter were on hand, too. Afterward, they all joined Don and Phil backstage, as did, discreetly, Bob Dylan.

Standing around and talking in a cramped office, Phil asked Bob, "Do you have any songs?" He played for them, too softly apparently, one that he'd written for the *Midnight Cowboy* movie but hadn't finished in time for it to appear there, something new called "Lay Lady Lay."

Phil would tell an oft-repeated story about this: "I couldn't hardly hear. You don't ask Bob Dylan, 'Hey, what's the lyric?' I thought he was singing, I swear, 'Lay across my big breasts, babe.' And I'm saying to myself, 'Why in the world have we got to hear a song and he's got a line like that? We couldn't possibly sing it.' So, when he finishes it I said, 'You could get away with that, but I don't think we could.' Now he's looking at me, [as if] saying, 'Why in the world is he saying *that* to me?'"

Don clarified that with his characteristic obliqueness they weren't at all sure whether Dylan was seriously pitching it to them or not, and so "awestruck," they let it pass. It would be one of his own major hits. Don and Phil would not get around to recording it for fifteen years. "I was there that night," Graham Nash notes. "I knew that Bob was a big fan of the Everly Brothers, so I'm sure that was disappointing for him; that's for sure." In the same period, Dylan reportedly offered Don and Phil a song he was calling "The Fugitive," but they didn't record that one either. It would emerge, after some tinkering with it by Bob and Johnny Cash, as "Wanted Man," on Cash's *At San Quentin* album.

They did continue to record individual sides for Warners after *Roots*, most unissued at the time, a good many with marked roots-scene connections—a take on Howlin' Wolf's "Down in the Bottom" with Ry Cooder on slide guitar, an unsuccessful single version of James Taylor's "Carolina in My Mind," several promising, little-known takes on Kris Kristofferson's "Casey's Last Ride," and a hushed, nostalgic version of Dolly Parton's "In the Good Old Days (When Times Were Bad)." There were country-rock sessions that included current Byrds Clarence White and Gene Parsons in the backup of a version of the hoary folk song "Cuckoo Bird" that became a little-heard single, and on another of those era-describing titles, the Don-written but Slater-credited original "I'm on My Way Home Again."

Gram Parsons, Chris Hillman, and Michael Clarke had departed the Byrds for the country-rock Flying Burrito Brothers, a band they'd describe as built on Everly Brothers vocal harmonies with Buck Owens' Buckaroos electric instrumentation. They would regularly perform "Take a Message to Mary," "Wake Up Little Susie," and an Everly-derived version of "Lucille" in their live shows. In 1969, Don would sit down with Parsons and show him how to work the vocal harmonies on "Sleepless Nights," a lesson made good on a few years later.

In an interview at the time, Gram, after describing the Everlys as band favorites, was not particularly gracious in commenting on his encounters with Don: "He's a little bit out of touch. They ain't the old Everly Brothers, if you know what I mean—not like those old Boudleaux Bryant tunes, that stuff, man.... They could still get that heavy, but I guess they've got one of those brother problems going." He did make sure to mention that he'd appeared on an Everly Brothers record—referring to a vocal overdub session, at which Don and Phil hadn't been present.

The Everlys' returning credibility was both evidenced and buttressed by high-visibility new recordings of their songs by stars of the era—Bobbie Gentry and Glen Campbell with "Let It Be Me," then "All I Have to Do Is Dream"; Simon & Garfunkel with "Bye Bye Love" on their massively selling *Bridge over Troubled Water* LP; Dylan with "Take a Message" and "Let It Be Me"; Linda Thompson (still as Linda Peters) and Sandy Denny, as part of the Bunch, with "When Will I Be Loved." And Doug Dillard and Gene Clark's version of "So Sad" on their album *Through the Morning, Through the Night* underscored the Everlys' foundational role for progressive bluegrass.

It was their appearance at the 1969 Newport Folk Festival, joined by Ike, who'd been invited along with them, that made it clearer to Don and Phil what new opportunities could be at hand. They were not fully cognizant of what an evolving Newport audience would want from them, but many who'd learned fingerpicking had heard that Ike had mentored Merle Travis and had once been a performer, as advertised on *Roots*. And, of course, there were far from traditionalist performers on hand at Newport now, too.

Four years after "Dylan going electric" was a controversial novelty, Newport Folk was much changed from its original "hard-core vernacular meets commercial folk boom" bent. More Nashville country acts had been appearing, more electrified roots-rock bands, and many more contemporary singer-songwriters—all of them accepted parts of an eclectic, Americana-like spectrum lacking only the name. Sharing the bill with Don and Phil that summer were Buffy Sainte-Marie, Doug Kershaw, John Hartford, Johnny Cash & June Carter (introducing newcomer Kris Kristofferson), Joni Mitchell, James Taylor, Van Morrison, Arlo Guthrie, Jim Rooney, and Jerry Jeff Walker. The classic subgenre standbys—Pete Seeger, the Muddy Waters Blues Band, Son House, Bill Monroe, Big Mama Thornton, Ramblin' Jack Elliott, and the New Lost City Ramblers—were still on hand as well.

Atlanta singer-songwriter Pat Alger, years later a friend and regular opening act for the Everlys, was in attendance at both of their Newport appearances. The main-stage show Saturday evening paralleled the "updated" Bitter End–style club approach, which included chatter and some slightly incongruous material for this place, such as songs from the musical *Hair*—"The Age of Aquarius" and "Let the Sunshine In." The daytime Sunday "workshop" set with Ike was an attraction for Pat, because he was a fingerpicker himself, aware of Ike's reputation.

"If you kept your eyes on Don, he kept his eyes on *Ike*," Alger recalls. "And you could see how much Phil thought of their dad." Indeed, Ike's presence seems to work like a tension buffer for them, with someone to focus on and follow besides each other. There would be more of this.

Some of the workshop set would appear on a 1995 Vanguard CD, *Nashville at Newport*, and the entire fifty-minute set later became widely available online. Ike's playing centered on jazzy blues and rags. He features a dazzling take on Travis's intricate, syncopated "Blue Smoke" instrumental after explaining that connection, and clarifying that he'd come first, as well as "Ike Everly's Rag." Then he mutters, "I'm hogging the whole thing here."

Don describes the Kennedy Jones and Arnold Shultz connections to the style, and how "basic components of country music come from a black man," a part of history not many were bringing up at the time. They all move on to the sorts of old-time country-meets-vaudeville songs they'd played on the family radio show—"Goin' Down the Road Feelin' Bad," "I Am a Pilgrim," "Step It Up and Go." It flows as if they'd never stopped. Then Phil and Don perform requested songs from *Songs Our Daddy Taught Us*—"Lightning Express," "Down in the Willow Garden," "Oh So Many Years," which they'd rarely performed since recording them.

It was all downright magical and powerful, the emotional connection to what they were performing restored. *Cash Box* would note, "The Everlys have matured and mellowed considerably since they were teenage stars, and their old material...sounded at the Festival better than it did on their hit records." There would be many encouraging press reviews in the months ahead. This appearance, as much as the *Roots* album's release and that Bitter End show, reestablished them as an integral part of a changing popular roots-music era. It said, "How we've managed where we've come from is foundational for what we—and *you*—play today."

More potential excitement followed before they left Newport. Just a few weeks earlier, Johnny Cash's new ABC TV show had joined Glen Campbell's in prime time as a home for music across the country-pop borderlines, followed by mom and pop and the hipper younger set alike—a sign of the current musical atmosphere in itself. It was set to run through the whole 1969–1970 season and beyond. As was the practice then with variety shows, rather than airing reruns over the summer, they'd need a limited-run replacement show for those months. In the face of the accolades and multigenerational response, Cash approached Don and Phil and their management with the idea that they might be good summer replacement hosts. It was a heady possibility.

Meanwhile, things proceeded much as they had—though personally complicated, with every appearance evidence of one "side's" venue in ascendence—nightclub casino, rock palace—and annoyance from the brother who wanted to be there least. They'd have a full month stand at the Riviera in Las Vegas alongside Connie Francis, and in the opposite direction, appearances at the Fillmore West in San Francisco along with acts such as the Sons of Champlin or Canned Heat, and at the similar Kinetic Playground in Chicago, with flashing light shows, on a bill with Cannonball Adderley and Aynsley Dunbar.

In early February 1970, a full Everlys stage show of this era was recorded by Warners at the Brand Hotel in Anaheim, California—including such current live staples as the *Hair* songs and John Lennon's "Give Peace a Chance." It would become their last album on the label under the decade-long contract, released as *The Everly Brothers Show*, because by then it was a lock that the Cash summer replacement show would happen. He'd proposed either Don and Phil or Marty Robbins as viable replacements, and when Robbins had to have open-heart surgery, the choice was simplified. It was to be *Johnny Cash Presents the Everly Brothers*, with ten hour-long episodes, taped in the spring before summer broadcast. The live album could not, of course, feature material from the upcoming show, but the implication was in the title.

Tensions between Phillip and Donald were in fact mounting in early 1970, just as production on the television series began, and it showed in multiple ways, small and large.

The Smothers Brothers were briefly headlining at Caesars Palace in Las Vegas and booked their old friends the Everlys to open for them. The Smothers' own new ABC network show, their return to TV, was going to follow the Everlys' that summer, every week, with the whole evening promoted together at times.

Tom, the older of that pair, would recall, "We knew the Everly Brothers, and we were exactly the same age...so we had Don and Phil open for us. Perfect!...The second night, their road manager comes down and says 'The boys aren't going on. Don is in his dressing room and Phil is up in his hotel room, and they're both mad. They're not talking.'...They came down to the show and never looked at each other." He elaborated on the follow-up on another occasion: "I told Dick, 'Tomorrow night, let's grab dinner with them. We're brothers to the sky; we've had our problems, we've worked together a long time, we can talk about how to get along.'...So, we all go to dinner, and we order drinks...and I said,

'I know you love each other,' and they said, 'We don't love each other; we don't *like* each other.' Inside of five minutes Dickie is siding with Phil; I'm siding with Don, and the two younger brothers got up and left. That's the truth about brothers."

There were other more serious changes afoot, and it's impossible not to see them as life-altering effects of all the tension and travel—and additional reasons Don and Phil were so on edge. In February 1970, Jackie formally filed for divorce from Phil after a year and a half of separation; they would have shared custody of son Jason. Phil said little about that at first, then commented to the British music paper *Disc and Music Echo* the following year, "I don't feel *anything* about my first marriage. It was just a bad marriage. Divorce is divorce."

More unexpected for its suddenness, after eight years together through thick and thin, Venetia filed for divorce from Don in April, on the grounds of "irreconcilable differences." Ann Marshall, who'd not been around the Everlys for the past few years, had seen their Las Vegas show advertised a few months earlier and flown there with a few friends. She'd met with the brothers and resumed her friendship with Don and Venetia in particular. According to her, Venetia had also heard stories of extracurricular activities by Don out on the road. The divorce would take months to finalize, and while Don was granted visitation rights to see their three children, he'd tell one interviewer that the kids didn't even notice the divorce at first, because he'd always been away anyway.

Ruefully, he summarized what had happened, as he saw it: "It doesn't work, being away from home all the time. It's hard to keep anything together.... There's no such thing as marriage in this kind of life." Later, Don would tell those who asked that he didn't see his California kids very often at all because he'd have to encounter their mother to do that. It got more bitter. He'd soon be saying, "It was a miserable marriage that made me feel like some country boy," an ending for a pairing that began with his attraction to her worldliness, and gossip magazines wondering about that very compatibility question.

Don's long absenteeism as a father certainly illustrated the darker side of his continuing, Peter Pan–like quests for personal freedom and adventure. He wouldn't be the first or last parent—traveling performer or otherwise—to choose personal gratification over responsibilities they'd signed on for, or the first adult to have a sense of social and professional responsibility that didn't quite include the personal. Venetia, who would essentially raise the three kids on her own, never formally remarried or resumed her acting career, but she went on to read scripts for Burt Reynolds's film production company, then became an executive at the production company Cinema Group Ventures, which released the feature *Star Trek III: The Search for Spock.*

With the TV show taping set to begin in Los Angeles in May (not in Nashville, where the Cash show was taped), Don took a side trip to London while returning from a multi-week tour of South Africa, for the express purpose of seeing whether the Beatles would be willing to be guests on the show. It proved to be an exquisite example of bad timing. The Beatles, he was informed, had just broken up for good. Paul McCartney asked whether, instead, Don and Phil might be interested in an as-yet-unreleased song he figured would be perfect for them; he'd even joked with John about being Don and Phil while recording it—"Two of Us" (riding nowhere). Don had to inform them that their contract with Warner Bros. had just ended. At the moment, the Everly Brothers had no record label where they could record it.

"When we were doing the television show," Phil recalled, "we were going through divorces, but we had to get up and sing anyhow—just like we weren't." Indeed, on the first episode that aired, Phil is singing a solo on Tom Paxton's "The Last Thing on My Mind," and when he gets to the line "I could have loved you better; didn't mean to be unkind," he breaks down crying, visibly, which may have puzzled home viewers at the time, but there's little doubt the recent end of his marriage was on *his* mind. The producers made a conscious decision to leave it in as it happened.

And that was only one aspect, if a personal one, of the broadly challenging context for the *Johnny Cash Presents the Everly Brothers* show's production, which began taping on May 9, 1970. That was the very day that a hundred thousand were protesting the Vietnam War's extension by "incursion" into Cambodia, on the Ellipse behind the White House—five days after the shooting deaths at Kent State, and three days after the confrontations at the World Trade Center construction site in New York, with blue-collar workers battling war protestors. It was reasonable to expect that, as with Johnny Cash's show, both the construction workers and the protestors would likely tune in to see Don and Phil and their guests. How to appeal across those social-political and generational lines had to be puzzled out, as well as working across rock and country boundaries. The show addressed these things in its very design.

Joe Higgins appeared weekly as a comically bossy Southern sheriff type, back before Jackie Gleason played one in the *Smokey and the Bandit* pictures—but he's really just a self-important parking lot attendant, lording it over these "summer replacement boys." He gives the Everlys ample chance to push back against him, like somebody in the bell-bottoms, flowery shirts, and vests they wore on the show might be inclined to try. There was also Ruth McDevitt, who took the name and role of their old Aunt Hattie and provided rustic stories of colorful folks in their alleged old Kentucky hometown, Minnie Pearl–style. There were always opportunities to come off as "country" as well as to read "hip," as both traditionally family-minded and rebellious. As if to underscore that these comedy bits were there to represent who the Everly Brothers were, they'd all be preceded by one of their most familiar hit songs, every time.

The show's producers, Bernie Kukoff and Jeff Harris, had previously produced Roger Miller's prime-time variety show and written for Glen Campbell's, and they had the experience to handle this. As Kukoff, nearing ninety at the time of our conversation, recalls, "You had a country singer, and you had a singer who was rock and roll—so then it's called a 'variety show'!"

There were episodes with guest pairings such as Marty Robbins (physically recovered by then) and Arlo Guthrie, the Statler Brothers and Neil Diamond, the Carter Family and Rick Nelson, Linda Ronstadt and Stevie Wonder, Brenda Lee and B.J. Thomas. Besides Rick and Brenda, other old friends, including Jackie DeShannon, the now famed Bobby Sherman, and Bill Medley appeared, as well as exciting unexpected guests such as Ike & Tina Turner.

This was, in fact, a great opportunity for two entertainers who'd been feeling trapped into performing the same material in the same way—even a safety valve. For the first time since the family radio broadcasts they were able to sing solos, sing material together they never had before, sing duets and group medleys with guests of various musical stripes, and touch on styles people had rarely heard them tackle—gospel, for instance, not a go-to field for them on record, or traditional pop, such as Cole Porter's "Anything Goes" performed with the Lennon Sisters. As in their old radio days, the format and hours to fill virtually demanded that all that be included.

In another first in all the years since they came to public view, they did not wear matching clothes. For all of the brothers' television experience, this was new, something they had long considered a goal—a flexible series of their own. *TV Guide* covered their first taping and reported finding Don scared enough to look pale and

Phil nervous enough to have kicked a bottle of Coke all over his bell-bottoms.

On the air, the atmosphere was energetic, sometimes even frantic, as Don, who tended to take the hosting lead, would excitedly announce guests and songs and lead heavy applause after numbers. It was another piece of tangible evidence of something Phil would admit much later: "He was always kind of out front, having to do the heavy lifting." They both responded demonstrably for each other after their solos.

A weekly on-air audience question time allowed them to show off their snappy answer wit, and the design of the single but variable set gave the proceedings a kicky, of-the-moment look. (There were Tiffany lamps and glowing autumnal trees; it's 1970.) Designed in the round, there was audience on all sides, close at hand, and the space was multilevel, the Everlys and guests performing up in scaffold towers and platforms, in a funky hanging biplane, on stairways. When navigating between them, the cameras sometimes flew overhead, moving if the people momentarily held still.

The song selections were Phil and Don's own. "We were not experts [on that]," Bernie Kukoff recalls. "We'd talk about it, and if they felt good about it, we'd do them. *They* were the experts." "Bye Bye Love" was the opening theme, "Let It Be Me" the sign-off to rolling credits— the latter modified with a stance-clarifying, Lennon-referencing line change to "Now and forever—give peace a chance." The Everlys' turn to Beatles songs was a consistent pattern across the episodes, from Don's memorable slow-ballad takes on "Ticket to Ride" and "A Hard Day's Night" and their duo "Here Comes the Sun," to rave-ups on "Ob-La-Di" and "Lady Madonna." The show-ending medleys ranged, depending on the guests, from Woody Guthrie songs to gospel numbers or "The Midnight Special."

The shows have been virtually unseen since their first run, and it would be a gift to fandom and good for history if a full release would ever become possible. Rights and costs on musical TV are complicated in the twenty-first century, but even a release of musical highlights as an audio album, DVD, or streaming special would be valuable. Besides some fascinating duets with guests from Doug Kershaw to Linda Ronstadt and Evie Sands, there are the Everlys' own takes on numbers they never put on record—Creedence's "Down on the Corner," the Stones' "Honky Tonk Women," the Box Tops' "The Letter."

All of the musical freedom, variety, attention, and excited camaraderie the show provided did not, in practice, alleviate much of the ongoing conflict between Phil and Don. It's debatable whether their differences would have lessened or been strained further faster had the show lasted longer. As producer Kukoff recalls, "You could sense the brotherly issues...two brothers and different temperaments, Don much tighter wound. The looser guy was Phil; I always found him more accessible...but I recall him snapping. There were clear kinds of tension off-camera, during rehearsals. I guess I was surprised about Phil especially, who was freewheeling with his sensitivity."

Ike Everly closed the first episode broadcast and also the last one, another indication of how the family music-making background and his picking mastery had become part of the general impression of the Everly Brothers story again. Margaret did not appear, but Ike was invited to play and talk guitar on college campuses, and appear at, for example, the University of Chicago folk festival along with her. The *Sun-Times* noted that they "sang sweetly, addressed the audience warmly, and won just about every heart in the house."

There was another important memory aid as the television series unfolded. After years of unavailability, the Everly Brothers original Cadence recordings came back into circulation, as Andy Williams started up the Barnaby Records label (named after his dog), with release of the Everlys' recordings the main impetus. Spring 1970's

The Everly Brothers' Original Greatest Hits was a revelation for the many who'd gotten to know the songs from the Warners do-overs alone. To this day, those recordings have been licensed to an endless array of labels, in releases of varying quality, but they have never again gone out of circulation.

There was some talk in trade publications such as the *Hollywood Reporter* that the Everlys were "close" to locking in a full 1971 season time slot for the show, and that Don and Phil were interested, but that appears to have been somebody's wishful thinking, never seriously pursued. It's telling that *The Johnny Cash Show* itself ended its run in March 1971, the network broadcast of *Hee Haw* in July 1971, and *The Glen Campbell Goodtime Hour* one more season after that. There was a chill blowing over anything with country connections on national TV; hit comedies such as *The Andy Griffith Show* and *The Beverly Hillbillies* would soon be off the air, too.

But this experience of being able to sing for people solo, and to sing what pleased them individually, surely escalated Don and Phil's thoughts of doing so more regularly. Those thoughts lingered—and festered.

Chapter Nine

TO THE BREAKING POINT
1970–1973

I F ATTENTION PAID TO THE *ROOTS* ALBUM AND THEIR TV SHOW brought the Everlys a new sense of relevancy, it also sparked encouraging new interest. "The bookings started coming in heavier again," Don Wayne recalls. "They had to turn down a lot of them." Recognition was bolstered further by media discussion of the Simon & Garfunkel, Dylan, and Gentry & Campbell recordings that brought a straightforward message to millions: you really ought to know and appreciate the Everly Brothers.

Don and Phil had both passed their thirtieth birthdays, so often a time for reconsidering the future. Both were single again, though Don's complicated divorce from Venetia wouldn't be finalized until January 1971. The long contract with Warner Bros. Records was done with, leaving them free to find a new label. The television series was over, and the Calliope Records business, too, though Phil had his own publishing company now, shared with Terry Slater, for songs they wrote—Bowling Green Music.

Don had been overoptimistic about the television show's likely effects, expecting to see a whole lot less of Las Vegas, for one thing: "We don't see our future in the cabaret scene, because we've got our own TV show now," he'd said, "which will change *everything*, completely. We'll be able to do just what we want musically." But reality set in.

Now he'd tell a Cleveland columnist that the TV show had been "too much work, and I'm not that much interested in TV to do it as a regular thing. . . . Once people see you, they think they know you. Everyone is image-conscious, and you have to conform to someone else's idea of what you should be." All of which said more about his current mood and general temperament than his relation to image-making; he'd been contributing to magazine photo spreads, dozens and dozens of TV appearances, and interviews for twenty-five years. In late 1971, the Everlys even attempted to return to national television directly with a syndicated half-hour show featuring them along with Ike, but it didn't happen.

Day to day, they were seeing less and less of each other. Don noted, pointedly, "We see each other often because of our work, and feel no need to have a social life together as well." A gig at the Landmark hotel/casino in Las Vegas, the very sort of situation Phil preferred and Don had come to detest, lasted a month.

Phil was living in Los Angeles's Touluca Lake and was often accompanied at the time by actress Jana Taylor, who'd appeared in several feature films and the daytime soap opera *General Hospital*. Like him, she'd recently been divorced. He told reporters that he'd only ever marry again if he wanted another child, then took that right back, mocking himself: "I'll probably go out and do it immediately." Meanwhile, there were still complicated alimony negotiations with Jackie.

Eight years after they'd briefly dated, Ann Marshall started seeing Phil again, as his marriage was coming to an end. She'd also maintained her friendships with both Venetia and Don, and was godmother to their daughter Stacy, who was now seven. As Don's marriage to Venetia came crashing down, it was Ann and Don who evolved into a serious couple, initially to Phil's chagrin. "He just said, 'That's the end for us,'" she recalls. Don moved into her apartment, and they nevertheless proceeded to attend Stacy's May birthday party at Venetia's together. This seemingly fraught situation was apparently all fine with everybody. "Well, it's Hollywood," Ann explains.

In early October, the Everlys played a week of dates that had to remind them of appearances of years before—at the Arkansas State Fair at Little Rock. Don was apparently feeling the pull of the rustic, as he purchased a twenty-four-acre ranch—or farm, if you will—in a location notably different from Arkansas or Muhlenberg County, Kentucky—north Malibu, California, overlooking the ocean. He'd say he went there to avoid the city smog; Ann relocated there with him. Their live-in relationship was public, and by these changing times there was no particular scrutiny or pushback about that.

They had a quiet life there, with only occasional guests. Don was growing organic vegetables and doing a lot of drawing, infatuated with pop art, in contrast to Phil's love of the antique. One of the more frequent visitors at Malibu was Billy Al Bengston, the celebrated Venice, California, custom car designer and painter of motorcycle themes, who had pop art connections himself. Billy would design the cover of Don's first solo album.

They rarely saw Don's West Coast kids. Margaret Everly would mention the following year that it was nice to get to see her "five gorgeous grandchildren...occasionally," though she didn't say where, exactly. It couldn't have been all five, because Don's son,

Edan, for one, was asking Ann what his grandparents were really like at about the same time. Ann describes Don as increasingly clinging in their time at the seaside place: "We got along great when he lived in my apartment. When we got the farm, if I would go down and collect eggs from the chickens in the morning, he'd be mad that I wasn't there holding his hand."

In late 1970, Don and Ann were witnesses for the generally forgotten Taos, New Mexico, wedding of her closest friend, the Mamas & the Papas' Michelle Phillips, to wild-man actor-director Dennis Hopper. Don paid for the marriage license; the marriage lasted one week. "A great investment," Ann remarked of the license fee.

Solo projects Don and Phil had shunned for years now became considerations—and the exposure singing solos on their TV show no doubt advanced the thought. The possibility became more real through their longstanding friendship with producer Lou Adler. After founding Dunhill Records in 1964, he'd signed and succeeded with the Mamas & the Papas, then sold Dunhill in 1967 and founded another label, Ode. Don's new living arrangement with Ann put Adler at close hand again.

As the last episodes of *Johnny Cash Presents the Everly Brothers* were being broadcast, summer 1970, Don was already in the Ode Records studio in Los Angeles with Adler producing what would become his self-titled solo album. Phil was seriously upset, and said so, because he hadn't been informed about it, and Lou had been *his* close friend—past tense. It may have been less charged to be peeved with Adler than with Don.

Within weeks, Phil changed his public tune, telling reporters that he expected to do a solo project, too, very possibly with Ode— and with no change in the status of the Everly Brothers as a duo. Not many months later, he'd admit this was, in truth, a turning point: "What it meant to me—well, I guess it was like cheating on a marriage." He wasn't referring to Lou as the disloyal one.

Don was explicit about his own motivation: "I didn't feel I was getting anything accomplished musically, on record," and there were "songs that I'd written over a period of time which really Phil and I couldn't do.... It was done apart as an experiment, only. It really was.... It's very important and necessary for the growth of the Everly Brothers to go on as individuals."

The instrumental backup for those sessions—and there was a lot if it—offers clues to where Don intended to go. The musicians included members of the Flying Burrito Brothers (Sneaky Pete Kleinow on steel, Chris Ethridge on bass), Spooner Oldham for keyboard soul, and Ry Cooder on slide guitar.

Eight of the eleven tracks were originals, the other three classic country. It's hard not to see his very slow, choral-backed solo take on the Sons of the Pioneers' "Tumbling Tumbleweeds" and his beautiful waltzing nod to the Louvin Brothers with "When I Stop Dreaming" as pointed comment for anyone who thinks celebrated "harmony numbers" couldn't be done well solo. His interpretation of Don Gibson's "Sweet Dreams," familiar to many from Pasty Cline's version, pushes it to the country/rock borderlands, with rock-ballad-style piano triplets meeting oozing steel guitar.

Don's new originals veer between country and singer-songwriter rock. He ventures into some political commentary on both South Africa and ecology in "Safari," and sings to a growing daughter in "My Baby." "Omaha" has a guy traveling around, forgetting details of all the places he's been, but finding "everything that I wanted" in that Nebraska city. Midwest nostalgia, perhaps? Other songs concern a relationship hanging in the balance (the caustic "Thinking It Over") and suddenly over ("February 15th").

The album caused no major stir, but there were those who were impressed. *Billboard* called the LP "a winner in every respect," though they couldn't have helped family relations any when adding, "In addition to this departure, Don will continue with his brother

Bob as one of the best and most durable of young acts around." (The codger reviewer who found them still all that "young" seems also to have confused Phil with big band singer Bob Eberle.) *Rolling Stone* suggested that Don had shown he could do "nearly" as well as the brothers together. In retrospect, Don would say of the whole project, "I was drinking a lot of tequila and smoking weed…and I think that was a mistake. But I wrote a lot of stuff during that time; it's…like looking back at a diary. It was kind of out there, and… self-indulgent."

In late November, the brothers appeared on Dean Martin's weekly variety show, singing "Mama Tried" and performing a goofy "Bye Bye Love"/"Your Cheatin' Heart" medley with Dean. In keeping with what seemed a family tradition of TV appearances yielding dates, Phil met one of the Golddiggers dancers who were regulars on the program and sometimes toured live as an act on their own. Her name was Patricia Louise Mickey. She was twenty; they began serious dating.

As Don's album was released in December, the Everly Brothers and Ike appeared on *The Johnny Cash Christmas Show*, along with June and Maybelle Carter and Tommy Cash, in a setting that put them sitting around a living room fireplace, trading songs. Guitar enthusiasts couldn't help but be interested in the "Ike meets Maybelle" aspect. He shows off Muhlenberg County picking in a short "Cannonball Rag" segment, and Ike and Maybelle do the two-players-on-one-guitar stunt, then Don and Phil sing "Kentucky," particularly slowly, with Phil nearly embracing Don's shoulder as the latter handles the guitar.

Ike then leads his sons and the Cash brothers in using bits of the lighthearted midsixties country song "Do What You Do Do Well" to connect his impressive performance of "Muskrat" with Don and Phil's "Silver Haired Daddy of Mine." Johnny adds the part of "I Never Picked Cotton" that tells how "my daddy died young, working in a coal mine," reminding audiences of a less-romanticized Kentucky background. Don appears disconnected from the proceedings throughout, unexcited to be there, and hardly looks at Phil at all.

Off-screen, much was happening. The Everlys were putting together a new, provocative touring band, changing accountants, replacing Jack Rael with Jack Daley as their manager, and signing on with a new major label, all before the year was over. It may have felt nostalgic when they returned to *The Ed Sullivan Show* for the last time on February 28, 1971, singing "Mama Tried," energetically and perfectly attuned.

That spring was marked by weeks more at the Landmark in Las Vegas, opening for country's Roy Clark, with Ike performing with them. There was a full week playing in the lounge at the Newport Hotel in Miami Beach, and another at the Circle Star Theatre in San Carlos, California, paired with Brazilian bossa nova star Sérgio Mendes. All of these bills were clearly designed to attract older audiences.

Don took to explaining to these more settled crowds that they were not "peacenik weirdoes," just "hippies with money." There was also a larger, outlier show on May 1, when they appeared at the Hollywood Bowl along with Joan Baez; Earth, Wind & Fire; the Association; and Country Joe & the Fish—a benefit for the Southern California Council of Free Clinics.

Phil was asked in multiple newspaper and TV interviews about the deaths of Jimi Hendrix, Janis Joplin, and Jim Morrison, labeling those losses "basic stupidity," lives wasted. At the same time, he had no reason to know, Gram Parsons was hanging out with Keith Richards in France, teaching him more country songs and licks, both in a druggy haze, singing Everlys songs and with the *Roots* LP the background music of choice.

For two weeks of shows in New Zealand and Australia, they were billed, perhaps ominously, as "The Everly Brothers—The

Living Legend." Reporter Tom McWilliams of New Zealand's *Play-date* magazine was surprised by how different from each other they turned out to be, and he reported some significant breaking news—that they'd negotiated a new three-year recording deal with RCA Records, calling "probably" for one Everly Brothers album and a solo record by each of them annually. Those terms represented a reasonable way forward that could take the Everly Brothers into the 1970s. Phil told the Melbourne *Herald-Sun*, "Don and I are as close as brothers can be and will never split up." With this new contract, "if anything, we should be doing more than ever before."

Their producer was to be the esteemed Paul Rothchild—who'd worked with Paul Butterfield, Joni Mitchell, the Doors, John Sebastian, and just nine months earlier, Janis Joplin's sessions for her final *Pearl* album. He was also well known as the owner of a house in Laurel Canyon that was, as author Barney Hoskyns put it, "a *de rigeur* drop-in for anyone interested in sex, drugs and music." There were a lot of anyones.

Rothchild wanted the Everlys to connect with strong songwriters and musicians he saw as both fitting and contemporary, and he'd choose most of the songs they'd record. In the typical style and pace of 1970s album-rock production, it would take five months interrupted by touring, involve many people, and the tracks would generally be built up in layers, not recorded with everyone in the room or even in the studio at the same time. It would be among their costliest albums to produce.

The promising throng of contributors to the sessions included illustrious music makers who crossed roots rock, country, and soul lines, called on as needed. They included Delaney and Bonnie Bramlett, Crosby and Nash, Ry Cooder, steel guitar great Buddy Emmons (who'd later work with the Everlys for years), Spooner Oldham, Geoff Muldaur, Barry Beckett, Clarence White, and Chris Ethridge. The songwriters, besides the Everlys themselves, would also be of the moment—Kris Kristofferson, Jesse Winchester, Dennis Linde, and John Sebastian; the latter two also took part in recording.

In initial August sessions, Phil and Don worked on a comfortable, straightforward duo take on Jesse Winchester's "The Brand New Tennessee Waltz"; strings were added on months later. R&B, while relatively downplayed, is raised in Delaney and Bonnie's "All We Really Want to Do," done in that duo's big choral soul style, arguably too much so.

Two numbers reflected Don and Phil's current situation and attitudes explicitly, as would be true of a number of recordings just ahead. Kristofferson's "Breakdown," reminiscent of the tune used with Woody Guthrie's "Deportee," is from the standpoint of a long-traveled musician: "You still got the same lonely songs to remind you of someone you seemed to be so long ago." That had to strike a chord. Their "Green River" turned out to be the last song on which Don and Phil ever shared writing credit; with its nostalgia for a lost Muhlenberg County home, they'd apparently intended it for inclusion in *Roots*. Smothered in production, the Everlys sounding like ghosts in the distance, it went unnoticed. It might have meant more.

With a tour of England and Europe set to begin on September 10, band adjustments were needed. Terry Slater, sticking to his publishing work, was unavailable, and they also wanted added flexibility to alternate between country and contemporary pop. That suggested to them adding a touring piano player for the first time, and they found one.

Phil had befriended that often forgotten Beach Boy, David Marks, as well as his sympatico parents, Marks's mother, Jo Ann, being into mysticism and his father, Elmer, old cars. They all clicked, and Phil was a frequent visitor to their Los Angeles home, in a building David had purchased with hit-record money. Phil mentioned needing a keyboard player, and Jo Ann brought up a struggling singer-songwriter renting one of their apartments—an unknown named Warren Zevon. Phil arranged an audition.

Warren would recall, "Don and Phil were both at the audition and I played 'Hasten Down the Wind' [which he'd just written]. Phil said, 'Can you play like Floyd Cramer?' I said, 'You bet I can.' Without asking me to play another note, they hired me."

He was hired both to play piano and to organize the new backup band for the tour, working with road manager Don Wayne. Among those Zevon signed up was a guitarist whom he tussled with regularly at first, but who could clearly do the job. They'd soon be an almost "telepathic" musical combination. It was Robert "Waddy" Wachtel, who idolized Don and Phil and knew much more about country music than Warren did at that point. They were both trained musicians, frustrated in their ambitions, and both would achieve recognition in the 1970s, beginning here. There was a quick practice appearance at the Knott's Berry Farm amusement park on September 3, with the new crew playing together for three quick shows.

The next day, Zevon joined the RCA album recording sessions, playing piano on a rocking Everly version of Rod Stewart's "Mandolin Wind," and on a loping country shuffle by Don with the self-explanatory title "I'm Tired of Singing My Song in Las Vegas," which pointedly laments the place's "plastic men and painted girls." It's sung by Don solo, and certainly earnestly. Years after, he'd laugh, "That's one of the songs I wrote from the heart."

Just a few days later, Don and Phil and this promising new band, including the rhythm section of Bob Knigge on bass and Gene Gunnels on drums, took off for England and the Continent. On the sly, the musicians were warned by Don Wayne never to try to be the one to unite the Everly Brothers: "They don't get along."

For the first time, they brought along Ike and Margaret, who'd never traveled abroad before, with some joint appearances, interviews, and a break from routine for the folks in mind. With the brothers' Everly Family background more widely known now, it seemed the time to do it. Don would quickly note how invigorating the revised backup was: "Since we've added a new piano player, it's made it musically interesting to me again. So it's kind of fun."

Martial Bekkers of the Dutch fan club, a local unit that the Everlys soon picked to head their international fan organization, recalled the opening-week show at Rotterdam: "It was a very big sports hall. Almost everybody was smoking pot, and it smelled like it. I got in with the Everlys' parents and we were invited to sit on the stage. Just before they started, the lights went down. There was some sort of electrical failure, and the only light was from a few windows—and it was said they should just play in the dark. Donald didn't want that, and he walked out and was interviewed on the bus. Phil stayed sitting on the side of the stage and asked his mother and father to sing along with him—and the three of them did. It was historic; you'd never see that again."

At the other, more typical Netherlands shows, Ike picked some, to much applause, and Margaret appeared, too, clapping along, but she wasn't singing, and when asked about that, Don would explain bluntly, "She's really not much of a singer." She didn't appreciate her obvious second-class status.

Multiple people in the Everlys' small and sometimes barely noticed traveling entourage, including Bekkers, Ann Marshall, and Don Wayne, saw squabbling between Margaret and a prematurely aging Ike that belied the press's picture of a "blissfully happy" couple on their "second honeymoon." Out of public view, she was often shouting at him bitterly and caustically, to the others' discomfort. The working situation only increased Margaret's grievances as the tour moved on to England.

"Everybody was wanting to talk to Ike all the time," Don Wayne recalls, "and I would get him and one of the boys to sing a verse or two to show how they were raised and what they used to sing on radio as a family. But no one seemed to be interested in her as much as they were interested in the father."

The brothers were booked for a two-week stand at the Batley Variety Club in West Yorkshire, known for featuring American acts, and they reverted to the nightclub style there, with Don's acerbic banter intact. At one show, Bekkers recalls, they were singing Merle Haggard's "Sing Me Back Home," slowly, "and people started whistling because it took too long, for them." Many in the audience were still just there for "Wake Up Little Susie."

Waddy Wachtel recalled, "Within a week, we had the both of them up every night, after the show, singing and playing. It's the Everly Brothers in my room, and it's the most incredible sound you've ever heard....That's when Donald showed me the open-G intro to 'Bye Bye Love.' I'll never forget that. It was like somebody slapped me in the face with a wet towel. On stage we'd been doing the songs all slick and wrong, and I hated it! I asked him if he'd let me teach the band the right way to play the songs, and he agreed."

The tour event that resonated with Phil and Don most, as an important life marker, was their October 12 show at London's historic Royal Albert Hall. Loudon Wainwright III was the opening act; tickets were sold out the day they went on sale, and it was as fine a setting as they'd ever been able to have Ike perform in.

Kathy Cole, who'd been the British Everly fan club secretary in the sixties, arrived at the show with a friend, and they were just outside the hall when Phil emerged from a taxi and introduced her to the woman with him—his mother. Phil offered them better seats than the ones they'd paid for, and they headed backstage to collect them. "The boys were running through some songs with their Dad," she recalls. "He was charming and very good looking for a man in his sixties; I noticed a lot of his mannerisms were identical to the way Don and Phil did and said things. Margaret was friendly and talkative; she said Ike was going on stage with the boys and I said that she should, too, and make it an Everly Family show. The three of them stopped and looked at us; I thought Don was about to come over and kill me, so it was maybe not such a good idea."

Margaret sat with Kathy through the show, watching the audience respond, making comments. Years later, she would tell her friend Penny Campbell Loewen of a decision that she made just then, after being essentially pushed aside on the tour: "If I'm disrespected like that, I don't need to go with them any more." She didn't, and it was by now apparent that however much she'd been a driving force in their early years, her role in her sons' professional life was now marginal. On her own, she stepped up her uncontested role as the family liaison to the fan clubs and fans in general, handling photo and merch requests and charming strangers, as she well could, while playing the role of Mother of the Everly Brothers for all it was worth. That would go on for decades.

The brothers themselves were delighted by the reception Ike received. "That really moved us," Phil would recall. "It was an important thing to see him take his guitar style out of Kentucky into this fantastically beautiful venue, and to see him getting a standing ovation."

Warren Zevon, unused to playing a venue anything like that, or to the surrounding hoopla, was struck by the whole scene, as well as Don and Phil's commitment to the work: "They played a sold-out gig in Albert Hall, and it'd be just like *A Hard Day's Night.* They'd send us out one exit to be trampled, so they could get out to their limo through another exit. And then a week later we'd be in an oyster bar in North Carolina playing to three people.... The best thing that I learned from them, and always admired them for, was that they always sang the same, as well as they could, which was incredibly good. We had chills all the time.... That was real impressive."

In early November, back home, work resumed on the RCA album, including several numbers by Nashville songwriter Dennis Linde, of "Burning Love" and "Goodbye Earl" fame—not particularly memorable, although one, the dark "Christmas Eve Can Kill You," would later be a favorite in collections of punk-rock Christmas songs. The Everlys and company were apparently just trying to be *done* with the whole endless project, even if it meant accepting weaker numbers. Fortunately, there were two stronger tracks still to come.

Rothchild thought maybe a change of scenery could help, and what became the album's title track, John Sebastian's "Stories We Could Tell," was due to be recorded, so he suggested they move recording equipment to Sebastian's house in Laurel Canyon, where there'd been some band rehearsals. John liked the idea, since his wife was quite pregnant, and he could stay close.

They got to it the night before Thanksgiving. Sebastian, another early Everlys fan, recalled, "Paul was not happy about all of the bickering that was going on between them. He said, 'Don, you take one mic. Phil, you take the other one, and John, you just sit in the middle and do your guitar part.' So, I'm just sitting there between them as kind of a peacemaker...while they're both singing a song I wrote specially for them....It was better than any childhood dream I could have possibly conjured up."

The final song that made the album, "Up in Mabel's Room," was old-school crooner pop written by Phil and Terry and sung solo by Phil. It wasn't recorded until mid-January, after club shows like that ill-attended club stand in North Carolina that Zevon mentioned. Each brother now had one cut without the other on it.

There were weeks more of overdubbing and tinkering with instrumentals; the whole process had become agonizing. Phil deemed it "hell on earth." Don decried that there was so much layered onto it just so "people could justify their existence" and please friends who wanted to contribute. "You couldn't hear anybody. One or two tracks I felt you didn't know Phil and I were *on* it." That was no exaggeration.

The critical reception was mixed. In *Rolling Stone*, Bud Scoppa praised it for demonstrating that "Don and Phil are not forever trapped in their own pasts," but questioned the production and lesser song choices. In the LA *Times*, Robert Hilburn called it "their best album in years, a coherent, confident, and contemporary undertaking with a theme—the trials of touring musicians." Julie Webb, at the UK's *NME*, was shocked by the obscured vocals and absence of harmonies. The commercial reception was meager, for all the endless tinkering.

In April, John Sebastian joined the brothers in singing "Stories" at the Palomino. In an interview with Mary Campbell of the Associated Press, Phil noted that he's "been interviewed so often he'd rather not go that route any more," then blurted out, "We cut this very expensive album for RCA and they're trying to get publicity to sell some!" These were not likely the sorts of comments the label was looking for. He goes on to mention solo albums he and Don would be doing under the contract.

Disappointed and talking vaguely of some "business hanky-panky" with the RCA Victor contract, the Everlys returned to their touring rounds with little changed but an uptick in tension. Don exchanged his "happy hippie" headband for a new dark beard, often accompanied by a scowling expression, quite a different image.

Phil admitted, "Everything was straining...I suffered from an acute case of stupidity; we'd get at odds. We always had a very volatile kind of thing, where we both were very opinionated about what we do. It was nothing that you could lay your finger on—more frayed nerves, frayed times, divorces, just life struggles, all the things you can be going through."

Both brothers began to cite alimony payments as a reason for the ever-constant touring, new for them to even mention, bitterness showing. "I'm sure we've earned millions, but we're not millionaires," Phil would say. "Don't forget, we're both supporting ex-wives, and they get expensive." Don said, "Our ex-wives own a piece of the Everly Brothers, so we're all on tour together—except they sit at home. In two months, I'll finish paying off a 10-year property settlement with my *first* wife. I'm glad to be rid of her; you can print that."

As their spring North American tour got underway, a show at New York's Philharmonic Hall, with Fleetwood Mac opening, was sparsely attended. (This was the version of that ever-evolving band featuring Bob Welch and Christine McVie.) During the same New York stand, they taped an appearance on *The David Frost Show*, which would have consequences, sooner and later.

On-air, they described writing "Cathy's Clown" together, a narrative that would later be contested, and Don, in keeping with their tradition of meeting women while doing TV appearances, met a coproducer of the show, Karen Prettyman. Dark-haired, with Native American roots, she was smart, had that TV production experience, and quickly evolved into being both his life partner and, in effect, his personal manager. Another sudden move, but Don Everly seemed always to have the next woman in mind as he left one.

Live-in girlfriend Ann Marshall had been traveling along with him as late as the recent North Carolina shows but wasn't able to join him on the oncoming tour promoting the new album. She recalls, "My sister had a son staying at the farm with us, so I was going to join [Don] a few weeks later, for my birthday. Well, by then he had met Karen. Years later he said to me, 'If you had gone on the road with me, we'd still be together.'"

Maybe so, or just something that cost nothing to say. Realizing that Phil had left her just around her twentieth birthday, and now

Don had, close to her thirtieth, Ann soon sent a celebrated telegram to Margaret: "Happy Mother's Day—and thank you for not having a third son."

A few weeks later, on July 15, 1972, Phil married his own TV-appearance-sparked companion, Patricia Mickey. Ike told Nashville columnist Red O'Donnell that he and Margaret couldn't make the wedding, the second of Phil's they missed, because "we're working on the weekends now and can't make it to the West Coast." Margaret tended to be standoffish with her sons' succession of women by this point, figuring they'd all just come and go. Patricia was initially busy in Los Angeles herself, shifting from chorus girl to actress, with parts in such television series as *Emergency!* and *The Sixth Sense*, and the daytime soap opera *The Young and the Restless*.

For their next album, Phil and Don were committed to avoiding the excesses of making *Stories We Could Tell*. "Hell, I can cut a record in three days in Nashville," Don told those at RCA concerned with *Stories'* expensive slog. "So, I called Chet up … and I said, 'We're probably gonna do that country stuff, like we've always done.'" It wouldn't take just three days to do the job there. It took four.

Chet Atkins, some eighteen years after they'd first met across that fairground fence, would be producing them outright for the first time. He was now a powerful force on Music Row, and at RCA Nashville in particular. Together, they'd make an efficient, universally applauded Everly Brothers album. Phil enthused, "It's amazing to go into the studio with him and see musicians performing differently. *We* sing differently … in front of Chet."

The personnel would be Music Row A-Team players, 1972 edition—Pig Robbins on keyboards; Pete Wade and Bobby Thompson on additional strings, banjo included, joining Chet himself; Weldon Myrick (a Lubbock-raised friend of Buddy Holly) and Hal Rugg on steel guitars; Johnny Gimble on fiddle. This was going to be a country record—modern country.

Don and his new companion Karen picked the songs. Some returned to the work of old compadres—Holly's "Not Fade Away," written for them in the first place, and "Rocky Top," the best-known song by the Bryants written since they'd last worked together. The brothers sang gleeful blood-harmony versions of some recent "outlaw country" songs—Waylon Jennings and Willie Nelson's "Good Hearted Woman" and "Ladies Love Outlaws," and Don essentially solos on Mickey Newbury's dark but nostalgic "Sweet Memories." They're understandably both right at home with Roger Miller's unflinching look at the exigencies of marriage, "Husbands and Wives."

Once again, there were some songs as personally significant as any they wrote themselves. They took up John Prine's famed song of Muhlenberg County loss, "Paradise," and even more on target were two songs by the comparatively obscure Texas singer-songwriter Gene Thomas, from the Acuff-Rose songwriting stable. His "Watchin' It Go" asks, "Where do you go when you've been watchin' it go?" Quite a relevant question now, and not yet answered.

The second Thomas song, "Lay It Down," is as pointed a description of Donald and Phillip Everly's "twenty-five-year fight" as anybody has written or would write, though it hadn't been composed made-to-order. They sing it on record as if their fate depended on it. It says what neither of them were prepared to admit—yet—so in retrospect it feels prophetic: "Tryin' hard to leave the load...It's so hard to lay it down...Lay it down, brother, lay it down...Take us from our self-made hell, find a way to lay it down." It became the devastating, deadly serious opening track of their album with the far less imposing title *Pass the Chicken & Listen*.

Multiple reviewers called this one their best album in years, strong contemporary country, but country radio ignored it, still viewing them as apostates. There were limits to what even Chet

Atkins and the generally unidentified, half-imaginary Nashville Establishment could actually make happen. "We all thought it might make it, but it's very hard to bring somebody back like that after they've been cold so long," Chet would comment sadly. "Lay It Down" and "Not Fade Away," pulled out as singles, didn't chart at all. It was the age of albums now, not singles—but the album was no commercial barn burner either. Don Wayne, recalling their disappointment, notes, "This was supposed to be a fresh start."

With little alternative, Phil and Don did as they'd been doing for years—they hit the road. They quickly assembled a new band, Zevon, Wachtel, and company being busy, with Sammy McCue on guitar, Ron Coleman on bass, and Gene Gunnels on drums. After a quick tour across Canada, it was back to England, Scandinavia, and Germany again. In London, Don suggested to Danny Holloway of *NME* that he was considering doing some solo shows in "underground clubs" when he got his projected solo project done—though he doesn't know what that will be, what it will sound like, or where it will happen, clarifying the lack of clarity.

A degree of "just going through the motions" malaise could overcome Everly Brothers shows once again, and weariness and cynicism in their public comments. It was noticed; that *NME* interview was headlined "Frustrations in Golden-Harmony Land."

"We've done it all, pretty much," Phil suggested. "I don't think there are any categories left that we haven't been put in during the last 15 years." In Canada, Don told reporters, "I can sing the old ones without feeling *anything*," as if this were a great new achievement for him. "Some of these tunes you might have heard in the back of an automobile. . . . We may be playing to kids who were conceived to our music. It's entirely possible."

A late October appearance on the British *Beat Club* TV show well illustrates what people were lamenting. The recent "Stories We Could Tell" and "Good Hearted Woman" songs come off well enough, but on "Bye Bye Love" and "All I Have to Do Is Dream" they look profoundly bored and remote, and sound like they'd rather be anywhere else. The light show behind them distracts from the proceedings, but not enough.

At year's end, Phil was in the studio in Hollywood beginning work on what would eventually be his promised RCA solo LP, produced by Duane Eddy. A range of musicians they'd been working with took part—James Burton and Earl Palmer, Warren Zevon, Buddy Emmons, and members of the current touring band. The songs were mainly originals cowritten with Terry Slater, but it would take the better part of a year to finish it, with life intervening. Phil, taken with ESP and the like in this period, would offer "special thanks" to psychic Jacqueline Eastland on the album cover when it emerged. It's unrecorded if she foresaw any of the events that would ensue over the year ahead.

The brothers' shows returned to the "some rock, some country" mode in the wake of their recent contrasting albums, so they'd appear in shows with Marty Robbins and Kenny Rogers on one hand, then in a Wolfman Jack–hosted "Superstars of Rock" lineup with the Who, the Hollies, and Badfinger. Warren Zevon rejoined on keyboards in the spring.

In early 1973, John Huddy noted in the *Miami Herald*, "Something is missing, as if they were performing their nightclub act by the numbers...[smiling] their distant smiles." The *Calgary Herald* scolded, "Everly Bros. don't try hard enough to deserve a comeback." The *Toronto Star* homed in on Don's louder and more aggressive new singing style, even on the country songs: "Too much of the music had apparently stayed in the city too long....The result was like walking into some small town restaurant and turning up the jukebox too loud to listen."

In May, they had a far-from-small two-week stand at the Sahara in Las Vegas, costarring with Nancy Sinatra, who'd been crossing the pop/country lines herself and knew plenty about show business families. Cowboy sidekick Pat Buttram appeared on the bill, too. The set featured breakneck-speed versions of their old hits, novelty "special material," and a turn on "Sweet Dreams" with Nancy, backed by Warren on piano. It all looked placid onstage, but during rehearsals Phil and Don got into a bitter argument, lashing out at Nancy, too. After shows, Don and Karen, Warren, and his fiancée, Crystal, hit the craps tables; Don won big one night and split the winnings with them—a momentary win at a tense time.

Opportunities never seemed to quite pan out, and Don and Phil were thinking seriously about bringing the Everly Brothers act to an end. Performing together had certainly ceased being any pleasure, and the money, while often still pretty good, was not enough to compensate. On top of that, Karen Prettyman was suddenly gravely ill with spinal meningitis. "And all the while," Don would recall, "my advisors were saying 'Hey, c'mon, we have a tour going soon.' The Everly Brothers were supposed to be more important than *anything*—and I was tired of that. . . . Miraculously, Karen recovered, fully. That changed my mind about what was really important in life . . . I told my people: 'I quit. I'm never going to sing as an Everly Brother again.' I took Karen home and looked after her."

Phil would later tell author Roger White that Don had called him, saying it was time to take time off from each other, two years with no working together, no contact even, and he'd agreed. The two of them would be asked about the reasons for the split for the rest of their lives, separately and together, and because they were reluctant to rehash it, then tired of being asked, speculation lingered about what single unnamed cause or event was "really" behind it. The simple, overriding truth was that they'd both just plain had it.

Phil said, "We had a big three-year deal in Vegas. Really a lot of money . . . and we put it all aside. It wasn't a matter of money. . . .

Donald decided not to do anymore—and we didn't.... We got off the treadmill, and very few people could."

In practice, there was one last set of shows coming up, already booked, and they decided to make those official farewell performances—shows back at the John Wayne Theatre at the Knott's Berry Farm amusement park, on July 13 and 14. Don Wayne was given advance warning, recalling, "They told me to start looking for another job, because they weren't going to perform after Knott's Berry Farm." After a decade as road manager with them through so many ups and downs, Wayne walked, their early warning providing time to move right on to another job elsewhere.

On the thirteenth, they announced publicly that the next day's show would be the last, and that they were canceling all of the rest previously scheduled. Don told Robert Hilburn, "I've been wanting to quit for three years now, and it's finally time to just do it. I'm tired of being an Everly Brother... I've got to find something else." The announcement meant press, friends, and fans from near and far would be there for the occasion.

They arrived separately. Phil and wife Patricia waited in his dressing room. Warren Zevon and Crystal were on hand as Don, distressed, nevertheless held court and had multiple margaritas before they came onstage for the first of three shows scheduled for that night. Don's timing and pitch were off; he was unfollowable. His stage ad-libs included telling the audience, "I don't know what you are doing here," and he misidentified band members. Phil tried to restart several miscued songs, with noticeable embarrassment and frustration.

Bill Hollingshead, the park's entertainment director, decided to engage the curtain of falling water that marked a performance's end after just five mangled numbers, saying it was the "emotionalism" of their last show together that had led to Don's below-par performance. Phil, heading for the side of the stage, suddenly halted, smacked his guitar on the floor, and spat out, "I quit!" as he left.

Don, foggy enough to imagine this had gone well, stood there saying, well, he'd just have to go on anyway. Hollingshead actually changed the marquee to read "The Don Everly Show." Though people left, he went on, skipping the usual duo songs. When an audience member asked where Phil was, he replied, "The Everly Brothers died ten years ago."

As global headlines were blaring news of the breakup and this final show fiasco, Gram Parsons and a young woman he'd had backing him on his first solo album's vocals were recording in Hollywood. They were working up Everly Brothers–inspired duets for his next album—the Bryants' "Love Hurts," "Sleepless Nights" (sung as Don had instructed him), and "Brand New Heartache." Her name was Emmylou Harris.

Everly Brothers and Bob Dylan songs had been mainstays of her repertoire since she was singing folk at the University of North Carolina at Greensboro in 1965. Gram had led her more directly into country music, and to these duets. Their recordings would add another way, and another generation of evidence, that the music the Everly Brothers had made together would stay in the public ear and consciousness—even when they were not promoting it themselves. This new duo would play in Houston on a bill with Linda Ronstadt and Neil Young, where Linda met Emmylou for the first time. They could soon be found, in private at first, working up close, sibling-like harmonies, which they loved. Ronstadt would recall thinking, "We should be the Everly Sisters."

For the next ten years, Phillip and Donald Everly would virtually never be in the same place, or even speak to each other.

How either would move beyond the working duo that family, success, and then audience insistence had imposed on them was about to be tested. Don would need to contemplate actually being the solo singer-songwriter he'd long speculated he should have been. Phil could now sing lead, following his own instincts, not his big brother's. They'd both be asked, constantly, if they'd be getting back together. Neither saw that happening.

Chapter Ten

DON
1973–1982

"THE EVERLY BROTHERS GOT TO BE SO SIAMESE-LIKE, IT WAS DEBILI-tating emotionally," he'd tell one reporter, on a rare occasion when he responded to questions about the duo at all. He'd add, "People were always coming up to me and asking, 'Which one are *you?*' For a while, I thought about changing my name." And, "I really regret that we hadn't made the split earlier."

In 1973, Donald Everly, of the famous Everly family, had been performing for some thirty years, virtually never alone. Now he tended to announce things like "I've always been a solo singer—solo first and foremost...I've *always* thought of myself as a solo."

Who he was and what he performed were evolving. Sometimes, he was in that "I'm absolutely always country" mode. Sometimes that would be modified now: "*Country rock*—that's what I've always done...I wanted to be Hank Williams—*and* Bo Diddley."

In the months following the breakup, he'd get back to work in that country-rock mode, fairly haphazardly, but far from "solo." Don was thirty-six, but he'd never had the chance to experience the "buddies as new family" period so many dive into in their twenties, postcollege or on a first regular job. He jumped at the chance to make up for that now.

The main location was a joint in Calabasas, California, about thirty miles from downtown Los Angeles in the San Fernando Valley, an area ranked wealthier even than Beverly Hills today, but not so much then. The Sundance Saloon was housed in a compact, rustic building constructed in the mid-1800s as a stagecoach stop; it was now a welcoming dive where area musicians home from touring could try out material without media glare.

Tuesday nights, typically off-nights everywhere, were packed, the small stage given over to a house band led by a sharp rhythm section—the Everlys' frequent bass player Ron Coleman, and drummer John Ware, known for work with Linda Ronstadt and Mike Nesmith's First National Band. Don became their regular lead singer. Sitting in, casually, would be country-rock cream—John Hartford, Glen Campbell, Doug Dillard, Byron Berline, Glenn Frey and Don Felder from the Eagles, Jackson Browne, and even Bob Dylan.

The celebrated Buddy Emmons, who'd remained close to Don, became the regular steel player, an attraction in itself. He'd recall attending Sunday chili parties at Don's Laurel Canyon apartment prior to taking the gig: "Someone always brought a little pot, for those who cared to indulge. There were always interesting people at Don's parties, from actors to artists to writers to musicians, a wide range of topics was open for discussion, for those who could keep up." He was struck by how "erudite" Don was. "After the feast and patter, Don would get his guitar and sing bits and pieces of new songs he was working on; those who'd brought instruments would join in." Harrison Ford was a guest on at least one occasion.

Don invited Crickets Jerry "J.I." Allison and Joe B. Mauldin, who'd relocated to LA, to take part, and they became regulars as well. The lineup kept getting stronger. Allison gave a call to his old guitar ace buddy—and since 1962, Phil Everly's buddy, too—Albert Lee, who had returned to the UK but was now back with a successful country-rock band, Heads Hands & Feet, signed to Capitol Records. As Albert recalled, "Don called Jerry, and Jerry said, 'I've got Albert Lee here from England,' and there was a kind of silence at the other end of the line and Don said, 'That's *Phil's* friend, isn't it?' We went out to the Sundance Saloon, and I sat in with Don and had a great time and I immediately became Don's friend...I think he really liked having a sidekick there, because he missed his brother, in a way." Albert and drummer Peter Gavin from his band joined the regulars.

A measure of the audience response was memorialized in song. Inspired by Don's performances at the Sundance shows, Ron Coleman worked up a number that, with some additional lyrics by Gary Stewart and Bob Melton, became the hard country ballad "Honky Tonk Man," recorded by both Stewart and Lacy J. Dalton. It goes, "All of the ladies that swoon at his name...come around, every time he's in town, just to see the honky tonk man."

A fledgling steel-guitar player, Vietnam veteran Jimmy Eaton began attending the shows weekly, sitting up front so he could watch Buddy Emmons's every move on the pedal steel. Recalling the three-hour, improvisational shows, he notes, "Don sang anything like Porter Wagoner, Ernest Tubb, Haggard, or Buck Owens. And not just the country bar band stuff, but more high-energy, more Eagles/Outlaws kind of stuff—country rock."

Emmons particularly enjoyed playing with Albert and would take part in sessions for Don's next solo album. He'd be invited to play on Phil's first, too, so he'd recall telling himself, "I guess I can say I've recorded with the Everly Brothers." When he left the area, assured he'd find more regular paid work in Nashville, he suggested this newcomer he'd been mentoring take his place, and Jimmy Eaton became the new Sundance Band steel player.

Of playing behind Don, Eaton recalls, "He could communicate quite clearly, in terms we understood. He was able to tell us what he wanted, and we just did it. Everything was cool. The one driving factor was that we were supposed to have fun with what we were doing; he had gone through that really hard patch where he and Phil broke up." There was just one taboo subject. "Don never, ever said a word about Phil—period."

As for the appearance of extracurricular substances on this scene, he comments, "The only real parking lot scene going on was, well, you know [i.e., weed]...but nobody would get so they couldn't stand up or anything. And there wasn't that much *alcohol* consumption; players could get a drink per set at the bar, but it was just beer and wine."

Musicians who popped in for the Saloon shows became the core backup for Don's second solo album, *Sunset Towers*, named for the apartment building he lived in and where, initially, it was being recorded. The sessions would take some fourteen months total.

The contract with RCA that theoretically offered both brothers solo albums had died quietly, so Don turned to Lou Adler and his Ode label, as he had with his 1971 solo outing. If loose live shows at Sundance had allowed him the fresh pleasure of playing music with buddies, with no pressures or demands, the recording sessions, similarly loose at first, proved chaotic and undirected. If Don wouldn't take charge, Adler wanted someone else to step up.

That turned out to be Heads Hands & Feet's vocalist Tony Colton, since that band's Albert Lee, Pete Gavin, and electric guitarist Ray Smith were already in on the sessions. As Albert would recall, "Tony...being the pushy kind of bloke that he is, took over everything....Don didn't really have a lot of input." The overall effect would be a production still under the influence of British psychedelia like *Sgt. Pepper* and *Satanic Majesties Request*. When they moved the work to the Ode studios for better focus, Carole King was in one adjacent studio recording *Tapestry*, James Taylor was in the other.

With his history of abiding (or instigating) take after take back at Warners, it's not surprising that Don liked the 1970s rock production atmospherics—essentially, just taking all the time you want. "Musicians can be more personally involved and reflective," he said, praising that work style. While proclaiming, despite much evidence, that his own concept of producing a full album on the theme of loss was being executed, he was clearly relieved not to be the project's overseer or even author of the music: "I like the freedom of being able to be an interpreter of songs, rather than the writer of them all."

And that's the most curious thing about the project, given the chunks of new compositions Don was showing people and his often-stated goal of featuring himself as a singer-songwriter. Just two of the ten songs that would emerge were contributed by him, "Helpless When You're Gone," a hard country weeper with a seemingly personal and revealing sentiment, featuring Emmons's steel, and "Evelyn Swing," a lighthearted, 1920s-style change-up, as close as Don would come to inventing an Ike-like ragtime number.

All of the other tracks were written by Colton and Ray Smith, some along with other band members. The ballad "Did It Rain," which has a strong, straightforward vocal from Don and memorable give-and-take between Albert Lee's guitar and Emmons's steel, is particularly effective. Don noted of the album as a whole, "It was sort of combined—country singing with the English rock sound. I enjoyed it; I really did."

When the record got generally positive reviews but didn't sell, his tune changed, crediting Albert for contributing strongly, but suggesting he really hadn't gotten along well with Colton. Ceding so much control to somebody else just didn't work for him very well. Albert viewed Don as still seriously pained and conflicted by the break with Phil throughout the process. That new "Helpless" song went, "A song can take so long...It reminds me of you; that's something you would do; I'm helpless when you're gone."

When released in August 1974, a club tour in support was organized, but Albert was already booked for a tour with Joe Cocker, so Don turned back to the recently married and still financially challenged Warren Zevon, initially joined again by Waddy Wachtel, who'd begun making a name for himself working with Carole King. When Waddy couldn't work extended parts of the tour after all, Don hired a still fairly obscure guitar player to join the band and sing harmony—Lindsey Buckingham, who was, of course, soon called on to join Fleetwood Mac along with his partner Stevie Nicks. Buckingham would say, "The tour was a real thrill for me, because I'd always been a big Everly fan—and I got to sing Phil's part on 'So Sad'...I still get chills thinking about that."

There was one show on that tour that meant a lot to the whole gang, particularly to Don himself, at the Exit/In club in Nashville, where Roy Acuff, Wesley Rose, the Bryants, Roy Orbison, and Chet Atkins all attended. The tour drummer, Eddie Ponder, recalled a union representative threatening to stop the show for back dues Don owed, and Chet stepping up with a wad of cash to pay up for him on the spot. The band all visited Ike and Margaret; she made biscuits and gravy. Zevon and Buckingham sat around picking with Ike—and were delighted to have the chance.

While Warren worked with Phil more than Don in these solo years, he was managing the rare feat of working with both brothers in this era of their separation—and liking it. Don was already on record as to how valuable he thought his keyboard work was, and Warren would say, "You don't have 'Bye Bye Love' and 'Wake Up Little Susie' without those guitar riffs we all remember, and they're *always* Don Everly. Don may say that he's playing Bo Diddley's lick, but it's the modesty of a genius. They're *all* Don Everly parts."

By this point, Zevon was also expressing how he'd come to view the Everlys, obliquely, in his song "Frank and Jesse James." Well known later, it places Phil and Don, unnamed, as more outlaw-like than they ever really were, but the important similarity for him was how those James brothers had kept at it, persevered against odds, "riding, riding, riding," as the song puts it. Warren used this same touring band on his demo sessions, a step that eventually led to his successful placement of songs with others, then to his own recording career, beginning in 1976. Both Everlys provided backup on those demos, separately, and Phil would appear on Zevon's 1976 album, harmonizing on "Hasten Down the Wind."

Liverpudlian connections continued. In 1974, George Harrison recorded a dark version of "Bye Bye Love" that functioned as a bitter kiss-off to the other Beatles, at about the same time Paul McCartney, recording in Nashville, was prying details from Chet Atkins about who played what on the Everly Brothers' hits.

Don's new solo album had not resulted in much new income, and now the sometimes meager tour audiences gave him pause—literally. "When that didn't make it," he said, "I figured it was really time to take a break." The mood back in Los Angeles certainly seconded that notion. Don found Lou Adler and Ode held him personally responsible for *Sunset Towers'* lack of commercial success, and other labels uninterested even in speaking with him.

"All of a sudden," he commented, "I was no longer asked to be at the party. I was off the 'A' list. There wasn't any room in the Mercedes for me.... The decision to move back to Nashville was made *for* me." To the *New York Times*, he complained, "Out there, everything is your last hit or your last movie. These people—they chew you up and spit you out."

And so, with the kind of abrupt change characteristic of him, Don and Karen Prettyman married, on May 5, 1975, and relocated to Nashville—the first time he'd lived there since 1960. It was the place he'd call home for the decades ahead. She kept on working as his manager once he got back to work, but for a while that break he talked about was real.

They moved into the Iroquois, a somewhat out-of-the-way, unflashy apartment complex, and kept a low profile. They didn't even own a phone, purposely, and Don was spending his time fishing with Albert Lee and occasionally checking in at Acuff-Rose. Royalties from his songs and Everlys records were enough to get by on—"mailbox money," as Nashvillians call it. "The hardest part," he'd say, "was all of a sudden not having anything to do, but...I had more friends [and] more to talk *about* than where I was playing next....I didn't sing or pick the guitar for a couple of years."

The places he tended to find those friends were Brown's Diner, country deejay Johnny Potts's Sutler Saloon, and Melrose Billiards—all favorite gathering places for local musicians, as Brown's remains to this day.

The Nashville Don returned to featured some music makers very different from those he'd known in the late 1950s, or even when making *Pass the Chicken*, drawn to the city by the country rock the Everlys had recorded themselves and Nashville-made projects from Bob Dylan, Ian & Sylvia, Joan Baez, and Kris Kristofferson. He had no interest in joining the mainstream country bar-and-fair circuit ("I'm not a good old boy; just can't do that"), but these more recent arrivals were relatively cerebral, renegade singer-songwriters. They were prone to downplaying their unmistakable intellectuality for the public, but they had many things besides gigs or gear to discuss.

In those circles Donald Everly found a crowd in which he fit right in, and in his own mind, could begin to carve out a new, individual identity.

Many of these artists were working with or simply hanging out for fun with the impish, Falstaffian ringmaster-producer "Cowboy" Jack Clement. Jack's history went back to producing Jerry Lee Lewis and others for Sam Phillips at Sun Records and George Jones in Texas, as well as writing hit songs such as "Guess Things Happen That Way" and "Just Someone I Used to Know." On any given day you were likely to find Don chowing down at Brown's with two substantial singer-songwriters Jack was producing—John Prine and Townes Van Zandt—or chatting with Jack himself about what they imagined they might do. Don tended to sit in the seats at Brown's along the front window, where you could surely be noticed while working hard to seem uninterested in it. His slow return to performing followed a similar pattern.

He began playing with some of those new friends in small Nashville honky-tonks such as the Sutler—essentially reproducing the comfortable, informal music-making situation he'd had back at the Sundance Saloon out west. As he'd explain, "Nobody knew who we were; I'd sing any song I liked just for free beer...I needed the stimulation of performing where my name wasn't plastered in big letters. It was good for me."

In June of 1975, Linda Ronstadt's dramatic, rocking take on "When Will I Be Loved" was being heard just about everywhere, as it reached number two on the US pop charts, and number one country, renewing media and popular talk about the Everly Brothers. Don claimed, not very credibly, that he didn't have time to check out Phil's new releases—but this unavoidable, huge chart success apparently grated. It was the one big commercial song Phil had had before, and here it was back on top again. And that was the unstated impetus, and certainly the background, behind one of the longest-lasting clashes the brothers and even their own nuclear families would have.

In Don's recollection, this was when he first began to question the writing credits for their biggest hit of all, "Cathy's Clown," sending a letter to Phil raising the issue. Del Bryant, who would watch this all play out over decades, recalls this clash as "the biggest fight they had," and the timing of its beginnings, as the Ronstadt record was exploding, no coincidence: "Don wanted his own huge hit. . . . And he wasn't one to easily give credit to other people."

Both brothers had described earlier how Don had been working the song up and Phil came over and contributed some verse modifications before it was ready. Don was now suggesting that whatever Phil had added had not added up to cowriting the song. Today, when the songwriting and motion-picture worlds both feature "credit bloat," where someone in a room as a record's made suggests changing the drum beat between two verses winds up credited as a song's cowriter, and movies credit the "assistant to the truck driver's hairdresser," it may be hard to grasp that smaller contributions once might have been excluded from the royalty payout.

The question was less cut-and-dried then. Recall how Felice Bryant sometimes added some bit to a song of Boudleaux's and would choose to not take credit for that; at other times she saw her contribution as more substantial, and she'd make sure she was named— though in their case the money was all going to the same house either way. When the "Cathy" authorship became a legal battle, that alleged questioning 1975 letter to Phil never surfaced, but the subject would arise more seriously by 1980—with lawyers involved.

One irony of any envy Don displayed concerning "When Will I Be Loved" was that, very shortly, he was honored for a major revival of a song that was indisputably his alone. A year later, Connie Smith would take "So Sad" back to the higher end of the Hot 100 country music chart. It was and remains always ripe for recording by others, and with that and other new versions, Don received a BMI award for the song having passed a million airplays.

More poignantly, there was a life-changing milestone event for the whole Everly family in the fall of 1975. Ike and Margaret performed one of their own shows back in Kentucky, in the hamlet of Drakesboro, southeast of Central City, then Ike began coughing seriously while stopping in to see his sister Hattie. Back in Nashville, the doctor found a spot on his lung, calling for an operation, and pneumonia followed. He was playing the Ike Everly–model guitar his sons had given him on that day he had to be rushed to the hospital. With Margaret, Phil, Don and Karen, and teenage granddaughter Venetia Ember on hand, Ike died on October 22, just a few weeks after that last show. He was just sixty-seven.

In the wire service report that appeared nationally, and even in Kentucky obituaries, he was referred to, inevitably perhaps, as "the father of Don and Phil Everly, popular singers of the 1950s and 1960s," and, incidentally, also a "country and western singer." Given the enormous mark he'd made on both of his sons, as both musician and father, his funeral and burial at Rose Hill Cemetery in Central City, Muhlenberg County, was one somber event that they both attended, seriously grieving.

Phil would recall, "We didn't talk for...five to six years, until we met on the day when Dad was in the hospital and had an operation, and then again at the funeral. And when we talk, we always talk like there's nothing, like we'd just seen each other the day before. It wasn't like we'd stood around and snarled at each other."

Don, who almost never attended any funeral, went into a deep depression, according to author Phyllis Karpp. First cousin Ted Everly, son of Ike's brother Leonard, observed, "Uncle Ike's death had completely overtaken him." The months that followed were a time of private contemplation. A strong reminder of what the Everly Brothers had had was Warner Bros.' issuing of the LP *Walk*

Right Back with the Everlys (20 Golden Hits), which introduced new audiences to strong but underheard parts of their catalog from those years, as well as more familiar Warners tracks.

For Margaret Everly, this was necessarily a weighty, pivotal time. That guitar Ike had in their living room would stay there. In fact, she would keep the entire house intact as it was just then, nothing removed—Phil's black bedroom, instruments, the collections of Don and Phil's stage wear, Everly Brothers memorabilia and correspondence from the fan clubs, paintings by Don.

She would point this out over the forty-six years remaining of her remarkably long and active life to guests who stopped in to talk with her there, and in her travels, and she'd keep on handling distributing Everlys merch to fans worldwide. In effect, she took on the role of ambassador of "the Everlys" and interpreter of their story to fans in the world at large. She would maintain and guard that identification, however up or down her relationship with her sons would be. For much of that time, she didn't actually see either of them all that often. She would never remarry.

When Don returned to music making, he again engaged in some musical identity remodeling, edging away, at least temporarily, from "We were always country rock" toward a focus on outright contemporary country. The changing Nashville scene and what "country" could now include made that relatively easy. He'd refer to rock and roll as *avant garde* country music," and summarized bluntly how he now wanted to be understood: "I want you all to know me as a good, modern country singer—and forget that I was ever an Everly Brother."

He sang some backup and wrote liner notes for Don Gibson and Sue Thompson's duo album *Oh How Love Changes* at Hickory Records, produced by Wesley Rose, putting him back in the vicinity of that complicated father figure. The most lasting product of that reconnection was an album he took up there in February 1976.

"We have always been good friends," Don said of working with Rose again, "and it just seemed the right thing to do. I'm always one of those persons who go on impulse." No question about that. Wesley put out a press release heralding Don's return to his roots in country, and, of course, Mr. Rose had never been excited by the Everlys' move toward pop in the first place.

The album would come together in three sessions spread throughout the year, and it would emerge as a collection of tracks of three minutes or less—the opposite of 1970s rock album construction. The veteran musicians behind him included Grady Martin and Reggie Young on guitars, Buddy Emmons on steel, Pig Robbins on piano, and Kenny Malone on drums; it was Music Row old-home week. When a reporter asked Don about that, he acknowledged the familiarity: "Yeah, I feel at ease. Actually, that kind of recording style I helped *establish* in Nashville in the early years." At times, a string section complemented them.

The four initial tracks recorded included just one Don Everly original, the jaunty "Oh, I'd Like to Go Away," in which a weary former world traveler expresses interest in getting out of Tennessee and visiting Iceland or China... or maybe just North Carolina. Two became a single promoted and played. The magnificently sung and touching "Yesterday Just Passed My Way Again," written by Mr. and Mrs. Whitey Shafer and first recorded two years earlier by Don's idol Lefty Frizzell, was coupled with "Never Like This," a contemporary country love ballad. This was Don Everly singing with his full lyric-painting power, the vocal tics and embellishments that had disturbed Phil and some audiences simply gone. It put him back on the country charts, where he wanted to be.

He happily attended Nashville's annual country deejay convention and the Fan Fair extravaganza, where country stars and fans met face-to-face. He'd recorded Don Gibson's "Legend in My Time" with singer-songwriter and Dylan sidekick Bob Neuwirth for

Neuwirth's solo album. They were taking in the deejay convention together when they ran into the multitalented Jim Rooney, who'd just relocated to Music City. Don had met him back at the Newport Folk Fest of 1969. Jim quickly became one of Don's regular eating, drinking, and socializing buddies, joining Don and Karen at their home while, as Jim recalled, "Don whipped up a gourmet meal and we talked about music, books, and art." Rooney joined the informal music-making get-togethers at the Sutler Saloon, which would soon lead to something new and ongoing.

In August, returning to recording, Don and company locked down two more love songs from Whitey Shafer, and the song that would provide both the album's title and a memorable single, "Brother Juke-Box." Written by famed Nashville songsmith Paul Craft, the track featured driving guitar by dependable earworm-creator Reggie Young. The song had special resonance with Don's audiences, given its metaphor that has "Brother Juke-Box," along with "Sister Wine," "Mother Freedom," and "Father Time," as the *only* family the singer's "got left." The single only charted at number ninety-nine, but it provided the model for later versions by honky-tonk heroes Keith Whitley and Mark Chesnutt and would be one of Don's lasting, impactful efforts.

The final four tracks, recorded in early November, were the most surprising, all written by Don himself. "Turn the Memories Loose Again," the album's closer, directly addresses how he looks physically different now (everyone notices the changes, and too frequently feel free to comment on them), and how he doesn't *sound* just like he did "back then" either, but he can sing and, as the title says, "turn the memories loose" again.

The other late tracks were new versions of "So Sad," "Oh, What a Feeling," and "Since You Broke My Heart," all first recorded by the Everly Brothers and now sung at the tempo and with the emphasis he chooses, as if he wanted to show how he would have done them alone if it had been possible. He does them well; they work, but they haven't made the harmonious brotherly versions any less the ones recalled. Don would say of this sudden decision to record from the catalog he'd avoided, "I got away from them for three years...it became very difficult to do them; I'm beginning to like them again." "Since You Broke My Heart" was released as another single, with its B-side a take on the Bob Wills classic "Deep Water," which had been written by Wesley's father Fred Rose.

A clear consensus has grown that of his three solo outings, this third album, released in 1976, was the most successful, effective, and lasting. It had the additional benefit of opening significant contemporary country shows and festivals to him. His full-tilt return to the country scene was in England in April, at the International Festival of Country Music staged at the ten-thousand-seat Empire Pool arena at Wembley.

It was a three-day fest that included, in days order, very established stars (Loretta Lynn, Don Williams, Carl Perkins), revered elders (Don Gibson, Jean Shepard, Hank Thompson), and on the third day, Don in a lineup culled from that hipper new country scene—Emmylou Harris, Mickey Newbury, the Dillards, and Tompall Glaser.

Announced, again, as "returning to his country roots," he sang "Brother Juke-Box" and his new slower version of "So Sad," then called on a somewhat nervous Albert Lee to join him not just on guitar, but on a vocal return to "Bye Bye Love," "('Til) I Kissed You," "Cathy's Clown," and "Walk Right Back," shocking people pleasantly with the vocal harmony. A few weeks later, after nearly two decades, Don returned to the stage of the *Grand Ole Opry* in its new, larger home, along with Albert.

In 1978, in addition to returning to that spring Wembley festival, Don and Albert toured across the UK with Marty Robbins. A reviewer in the UK's *Country Music People* actually complained that they'd performed too *many* Everly Brothers oldies. Don had his wish about being taken for a contemporary country artist, not an Everly Brother—and that's what he got for it. There'd be a similar performance at a three-day country music festival at Rotterdam on the same trip, with a virtually all-mainstream country cast.

Despite the charting singles, the intractable Wesley Rose was predictably unenthusiastic about the contemporary, mildly rocking version of country Don was pursuing. "Again, it got difficult to work with him," Don said, "so I got myself off that deal." He would do next-to-zero recording in the years that followed, but the environment remained essentially country—by way of that emerging Nashville singer-songwriter scene.

He sang backup harmony along with Albert and Rodney Crowell on troubadour Guy Clark's self-titled album, and then early in 1979, he harmonized with Emmylou Harris, now Nashville-based herself and more strongly country-oriented, on her recording of the Louvin Brothers' "Every Time You Leave." This was tight harmony singing as he'd been used to, with a duet partner adept enough to pull it off.

Don would later expound on how this Nashville environment became his permanent home: "People ask me why I live where I live. It's because I can stay a songwriter for the rest of my life here . . . I was very frustrated musically before I started writing again." His writing output would not be huge, but it would be steadier.

Coincidentally, his perennially ambitious mother Margaret, who'd occasionally worked on writing songs with Ike back in the Shenandoah days, was now writing some herself, collaborating with writer-producer Norro Wilson, known for his songs for singers in the Billy Sherrill "countrypolitan" stable—George Jones, Tammy Wynette, and Charlie Rich. One of their collaborations, "Move Over Juanita," appeared on a single by country singer Margo Smith, whom Norro was producing.

In September, Don made a surprise appearance at the annual Buddy Holly Week of shows and festivities in Hammersmith, London, overseen by Paul McCartney, who now owned and was promoting the Holly song catalog. Close Holly associates including María Elena Holly and Bob Montgomery flew over for the events, and Don was invited to join in by Crickets Allison, Mauldin, and Curtis, Nashvillians now as well and part of Don's regular social life.

Wife Karen accompanied him on the trip, and Albert Lee appeared for a "Bye Bye Love" duet. Don backed Wings' Holly-crazed Denny Laine on "Raining in My Heart" and sang "Maybe Baby" and "It's So Easy" with Paul and the Crickets. It had to have been a kick for them all; it certainly played like it was. The finale was "Bo Diddley," with Wings and the Crickets, Don, and Albert all performing a number from a performer who'd inspired them.

At the after party, Don first met Rockpile's Dave Edmunds, a devotee of '50s rock of all flavors. They sat up late at the hotel where both were staying, singing the old Everly Brothers songs, with Edmunds taking the high Phil parts. The following year, Edmunds and Nick Lowe, his Rockpile partner, recorded a four-song Everly Brothers tribute, included as a seven-inch bonus record alongside the only album issued under their band's name. That Everly-Edmunds-McCartney combination would have further reverberations up the road.

Don was meeting new people back home, too. Among the evolving regulars at Brown's Diner were several who'd feature prominently in the next years of his life. Jim Rooney introduced him to singer-songwriter Pat Alger, a Nashville newcomer who'd once been a folk musician in Atlanta but was better known for upstate New York work with the Woodstock Mountains Revue, alongside Eric Andersen, John Herald, and Happy and Artie Traum. Though he'd seen the Everlys at Newport, he'd never met them.

"At Brown's," he recalls, "guys like Don could go be themselves and nobody would bother them at all. It was great for him to just shoot the shit in a bar and maybe go play some pinball." Don would give him the chance to jump-start what had felt like a fading career and he'd eventually emerge as the cowriter of massive country hits such as "Small Town Saturday Night" for Hal Ketchum and "Unanswered Prayers" for Garth Books—a unique folk-to-chart career path.

Alger's opportunity, very low-key at first, came as Rooney talked Don and his buddies into organizing into an actual band—the Dead Cowboys, with Don as lead singer. (If the name was inspired by how they felt after a night painting the town with Cowboy Jack Clement, they never said so.) Pat was recruited to be the regular solo opener for Dead Cowboys shows.

The band's international cast included Phil Donnelly, Irish guitarist; Tony Newman, who'd played with David Bowie and Jeff Beck in England, on drums; Lamar Hill, who'd been in Doc Watson's band, on keyboards; and Rachel Peer, then John Prine's wife, on bass and vocal. Jim Rooney was often in there with them, too. Don was admirably protective of that band, whose players certainly weren't joining in for money; he'd see to it that venue operators they dealt with treated them well.

"Don had a sense of himself of being the boss," Alger observes, "but with the Dead Cowboys band, most of those guys were pals, so that was less so; he didn't seem like the person telling everybody what to do." In this informal setup, Don would sing everything from "T for Texas" and "Tumbling Tumbleweeds" to occasional rearranged Everlys hits with Rachel taking Phil's part, some of his solo material, and on to "Good Golly, Miss Molly" and Blondie's "Dreaming"—one more dream song for the collection.

Rooney recalled, "Our standard of success was that Phil Donnelly needed to be levitating at the end of the evening. He'd get excited and started hopping...until finally both feet were off the ground." Mission accomplished. Music journalist Bob Oermann, who'd review their first scheduled show, suggests that their sound is best understood as "cowpunk," the harder-edge country-rock style of the time, and a term usually applied to outfits such as the Long Ryders, Rank and File, Lone Justice, and Jason and the Scorchers.

Oermann had only recently moved to Nashville himself and was stunned, his first week in town, to find Don and John Prine casually eating at Brown's on either side of him. As the Dead Cowboys began regular Monday night shows at J. Austin's, a club in the basement of the building that would later house the Bluebird Cafe, he'd note of Don, "He's maintained that sweet, angelic quality that the Everlys always had, but he's toughened up enough to give his stage presence an edge." Don sent Oermann a thank-you note for the review—an unexpected, unusual performer response.

Don would sometimes get away from the music business by taking time to fish on Nashville's Percy Priest Lake. Food and drink played a noticeably large role in the gang's ongoing talk and time together—not unusual among performers in general, but more marked given Don's foodie tendencies.

John Prine, then in his self-described "wild years," recalled arriving at Brown's at about three thirty in the afternoon to meet up with Don and Townes for late breakfast, then heading to Melrose Billiards for a beer. (By this point, John and Don had figured out that Prine's grandfather had sometimes picked with Ike back in Muhlenberg County.)

Pat Alger, another regular dinner guest at Don and Karen's, recalls, "We *never* talked about music; Don and I were swapping recipes...I had taken a cooking class with Jacques Pepin, and I had some specialties—one of which was this tomato sauce. It was almost too simple for Don to wrap his head around, so I cooked it for him, and then it was 'Oh, wow; this is incredible!' Karen was a real pleasant person, and had a good sense of humor, and she liked to eat and have a good time, too. They were interested in a lot of things....I did get the feeling she was keeping an eye on him, though."

The now annual Wembley festival, drawing over thirty-seven thousand in its 1980 edition, had expanded to play multiple European cities in France and Holland as well as the UK. With the "Yesterday Just Passed My Way" single charting, Don played those with Albert Lee, on an all-star bill that included, at Rotterdam, for instance, such twang standard-bearers as Roy Acuff, Faron Young, Bobby Bare, Charley Pride, and Stonewall Jackson. *Billboard* saw these festivals as important expansion outlets for country music.

Don took the trip as an opportunity to bring the Dead Cowboys with him for their own appearances—for a month across France on a bill with Wanda Jackson, then back to England for a few more stops. At the Venue club in London, Jim Rooney recalls, the audience expected them to show up looking like leather-clad Teddy Boys, apparently unaware of Everly evolution. Don, with Karen, Phil Donnelly, and Jim, then went on to an Irish folk festival, as a folkie acoustic group, before heading home.

Just one recording emerged from these early Dead Cowboy days, a single with Don and Rachel Peer singing he-said-she-said-style, on the pounding "Let's Put Our Hearts Together," a new one from Don produced by Rooney and backed by a "So Sad" solo update. "It was released by Polydor, in the U.K. only, while the band was on tour," Don noted. "It's a thing I wrote at Acuff-Rose. Got it put out in England and...nothin'!" It would be his only released record under his own name in this period.

The icy state of Don's relation with his West Coast family is well illustrated by the fact that he turned down Albert Lee's request to be best man at his Malibu wedding because, as Albert recalled, "he didn't want to come back to L.A., where there were too many bad memories."

His uncommunicative long-distance relationship with Phil now descended into the beginning of a long legal struggle. Don apparently got Phil on the phone, demanding that he take his name off of "Cathy's Clown," a move which, as we've seen, he'd been contemplating for some time. Their old buddy Joey Paige, called on to testify about the incident, said he was there with Phil when the call came, described it as "verbally violent," and that he'd heard Phil reply, "You know I wrote half that song," then relent to the demand.

In 1980, both brothers signed a document releasing all rights to Don. From then on, it was listed as a song by him alone, and that's where the ongoing songwriter royalties would go. Anyone familiar with the basic dynamic between the two brothers would have to conclude that with the authorship somewhat fuzzy from the start, and the haranguing about it hard, Phil simply acceded to Don's demand rather than go on fighting about it. It was the easiest course, and the way things tended to go. Battling was the only way they interacted now at all.

There were unquestionably long-simmering emotions still lurking behind the legal scuffling, complicated ones, as Pat Alger noted when he gave this angrier Don an unseen photo he had of the two brothers with Ike at Newport. Don was tearfully grateful to have it. In retrospect, Don would say of his feelings at the time, "It's like after a marriage has broken up; you miss the other person, but when you think about getting back with them, you start thinking about losing your personal freedom. It's hard, two voices singing as one."

He was hardly sitting around brooding all the time. His Nashville eating, drinking, and general carousing scene was well populated. One of the characters everyone around it mentions was a suave, pencil-mustached fellow known as Roberto Bianco, "the Romantic Voice of Our Time." He was not really Italian (real name: Robert Biles), and he became known for bringing incongruous, grandiose Las Vegas–style balladry to the Bluebird Cafe, haven for quiet, contemplative singer-songwriters. He'd been a bartender at J. Austin's when the Dead Cowboys played there and became part of Don's entourage. Journalist John Nova Lomax, then working as a waiter at their favored Faison's restaurant, recalled Bianco as Don's court jester, "human shield" for charming and distracting strangers who wanted to crash the proceedings, and also his "weed carrier," which meant grabbing the stash if local police got inquisitive.

Back at Brown's, Don met another person who would bring more dramatic changes to his life. Her name was Diane Craig. Dark-haired, notably sharp-minded, she was the daughter of Hollywood movie actor James Craig, and was a secretary for the Nashville musicians' union, where she'd met all the performers in town as they stopped by for their checks. She was also the former wife of acclaimed but troubled singer-songwriter Joe South; they'd had one son, who was now seven.

"I walked in, and Phil Donnelly and Don were just sitting at the bar at the entrance," Diane recalls. "Don was in his Peabody Hotel sweatshirt. He wasn't an 'Everly Brother' to me, he was a Dead Cowboy, and we had this shared circle of friends; I met him through Phil Donnelly. My first feeling was feeling sorry for him, understanding the industry. Like—what was he *doing*? Don and Karen were not on my radar in any way, shape, or form when Don came into my life. And I never got to know Karen well."

Don was about to make one of his abrupt choices. "The best way I can explain that," Diane suggests, "is that there was a basic, tragic insecurity in him. He loved women, and then he was really upset with them, and he was always...looking. Don could not leave one woman without being attached to another." That was certainly what the record showed—when he broke with Mary

Sue, with Venetia Stevenson, with Ann Marshall, and now, with Karen, he had a "next one" readied.

At a Nashville restaurant, Don and Diane parlayed with Karen directly as their relationship began. Diane recalls the subtext: "'Am I stealing your husband? I'm not that person.' And she says, 'You can *have* him.' So, I helped them with the divorce, and getting him money from BMI he hadn't been paid yet." Don moved into Diane and son Craig's apartment.

At the time, Karen was a known, working name around Music City herself. She became director of a go-to, three-thousand-listing directory of Nashvillians in music, the arts, and support companies, *The Nashville Hotline*, which was a bible for locals in the industry for a number of years. She put her video production skills back to work, too, linking film and music people in town. She'd have production roles on Johnny Cash specials, Waylon Jennings videos, and the well-recalled Hank Williams Jr. video for "All My Rowdy Friends Are Coming over Tonight." By March 1984, the *Tennessean* paper could headline "Karen Everly Key Figure in Nashville's Music Video Production." In 1987 she was diagnosed with multiple sclerosis, which severely limited the work she could do. She died at age fifty-three in 1997. Many of Don's closest associates had had nothing but positive things to say about her, calling her sweet, kind, and special, so some started out with serious doubts about this new Diane Craig person.

In the following months, Diane learned more about the kids out west Don was barely in touch with, and about the intensity of the break with Phil, and she began to press him, even nag him, suggesting that the brothers really ought to get back in touch or they'd regret it.

Later, Don would spell out some things he'd come to understand about his relationship with Phil: "When you grow up together, working together day in and day out...you don't know any other way, any other life. You tend to blame each other for all the things that go wrong in your personal life—divorces, whatever."

He was able to move past that now. He was indeed the one who loved to experiment, to close chapters, leave the past behind— except when he didn't. He was also the one who'd stuck with Acuff-Rose, who'd returned to working with Wesley Rose despite everything, who'd come back to country music and returned to Nashville from California. He did all of that.

And in November 1982, Donald called Phillip.

Chapter Eleven

PHIL
1973–1982

Looking back, Phil once remarked, "When we finally split, I did basically *nothing* for ten years...just quit thinking about it so much."

He was sometimes much busier than that remark suggests, but he did have periods when he didn't perform for years at a time, and didn't seem to miss it either. He was able to focus on things he'd rarely had time for—fishing, following baseball, and tinkering with the cars he loved and collected, which at times included a 1920s Duesenberg, 1930s models from Packard and Studebaker, and new Corvette and Jaguar sports cars.

"I'm happier," he'd say after just a few months of relaxing, "happy being in one spot, happy watching television. That's what I never had before." He'd mention that checking the tomato garden and feeding the dog were daily highlights.

He could also have more meaningful time with his son, Jason, who'd go from seven to seventeen in those years, and with his nieces and nephew as an active surrogate dad for Don's West Coast kids— Stacy, who'd go from ten to twenty in that span; Erin, from eight to eighteen; and Edan, from five to fifteen. In those life-shaping times for them all, their uncle really mattered. Phil spent the better part of the first post-split year at home with wife Patricia, who was expecting. On September 25, 1974, she gave birth to Christopher, Phil's second son.

As Jason, his first, later told *Rolling Stone*, "My father was a regular guy—the guy hanging down at the Home Depot or Walmart.... When I was in grade school, kids were saying, 'What's your dad do?' and I was like 'Oh, he's a singer,' but nobody had ever heard of him.... To me, he was just the guy who shot hoops with me... taught me how to sing and play guitar and spanked me when I didn't do my homework.... He was also a closet inventor.... He wanted to make a guitar with a speaker in it. It was heavy and it really didn't work."

Phil's RCA solo album, begun back when *Pass the Chicken & Listen* was still in the works, was finally completed late in 1973, and wound up with the less than enticing or enlightening title *Star Spangled Springer*. An illustration of said patriotic spaniel dog, dressed in a suit, graced its cover. Phil would attribute the title and image to having drunk too much wine.

He was less than motivated to get out and promote it, or to start performing solo, so the label showed little interest in the record either. Embarrassingly, it was released in Europe with a note from Phil addressed to international Everlys fans, written way too soon, assuring them of the duo act's "continuance" despite any "rumors" they may have heard. He goes on to acknowledge contributions to the project by Terry Slater, Warren Zevon, Duane Eddy, and wife Patricia.

As lightly as he took it, this was arguably Phil's most intriguing solo album. Seven of the ten tracks bore songs written by Phil with Terry, and two by Phil alone. Patricia appeared singing with him on two—and in a frisky, romantic photo on the album's back cover. The set sits squarely in the pop arena, though steel players are employed (Buddy Emmons, J.D. Maness) and, given that Duane Eddy produced the set, the guitarists were mostly associated with twang (James Burton, Richard Bennett, Duane himself). There are also delicate, sophisticated keyboard and horn arrangements by Warren Zevon, so the sound palette is varied and interesting. Phil had nothing but praise for Duane's production: "He has a great ability of getting the essence out of people, and also a tremendous eye for songs."

Phil's sensual side is more explicit; singing solo may have made that feel more appropriate. Bedroom sheets make several appearances in the lyrics. Also, British references are legion, so it's not all *that* star-spangled. It's an album about turning the page, and it goes for the unexpected—for the most part, quite well. Many of the songs turn the bucolic longings of country rock inside out, presenting nostalgia and longing for sophisticated women in the cities of Los Angeles and London while stuck out in the country. The best-remembered Phil original, the metaphorical closer "Snowflake Bombardier," is explicitly about page-turning ("Yesterday's dead and buried...but tomorrow's another story").

In a then-surprising twist, the Phil who'd been joining in on "Give Peace a Chance" on the brothers' TV show and was teary-eyed over the divorce from first wife Jackie, now sang "America—love it or leave it; think about signing up for the marines" ("Red, White and Blue"), and quoted state divorce decrees in an acerbic plea for poor put-upon male alimony-payers ("La Divorce"). "Poisonberry Pie" proceeds to mock bra-burning women's libbers while he's at it; this allegedly "relaxed" Phil actually seems testier. "Our Song," with its admission that "Lately singing don't come quite as easy, and I believe it's because we're both alone," may suggest one reason why. These songs marked Phil's more public turn toward social and political conservatism.

The one non-original on the album is a great what-might-have-been. Written by Mike Hazelwood and singer-songwriter Albert Hammond and first recorded in 1972 by Hammond himself, virtually unnoticed, the song, brought to Phil's attention by Duane Eddy, was the sweeping love ballad "The Air That I Breathe." In Phil's nimble hands, and with Zevon's orchestral and vocal arrangement applied, the song becomes a dramatic, moving anthem—pretty much the one the world would come to know, but not from this version. While producer and close buddy Duane saw it as a single, Phil nixed that idea on the grounds that it was too slow for that.

The Everlys' old friends the Hollies had plowed ahead since Graham Nash's departure in 1968, finding renewed success with songs such as "Long Cool Woman in a Black Dress" and "He Ain't Heavy, He's My Brother." (Now *that* one would have made for an interesting Everlys single.) As Holly Allan Clarke recalled, their producer Ron Richards's secretary had listened to Phil's album and suggested that "Air" could be a strong song for him: "I listened to it, and obviously felt that I wasn't going to be able to do it as well as Phil.... So they said, 'Do it the way Phil would sing it.'" Their version had Allan and Terry Sylvester, who now sang the Hollies' high parts, harmonizing Everly Brothers–style. It was a hit.

Bud Scoppa praised Phil's album in *Rolling Stone*, saying "With the past resonating just below the surface, and with...surprising poetic depth...there's a lot to be dealt with beyond the first few pleasant listenings." In practice, since it wasn't much promoted, not many people got the chance to hear any of it on release.

An opportunity that Phil did jump at was to host *In Session*, in 1974, a syndicated TV interview show focusing on pop music makers, particularly roots-music-identified ones, with thirty-nine episodes projected. He remarked of the career adjustment, "There are *other* things to do... I'm 34 years old, and I don't want to live the rest of my life as if the best part has already passed." With the disparaging interviewers of his youth clearly in mind, he added, "*In Session* is a concept I firmly believe in... because the performers can come on the show and relax... treated with respect instead of indifference. It's low-key; no pressure."

Six half-hour programs, videotaped in recording studio settings, RCA's and Capitol's among them, featured such guests as Kris Kristofferson, John Prine, B.B. King, Jackson Browne, and Dory Previn. Phil was adept as the interviewer, but the show tended to be broadcast spottily and in late-night slots, following the popular *In Concert* series. The show and the job would be over after just the six appearances.

Even while lying low at home, Phil had some notable interactions with old friends. When John Sebastian got around to recording "Stories We Could Tell" himself, for his *Tarzana Kid* album, Phil sang harmony; Lowell George of Little Feat was also on hand, as his "Dixie Chicken" was also recorded by John. A brief outcome was George's proposal that he should join Phil and Sebastian in a new supergroup, which were all the rage at the time. They tried some things; Lowell quickly realized that generationally and temperamentally, it was no-go: "Real great three-part harmony... but it could never have come to fruition, not in a million years. We were just not aligned."

Warren Zevon, still trying to write a hit that could spark his own frustrated career, was "hiding out" in Phil's guesthouse when Phil tossed an idea his way that worked. Among the late-night movies on TV that he now had time to watch was *Werewolf of London*, a 1935 horror film that struck a chord, at least as an image and rhythmic title. He suggested that Warren might be able to do something with that in some sort of dance-craze novelty.

Waddy Wachtel had a catchy riff waiting to attach to something; this was it, so the two of them tossed around comical lines. Waddy added the "ah-oo's," And that's where the "Werewolves of London" single that launched Warren Zevon came from. The Zevon-Everly connection wasn't well known at the time, but people might have noticed that Zevon's "Excitable Boy" song has one "Little Susie" murdered at the junior prom, Warren's idea of a salute.

Phil and Don, separately, both added backup vocals to Zevon's demo version of "Poor Poor Pitiful Me," recorded in Hollywood. Producer John Rhys, leading those sessions, recalled, "Warren got Don in first because if Phil hears it, he won't sing. So, we put both of them on, unbeknownst to each other."

By this time, Phil and Terry Slater had a relationship so tight that Phil considered him as virtually another, very different brother, the person who'd come to know more about him than anyone alive. Terry wrote with Phil regularly and arranged a new multi-record contract for him with England's Pye Records. Phil said, "I could have done a deal in the United States, [but] I didn't want a deal with any more gigantic record labels. Not that Pye isn't a big label, but you are aware of who is controlling what, like we had at Cadence."

Phil and crew were in London for months while those sessions ensued. He rented a flat in Knightsbridge for the duration, with only a short break between records. He learned to play cricket, drank a lot of tea, and briefly thought this might be where he wanted to live, before realizing that he was homesick for Hollywood. Patricia was initially there with him, but as her pregnancy progressed, she needed to head home, and Phil noted missing her terribly. His only performance while there was an appearance on Cilla Black's TV show, dueting on "Let It Be Me."

He did agree to interviews. Reporters just kept asking about his relationship with Don. "I don't know if we'll ever see each other again. . . . I just don't feel I want to see him," he told the *Evening*

News, adding poignantly, "When Don and I split, my father told me that I would never be able to match the Everly Brothers. But if I believed that, I might as well walk out into the ocean and start swimming."

Of the twenty-two tracks total on *There's Nothing Too Good for My Baby* (known in the US as *Phil's Diner*) and the follow-up, *Mystic Line*, Phil and Terry wrote thirteen. The album cover of the American version of the first one has Phil grinning in front of said diner, a beloved, repurposed-railroad-dining-car joint in the San Fernando Valley, an everyday-grub hangout for local musicians. Phil considered buying it, but he was turned down.

The *Phil's Diner* LP included a bouncy version of Eddie Cantor's 1931 Charleston number "There's Nothing Too Good for My Baby," origin of the British album title. Phil had been a Cantor fan since Ike exposed the boys to pop of the era in their childhood. Most of the new originals work hard to be MOR "easy listening," if with Phil's voice buried in piles of chorus and reverb.

Most attention has gone to the single "Invisible Man," a rocker about a call for his return by a girl he's ghosted, and to the dark track "It's True," to which Warren Zevon contributed writing along with Phil and Terry. It's about how heat and monogamy are strongest when they're fresh. On simple ballads such as "Too Blue" and "Caroline," a "girl back in Kentucky" song, Phil is perfectly effective, as would be expected.

During a brief return home, he made one of his rare live appearances of the time—a pair of shows at North Hollywood's fabled Palomino country music venue, emphasizing newer material. It would gradually become one of the most likely places to see him. He also attended a party Paul and Linda McCartney threw aboard the *Queen Mary* in Long Beach, attended by everyone from Bob Dylan, Joni Mitchell, and the Jackson 5 to Tony Curtis, Dean Martin, and Cher. The chatter may have been interesting.

With the first contracted album greeted with little more than yawns on either side of the Atlantic, when noticed at all, they changed the tone for *Mystic Line*. Zevon was back on keyboards and arrangements; he wrote the dark "January Butterfly" with Phil, which manages to be both ominous in sound and—since January butterflies are unlikely to last—a straightforward declaration of brief yet transforming love.

Phil's new "Words in Your Eyes" proceeds with almost military-march relentlessness—fitting for a ballad about realizing that the lover addressed is inevitably going to leave. He found himself, he'd reveal, "progressively...more emotionally involved with what I was writing....If I've written one by myself, it's straight from what I've lived." He also revisits two of his older songs—"Patiently," which had graced that Larry Barnes single on Calliope Records, and "When Will I Be Loved" taken hard-reggae-style, with a close seconding vocal by—himself.

Disappointed with Pye's ability to get either record heard, he pulled out of the contract with just those two of three projected albums recorded. Phil would dismiss both releases, saying that they "never really were an effort," and that "we were busy running around having a good time...and we did those very fast." He'd add, "Maybe the material was at fault, too....It was a little more abstract than most of my music."

Terry Slater, focusing more on music publishing, made a connection for Phil that helped. He was working for Sam Trust, a veteran of BMI and Capitol Records' Beechwood publishing arm. Sam was an innovator in the arena, founding a management firm that specialized in handling the administration work for small publishers—such as getting royalties paid and collected. Phil was among many Terry introduced to him. Trust discovered considerable payments Phil had not received from the Cadence years—inadvertently unpaid, apparently—and worked to get that error corrected. The amount retrieved was substantial; the working relationship would last.

And then, further into 1975, Linda Ronstadt's smash version of Phil's "When Will I Be Loved" put his most celebrated song and his writing back into popular consciousness, and also produced the most new income he'd seen in some time. Tanya Tucker recorded the song in those months, too, and Phil would be awarded BMI's Robert J. Burton Award for the most-played country song of the year. Felice and Boudleaux Bryant joined him at the award ceremony, proudly saluting their old friend and disciple.

When Phil returned to the Palomino, backed by Warren on keyboards and Sammy McCue on lead guitar, Patricia commented to fan-club eminence Heidi Ploen that Phil was visibly nervous before the show. The nerves continued; Art Fein reported in the *Los Angeles Free Press* that onstage "the look in his eyes could be accurately described as terror."

Phil was at ease on the public television series *Soundstage*, though, in a nostalgic dual appearance with Dion DiMucci—whom he'd known for years, though they'd not appeared together because the Belmonts and the Everly Brothers were both "white harmony groups" and promoter Irving Feld had kept them on separate Show of Stars itineraries. They sang Jimmy Reed's "Baby What You Want Me to Do" together and introduced Dion's "Queen of '59," which they then recorded. Phil also performed his new "The Words in Your Eyes" and poppy "Lion and the Lamb."

That pleasing 1975 career uptick was shattered by Ike Everly's death in October. Ike's illness and unexpected turn for the worse had come fast, and happened when there was no sign the Everly Brothers could be put back together, as Ike had hoped. This naturally hit hard for both brothers but Phil, as usual, snapped back faster. His penchant for at least seeming to put setbacks aside and moving on was evidenced in his quick return for two scheduled Palomino shows, just past two weeks after Ike's funeral.

The *Los Angeles Times* found in these appearances an "aura of insecurity" and "self-deprecation" at odds with the quality of the set. Phil would simply recall that they hurt: "I wasn't satisfied. I don't want to sing like that." He meant it; he began three full years with minimal public appearances, punctuated by some songwriting and a few media performances, but not before audiences.

There was another looming reason for his tenseness and that next long performance break. "I was getting divorced," he explained. "I was getting a lesson in life, and I was still a little *sick* . . . I'm the only person in California with a divorce lawyer on retainer."

And yes, the tone was the flippant one, self-deprecating indeed, he often took to announce hard news. Just a year and a half after Christopher's birth, Phil and Patricia were at loggerheads, and they would legally divorce in December 1978. "I should do 'La Divorce Number 2,'" he'd quip. "But I won't."

Some have suggested that one reason for clashes between them was that Patricia wanted to resume her acting career, and with his insistence on traditional gender roles, he opposed it. Ms. Mickey would go on to have one-shot television appearances on shows such as *Fantasy Island*, *Simon & Simon*, and *Empty Nest*. What lessons in life that Phil was suggesting he took from all this, he never spelled out—but he wouldn't marry again for two decades.

According to Don, he did call Phil on January 19, 1979, to wish him a happy fortieth birthday. There was zero music talk, but he no doubt heard at least a little about his brother's reasons to be less than cheerful. Phil moved to a house in Burbank, not far from the Warner Bros. lot, a few doors down from Andy Griffith, alone except when the kids stayed with him. A guest cottage in the back became his recording studio. He'd live at that address for fifteen years.

For less personal genre songs, he'd write with two collaborators—old marines and touring buddy Joey Paige, and veteran musician and songwriter John Durrill, best known for his role in the Ventures and Five Americans rock groups, and for composing movie soundtracks. They were still placing songs with others through those low-profile years.

In 1978 Tanya Tucker recorded the upbeat "Lover Goodbye," written by Phil and Joey, with Phil supplying close vocal harmony on her record. It's a kicky kiss-off song. It was around the same time that Phil contributed to the first of two Clint Eastwood "comedy with orangutan" movies, *Every Which Way but Loose*, playing himself at a club, singing "Don't Say You Don't Love Me No More," which he'd written with Paige, in a duo with Sondra Locke. Their song "One Too Many Women in Your Life" was used in the *Any Which Way You Can* sequel, and Phil and Locke sang "Too Loose" in that, written by others. He was finally dressed like a cowboy in a Warners Bros. picture, twenty years after trying to get there.

Producer Snuff Garrett, an old friend, worked with Phil on the Eastwood movie music, and he now produced Phil's return to album recording, the 1979 *Living Alone* LP on Elektra Records. Of the ten tracks, six were written with Durrill, two with Paige, one they all worked on, and just one, the title track, was by Phil alone. It sets the tone for the collection in its breezy sound, and it's certainly personal. It goes, "Living alone, love can never make you cry."

Once again, his vocals on the slower ones ("Love Will Pull Us Through," "Charleston Guitar") hold up best in retrospect, but the majority of the tracks are transparently trying to fit into the current disco-pop mode, with heavy orchestrations. Phil tries shouting over the din and it doesn't work so well. We're very far removed from country honky-tonks, even on "Buy Me a Beer," which has lyrics that would have been at home in them. The album was never widely released in the United States, but Phil's "Living Alone" song was also recorded by Johnny Rivers, and by his old acting-school buddy Dean Reed.

Reed had had a harrowing life since they'd been in Paton Price's class in Hollywood, having sung in Chile with leftist martyr-hero Victor Jara, been exiled from there by the Pinochet regime, and since been operating as a sort of prized-catch American movie actor and TV host working for the Stalinist East German state. "Comrade Rockstar" is how his biographer referred to him—or "the Red Elvis," forgotten in the West, a star in the East. It's a testament to Phil Everly's sense of personal loyalty that however politically conservative he'd become, he actually went through the checkpoints in divided Berlin to appear on the East Berlin–based *Dean Reed Show* in 1979 to sing "When Will I Be Loved," the part-German "Ich Bin Dein" ballad from the *Living Alone* album, and several Everly Brothers hits in a duo with Reed. Phil would be called on to talk about Dean and their relationship in multiple documentaries that emerged after 1986, when Dean was found drowned in a lake near his home, with a suicide note, real or planted, found in his car.

At the turn of the '80s, Phil was gradually regaining his appetite for performing, and began appearing regularly at the Palomino on Friday and Saturday nights. He said of that stand, "We do ten days to two weeks of rehearsal to play the two days.... When I open, I feel like my blood's really up and I'm really excited.... On Saturday nights I bring my kids and they sing." (Those kids included Don's. For instance, he'd sing "Bye Bye Love" there with teenage niece Erin, Don's daughter.)

"It costs me more than I make to do it," he'd admit. "I have people that fly in all the way from Texas." He particularly liked that he could introduce obscure newer songs; refreshing his Palomino sets became an impetus for writing more new material. Sometimes he performed with Joey Paige, testing songs they were writing together.

In lieu of the blood harmony he was most lauded for, he liked having crowds sing along, and never tired of finding singers for occasional duets. Johnny Rivers recorded a second side with him, the ballad "Dreamer," another dream song, of course.

In 1980, even as Don's legal maneuvers regarding authorship of "Cathy's Clown" ensued seriously, Phil's thoughts about his estranged brother were softening, which probably adds some additional context for Phil's decision not to fight having his name removed as cowriter. He didn't want to worsen the relationship just then, and he'd begun to admit that he just plain missed Don.

If Don claimed he wasn't paying much attention to the albums Phil was releasing, Phil noted hearing one of Don's Wembley festival broadcasts with Albert: "The one thing he sang which wasn't an Everly Brothers song was a Louvin Brothers song...I just thought, 'Don, why on earth don't you just record an album of songs like that?' It was so good...Don is possibly, if not the best singer in the world, close to it."

By 1981, he told celebrated interviewer David Wigg of the UK *Daily Express*, "All I know is that we need to resolve our differences at some point of our lives. I wouldn't want to die with this kind of problem." Then came further admissions about events going all the way back to childhood, their complex, different relationships with their mother, the hit years' pressures to keep finding more big ones, and the prescription drugs' effects.

The realizations had been hard come by; it was certainly brave of him to put these thoughts out there: "Donald was older, and so he had to carry the brunt of everything. I was sheltered, and I think that, in itself, was an asset. I didn't realize that until much later in my life. He also had more talent than I did. I hate to admit it, but now I'm 43, I can say it: His hands and ear for music are faster."

He was in England to promote a new song he'd written and recorded as a single for Curb Records, "Dare to Dream Again," potentially the lead-in to an album; the single was taking off. In what had to have been as much a surprise to him as it was for many, he now charted a series of singles—on different charts, on different labels, and in different countries.

"Dare," which he'd produced along with Joey Paige, reached number nine on the *Billboard* adult contemporary chart and number sixty-three on country. It's a love song that, not for the first time, suggests other contexts, too: "Dream again the dream we dreamed the first time . . . without you, I know I'll never dare to dream again." Fans could not help but be reminded of the first big "dream" song and who'd been in on that.

Phil would perform it on a London BBC TV special and talk vaguely of maybe touring behind it ("I want to stay in a very loose situation"). He performed it again in a Palomino show broadcast in May 1980, singing with "Everly sister" Emmylou Harris. They offered a duet medley of what she called, reasonably, "the dream sequence"—that new "Dare" number, followed by Roy Orbison's "Dream Baby" and "All I Have to Do Is Dream." The set put her on a short list of people who've ever sung harmony with both Phil and Don—separately.

It might be noted that Emmylou owned and was using regularly a Gibson J-200 acoustic, that first model guitar Don and Phil used, established by then as a go-to for country rockers. George Harrison used one, and in the first days of 1982, solo in a hotel room, Bruce Springsteen employed one as the central instrument in recording his celebrated *Nebraska* album.

The Curb single was followed by another, the peppy Phil-and-Joey-penned "Sweet Southern Love," which reached number forty-two adult contemporary and number fifty-two country early in 1981, either despite of or because it rhymed "land of cotton" with things "not forgotten" and mentions that he's a "ramblin' man." While the Curb deal did not yield an album after all, Phil was quickly picked up by Capitol Records for another charting single, the ballad "Who's Gonna Keep Me Warm," written by pop song-writers Kevin McKnelly and Don Stirling. It was a hit in the UK, which led to a bigger, more often recalled hit, at least over there, the top-ten "She Means Nothing to Me," a duet with Cliff Rich-ard, who had tremendous nostalgia value in Great Britain that he's never quite managed in the US of A. Singing backup on the single, and the Capitol LP *Phil Everly* that followed, was Fleetwood Mac's Christine McVie, a longtime Everlys fan; Dire Straits' ace guitar-ist Mark Knopfler was among the musicians—stars of yet another generation.

A half dozen of that album's songs were again written with Terry Slater. They'd come up with some fairly cute keepers, such as "God Bless Older Ladies," which surely spoke to a segment of Phil's audi-ence by this point, and "Never Gonna Dream Again," which posi-tioned itself to be the last in any future dream sequence.

The Capitol album was not rushed out in the United States, where they'd been marketing Phil, as Don was elsewhere, as *coun-try*, not pop. With the compact disc format breaking through, it would emerge in the States, slightly expanded, a few years later, as the CD album *Louise*, under much-changed circumstances.

Were Phil's charting songs suddenly "better," or these record labels more on top of marketing what he created? It's hard to make a strong case for either. What is clear is that what Phil was inclined to do, and how it sounded, was beginning to gel very well again with what substantial contemporary audiences *wanted*.

A glaring example: the song from the Capitol album that became an album title, "Louise," had been introduced by Ian Gomm, who like Everlys acolyte Nick Lowe was a veteran of the British pub-rock band Brinsley Schwarz. It was exactly the sort of breezy power-pop song (as such things came to be called) that suited Phil—and the Everly Brothers—perfectly. The "new wave" trend had the potential to reintroduce the Everlys sound, rather than to upstage it, as the British Invasion had.

It had become clear, though, that even as Phil found this level of success charting singles, there were limits to how far that could go as long as he was a solo act. He knew it, and spoken or unspoken, his friends knew it, too. As Warren Zevon put it, "People are used to the cake with the frosting, and they're reluctant to give an ear to half the recipe.... They were great singers individually, but together, they were sublime."

In November 1982, Phil told Peter Holt of the *London Standard* that from what he'd heard at second hand, arranging a show with Don back at the Royal Albert Hall might be conceivable. "Our kids want it resolved, and we want it resolved, but until Donald and I speak, nothing will happen."

A few days after Thanksgiving in the United States, Phil was interviewed on a Scottish-based country music show on BBC radio. The host, Barry Knight, played "That Silver-Haired Daddy of Mine" from *Songs Our Daddy Taught Us*, and Phil said, "My father used to sing that song, and when he would sing it, it would bring a tear to my eye. I never, ever hear the song without having that real great feeling a son can have for a father."

They finished up talking about "Dare to Dream Again," with its barely hidden brother-related subtext, which Knight referred to as its "overtones."

Don, at the split, had said not to bother even to call, so Phil hadn't. It was just short of a decade later. Donald called Phillip.

Chapter Twelve

REUNION
1983–1984

FOR ALL OF THE TREPIDATIONS THE BROTHERS EVERLY HAD HAD about getting back in touch, when it finally happened, it proved comically easy.

"We had sort of been in the back of each other's minds, I guess," Phil admitted. "It just took one little phone call to put everything behind us." And Don said, "We both knew we wanted it; words had been passed back and forth through friends. And then I just called Phil one day and said, 'How ya doin'?' And he said, 'Fine, how you doin'?' And that was it."

Accounts of their reconnection have generally focused on their shared interest in a musical reunion as the cause, some even suggesting they'd only reunited to make more money. That's not true, and harsh, if understandable. The way they spent the first six months following that call certainly suggests those narratives are well off base. This was foremost about reestablishing being brothers Donald and Phillip.

Don said, "I missed the relationship more than the singing.... The *first* thing people want us to do is sing. That's the same way it was when we were kids. People'd come over and say, 'Come on, Don and Phil, sing us a song.'" And as Phil detailed, "We settled it in a family kind of way; a big hug did it.... It was a personal thing... we started hanging out, just meeting to talk and going out to dinner like friends do—like *brothers* do."

Phil brought along more than a hug. Before they got together face-to-face, he'd turned his attention to an idea that was both sentimental and practical, that would salute the family past but also be of potential use now, commissioning Portland, Oregon, luthier Robert Steinegger to make him two identical custom guitars, signed "Everly" by Phil. They were dubbed "the Ike Everly model," and designated the D-50 because Phil had intended to present one to Don on his fiftieth birthday—February 1, 1987—father and brother guitarists both acknowledged. He just didn't wait that long.

These were flattops smaller than the familiar J-200 Gibsons they'd played for years before the breakup, with a different bridge, fancier gold inlays, and mother-of-pearl borders, but still with the signature double pickguards that said "Everly Brothers guitars." They would play them for the rest of their careers. Only fifty-seven were made, all ebony in color at first, then varied, and the originals would come to be owned and prized by select Everly admirers, including Paul McCartney and George Harrison, and the two Norwegian guitar players in the band a-ha (Terry Slater would become their manager). Gibson eventually made a model more like it.

Phil's son Jason said of the original his father gave him, "Fantastic proportions, beautiful sound and magnificent to look at.... It has [a] beautiful cherry wood back and a black Everly pick guard.... The Ike Everly shape is the best.... My father liked the Gibson

Everly models, but they were narrow. A fantastic stage guitar, but it was missing the fuller sound he was looking for."

That this peace offering to Don would be named for Ike is an indicator of something both brothers fully understood they'd never stopped sharing, separately or together—their reverence for their father's playing and desire to have him remembered and esteemed. It was no accident that they'd each been toying with the idea of returning to the Royal Albert Hall, the venue where they'd brought Ike Everly to his largest adoring audience.

Don was still living with Diane Craig and her son in her Nashville apartment. She recalls how in the summer after the ice-breaking phone call, the brothers reunited personally: "Phil and Terry Slater came to Nashville, and that's when the brothers got together. . . . We all go to the fanciest restaurant then—Arthur's—and Don and Phil are having a wonderful time. Don wants to come back to my condo, which we do. Terry is exhausted; he says, 'I think I'll just go back to the hotel.' Phil and Don that evening wound up just getting shit-faced; they had such a good time together. And that was when they started to make plans. Over the months from the beginning of 1983 through late September, they got the band together, found producers, and set up the concert."

Slater, back home in England again, but talking to Phil by phone virtually every day, would be the central mover and shaker in that succession of events. His and Phil's publishing company was still being administered by Sam Trust, who'd looked further into royalties both Phil and Don were owed, this time by Warner Bros., and as he'd recall himself, "got a ton of money" for them. That sat well with both brothers, of course, although it was Phil alone who paid Sam's administrative fee, as he had with the Cadence-era royalties.

Terry, Sam, and the Everlys began to consider business arrangements to make the most of a projected reunion, looking at Royal Albert Hall with a one-off, maybe two-night event in mind. Terry knew the management there, as well as top London promoters. Don and Phil had to consider what these performances would be, which ended their "much talk, no music" stage.

"We talked a long time before we ever played," Don told the *Washington Post*. Just to see how and if their voices still meshed, they staged early run-throughs with local musicians in Nashville, out of public view. Don would tell banker fan turned writer Roger White, "We just walked up to the microphone and said 'Right. It's "Bye Bye Love" in the key of "A."'" Phil recalled, "The first few notes were weird. It was like jumping into a pool not knowing whether the water was warm or cold.... But when we went into 'Bye Bye Love' I knew we could do it—even if I have to stand on tippy toe to hit the high notes."

Test passed, the brothers, Terry, and Sam got together for project discussions at Margaret Everly's house. Sam Trust recalls, "The first big Cadillac that they gave to their mother was still there. Don was very standoffish to me at first, knowing I was a close friend of Slater's." In their discussions, the idea arose of producing a video version of the concerts. Sam had packaged the lavish *Compleat Beatles* multimedia box set in 1981 and retained American Stephanie Bennett to produce a video documentary for it. He recommended Terry sign up her Delilah Films outfit to tape the Albert Hall shows, and everyone agreed to it. "Terry got together with the promotion people in London, where the Everlys were very popular," Sam recalls, "and they did a hell of a job putting it together and pulling it off."

It was time to assemble the band. Albert Lee was quickly agreed on by both brothers for lead electric guitar. This certainly appealed to Albert, who'd note, "I'd always hoped if they got back together, that I'd do at least *one* gig with the Everly Brothers." He was appointed musical director of the shows and would be playing with the Everlys, in practice, for over twenty years to come. Terry was assigned the role of hiring the rest of the band, which turned out to be three from Cliff Richard's outfit—Martin Jenner on guitar and steel, Mark Griffiths on bass, and Graham Jarvis on drums—plus Pete Wingfield on keyboards, an experienced blues-circuit player who'd become another Everlys band regular.

An Associated Press announcement of these Albert Hall plans was widely published, as well as the plans for a TV cablecast, a related album, and very possibly a tour to follow. *Variety* reported on the deal with Delilah Films to produce a videocassette and HBO cablecast version of the show for the United States; the BBC *Arena* series was the producer in the UK. Phil was pressed to explain what had caused the breakup in the first place, as he and Don would be virtually every time they talked to reporters. To the AP reporter, Phil answered, vaguely and briefly, that it involved personal family reasons, and that "I'll just mark it down, forget the yesterdays and move on to the tomorrows."

On this aggravating question, it was both brothers' way. They stopped detailing any of that for others, and very likely never really thrashed it out with each other, but their reluctance to discuss it only fueled speculation, some scurrilous. Don said, "Mostly I look forward to the next place I'm going to, the next audience, the next song. I'm having a good time."

As the September 22 and 23 show dates approached, Phil and Don flew to London and the band assembled for ten days of rehearsals, working up versions of the Everlys' songbook they would play. Albert would recall musical tensions in the early rehearsals, arising from the differing ways Phil and Don had been approaching the hits while they were apart, and the return of Don's unpredictable, ever-changing vocal attack. Phil even stayed away from rehearsals for a few days, and to make matters worse, some of the band's gear was stolen. They soon got back to their patented, eyes-in-contact, locked-in harmony, though—updated, with new arrangements that had room for live guitar leads from Albert and other '80s modifications.

Hanging around during the rehearsals was rocker Dave Edmunds, who'd met Don during that 1979 Buddy Holly Week after-party and known Albert for years. After one rehearsal, Edmunds related, the three of them "ended the day by putting away several pints of beer in a local pub." Dave attended the opening show, along with an English songwriting buddy, Paul Kennerley. The camaraderie would have musical aftereffects.

At a London press conference, Don and Phil explained how things would be sounding different now. Don said, "There's a lot more maturity in our voices and you can hear it," to which Phil added, "You can sing the blues at 20 and be blue; you can be sad at 20—but when you sing the blues at 40 you've got 40 years of blues and sadness. At 60 it'll be some other way." He was apparently already envisioning a long-term recommitment to the brotherly duo.

Virtually all of the journalists commented on how different they looked, Don especially, with his added weight and much-changed face, but they were comparing two men in their midforties to how they appeared when half that age or less. Don could confide when asked about it directly that he loved food and didn't care in the least anymore how he looked to people. That was an act of defiance of the audience's—and his image-oriented mother's—expectations.

By the time the show dates arrived, there were reportedly over sixty thousand requests for tickets; the hall seats twelve thousand. Some advised the Everlys to have a run-through somewhere more obscure, but they decided to forgo that. Phil recalled, "I remember how we felt having dinner in the hotel before the show . . . Pete Wingfield and I kept wondering how we had the nerve to go out there and do it without trying it out someplace else first."

And so, a highly expectant crowd, thrilled even to get in, was in place on the night of September 22, 1983, as dramatically, without hoopla or even an announcement, Phil Everly descended a staircase on the left of the famed Albert Hall stage and Don Everly descended one on the right. They wielded twin Ike Everly–model acoustic guitars. The crowd greeted them with cheers. The opening number, surely pointedly chosen, was "The Price of Love," in a hard-rocking, energized version that said instantly "This will not all be gentle, lilting balladry tonight, folks."

They sang into separate microphones now, instead of breathing on each other over just one. Albert was close behind them on electric guitar; pianist Wingfield was particularly conspicuous, standing and pounding the keys rockabilly-style. It was during a number that they'd sung hundreds of times before that the brothers began to make visible, emotional eye contact, sometimes tearing up, as they sang the opening lines of "Walk Right Back." Because now, face-to-face and eye locked to eye, it played quite differently, electrically so: "I want you to tell me why you walked out on me / I'm so lonesome every day / I want you to know that since you walked out on me / Nothing seems to be the same old way... / Walk right back to me *this minute.*"

Most all of the songs played differently. By the second night, the show preserved on the concert DVD, they both broke into perceptible, ironic smiles when the old narratives evoked histrionic teenage angst, twenty-five years after they were introduced. A familiar line like "I wonder if I care as much as I did before" had added context and personal implications impossible to miss, and they didn't miss them. Neither did the audience. Phil would tell Jim Jerome of *People* magazine, "During 'Love Hurts'... I got chills. You have to have been us and gone through it to have that moment. It was just that simple—and that complicated."

It all flowed, the songs hitting home, to the audience's visible and audible excitement, from that stately take on "Love Hurts" Phil mentioned to "Cathy's Clown," with its classic rhythmic chords slammed harder than ever before. Mid-show, the band stepped away and Phil and Don went into an acoustic set of old-time country songs their daddy taught them, very much with Ike in mind, ranging from a delicate take on the ancient "Barbara Allen" to the frisky hillbilly chestnut "Step It Up and Go," which Ike had performed on the same stage in 1971.

Inevitably, Don rammed improvisational vocal takes into some of his solo moments—notably in "When Will I Be Loved," announced as one "written by Baby Boy Phil," yet it all still fit. The range they handled across thirty-one songs, after all that time away from each other, was a testament to both brothers' professionalism, and also their real-time response to the moment. The days of autopilot run-throughs seemed far behind them. These were the Everly Brothers.

Don confessed to Patrick Carr of *Country Music* magazine that, during the show, "My song list and my lyrics fell off, so I was having to remember all that stuff after all these years, and I was sweating a little.... Phil was like the Rock of Gibraltar out there," to which Phil added, "Donald just says that.... Really, we're pretty stable. When we get on stage, we're on stage."

Don told the Albert Hall crowd, "We hope to keep doing this forever." And afterward, he suggested to UPI journalist Mark Schwed, "I think we sing *better*.... We're like a fresh group coming back out on the road." He bumped into Sam Trust backstage, walked up to the man he'd first been suspicious of as Phil's publisher, and said, "I want to shake your hand.... None of this would have happened without you." Flabbergasted and touched, Sam thanked him back.

Phil said, "That night was magical. Even separate from...what it meant just to my brother and me, it was something else. The audience was amazing. There was a flow of emotion as you rarely feel."

Diane Craig, on hand with Don for the duration, recalls a poignant, private moment from later that evening, at London's lush Allen House hotel: "At a wonderful party after the reunion concert, Phil was sitting in a chair, and Don was sitting on the arm of the chair. It was just a casual conversation; I don't know how it started or where it came from, but Phil thanked his brother for being the buffer between him and their mother—from the pressure she'd put on those little boys then, and since." Diane saw that as a perfect illustration of how thoughtful, accommodating, and conflict-abating Phil could be, and also how rarely the two brothers spoke about their mother's often-aggravating tendencies toward attention-seeking and agitating, however much she'd seen herself as "a buffer."

Margaret was not in London, and apparently hadn't been invited to be there. In this new flurry of interest in Don and Phil, she did see new opportunities for her own media appearances as the Everly Brothers' mom, however. She'd sometimes contacted local papers or TV stations when she visited friends in towns around the country, and as the reunion plans unfolded, she made herself available for interviews to multiple papers. She tended to focus on her own role in her sons' story.

She told the *Des Moines Register*, "I stayed neutral and out of the way all during the time they were apart. I didn't push them to get back together, but now that they are...I'm just as happy as you'd expect their mother would be." On Archie Campbell's Nashville Network cable TV country talk show, they discussed Everly family musical history. Since Campbell had known them back in Knoxville, she gave him some straightforward answers, but her more hesitant answer as to whether Don and Phil were "normal kids even after their success" would be, "Well—*yes and no*. You're bound to change when you meet success. I often wondered if I'd fitted them for the outside world....We had close ties with each other and that made the difference."

Reviews of the reunion concert were ecstatic. In the *Guardian*, Robin Deselow enthused, "Last night's stirring, highly emotional event was something truly special...quite extraordinary." Long-time fan Ray Connolly, writing for the London *Evening Standard*, said the Everlys "demonstrated to perfection that they have lost none of the extraordinary magic...those wonderfully plaintive voices as resonant as when we first listened to them," and lauded Albert Lee and band for underscoring "what terrifically inventive and exciting musicians the Everlys are." In the *Telegraph*, Charles Clover called the show "a triumph....The Everlys performed... with such immaculate phrasing and delicate, glistening harmonies that it was as if hearing them for the first time."

Afterward, Phil headed home, while Don and Diane joined Albert Lee and his wife, Karen, for some vacation time on the Continent, eating their way from Paris to Venice and Florence, with Don and Diane continuing on to Rome and Naples for some couple time alone. By the time the late December/early January TV versions of the show ran on both sides of the Atlantic, Don and Phil were encouraged enough—and in demand enough, once again—to have signed a new recording contract with the Mercury/PolyGram label, mentioning a projected new album wherever they were interviewed about the reunion show broadcast.

The Everly Brothers were back in business. And they had arrived at a point in their lives where, for now at least, they could be something they'd never quite managed to be before—adult friends.

Chapter Thirteen

BACK AT IT
1984–1988

Back home in Nashville, Don called Dave Edmunds to feel him out about producing that new album. Don said, "I was struck by what a pleasant guy he is. Then I thought, 'Well, we need a producer; Dave Edmunds would be a perfect choice.' I knew the record company would go for it." The brothers met with Dave in New York to make plans.

Some found the choice puzzling; as a producer, Edmunds was known for amiable yet raucous, updated rockabilly with the Stray Cats on one hand, and for dolloping on layers of synthesizer sounds on his own recent records on the other, neither typically parts of the Everlys' sound. In fact, the Everly brothers wanted to arrive at some contemporary combination of both, while maintaining their vocals as central. As Don put it, "We'd like to keep one foot in our original sound, but then we'd like to break some new ground, too... I think we're going to add some synthesizers." Edmunds was thrilled, but admitted, "I was terrified, but I said yes because I believe in saying yes to most things."

Scheduled to return to the recording studio together for the first time since 1972, the question was what songs to record. Phil proposed no originals, fearing the sorts of pop songs he'd been writing wouldn't be fitting, and left it to Don and Dave to find material. Don brought forward one song, the haunted breakup ballad "Asleep," from a set he'd written with Phil still singing harmony in mind, back before he'd even moved to Nashville. He also provided "Following the Sun," about leaving behind a "cold heart," a nod, perhaps, to his teenage hero Hank Williams, written by a man who'd now lived a whole lot more. And he suggested that they should finally get to "Lay Lady Lay," fifteen years after Bob Dylan had brought it to them.

Diane, whom the press was frequently mentioning as the highly trusted source of stability in Don's life and would be thanked in the LP liner notes, recalls, "When it came time to do these albums [this and its follow-up], it was Don and me going back and forth in a Toyota van listening to demos and music while Don chose the playlist. It was Don's party." He'd recall, "We literally went through hundreds of songs to find the right ones for us."

From his Nashville friend Pat Alger, came the driving "I'm Takin' My Time," about getting back together with a departed love—slowly. "Phil," Pat recalls, "said, 'If I were you, I'd write a song. I'm not guaranteeing it will be in there, but if Don and Dave Edmunds like it.' . . . So I called my friend Rick Beresford, a great harmony singer, and said, 'Maybe we can write something for the Everly Brothers, reminiscent but not just a copy of their old songs.' After that, Brenda Lee also used it, as a single."

Naturally, many of the demos Don and Diane were checking out had arrived via Edmunds. He detailed, "Mark Knopfler sent me a beautiful song called 'Why Worry,' and Jeff Lynne chipped in with

'The Story of Me,' a haunting song." The former was turned to later. The latter was projected as the album title for some time. Phil would mention how it raised a very old issue, which they were now able to take very lightly: "Don and I are two individuals, but.... you can't say 'the story of me-s,' you know, which we... laughed about. It's really the story of 'me,' the Everly Brothers." The romanticized video for that one places them in a huge British stately home.

Next, Dave recalls, "I flew to Nashville to discuss all aspects of the project with Don and Phil, and to sift through the material we had gathered.... Oddly, any song sounding remotely like 'The Everly Brothers,' would be automatically discarded by them."

That was not a universal perception—or experience. Dave's British friend Paul Kennerley, a longtime Everlys fan who'd, for example, collected all of their UK EPs, had made a name for himself with the "country opera" concept albums *White Mansions* and *The Legend of Jesse James*, harbingers of the Americana format ahead, featuring Waylon Jennings, Johnny Cash, Levon Helm, Albert Lee, and Paul's future wife Emmylou Harris. He'd since written singles for Jennings, Cash, and Harris including her hit "Born to Run," a song built on Everlys-like guitar riffs. After relocating to Nashville, he was doing demos in his home studio, one of which was for his moving, very Everlys-appropriate ballad, "The First in Line."

As he recalls, "I couldn't keep doing my own demos, and Emmylou said, 'Well, there's this young boy who's just moved here from California, called Vince Gill.' I paid him forty dollars a day. I'd done the track for 'First in Line,' and he sang it; the demo is fantastic. I sent a cassette to Dave, not knowing he was producing the Everlys." It would be the second single from the forthcoming album, a fan favorite that would chart country.

Edmunds made another significant call, with some trepidation. It would lead to Phil and Don's biggest multi-chart hit in over twenty years, some new "classic" Everly Brothers: "I decided to call

Paul McCartney. It was a harrowing ordeal, dialing the number of history's most prolific and successful songwriter, just to ask for a song. He...readily agreed to come up with something. 'Give me two weeks and call me.'... True to his word, he sent me a demo he had recorded of a charming song...which sounded perfect for Don and Phil."

Paul said at the time, "Dave had a lot of people asking him to contribute, and I said 'Yeah, please,' because they were one of the very first acts that influenced people like me.... The Everlys were very special.... So, when I got asked to write a song, it was a privilege—and an honor...I didn't want to come up with something that was wrong...and I came up with 'On the Wings of a Nightingale.' They liked it." Paul's song was chosen as the first single from the album known as *EB 84* in the United States and simply *The Everly Brothers* in the UK. Don loved its prospects from the first: "It's a...really melodic song. I'm thrilled with it, to be honest. He really put some thought into it."

It would rise on both the pop and country charts and to the upper reaches of the adult contemporary chart. This being the mid-'80s, there was a video, an utterly appropriate one, which had the brothers Everly resurrecting a junkyard '57 Chevy Bel Air and taking off in it, refreshed, as they sing, "I can feel something *happening*." It would be seen everywhere and contributed to the song's meaning—reclaiming that car, and themselves. Visuals worked for them once again.

After months of selecting songs, the sessions began in April, at London's Maison Rouge studios, with backing tracks recorded before any vocals. The band included Albert, Dave Edmunds himself and Phil Donnelly on guitars, Pete Wingfield on keyboards, Terry Williams or Gerry Conway on drums, with John Giblin or Jeff Lynne on bass and, at times, Gerry Hogan on steel guitar. Phil and Don had expected to record their vocals separately, but that wasn't optimal, so instead Don would work out the lead vocal in the studio, then be joined by Phil just as it was time to record, limiting time for disagreements. Without a word, they went right into their eyes-locked pairing.

"Suddenly," Edmunds would say, "their parachutes open, and when that happens—look out. You've never heard singing like it." Albert did recall some issues during production: "It was an odd situation. How can you tell the Everly Brothers how to sing? They didn't like being told what to do. Poor Dave had that thankless task."

The resulting album, coming on the heels of the reunion show cablecasts and the associated live recordings and videos, made Phil and Don Everly rock stars all over again, 1980s-style, and it enhanced their reputation as legends of both rock and country.

Rolling Stone's Kurt Loder said, "It would be wonder enough that a comeback album by the greatest white harmony singers in the history of rock and roll would in any way approach the timeless brilliance of their classic hits.... That *EB 84* not only equals the artistic peak of their youth, but in one case—with a song called 'On the Wings of a Nightingale'—possibly surpasses anything they've ever recorded, is surely cause for jubilation."

In *Country Music* magazine, a sophisticated bimonthly that could not have existed back when they entered recording, Rich Kienzle singled out Albert Lee's playing and the notably country "The First in Line," exclaiming, "That Don and Phil reunited was a pleasant surprise; that *EB 84* reveals them to be as vital as they were nearly 30 years ago can only be considered a triumph."

Rare dissenting reviews focused on what some experienced as a lack of sonic clarity, with the layers of synthesizers enveloping Don and Phil's vocals. In truth, the album was quite au courant in that. *Stereo Review* would praise Edmunds's production, specifically if peculiarly, for supplying the Everlys "a brilliant combination of Eighties sophistication and backwoods primitivism."

The Delilah Films team that taped the Albert Hall concert followed up with their projected TV documentary for the UK *Arena* series, *The Everly Brothers: Songs of Innocence and Experience*, later broadcast in the United States as *The Everly Brothers' Rock 'n' Roll Odyssey*. It has had a continuing role in the persistence of the exaggerated "Kentucky origin" story. The film takes substantial time portraying Don and Phil's visit there with relatives such as preacher cousin Ted Everly and Ike's surviving brother Roland, the union organizer, and even has them visiting a closed coal mine—a workplace they'd never entered in their lives. Muhlenberg County is presented as charmingly exotic, as if this were an anthropology special. Not for nothing did the destination sign on the crew's bus, off camera, read "WHERE IN THE HELL R WE."

Truthfully, their parents' place of origin did hold added sentimental pull for Don and Phil, now well into their forties, with Ike gone for nearly a decade. Producer Stephanie Bennett suggested the time in Kentucky sparked added connection between them. Still, while the film features meaningful interviews with the Bryants, Mose Rager, and Chet Atkins, it begins and ends implying that Kentucky church hymns and their summer visits as kids were central in forming their characters and style. Chicago, Maxwell Street, and even Shenandoah are barely portrayed, and Knoxville barely mentioned, formative as they all were in reality.

When Phil, puffing on a cigarette, is pressed to answer the wearisome question "Why did you two break up?," he brushes it off, firmly, as a piece of the past he won't let intrude on their present. Avoiding rehashing, limiting their months on the road together, and using separate buses and hotels had been carefully agreed on by the two of them precisely to avoid the all-too-familiar irritation of unending entanglement. Shallow accounts take those arrangements as evidence "they hated each other," when they were in fact intended to assure that sources of potential irritation would never reach that point. As Don told *People* magazine, "We're not taking any chances, this time."

Back in Nashville, bookings had begun for what would be the extensive 1984 Reunion Tour. For that, joining Albert on electric guitar and Pete Wingfield on keyboards, was busy session man Phil Cranham, on bass. They would be the heart of the Everly Brothers band for some eighteen years. Phil Donnelly, Nashville-based Irish buddy of Don and John Prine, played additional guitar for the next few years, along with the experienced, much-loved studio drummer Larrie Londin.

The tour reached across the United States and Canada that summer, then made seventeen stops in the UK from mid-October. There were no shows in California until the tail end of the American schedule, even when they reached the West Coast; the reasons were personal. Phil had to broker a family truce and reunion for Don, who was still saying of his continuing distance from his kids, "It's just the way it is. When you have nothing, *nil*, with their mothers but a lot of strain, it's better to stay away."

He apparently was getting reports about his daughters and son out there, was sometimes in contact with them by phone, and well aware that his son, Edan, now fifteen, and Phil's son Jason, seventeen, had begun singing together. He'd comment, "We aren't pushing them. We wouldn't do that to them." The only public photo that puts Don with his four kids together with Phil and his two would be taken backstage at one of those California shows, with broad smiles all around.

Don had been based in Nashville for close to nine years—which didn't mean he was stopping in at Margaret's regularly, no matter which woman he was living with. Multiple people close to the brothers have noted that their mother could be harshly critical and sometimes manipulative in private, even while presenting herself as hands-off and supportive in public. Nevertheless, Don did see her on occasion. There was a point around this time when Margaret was in the hospital being treated for a kidney issue, and Don and Diane visited her there; they also had her at their apartment for a relaxed Christmas dinner. It could happen.

Out on the road, with over forty stops at fairgrounds, casinos, and amphitheaters across the country, the crowds were substantial and enthusiastic, some there out of nostalgia, others, including new younger audiences, quite ready for the Everlys' updated sounds. Phil Donnelly would tell the *Los Angeles Times'* Robert Hilburn, "You ought to have been with us on some of the state fairs. The audience screamed so loud it hurt my ears. In Iowa, the state troopers had to hold the audience back."

Albert Lee described how Don and Phil were dealing with this return to the road: "They kept...to themselves, and when they wanted to go out to lunch together, they would, but they traveled in separate buses, and they had separate limos to the gig, but they'd chat and say, 'How was your day?' 'Oh, it was fine.' They'd get on okay, but sometimes it would get a little tense.... They learned to live with each other, and, fortunately, we had 20-odd great years."

Comedian David Steinberg was scheduled to join them as the opening act but couldn't make it, and for a last-minute replacement Don called on Pat Alger as a temporary fill-in. A highlight of Pat's set would be his own "I'm Takin' My Time" from the *EB 84* album. He recalls, "I had pretty much decided I was quitting music. I had a three-year-old son, and I wasn't making nearly enough, so I'd gotten a freelance job designing books that was supposed to start that week. But Don asked me, and I said, 'Sure, of course!' Phil only knew I was one of Don's friends, so I got a little side-eye. Our first gig, we were playing the new Cincinnati Reds baseball stadium, and I see Phil at the side of the stage watching. That continued for the first three or four gigs, then he came up to me and said, 'You're doing a good job; I think it's going to work out.' I went on to play literally hundreds of gigs with them over time."

In Columbia, Maryland, early in the tour, Don greeted the crowd with "I'm glad to be here. After all these years, I'm glad to be anywhere; this is wonderful, the second time around." The *Washington Post*'s Geoffrey Himes noted that the concert "offered welcome evidence that it is possible to...recapture something of past inspiration. The Everly Brothers...clearly savored the pleasure of a harmony sound greater than the sum of the parts."

The set list was similar to that of the Albert Hall shows, but without the acoustic break. In his report on the August show in Las Vegas, Hilburn noted, "The pair has put together an outstanding, rock-conscious band that gives their music a fresh, dynamic edge.... The Everlys have returned with more character and maturity in their vocals."

As might be expected, in the UK the reception was rapturous. There were shows in Liverpool and Manchester, Belfast and Cardiff, but the centerpiece was the closer at London's Hammersmith Odeon. Reporter Mick Greene expressed surprise to find "a lot of youngsters in the audience screaming along.... The standout song of the night [was] a really raunchy 'Lucille,' which had keyboard player Pete Wingfield...ending up lying on the floor playing his solo. That really took me back." Pat Alger recalls George Harrison stopping backstage to see Phil and Don after the show, asking Don the very Harrison question so many musicians did, "How did you get that sound on that guitar? Do you mind if I see that?"

Offstage, Pat recalls that Don and Phil "almost always picked up the check; that's not typical, and they paid all the expenses. We stayed at the Kensington Gardens, a wonderful old hotel where they had tea in this lovely appointed room. The first time we sat there, we ran into Peter Blake, the guy who designed the *Sgt. Pepper* album cover. Talking with him and Don Everly, in England, near the palace, well.... Phil was very good friends with a lot of singers there, but Don was just so...erudite." There's that description of Don again.

They finished 1984 with three nights at Harrah's Lake Tahoe in Nevada. On the last show, Phil and a beaming Don were joined onstage by the latter's teenage son Edan, playing "Be-Bop-a-Lula," "You Send Me," and "T for Texas" together. Edan would say, "I remember getting goosebumps listening to them sing together every night."

Don would note of the tour, "We made more money in the first year back together than we had in the last ten we'd worked together before."

His predilection for taking off and going fishing reached a new level as he and Diane headed to Captiva, Florida, not far from Fort Myers, where he took a course in piloting substantial sailing vessels. Don was again contemplating purchase of a sleek boat of his own; a model for it sat in their living room. In the months ahead, a new song and album title supplied it a name—the *Born Yesterday*. The fantasy boat never got purchased; the album worked out fine.

The Mercury/PolyGram people were anxious to see the Everlys begin work on a follow-up to *EB 84*. Phil reasoned that the audience reception since the reunion hadn't really depended so much on material, new or old; people came to hear them *sing*, and he again deferred to Don and Dave Edmunds, who was returning as producer, for shaping the new project.

They suggested that things be kept simpler, in part because the time set aside for recording was compressed. The backing tracks were recorded at the same London studio as before, but the vocals were grabbed later, at the Record Plant in Los Angeles. The sound would be relatively straightforward, and the album's flavor cleaner, with vocals clearly up front. That worked for the end result—in the album's favor.

There might well have been no Everly originals on the new album at all, but as the end of the sessions neared, they still needed one more good song. Diane had the lyric of what would become the album's title track in her handbag and asked, "Well, what about this?" Don had labored over "Born Yesterday" at their apartment for some time. A moderately paced but searing ballad about the lingering hurt on both sides of a broken relationship, and—so country-like—how others responded to that break, it was distinctly personal. Don told Patrick Carr of *Country Music* magazine, "That song came out of Brown's Diner. People write on the walls there, but it's not limericks like you find anywhere else; it's about the music business, people's breakups, who's going with whom and why—small town talk. I've been the subject of a lot of that kind of talk in Nashville."

He wasn't speaking to that magazine by accident. As a single, "Born Yesterday" would reach the US country music chart top twenty (number seventeen), the highest run of an Everlys single as country since "('Til) I Kissed You" twenty-five years before. "Country or pop" hadn't been a particular consideration. The emphasis for this second PolyGram album was on keeping the song choices contemporary, exploring particularly sources influenced by the Everlys in the first place—an effect, no doubt, of Paul McCartney's song having worked out so well.

The album's opening track, "Amanda Ruth," had been written and introduced in 1982 by a pair of Everly-aware brothers, Chip and Tony Kinman of the seminal Austin cowpunk band Rank and File. That latest version of country rock, fusing country and punk rock sounds, was so unexpected that the country tinge could be fresh again. The Everlys' version starts the album off with slashing electric guitar so twangy that it lays down a country marker for the whole LP.

Phil would call Mark Knopfler's "Why Worry" "one of the better ballads we've had in our hands in a long time." The melodically elegant yet simple, Everly-influenced song, introduced to them earlier by Dave, had appeared on Knopfler's band Dire Straits' popular *Brothers in Arms* album that May. As a song about perseverance when things are bleak and finding comfort in love, it was perfect for the Everlys in both concept and sound. On Don and Phil's slightly faster version, Albert supplies a haunting guitar intro, and, of course, there are those harmonies. The album track "These Shoes" would prove a fan favorite; it's a sort of pop update of Ernest Tubb's "Walking the Floor Over You," with the agitated pacing taken out to the streets. It was paired with the catchy "I Know Love" as a single that again charted country, reaching number fifty-six.

It wouldn't all read "country," though. One of the most often played tracks would be a mesmerizing version of Bob Dylan's relatively obscure and melodic "Abandoned Love," one of the better recorded interpretations of his songs ever, with Irish pipes and whistles courtesy of Liam O'Flynn—Irish American roots rock. Phil and Don also got around to recording Sam Cooke's romantic "You Send Me," a live-show staple for them, although, in the marketing style of the time, it was added as a cassette and CD bonus track only and wasn't on the original vinyl LP. They came to see it as recorded too hastily, and it did drag, compared to the versions live audiences were regularly treated to.

Total sales for the *Born Yesterday* album, released in November 1985, would not be quite as solid as expected, despite the hit singles and the lasting quality of the record, as good or better than its predecessor. The hubbub and publicity surrounding the comeback album and tour couldn't quite be duplicated. Phil would say, "This one is better. I think the songs are better. . . . If the slow ones make you feel romantic and the fast ones make you want to dance—well, that's my criteria. This album comes pretty close to that."

The critical reception was all they could have asked for. In *Rolling Stone*, David Fricke noted, "There is a sense of frisky adventure . . .

in their daring song selection and the gutsy understatement...
which establishes the Everly Brothers as vital song interpreters
for the Eighties." Perceptively, in the Los Angeles *Herald Examiner*, Mikal Gilmore deemed it "their most cohesive and probing
effort since the '68 masterwork *Roots*.... It establishes firmly that...
these country-bred tenors have come back together because they
have found they now have something to say about the ways of the
human heart as it ages, as it rends and heals, time and time again."
The Everlys would receive a Grammy nomination for the album
for Best Country Performance by a Duo or Group with Vocal. A
newer blood-harmony duo, the Judds, won.

The album-supporting 1985 tour largely retraced the previous
year's North American itinerary, plus traditional Everly Brothers
stops in Australia and England. Phil, who was spending a lot of
time at home with his kids, admitted that he wasn't that thrilled
about touring anywhere anymore, comparing it to another marines
stint—and said so to the *Stars and Stripes* military newspaper.
When they got to Australia, they'd confess to local reporters that
they couldn't even recall just how many times they'd been there; it
was a blur.

When the tour began in Dallas in July, Don was suddenly rearranging his relationship situation again, for another in his string of
"adventures," as he called them. Diane Craig recalls, "That was the
point at which Don decided that he was going to go after this good
friend of mine, Victoria Ballard. I'd met her when she was working
at [steel guitarist and producer] Pete Drake's studio. There was a
night at my condo when she asked to come over just to talk to me,
and Don comes home and Victoria is sitting in a chair, and though
she knew Don already, she says hi. Don told me later it was at that
moment that he decided that Victoria was going to be his next girlfriend. Honestly, there was a part of me that knew that shoe would
drop."

Victoria, a blonde, had been married to country singer-songwriter Larry Ballard, who'd had a series of honky-tonk albums for Capitol Records in the mid-1970s, produced by that same Pete Drake; they had a daughter. She would accompany Don on multiple public events over the following months.

"I was at the venue in Dallas," Diane recalls, "and I knew that all of this was happening, and I left and went back to Nashville. They were getting ready to go to Australia and he took Victoria with him for the shows there, and that was pretty much it." Full disconnection took time. Months later, Don referred to all this in the brothers' interview in *Rolling Stone*: "My personal life . . . is sort of strange. I guess I'm with a girl called Victoria right now—but I'm still with Diane, too. I don't know how to describe this. . . . You get your career straightened out and, all of a sudden, your personal life goes."

Go figure.

The *Born Yesterday* album, with its more country tinge, arrived as Steve Earle, Randy Travis, and Dwight Yoakam were appearing on the Grammy Awards telecast as representatives of "new country," a style with which this album and the ensuing Everlys tour fit in perfectly well. But they were on rock recording agendas, too. Paul Simon had them provide backup harmony vocals on the title track of his classic, if sometimes argument-inducing, album *Graceland*, and Keith Richards was privately recording soon widely bootlegged versions of "So Sad" and "Cathy's Clown," with the emphasis on the slamming guitar.

In January of 1986, Phil and Don were on hand for their induction into the Rock & Roll Hall of Fame's first, original set of honorees. This was certainly another indication of how firmly they now lived in the public musical consciousness, had carved a place in pop music history, and made rock contributions understood to be worthy of memorializing. While some would always wonder if allegedly rebellious rock should have any establishing canon, hall or museum, the Everlys, having been in the field for some thirty years, enjoyed this new sort of respect.

"We fought the battle together with the rock acts," Phil would note of that history, "and there were people who supported it and us over the years. It's nice to see the taste glorified. I mean, they all said it wouldn't last—and here we still are." They were ready to accept *this* recognition together.

"I did think," Don told *Rolling Stone*'s Scott Isler the day of the inductions, "being an Everly Brother for the rest of my life is just like being put in a bag when you're nineteen.... That's the end of it. But when you...see what the world's like out there by yourself, it's not so bad. Being an Everly Brother doesn't bother me now at all; in fact, I'm proud to be an Everly Brother."

That was one hard-won sentence. The induction ceremony was a black-tie affair at New York's Waldorf-Astoria—incongruous enough to raise some eyebrows. Also on hand from the first set of inductees were James Brown, Chuck Berry, Ray Charles, Fats Domino, Jerry Lee Lewis, and Little Richard, all having a swell time reminiscing along with the Everlys and basking in the recognition. They'd indeed been through wars together. (Buddy Holly, Elvis Presley, Sam Cooke, and Alan Freed were among those inducted but not alive to experience the moment.)

Don and Phil—the only duo, let alone group, included—were inducted by Neil Young, who recalled trying to get a sound like the Everlys' for his first high school band's vocals. "We never did get it," he laughed. "But years later I found myself in Los Angeles, putting together a band [with] Stills and Furay, we were working on the vocals...trying to get that sound. Still couldn't get it!... It's such a great honor...and I'm so proud to introduce you to the Everly Brothers."

They looked genuinely thrilled to get their two induction trophies, at which point Phil quipped, "Thank God, they gave us two;

we won't have to fight over it," and then, "I think this speaks well of all of us; we made good choices when we were real young." Don added, "This is kind of a hats off to rock and roll, which has changed all of our lives—the way we dress, the way we look, the way we think, the way we interact amongst each other. . . . Rock and roll's been good to us. Hope it's been good to you."

Career and life-spanning interviews followed, particularly about their lives as brothers. Phil commented to Jay Cocks at *Time*, "Don and I are infamous for our split, but we're closer than most brothers. Harmony singing requires that you enlarge yourself, not use any kind of suppression. Harmony is the ultimate love."

Don suggested to *Playboy*, "My advice to anyone who hasn't spoken to his brother for a long time is—call him up." And he told country music reporter Jack Hurst, "It was painful being a teenager and it's painful being an adult. . . . Our audience went hither, thither and yon, just like we did. They all had kids and divorces, then they see us come through town and they say, '*They're* back together.' . . . I can tell they're separated, and they say to the kids, 'That's what I intended to do.' And the kids kind of look like they're thinking, 'What *is* this?' Then they get into it, because we're still rock and roll."

There was an aspect of their own family's life the brothers didn't talk about much at all—their dicey, arm's-length relationship with their mother, which made news just weeks after the Rock Hall induction. Margaret was sixty-seven, remained single, and, Nashville-based Venetia Ember aside, had little to do with any of the grandchildren, as little as she'd had with the wives and girlfriends that had come and gone. She was handling a good deal of fan club merch, souvenirs, and correspondence, even regularly receiving fans and club eminences from the United States and abroad at her Nashville home, which she continued to maintain just as it had been, as a sort of shrine.

She unquestionably won plenty of admirers doing all that; she could be charming and welcoming, sharp and witty—if vague about ongoing relationships and why visits from Phil and even from Don, who lived nearby, were so rare. A general impression of family harmony with a dedicated, upbeat mom prevailed. That image was cracked when on February 18, 1986, a disturbing story broke that made headlines worldwide: "Don Everly's Mother Sues Him to Get Title to House," "Weeping Widow Caught in Everlys Feud," and "Wake Up, Little Donny, 'Cause Mom Is Suing."

In a lawsuit filed in the Chancery Court in Nashville, Margaret asserted that Phil and Don had bought the house for her and Ike in 1958, putting it in Ike's name. (It had been one of the first things they did with early hits money.) They'd also made the ongoing mortgage payments on the place, so they were taking tax deductions on it until the midsixties, when the Internal Revenue Service questioned those deductions. Ike and Margaret then signed title of the house over to their sons to remove the question of ownership. Margaret now claimed that they'd promised to return title of the house to her again once the tax deductions were over with. Phil acquiesced and signed over his 60 percent interest, but Don said no. Her suit asked for a court ruling that Don had "abused his confidential relationship with her" and should be forced to turn over his 40 percent.

However much this was about causing an attention-grabbing ruckus, Margaret's basic, understandable concern was that if the house stayed in her sons' names, sooner or later they'd lose it to some new wife or other in another divorce. That's how she explained it to her friend Penny Campbell Loewen. As it happened, neither Phil nor Don would ever divorce again.

Elements of the press lapped this up, particularly in England. Loose with facts, and at once tear-jerking maudlin and nasty, the celebrity press there portrayed Margaret as a frail old matriarch decades older than she was, Don in one case as a "truculent over-weight crooner," and the brothers as trying to throw their mother out into the street. Creative stuff with little relation to the reality.

The London-based *Globe* scandal sheet outdid itself, printing such comically misleading remarks as "When the boys were fight-ing, Don always tried to put his mother in the middle and tried to make her take sides.... For months, the poor woman has cried herself to sleep over the way Don treated her;" and even "Imagine Margaret's pain. It really took a lot out of her to go public like that." The last thing either brother wanted was to pull their mother into disputes, and taking stories public was practically her hobby. They failed to supply Don with a black cloak and mustache to twirl. The court reportedly ruled in her favor, though ending the press bar-rage might have contributed to Don's decision to go along. Title to the house shifted, records show; it was now hers.

This was all put behind them as the Everly Brothers 1986 tour got underway, running through the summer into fall across the United States and Canada. They now preferred playing big state fairs, with their all-age family audiences, or theaters in the round, where they could be closer to the attendees. About getting there, Pat Alger recalls, "They each had a bus; initially I rode on Don's, but that stopped a lot and was dull; I wanted to *go*. So I started rid-ing on Phil's—and that's when I got to know Phil better. We had a great time."

The tour high point for both brothers was a nostalgia-evoking Homecoming extravaganza in Shenandoah, Iowa, over the Fourth of July weekend. Just days before, another memory-evoking fes-tival, the traveling Golden Age of Radio Reunion had played Shenandoah, and Margaret was there in her cowgirl suit, answer-ing questions about the family's time there and announcing that she was at work on two projected memoirs, "The Growing Years" and "The Innocent Years"—never published or turned into a movie as she'd hoped. In fact, the brothers made clear to the global fan club head Martial Bekkers that they were no happier about her controlling how their story would be told than they liked the idea of either of them relating their different versions themselves.

Margaret shared the spotlight in this event with early country legend Patsy Montana, who lived there at the time and performed for the crowd. When called on to join in on a song herself, it wasn't on one of the *Ike Everly Family* show country oldies; it was, incongruously, on "Bye Bye Love." There's no record as to whether her sons asked her to stick around for their arrival soon after, but she didn't.

Days later, Phil and Don were taken aback to discover just how much fond feeling they still held for the place. Phil's comments to Des Moines radio interviewer Brian O'Brien underscored how much they saw this place, fundamentally, as their home, however "Southern" people wanted to see them: "That formative period, growing up around Shenandoah, is what I really remember in my lifetime. . . . It gave us stability and a work ethic and all of the things that people know come out of the Midwest, that serve you better than anything else, because you never get to take anything for granted. . . . Life is something that has to be *pursued*. People from the Midwest don't forget those kinds of basics."

The excited Iowa press previewed the multiple events planned, which included an evening concert, a parade, and renaming the main street on one end of town Everly Brothers Avenue. The celebration was largely promoted and financed by local entrepreneur Bill Hillman, who would play a continuing role in memorializing the Everly family's Shenandoah period thereafter. When the *Des Moines Register* asked Phil if the brothers could have imagined as kids that they'd be so many times "bigger" and better known than Earl May and Henry Field—the Shenandoah seed companies owners—Phil said, "Not only could I not have conceived that then, I still can't make myself believe that now. . . . They were the giants."

Together, Phil and Don, who'd had so little in those days and never forgotten it, made a generous commitment to the kids of the town—donation of most all of the proceeds of the Homecoming events to a new Everly Family Scholarship to go to Shenandoah High students toward college, and to grade school and high school kids who couldn't afford equipment for extracurricular activities. That sort of generosity was becoming typical of them both.

Hard-core fans flew in from around the country, as did some national press. Local merchants featured poodle dresses and other fifties paraphernalia in shop windows, and there were events of sorts the Everlys must have enjoyed back in the day—a pet show, a water fight sponsored by the fire department, a hot rod show, a sock hop, and a pancake feed—plus a new Everly Brothers lip-synching contest. In the parade car, the waving brothers were accompanied by Don's new lady friend, Victoria, unidentified in local reports, with homecoming queens of many football seasons following on floats, and high school band members from the '50s marching along playing. The Everly Brothers performed some seventeen songs at the scheduled concert, even though it was cut short by torrential rain and winds. Don told the crowd, "There are milestones in everybody's life.... This day is going to stand out forever."

New to many there, apparently, was their opening performer, added just days before—Texas singer-songwriter Nanci Griffith. The distinctive "folkabilly" singer, as she referred to her genre-line-busting music, already had four albums out, and had appeared a number of times on the nationally viewed *Austin City Limits* TV show, but she was probably best known then as the writer of "Love at the Five & Dime," a hit that year for Kathy Mattea. Her own fame as writer and vocalist would increase substantially a few years later, particularly for her memorable interpretations of songs such as Julie Gold's "From a Distance" and John Prine's "Speed of the Sound of Loneliness."

She was in these circles now. Jim Rooney produced multiple albums for her, she'd often tour with the Everlys, and she would record the duet "You Made This Love a Teardrop" with Phil in 1989. Not well known because they kept it away from any publicized glare, Nanci and Phil dated for a time during those touring years. She'd say a few months into the tour, noting how she was treated like a special guest every show, "Don's a very quiet person. Phil is very sweet—and funny. They're both so kind."

There was another memorializing event in the fall as the Everly Brothers were added to the Hollywood Walk of Fame— in the recording category, naturally, not the movies. At the sidewalk induction ceremony, they were officially added to the walk by a next-generation friend, Tom Petty. He'd long been an Everlys admirer, a student of their recordings for what he could learn from the harmonies and riffs. Fetching his daughter Adria after school one day, he'd noticed her classmate Chris Everly being picked up by his dad, Phil, and according to Adria, after that Petty kept picking her up daily until he managed to bump into Phil directly, and they became friends. Two years later, Petty would sign on for a part-time job with the Traveling Wilburys supergroup, in which all of his fellow members—Bob Dylan, George Harrison, Roy Orbison, and Jeff Lynne—had had significant musical relations with the Everlys.

Some were questioning the Everly Brothers' near-complete reliance on old audience favorites, performing live, when they were making such relevant and strong *new* music: "One measly song from those sessions," Don Waller complained of a show, in the *Los Angeles Times*. "The Everlys are selling themselves and their fans short." He was touching on an issue Phil and Don wrestled with, and had concluded that "safer is better," a tacit if not locked admission—or fear, perhaps—that they had entered "legacy act" territory.

They continued to have an influential, uninterrupted hold on oncoming generations of roots rockers, though. In the documentary

Athens, GA: Inside/Out, released early in 1987, the loud/soft, gentle/ clanging, innocent/cynical, and often misty sounds of R.E.M. are featured, with Michael Stipe and company taking on "All I Have to Do Is Dream." Who but the Everlys could have been a more natural model?

An older set of longtime admirers, the Beach Boys, invited them to join them on their own twenty-fifth anniversary TV special, taping at Waikiki Beach in December, with the two sets of harmony-singing families merging for a medley of the Boys' "Don't Worry Baby" and the Brothers' "Wake Up Little Susie." The Everly's own studio version of "Don't Worry Baby" would be pulled by Mercury/PolyGram as the single from their third and last album on the label, *Some Hearts . . .*, but they were not pleased with that call. Don and Phil had supplied seven of the ten songs recorded for it, with the theme throughout, as the album title suggests, love— desired, lived, lost, recalled, rekindled. To have more direct control on how it would all sound, they produced it themselves, at New River Studios in Fort Lauderdale, Florida.

They fell into a familiar production muddle, reminiscent of some of their unsupervised studio adventures of years before. On the released album, the vocals are so drowned in reverb that they often seem to be coming from some other, spooky room, and they're regularly overtaken by the sheer volume of the instrumental layers, an unfortunate presentation style for songs about such intimate emotions. The "wall of sound" here is a wall between the songs and the listener.

Phil's songwriting contributions are all cowritten with his frequent collaborator John Durrill, and two of the three, "Angel of the Darkness" and "Brown Eyes," are about being haunted in dreams by a former lover, darkly in the first case, longingly in the second, stronger song, and both apparently sparked by memories of ex-wife Patricia Mickey. Don's songs, mainly sung solo in his free-form athletic style, focus on heartbreak, as his songs did when he was seventeen. "Three Bands of Steel" and "Be My Love Again" are lyrically and melodically strong, but they're difficult to get close to for the production's interference. Songs from other sources were the poppy "Julianne," by buddy Pat Alger with his Music Row collaborator Fred Knobloch, and John Hiatt and Mike Porter's "Any Single Solitary Heart," the strong, harmonious album closer.

The brothers eventually gave up on the producing side of the project, frustrated with getting what they wanted, and turned that over to drummer Larrie Londin. In retrospect, they were almost always really better off working with a strong, focused producer. Don admitted later: "My part was self-indulgent. . . . I didn't think of anything but this vision I had in my head."

Neither brother showed interest in doing much of anything with the new material after getting the album done and over with. Where *Some Hearts . . .* was reviewed, on first release or a rerelease that came the following year in an attempt to relaunch it, it was generally pegged as less successful than the two predecessors, and as *Goldmine* put it, "No single song stands out as a potential hit." That's why Mercury/PolyGram took "Don't Worry Baby" as the single, barely promoted the album as a whole, then dropped the Everlys from the label.

They would continue to make music and draw enthusiastic crowds for nearly twenty years more, but there would never, it turned out, be another new Everly Brothers album.

Chapter Fourteen

THE HOME STRETCH
1988–2000

THE EVERLY BROTHERS' RECORDING ERA MAY ONLY HAVE EXTENDED to occasional contributions to projects by others at this point, but they had such a tight musical and personal bond with their immensely capable band that audiences remained riveted by what they offered. For many, the Everly Brothers coming to town now meant an exciting band was on the way, not simply a duo. Whether a number was leaning country, or rock, or rootsy Americana, this outfit could deliver.

Albert Lee, often referred to as the "guitar players' guitar player," renowned especially for his clean, fast country licks, led the outfit; Phil Cranham was on bass, Larrie Londin on drums, and Hank DeVito on steel, joined by Glen D. Hardin on keyboards. Hardin, like Albert and Hank, had been a member of Emmylou Harris's celebrated Hot Band. When DeVito left the

Everlys in 1988, Londin informed Don and Albert's old Sundance Saloon partner Buddy Emmons that the job was open, and that steel guitar giant joined the band for a dozen years. Emmons would recall thinking instantly when Don signed him, "Here we go again: buses, billboards and 'Do Not Disturb' signs."

Right through the 1990s, the places they played tended to be ones where they'd found success for years. The shows became more patterned—one-hour gallops that squeezed in some of the big hits by mashing them into medleys, with newer numbers relatively rare. Pat Alger was often the opening act.

The reception for this Everly Brothers band was usually warm. In 1987, from Wilkes-Barre, Pennsylvania, June Bell wrote, "The band provided a dynamic accompaniment." At an Owensboro, Kentucky, show the same summer, Don warned the crowd, as he would many places, "We're going to sing some old songs and some new songs, but they're all about love and relationships because Phil and I are romantics at heart." And then he'd point out that many of the songs bore women's names, and that "we were married to about half of them." In Milwaukee, Chris Lathrop observed, "Although the Everly Brothers' five-piece band was introduced as a rock'n'roll outfit, the sound was predominantly country . . . but these guys sure could bring it, anchored by superpicker Albert Lee on guitar."

Some of the nostalgia-frozen reviewers and audience members had apparently failed to notice that the Everlys had been touring with electrified bands for over twenty-five years, and still expected to hear duplicates of the earliest, gentlest records of thirty years earlier. In Northern California's *Contra Costa Times*, Marcy Bachman-Hartman fumed, "I looked forward to one more relaxing evening of sheer pleasure . . . basking in the sounds that recall memories precious to many of us. It was not to be. . . . Speakers blared ear-splitting chords before the brothers even stepped on the stage. . . . The majority of familiar hits had been torturously updated.... That the Everly Brothers are bastardizing their considerable talent in the name of attracting a more up-to-date audience is a disappointing commentary on the times and on the singers."

While they were doing exactly what they wanted to, and what much of the audience wanted to hear, at a St. Louis show in the period, Phil actually apologized, slightly, for the volume: "When you're in the Rock and Roll Hall of Fame," he explained, "you have to do that once in a while."

On the other hand, in the popular little tourist town of Nashville, Indiana, at the Little Nashville Opry, which often attracted major country acts, Jill Warren of the *Indianapolis Star* was fine with the band, just as it was, but was primed to hear the Everlys' recent country chart hits, and more new songs like them, finding instead: "Don and Phil Everly filled most of their disappointingly brief 60-minute set... with a string of oldies.... Perhaps as a concession to the crowd, most of whom sat like stones... the Everlys included their bona fide country hit 'So Sad.' Don felt bound to remind fans that he and his brother performed the tune on the esteemed stage of the Grand Ole Opry."

They'd appealed to multiple audiences, and they couldn't thrill all of them at once. But then, who could?

While back in their British home-away-from-home in 1989, things took an uneasy turn—at least, as the tabloids described it and even promulgated. The *Daily Mirror*'s William Marshall "innocently" asked Don, "the roly-poly one with the short, smoking fuse," why the Everlys were back over there again at all, when "at the ripe old age of 52, he should be home toasting muffins in Tennessee." Don swore at him from that photo opportunity event all the way back to their hotel's bar, adding, "What the hell. I don't have to ask people like that for a passport to come here. I've been coming here for thirty years." Cooling off after a few drinks, he confessed to the same infuriating reporter, "If I don't write and perform and play my music, I might as well die."

The *News of the World*, taking off from the brothers' shared dismay that Mercury/PolyGram had made "Don't Worry Baby" the new single, somehow twisted that into evidence that old conflicts between them were renewed: "The Everly Brothers' feud boiled over in fury last night when they were DROPPED by their record company."

Phil did say, "This is the last major tour we'll ever do; I've had enough," which meant "in support of a record." It was hardly the Everly Brothers' last major tour. Don commented, "You can't keep doing what people expect. You just do what your heart tells you to." They would still work a new number or two into the sets—Don's memorable rendition of George Jones's signature hit "He Stopped Loving Her Today" was one—a song few have dared to cover. They didn't stand still. They kept right on going, to positive effect.

By 1993, Todd Everett of *Variety* could update, "The Everlys... have come as close as possible to revamping their show without leaving out...major hits, or substantially changing their band. They've left their trademark tuxedos at home.... Don has finally stopped ridiculing his younger sibling. Some songs have been slightly rearranged...Albert Lee, Buddy Emmons and Pete Wingfield [back on piano] took solos that weren't on the records, and occasionally Don...would kick off songs with a deceptive introduction, a funny 'Pinball Wizard' strumming intro to 'Wake Up Little Susie,' for example." (Of course, Everlys' fan Pete Townshend would have been the first to point out that celebrated strum from *Tommy* owed much to Don's original in the first place, as had the intro to "I Can See for Miles.")

Don credited the band with the act's continuing energy. "We have a real band," he told Paul Freeman of the *Los Angeles Times*. "It would be embarrassing to not be up to par and snuff, because they'd say, 'Gee, they're getting too old to do it, aren't they?'... When I get discouraged, I look over and there's Buddy Emmons, there's Albert Lee and the rest of the guys.... I love going on the road with them. It's like a field trip with your best friends."

Clearly Albert felt similarly. "I had to pinch myself a number of times," he'd recall. "You start to take it for granted, not only being able to play with the Everly Brothers, but that it was a great band, too. We had Buddy Emmons for a long time and Larrie Londin; they were two of the best there ever was. But it was always a good band, no matter who was in it."

The musical relationships the Everlys had generated over the years played a strong part in one-off collaborative recordings and television appearances they'd take part in over the years immediately ahead. They were prominent on a 1987 TV salute to Chet Atkins, where Chet backed them as only he could on "Bye Bye Love" and "Wake Up Little Susie" and Mark Knopfler joined them all for a beautiful rendition of his "Why Worry." Don and Phil soon joined Johnny and Rosanne Cash on a new chick-a-boom recording of Cash's '50s hit, Jack Clement's "Ballad of a Teenage Queen." That one charted country and was nominated for a CMA Vocal Event of the Year award. The sweet, airy Phil and Nanci Griffith duet "You Made This Love a Teardrop" was not many months behind.

There was a personal loss for the Everly Brothers and so many others in Nashville and for music everywhere that June with the death of Boudleaux Bryant from lung cancer at a Knoxville hospital. That he'd played a central role in the Everlys' musical story was well understood; that he had mattered so in their personal lives, too, less so. Like Ike at his death, he was just sixty-seven.

A favorite part of Phil and Don's annual calendar for fourteen years, both personally and professionally, began in 1988, when Don saw on a news report that Muhlenberg County's Central City (population five thousand; *that* size "city") was economically depressed again, after a recent cut in federal revenue-sharing, and needed an up-to-date police radio system. Don and Phil donated $6,500 to cover it.

Town leaders had in mind a small one-time ceremony to thank them, but, encouraged by cousin Ted Everly, and with memories of how much the Shenandoah homecoming had meant, Phil and Don saw that a similar annual event could serve as a fundraiser, contribute to the local economy, and honor the music born in the hands of daddy Ike and others from the area.

Locals, extended family included, knew very well that Don and Phil had always lived elsewhere, and that Phil was born in Chicago. (At the first Homecoming, wry local officials presented him with an "honorary Central City birth certificate.") Phil would say, with Ike's life no doubt in mind, "When the rest of the nation thinks of Kentucky, they think of horse racing and the Kentucky Derby. When we think of Kentucky, we think of the coal-mining region."

Local media called the first August 1988 Homecoming edition the biggest event ever to happen in Central City. National media rolled into town to cover it, and fans showed up from as far away as California, Utah—and England. Don and Phil (accompanied by his son Chris) put their handprints and autographs in cement, attended a ribbon-cutting where the town's Chestnut Street was renamed Everly Brothers Boulevard, and were in the parade from there to the city hall, where they were publicly thanked and discovered a monument had been installed.

That read, with admirable accuracy and inclusion, "From Brownie, to Iowa, to Knoxville to Nashville, to Hollywood, to England and around the world...Don and Phil have taken the music of Kentucky, as taught by their parents. And now they are bringing it back home to Central City." That evening they headlined a concert attended by ten thousand, featuring also their buddy

John Prine. His famed song of coal destruction and personal loss, "Paradise," with its "take me back to Muhlenberg County" chorus, was the full-cast event closer.

Don and Phil established an organized fund to finance area projects and multiple annual scholarships for local high school students—the Everly Foundation. The fund also managed future editions of the Homecoming, the proceeds eventually becoming an ongoing endowment of well over $100,000, with as many as six hundred local residents contributing to the foundation's work. Phil could say of the organization and its projects, "It's maybe the best thing we've ever done in our lives . . . something that has some permanence." The Homecoming was "one of the main things we look forward to each year."

By the second year, the Everly Brothers Homecoming Festival was already a regularly scheduled three-day affair set around September's Labor Day weekend, and a number of the brothers' performing friends would be on the bills with them, one time or many—Prine, Duane Eddy, Chet Atkins, Bo Diddley, Sonny Curtis, and also less obviously connected country stars such as Tammy Wynette, Billy Ray Cyrus, and New Grass Revival. At Don's suggestion, there would also be a spin-off, a separate annual thumb-picking contest sponsored by the foundation to honor and further the music of the area's famed pickers—Ike Everly, Mose Rager, Kennedy Jones, Merle Travis, and Arnold Shultz.

Home as many as eight or nine months of the year now, Don went on playing with his Dead Cowboys band. That loose outfit had a gig as far afield from Nashville bars as they'd ever get with a late 1988 taping of an episode of the Irish musical TV series *The Session* at Dublin's new Point Depot venue. Invited there by Phil Donnelly, who'd returned home, Don, Jim Rooney, Cowboy Jack, and Rachel Peer flew over to join him along with Marty Stuart and John Prine, who'd recently been working with producer Rooney as well. Lyle Lovett happened to be in Dublin, so he joined in, too, with Clement as ringmaster, Don as lead singer.

They took up the country side of this outfit's range—"So Sad" and "Yesterday Just Passed My Way Again"—and Rooney and Don with Johnnie & Jack's "Down South in New Orleans." They then veered toward rock—"Lucille" and "Good Golly, Miss Molly"—and closed with Cowboy Jack's terrific bluegrass-meets-rock version of the Stones' "No Expectations." Stuart, Prine, and Lovett joined in. Don, Albert, and Buddy Emmons did some strong club dates in the UK, piggybacking on the same trip.

To mark Don's fiftieth birthday in 1987, Phil presented him not with another guitar, but with a restored 1960 Cadillac. Both brothers tended to say yes to appealing invitations now. When the determinedly folksy Garrison Keillor of the popular *A Prairie Home Companion* public radio show chose to present them as contemplative down-home gospel singers, joining him on "Softly and Tenderly Jesus Is Calling," they went along with it, as if they'd ever performed much of that sort of material publicly in their entire adult careers. Invited to join Jerry Lee Lewis, Chuck Berry, Bo Diddley, and Leslie Gore on a Legends of Rock package show in Melbourne, Australia, soon after, they said yes to that revival show, too. Don even signed on for recordings with "America's Polka King" Frankie Yankovic, on "That Silver-Haired Daddy of Mine." He had to have had that Midwest/Chicago upbringing in the back of his mind, where nostalgia could get a little bouncy. They enjoyed all of those gigs.

In 1989, Reba McEntire took her slow-ballad version of "Cathy's Clown" to number one on the country music charts, with a fresh point of view in the lyric that made the singer a woman (a nineteenth-century cowgirl in the video) who loves the man people dismiss as that dang Cathy's pushover.

Guitar Player magazine, in a lengthy September 1990 profile by Bill Bush, "Don Everly: Rock's Acoustic Rhythm Pioneer," heralded

Don's important contributions as a rhythm guitarist, a focus not much recognized with such clarity in the press before. Bush said of the Everly Brothers' initial breakthrough, exhilaratingly bluntly: "The music had balls—big, percussive, choked acoustic chords that cut through, providing not only a strong rhythmic background, but a key element of the song itself. Don's open-tuning experiments and inventive rhythm patterns gave their guitars a more metallic, drum-like ring than the traditional country acoustic sound."

Don reveals in the portrait how the obvious differences between his style of playing and Ike's came about. Aware that all the good money went to singers, Ike had encouraged him to play rhythm, and so "the guitar was just a tool for me as a singer."

It's debatable how literally "Irish" the Everlys had ever considered themselves to be, but when Jim Rooney was overseeing Nashville elements for *Bringing It All Back Home*, a BBC documentary series on Irish music connections around the world, he recruited Phil and Don to trace that connection in American country music right through to rock and roll. They revisited one of the songs from *Songs Our Daddy Taught Us*, "Down in the Willow Garden," as "Rose Connolly," one of its historic titles, in an Irish-saluting version, and took on another early favorite they'd never recorded, the York Brothers' "Don't Let Our Love Die." Rooney would recall that the unrehearsed taping at Jack Clement's studio started awkwardly, then "suddenly, out of the speakers came the Everly Brothers," harmony in place, eyes locked. Irish pipes master Liam O'Flynn, the same fellow who'd backed them on "Abandoned Love," joins in, showing how the sounds were related. They're visibly moved, and they deliver some of their strongest documented performances from the post-record-making period.

They toured Europe with Duane Eddy in 1991 and in 1992, then in Toledo, Ohio, crossed paths with Graham Nash, who was in town to appear next at the club they were playing. They invited him to their show, then to sing "So Sad" with them, in a third part even higher than Phil's, fulfilling his self-described "lifetime dream." Phil also backed John Prine on the chorus of the upbeat "You Got Gold" track on his 1991 album *The Missing Years*. Fiona Prine, who'd become John's new wife, says, "I know that was something John really appreciated. He just loved having Phil's voice on that record."

Neither Don nor Phil was showing up in news reports about their dating lives, which must have been a relief, but one next-generation Everly, Don's daughter Erin, a knockout Wilhemina agency model and actress who resembled both her father and her mother Venetia, made some headlines of her own in 1990 when she married her longtime boyfriend Axl Rose, the singing, songwriting leader of the hot hard-rock band Guns N' Roses. Famously, she was the subject of Rose's change-of-pace, breakthrough ballad "Sweet Child o' Mine," which went to number one on the *Billboard* Hot 100 chart. Better than being the heavy in "Poor Little Fool," as her dad was, but their marriage was short-lived, annulled after ten months with charges of abuse by Rose filed.

Don was proud to note that his son, Edan, twenty-four in 1992, had a recording contract for his band now, itself called Edan, on Hollywood Records, the Disney-owned label that brought records by Freddie Mercury's Queen to the United States. Edan referred to the album, *Dead Flowers* (with no connection to the Rolling Stones song), as "party rock," though it was often categorized as glam metal; there was enough highly tended hair involved to make an Everly proud. It was the nineties.

"Edan's a great name for a group, I think," Don said, and he'd note that his own hard-struck guitar chords, played loud enough, sounded like metal themselves. Edan was the band's lead vocalist, guitarist, and main songwriter; Frankie Avalon's son Frank was the drummer. The band's commercial timing was not optimal, as the grunge trend was taking hold at just that time.

Phil's son Jason, twenty-seven in 1993, was pursuing a musical career of his own, and had an album out from Polydor's Hamburg division, *No Ordinary Music*. It's a varied, poppy set, with some lavish, string-backed ballads. Jason wrote ten of the twelve tracks, alone or in collaborations, and he sings with Phil on three of them. They take on Simon & Garfunkel's "Cecilia" with a reggae beat; Jason recalled Phil telling him to just "go ahead and sing the melody; it's easier." The breathy "All I See Is You," with a son-father chorus, might have been a latter-day Everly Brothers ballad. Jason would go on to have a career both in music and as a film actor, including a starring role in a Filipino romantic comedy, *Isang tanong, isang sagot*. On occasion, Jason and Edan would get together and perform a set saluting their dads. The vocal combination is not precisely the same as Phil and Don's, and it would be silly to expect it to be, but you can certainly hear family resemblances.

Then, on New Year's Eve 1994–1995, at a party at Phil's in Los Angeles, Jason introduced his father to a woman who'd arrived at the festivities with some of his own buddies—Patti Arnold, thirty-seven. She was working as a dispatcher with the Los Angeles Police Department, and while she was eighteen years younger than Phil, Jason thought she and his dad might hit it off. Years later she would recall Phil's initial lack of enthusiasm on their first date: "I'm not looking for a girlfriend, I'm never getting married," he'd told her. And she figured, "OK, at least this'll be a nice dinner."

She was unpretentious, smart, loyal, and it quickly became apparent to both of them that they cared about each other. Marriage-wary, even as far behind him as his divorces were, they agreed that if they were still together in five years, then they'd wed.

Things had quieted down for Don. He'd tell country/rock borderlands authority Chet Flippo, then *Billboard*'s Nashville bureau chief, "I *like* my life the way it is now. I've kept a low profile....We tour about two or three months a year. We do the fair dates and get on the bus with the band. Hell, to me it's like camping! I even like Vegas now. We don't have to work that hard. You get old and you get more mellow."

Soon after, at a Nashville bar, this mellower Don met the woman who'd be with him for the quarter century in his life still ahead. Adela Garza was just twenty-five, a year younger than his eldest daughter. She and her twin sister, Adelaida, had first come to town from Texas to try to make it as country singers, a familiar-enough story. She was often described as relatively "businesslike" as country singers go, but Adela, to a degree, resembled ways he'd been himself when younger, with a fuse that could go off at times.

Fiona Prine suggests that when Townes Van Zandt died on New Year's Day 1997 from effects of acute alcoholism, her late husband John and Don and much of that once-wild Brown's Diner/Cowboy Jack gang saw that as a "there but for the grace of God" event and veered toward more restrained, even domesticated lives. "The eighties were definitely over," she recalls. Don certainly followed that path. Just a few weeks later, on March 27, 1997, he married Adela at his place in Nashville. He'd say of how that changed his life, "I was hanging out with other songwriters, drinking and carousing around. I think it was 'cause I was bored....Now my life's opened up....We hang out in the kitchen and get guitars out and sing. When Adela came into my life...guitars got into tune, and there was recording equipment. It brought me back."

He bought her a Telecaster, then began using it himself to explore, for the first time, whether he could bring Ike's Muhlenberg County fingerpicking to an electric, and attempted to put together a Kentucky "superpickers" touring group, but that didn't come to fruition.

The recharged feeling of connection to Kentucky did show itself, though. He appeared on several public TV shows on Kentucky's KET that year. On *Tim Farmer's Country Kitchen*, he's shown fishing with a Mr. Pace, his junior high school science teacher from Shenandoah, and he takes the host on a tour of the charming, rural Lake Malone Inn and restaurant, which in fact he's just purchased. It became Everly's Lake Malone Inn, and before long Don renamed that adjoining body of water Lake Adela. He now had at least an alternative address in Kentucky, for the first time since he was six weeks old.

He would say of the purchase, "I believe as you get older, you begin to appreciate your roots.... For years I had been looking for a cabin near where I was born, and I found one—with 55 rooms." A small Everly Brothers memorabilia exhibit was put up, and informally, friends such as John Hartford and Buddy Emmons would play with him there from time to time. Occasionally, Phil would, too.

Recognition of the Everly Brothers' lasting contributions to popular music continued and began to add up to a fuller picture. In that busy 1997, they were the first duo to be awarded the Grammy Lifetime Achievement Award, joining the likes of Bing Crosby, Billie Holiday, Louis Armstrong, Charlie Parker, Roy Acuff, Hank Williams, Chuck Berry, and Bob Dylan as performers who'd made course-altering contributions to the recording field.

A few months later, in an unexpected way, they got down the last new Everly Brothers studio recording they'd ever make. Andrew Lloyd Webber, known for his big operatically influenced musical shows, and Jim Steinman, who wrote the over-the-top *Bat Out of Hell* Meat Loaf numbers, were turning the 1961 all-child-cast crime film *Whistle Down the Wind* into a musical. None of these factors scream "get the Everly Brothers," but they were invited to record the song "Cold" for use in the stage production. Don and Phil, in their separate hometowns, recorded their parts and the two tapes were amalgamated into the duo for the show. It's a chugging sort of "really cold winter" number, a reasonably charming change-up, redolent of their early sound, to close out their recording era.

In late April 1998, Don and Phil played Nashville's Ryman Auditorium for the first time in close to forty years, introduced by Chet Atkins. Don told the crowd, "Nothing's gonna top this." In the Nashville *Scene*, while heralding "Everlys affirm their place in pop history," Michael McCall answered his own question: "How does that youthful sound hold up, coming from men who are now 61 and 59 years old? Remarkably well, it turns out."

A few weeks later, they'd experience a peculiar sort of later career pleasure, when in the same auditorium *Bye Bye Love*, a family-friendly stage show they'd approved, premiered there, with Jeff Boyet, who'd had country records as Dale Jeffreys, and theme-park singer Matt Newton as Don and Phil. It wouldn't have the impact of Broadway's *Beatlemania* re-creation, but it was an indication of how the Everlys were appreciated and reconfirmed their music's continuing appeal. Mother Margaret, not untypically, indicated to friends that she didn't like the show because she hadn't had input into its book's narrative.

For Phil's sixtieth birthday in January 1999, wife Patti, with help from Terry Slater, staged a lavish surprise party at their Los Angeles home, described to Phil, misleadingly, as a casual get-together of a few friends. He dressed in what was already becoming a surprising everyday comfort-first offstage outfit for a guy raised to pay immense attention to his attire—an electric-blue sweatsuit and sneakers. Terry had convinced Phil's old touring band and other UK-based musicians to fly in for the event—and they all greeted him wearing the same outfit as his, then presented him gag gifts such as an old-age walker with a built-in microphone. Patti arranged with her LAPD friends to have a police helicopter fly overhead blaring the loud bullhorn warning "All you people down there: enjoy yourselves! Happy birthday, Phil."

On August 23, following a well-received two-week Everly Brothers stand at the Desert Inn in Las Vegas, Phil and Patti decided the five-year safety waiting period was up and they were married at the Caesars Palace wedding chapel. They reportedly mocked their own age difference by putting photos of Phil at twenty and Patti at two, same time, on the 120 guests' tables.

A few months later, the two of them bought a notable, substantial house, south of Nashville in Columbia, Tennessee, so they could spend the springs and falls there, besides winters in Los Angeles. This was a ten-bedroom 1846 mansion, six Southern pillars out front, right in the town. It was, historians knew, a place where the flamboyant, notorious Confederate general Nathan Bedford Forrest had recuperated after an argument with one of his own lieutenants that left him shot in the hip and the lieutenant dead. Forrest was later a founder of the Ku Klux Klan; Phil was careful to point out that, no, he wasn't living in Forrest's house.

He'd come to refer to it as his real home, a place where his extensive antiques collection fit well, where he could sit on the back porch and ponder, and where he'd set up a music room where visitors would work on songs with him. Sometimes Don came by.

If brothers Phillip and Donald Everly were rarely in perfect harmony in their offstage lives—and how many siblings are—they were now more in synch. While two years apart in age as always, they both had married for the last and lasting time at the age of sixty, committed and comfortable settling down. With Phil's purchase of that Columbia mansion, they were near each other for a good part of their off-the-road months for the first time since 1975. That's where they lived and how they stood, working right on into a new millennium.

Chapter Fifteen

ANOTHER CENTURY
2001–2021

A S THE TWENTY-FIRST CENTURY ARRIVED, "COUNTRY" MEANT BROOKS
& Dunn, Toby Keith, and Faith Hill, and "pop," in the mood for
harmonizing again, might be the Backstreet Boys, Destiny's Child,
or 'N Sync. Contexts change, but with Don and Phil now in their
sixties, they were still a live draw—a working, honored legacy act.
Grand gestures of recognition piled up.

In October 2001, the Everly Brothers were inducted into the
Country Music Hall of Fame, in the big catch-up edition marking
the Hall's move to their new expansive home. Multiple brother
duos were among the dozen acts inducted—the Delmore Brothers,
the Louvin Brothers, and the Everly Brothers. At a private black-tie
event, Phil sat smiling and joking with Charlie Louvin and Sam
Phillips (also inducted that night). Don didn't attend; neither did

Margaret. Phil's boys, Jason and Chris; his wife, Patti; and Don's daughter Venetia all did.

The plaque in the Country Music Hall of Fame reads, "The Everly Brothers updated country's duet harmony tradition, influencing generations of pop and rock & roll musicians.... The Everlys' music is known and loved all over the world." Accepting the honor at the installation ceremony, Phil said, "I want to thank my father for teaching us; I want to thank my mother for dreaming us. I want to thank Boudleaux and Felice for writing us. I want to thank Chet for guiding us. And I want to thank you all for honoring us."

A few weeks later, the Everlys' induction into the Country Hall was announced during the thirty-fifth annual CMA Awards, broadcast nationally from Nashville's Grand Ole Opry House. Inductees were no longer making acceptance speeches on-air, just given a moment to stand in place and accept the mention. Broadcast network minds had reached their dubious but hardening conclusion that the mass audience could only stand a few seconds of historical recognition.

The copy to be read was handed to the always charming ceremony host Vince Gill, who told the audience, "Inspired by the Louvin Brothers, Kentucky's Don and Phil Everly had hits with 'When Will I Be Loved,' 'Cathy's Clown,' 'Bye Bye Love,' 'Let It Be Me,' and so many more great records.... The Everly Brothers represent the country style called rockabilly—and nobody discovered more rockabilly talents than this next Hall of Fame member, producer Sam Phillips..." That was it. Two and a half sentences and on to Sam.

It's not certain whether Phil was listening closely enough to take in the quick, debatable part tagging them unequivocally as "rockabilly." He certainly heard the only *somewhat* true part about coming from Kentucky, and definitely heard the "inspired by the Louvin

Brothers" start, because that provoked him to bolt from the auditorium moments later.

The Bryants' son Del, by that time a senior executive at the BMI music rights organization, sat right behind him. He recalls, "I was very close to Phil....Well, they came to the part where they said one of their early influences was the Louvin Brothers. Phil all of a sudden gets up and walks out. I found him in the back and said, 'Phil, are you okay?' And he said '*Dammit*, we weren't influenced by the Louvin Brothers. I don't know if we'd even *heard of* the Louvin Brothers. That just pisses me off!' And he went on for over a minute. It was like lightning struck."

The "influenced by the Louvins" trope has been repeated and published hundreds of times, though even a quick check of where the Everlys and Louvins were working and heard before the Everlys were recording reveals they hadn't crossed paths or even shared radio listening range; the influence was minimal at most. A decade older than the Everlys, Charlie and Ira Louvin, focusing especially on gospel music, hadn't charted a hit single until the stellar "When I Stop Dreaming" in May 1955, and their way to share vocals and create harmony was really quite different from Don and Phil's approach. Because the news that the Everlys were joining the *Grand Ole Opry* cast came the same day the Louvins announced they were leaving, some thought Ira and Charlie were peeved by the hiring, but Charlie always maintained the timing was completely coincidental. The Everlys and friendly Louvins mingled easily in places such as the Nashville deejay conventions and valued each other as country contemporaries.

That same autumn of 2001, Don and Phil were each inducted into the Nashville Songwriters Hall of Fame as well, by their buddy Sonny Curtis, reflecting their writing's continuing impact and repeated recording by so many others. When the state of Kentucky established its own Music Hall of Fame and Museum in 2002, near the historic Renfro Valley Entertainment Center, the Everly Brothers were in its inaugural class of inductees, along with Bill Monroe, Loretta Lynn, Tom T. Hall, Rosemary Clooney, and Jean Ritchie. In 2004 came yet another induction, into the Sharon, Pennsylvania-based Vocal Group Hall of Fame, where they joined classic pop groups from the Mills Brothers and Andrews Sisters to Peter, Paul and Mary, and the Spinners. It was yet more comfortable company.

The shows went on. In October 2003, Phil and Don were invited by Paul Simon and Art Garfunkel to appear at the opening edition of their Old Friends reunion tour, at the Wachovia Arena in Wilkes-Barre, Pennsylvania, a one-off where they'd sing "Wake Up Little Susie" and "All I Have to Do Is Dream," then join their hosts on "Bye Bye Love," which was by now associated with both duos.

Don and Phil were visibly older, but the performances were energetic and touching, seemingly inspired by the invitation, the enthusiastic crowds, and the realistic possibility that they were nearing the end of their performing years. It was not quite time for that. As Simon detailed later, "I said, 'Phil, look, if you're going to retire, you might as well come out one more time and take a bow, and let me at least say what it is that you meant to us and to the culture.'"

They joined the whole tour, their excursion together proceeding east to west across the country, then back to the northeast, including multiple shows at Madison Square Garden. By the summer of 2004, the dual shows had extended from the Hollywood Bowl to Hyde Park, London. Long-standing tensions between Paul and Artie themselves were by now the stuff of stage jokes, and somewhere in the course of this adventure Paul first made his oft-quoted crack, "See, you don't have to be brothers to hate each other." A DVD video and double CD were released chronicling the tour, and the Everlys' set was included on both.

Phil's experience with guitars and penchant for tinkering in his workshop along with his sons led to his development, with Jason, of a guitar-string coating that made strings last longer and play louder. Patented, they'd be marketed by the company they set up for it, Cleartone Strings, run by Jason, with electric guitar versions sold as Everly Strings or Everly Rockers. Phil told *Guitar Player* magazine, "I've always had an interest in how things are made, and I felt that guitar strings could be improved upon with more modern machinery.... Both of my sons are musicians, so I thought it would be a real good thing if they had a business to fall back on...Jason became an expert.... They've made a good success of it."

At about that time, a Dutch TV series, *Star Children*, ran a program focusing on Jason and Phil, their affection and shared experiences sweetly obvious. They're seen in Central City, Kentucky (the down-home location still irresistible for European television, it seems), singing "In the Pines." Jason points out that the area and its stories are interesting and sad—even for a guy like him, brought up entirely in Los Angeles. It isn't mentioned, but at times Phil is huffing for air, just trying to speak.

Singing must have become challenging for him, but stimulated by the Simon & Garfunkel tour, the Everly Brothers decided they'd go on, with another tour of their own, beginning in the UK in November, with shows scheduled in a dozen cities, maybe more. It would turn out to be their valedictory go-round.

The year 2005 had a certain round-number symmetry about it; it was exactly fifty years since they'd walked into a studio to record their first records for Columbia—and just about sixty since they'd gone on-air in Shenandoah. Don was sixty-eight, Phil sixty-six. Albert Lee, their lead guitar player for decades by then, recalled, "When we got together again to tour the U.K., Phil was struggling a bit on the high notes, and if he couldn't make the high note, he'd sing in unison with Don—and Don hated that.... A couple of times,

Phil suggested maybe lowering the song a key or two. Well, Don wouldn't hear any of that."

The dozen nostalgic UK shows went well enough. Don would announce at each performance, sounding more or less resigned to it, "I'm still Don. He's still Phil. And we're still the Everly Brothers." The audiences would cheer. They introduced some of their old-school acoustic country songs by playing a recording of a 1951 Everly Family radio show where they sang "Don't Let Our Love Die," then faded into it live, these fifty-four years later.

At Manchester, Graham Nash joined them for energetic three-part harmony versions of "So Sad" and "Bye Bye Love." It worked well, but their final, shaky return performance at the Royal Albert Hall six nights later was diminished by the vocal issues Albert recalled. Betty Clark reported in the *Guardian*, "Watching Don struggle with his solo and Phil twitching as he adds high harmonies is heartbreaking....Still...if, as is rumored, this is the last Everly Brothers UK tour, it's a warm goodbye."

By some accounts, Phil had already told Don privately that he couldn't go on like this. The last show was at the Regent Theatre at Ipswich on November 28, 2005, the final song Sam Cooke's "You Send Me." It was dirge slow, and to these ears, on the recording grabbed there, so sad.

Albert recalled, "We were supposed to go on to Vegas and Reno...but Phil decided he'd had enough. We were in the bus with him on the way back to London celebrating the last gig and he told us that was it."

Predictably perhaps, how Don and Phil envisioned semiretirement differed sharply. The more gregarious Phil often got together with other music makers, while Don would spend most of his time at home or eating out locally with Adela and her twin, Adelaida, who lived with them as well. He might stop up at the lodge in Kentucky, and occasionally would do local Dead Cowboys shows, but that low profile he'd been keeping just got lower. Asked what he'd been up to in 2011, Don replied, "I listen to the music in the car.... I switch between WSM, the country music station and NPR....I don't write too much with people.... The only thing I've written about lately are my poodles."

Within months, Phil recorded a bouncy Everly Brothers–like tune, "Sweet Little Corrina," with Vince Gill, now far from a forty-dollar demo singer, who'd call the pairing one of his "greatest career blessings." In a confluence of harmony singers, Phil joined Righteous Brother Bill Medley and Beach Boy Brian Wilson in a stately new version of Wilson's "In My Room." And when the Crickets were inducted into Nashville's Musicians Hall of Fame in 2008, he sang "Let It Be Me" with them, and caught up with Keith Richards, who inducted them. He also backed nephew Edan Everly on "Another Shade of Blue," a track on his 2011 album *Songs from Bikini Atoll*.

Phil and Patti now had three addresses—the Burbank place for the winters, a beach house on Alabama's Gulf Coast for the summers, and the Columbia mansion south of Nashville for the springs and falls. He'd have friends in to play music and write songs in all three.

Both Pat Alger and Sonny Curtis wrote with him at the mansion fairly regularly. He wrote with buddy Duane Eddy on the porch of the Gulf Coast house, during Eddy family visits there. Newer name Nashville writers such as Bobby Tomberlin and Shawn Camp would come to Columbia, too. Tomberlin would recall, "I was very nervous the first time that I was going to write with Phil....It didn't take five minutes for me to feel relaxed around him. He and his wife Patti became extended family."

Shawn Camp, bluegrass singer, writer of number-one country songs for Garth Brooks, Brooks & Dunn, and Josh Turner, and guitar player with both Cowboy Jack Clement's and Guy Clark's bands, wrote with Phil in Columbia on multiple occasions, along with Billy Burnette, also in Jack Clement's band and a friend of Patti's, and at other times alone with Phil out in Hollywood.

When Shawn mentioned that he'd bumped into Don at a Nashville grocery store and found that he was headed to the hospital for a knee operation, Phil had known nothing about it. Once again, the brothers were not much in touch. "I never let on to Phil that I knew Don very well," Shawn admitted, finding that wise. "But they were connected at the heart whether they liked it or not. Phil told me that he felt like harmony singing was the purest form of love on earth, just following someone wherever they went. He loved Don *that* way." Shawn was visiting Phil and Patti in Hollywood when, on the way to lunch, she barely tapped the bumper of the car behind them and they had words, as spouses will. "It was a playful thing," he recalls. "You could see the love in the way they bickered."

In 2009, Phil was on hand at a Rosanne Cash concert at the Country Hall's Ford Theater, where in introducing her take on "Love Hurts," she referred to it as a song she'd picked up "from Gram and Emmylou." Phil stood halfway up in his seat and shrugged demonstrably, sad-sack "Whatcha gonna do?" style, to the appreciative laughter of the crowd.

He spent most of his time living the daily life of the "regular guy" people perceived he was, immense talent aside, exactly what he very much wanted to be. He'd eat at the Olive Garden chain Italian restaurant, shop at Home Depot, watch old Westerns on TV, barbecue burgers for guests, and attend local high school football games. And he played with Jason's two daughters, the grandkids.

The surprise to Shawn on that Burbank visit was that Phil greeted him at the door strapped to a breath assistance device, hooked up to oxygen tanks. As early as 2001, he'd stopped smoking because he was having those breathing issues. In 2011, he was diagnosed with chronic obstructive pulmonary disease, COPD, no doubt a result of his years of smoking. Patti would say of living with that affliction, "In the middle of the night, you look over to see if they're still breathing." Through his years left, Phil would have the oxygen with him. His last public appearance was that same year, joining María Elena Holly as her late husband Buddy Holly, Phil's friend of fifty years before, was added to the Hollywood Walk of Fame.

Don was rarely seen out and about. Songwriter Paul Kennerley recalls, "In around 2010 we met at Starbucks, and I asked him, 'Don, don't you ever want to record or play?' . . . He just wasn't on fire. I said, 'Look, come back to my house; I could hook you up with people who'd just sing with you and play, somebody like Buddy Miller'—low-key. I'm thinking maybe he'll cut a track with Don to get him going. Just sitting in the kitchen, they played a couple of Hank Williams things, and I said, 'Don, it would be great to just get a group of musicians around; Buddy has a studio.' But he just didn't seem interested."

Phil was writing with his own mortality in mind. Duane Eddy detailed, "We wrote this song together, 'After I'm Gone.' You know, his wife Patti adored him. . . . The chorus ends with, 'You will love again, after I'm gone.' After we finished it, there were tears in his eyes. . . . Phil sang harmony with himself. . . . If we mixed in the harmony vocal too much, it sounded just like a song with his brother." On hearing the mix, Phil said, "Oh good. It's not another damned Everly Brothers' song." As of this writing, the recording has yet to be released.

Jason reported, "I don't remember the last time the brothers actually saw each other. It's possible they had a meeting here or there. . . . There's always some business stuff to chat about, and their mom [was] still alive. Periodically, you know, birthdays, holidays, they would chat. Don would be like, 'You look grayer now.' 'Ah, you too.'" In 2013, their original recording of "Cathy's Clown" was added to the US Library of Congress's National Recording Registry, naming it as an American recording worthy of permanent preservation. There was no disagreement about that.

In a late 2013 piece in the *Wall Street Journal*, Phil said of the Columbia mansion, "The house makes me feel kind of solid... I like things that are way older than I am and are going to outlast me.... My favorite space is my music room.... Occasionally Don comes by from Nashville. And, no, we're not getting back together. We're retired, and there's plenty of music people can buy if they want."

He was certainly right about that. The extraordinary German label Bear Family had by that point carefully curated and released three enormous box sets of Everly Brothers recordings, including everything released and more from their first Columbia sessions through the Warner Bros. years and the RCA recordings of the 1970s, unheard outtakes and live material included. The Mercury/PolyGram recordings were still available and eventually anthologized, too, and Warners put out additional CDs with further alternate takes. A short-lived, adventurous Nashville wing of the Varèse Sarabande label released revealing early demo records by both brothers.

Phil's struggles with COPD had gone on for years. Then the symptoms took a sharp turn for the worse. He was admitted to the Providence Saint Joseph Medical Center in Burbank, and he passed away there on January 3, 2014.

There was an immediate outpouring of grief from everyday fans, seen broadly in social media. Admiring music makers marked his passing, if often within newspaper obituaries that talked more about the Everly Brothers act, less of Phil the man and singer. Headlines heralded loss of "half of the brilliant duo." Art Garfunkel, to his credit, was quoted saying simply, "Your sound, dear Phil, was my model of beauty and charisma when I was 14." Paul McCartney posted on Facebook, "When I finally met Phil, I was completely starstruck and at the same time extremely impressed by his humility and gentleness of soul. I will always love him for giving me some of the sweetest musical memories of my life." Linda Ronstadt and Graham Nash shared personal and professional empathy for Phil's life and career in newspaper and radio interviews. *Mojo* magazine lamented the loss of "a prince among men."

The humility so many spoke of when describing Phil had become for him a watchword. As the preacher at the memorial service quoted him as saying, "If your ego is in check, then your life is in check."

Don, as was his pattern faced with any death, stayed out of sight, but he released a wholehearted, even mystical statement the morning after Phil died: "I was listening to one of my favorite songs that Phil wrote and had an extreme emotional moment just before I got the news of his passing. I took that as a special spiritual message from Phil saying goodbye. Our love was and will always be deeper than any earthly differences we might have had. . . . The world might be mourning an Everly Brother, but I'm mourning my brother."

Don would not attend either Phil's memorial service in Columbia or burial of his ashes at Central City, Kentucky, close to Ike's burial spot. The Everly family established a Phil Everly Memorial Fund, contributions going to the fight against COPD.

The roots-music world was seeing a marked revival of interest in harmony singing just then, synchronicity at work, often with the Everly Brothers as models. In Phil's final interview, in *Paste* magazine, he commented on this emerging trend, praising the vocal work Norah Jones and Green Day's Billie Joe Armstrong were doing in particular. Their salute album, *Foreverly*, replicated the entirety of *Songs Our Daddy Taught Us*, song for song, a little faster and electrified, but with dead-on harmonies and a good deal of Everly-like tone. Soon, there would be full albums of Everlys material interpretation by Abigail and Lily Chapin (the Chapin Sisters, *A*

Date with the Everly Brothers), Dawn McCarthy and Bonnie "Prince" Billy (*What the Brothers Sang*), and the band Dead Rock West (*It's Everly Time!*). All evoke cruxes of the songs, but none are retro in sound or production—fine, smart, and appropriately varied salutes. Additional young, clearly Everly Brothers–influenced duos were gaining notice, too, including the Milk Carton Kids, the Cactus Blossoms, and the Secret Sisters. Peter Asher, of Peter & Gordon, long an important roots-rock producer, noted, "Every duo that came after them tried to sing like the Everlys, but none of us could match them. It remains everyone's idea of the ideal duo."

A few weeks after Phil's passing, the Americana Music Association staged a pre–Grammy Awards salute, recognizing Phil and Don's absolutely foundational role pioneering that genre, which is all about contemporary change-ups on American music rooted in time and place. The all-star revue included performers Bonnie Raitt, Ry Cooder, Rodney Crowell, Rhiannon Giddens, and the Haden Triplets—daughters of Charlie Haden from that other Iowa radio family. Patti Everly was in the audience; Rodney Crowell read a note from Don sending his regrets for not being there, still feeling too brokenhearted to be out and about.

Mourning, he was out of sight for months. An Everly Brothers tribute was scheduled by the Rock & Roll Hall of Fame for October 2014—a major weeklong edition of that Hall's American Music Masters series, with panels, interviews with Everlys band members, and films, at Case Western Reserve, climaxing with a concert, and all about Don and Phil's continuing influence. Speakers included country music historian Colin Escott and pop critic and author Ann Powers, who delivered the keynote address. "Everly Brothers music," she suggested, "was the sound of young people thinking. It gave sonic shape to the motion of emotions, especially the ones that kids tended to keep to themselves: yearning, self-doubt, resentment, shaky hope."

Don agreed to attend the week-climaxing musical gala, but not to perform. With Rodney Crowell the emcee and Albert Lee leading the band, that October 25 show featured a series of special duet combinations performing Everlys songs—Emmylou Harris and Alison Krauss, Vince Gill and Keb' Mo', Allison Moorer and Shelby Lynne, Peter Asher and Vince Gill, Waddy Wachtel and Graham Nash.

As the evening's end approached, Don was brought to the stage to accept the American Music Masters award from the Rock Hall's CEO Greg Harris. He was seventy-seven and looked noticeably older—thinner now, the hair silvered, the cheekbones that once gave his face its edge showing again. He changed his mind in the moment—as was his way—and sharing a mic with Graham Nash, led the full cast in "Bye Bye Love." The crowd was both excited and teary-eyed. Nobody had seen him sing that in nine years.

Though most of his time was spent at home, he occasionally checked in with Paul Kennerley. Paul recalled, "It was a year or so after Phil died; I hadn't seen him since. He came over to the house, and Adela was with him. He was using a stick because he'd had a knee replacement, but he was still driving. I said, 'I'm very, very sorry about Phil.' And he said, 'All I do is sit in the car and listen to Phillip. That's *all* I listen to.'"

After all of the conflicts, all of the long silences, the meticulous arrangements for peaceful coexistence, the harmony and disharmony, Don Everly missed his brother.

On a visit, Kennerley was concerned to find that he was virtually never playing music: "And leaning against the back of the sofa was a guitar, and I could see the bridge was coming away from the wood. He clearly hadn't played it. I said, 'This is one of the most important guitars in the world.' It was the one featured on all the key records. In the basement was a Cadillac Green Gibson 335 electric, leaning with its headstock fused to the wall."

"We gently got it off," Paul continued, "then drove to Joe Glaser Instruments in Berry Hill and Joe is in seventh heaven, because he knows what the first one is. So we leave it with him, and Don worked with him on that. The guitar was restored, and the electric, too. Glaser would say, 'It was not lost on me what an honor it was to work on those.'"

In a 2016 phone interview with his childhood home base, KMA radio in Shenandoah, Don admitted that Phil's absence haunted him: "I think about him every day . . . I have a bit of his ashes here at my house, and I go by, and pick the ashes up, and I sort of say good morning to him."

Don turned eighty on February 1, 2017, and since time had evolved his appearance, there are multiple stories of Nashville locals not quite recognizing who he was anymore. Tour guides at the old RCA Victor Studio B mentioned to visitors that Don showed up one day wanting to have a nostalgic look around where the Everlys had recorded "('Til) I Kissed You," and the person at the door checked his driver's license before recognizing who he was. Margaret related a phone call to her good friend Penny Campbell Loewen: "Don said he had gone to the store and as he was walking down the aisle he noticed a couple of ladies staring at him, so he'd reported, 'I may have sung a couple of Everly Brothers songs as I was shopping to let them know that it's really me.'"

Margaret was approaching her one hundredth birthday; as her neighbor Brenna Davenport-Leigh, onetime head of A&R for RCA Nashville, recalls, she was still living an active, engaged life, taking karate lessons and getting dressed and putting on makeup every day, even when she wasn't setting foot out of the house. She kept in touch by phone with people across Everlys fan circles, but not so much with Don. Martial Bekkers of the international fan club recalled, "Donald really avoided her. There was one time when he'd bought a special car he was going to show her, and he went up the driveway hill and parked it there, and she came out of the house to talk to him about it a little—and that was it. He wouldn't step further on, and her coming out was a signal that he couldn't go in."

In 2017, the old question of songwriting credit for "Cathy's Clown," seemingly settled in 1980, surfaced again, on the question of writing credit, not royalties, which are distinct. In the epic *Everly v. Everly* legal battle Don himself and Phil's heirs both filed notices under copyright law to terminate previous agreements on the matter—Don's to formally end the 1960 song assignment to Acuff-Rose as publisher, Phil's family's to terminate the 1980 agreement that removed Phil as cowriter.

Don sued Phil's heirs seeking to confirm his status as sole writer and so able to break with Acuff-Rose as the publisher on his own. A first court found against him on the grounds that the authorship was still in dispute. Court decisions went back and forth until a final one in February 2023, which decided that Phil's family's effort had been made past the statute of limitations for reopening the case. None of this changed how people care about "Cathy's Clown."

In June 2018, Don made another rare performance appearance, joining Paul Simon onstage at Nashville's Bridgestone Arena during Simon's farewell tour. Naturally, they sang "Bye Bye Love" for the large arena crowd. Paul then announced, "Well, that makes my night; I got to be Phil Everly."

Life with Adela was not always tranquil—or private. She had some issues of her own. In July 2019, for instance, she made local headlines when she was arrested by the Tennessee Highway Patrol for driving recklessly—speeding, driving off the road, barely avoiding crashing into multiple vehicles, then plowing into a patrol car. The charges, piled on heavily at the time, were apparently not seriously pursued. She and her sister had little to do with Don's family at all, which tended to keep him away from them, too.

Don's devotion to her was unabated, though he did take an occasional time-out. Sonny Curtis recalls, "A year or so before Don died, while his wife was in Texas, he spent a week out at J.I.'s [Jerry Allison's] house. J.I., Don, and I hung out every day, had a few beers, and even visited the Johnny Cash Museum. We saw Don a lot."

That October, he received official recognition long due from *somewhere*, for his creation of the groundbreaking, slashing guitar intro to "Wake Up Little Susie," in the form of the Musicians Hall of Fame's Iconic Riff Award, which proclaimed it "one of the most recognizable guitar riffs of all time." It was certainly one of the most influential. He turned up for the awards ceremony at Nashville's Schermerhorn Symphony Center to receive it.

Before that, though, he took a private walking tour of the museum itself with Jay McDowell, bass player and cofounder of the revivalist country band BR549, Everly Brothers lovers all. Jay was then head of the video department of the Musicians Hall, and recalls, "Jerry Allison was there, and he introduced me to Don as 'one of us,' the coolest thing anybody ever said to me or about me. But the beauty was seeing what sparked Don's memory."

The place is designed with sections on different recording centers. There was Music Row, and Don recalled and talked about what Chet Atkins, who'd died in 2001, had meant for them and for him. There was Motown, which he could recall visiting and their show with the Four Tops. There was the Los Angeles Wrecking Crew gang, so many of them close friends and recording partners. It was a walking tour of an American musical life in review.

Paul Shaffer, the awards show emcee, read a note from Paul Simon, who was unable to attend, underscoring how Don's guitar playing had influenced thousands around the world. Ricky Skaggs inducted Don, calling it an honor for another boy from Kentucky, and reminding all of what collaborative work the making of the

"Wake Up Little Susie" record had been, and how Boudleaux had left room in the song for Don to add those riffs.

Don was determined to walk onto the stage without the cane he'd been using, and he did. He told the crowd, breathily, "I appreciate it, I really do, after all these years—sixty years—have gone by. . . . It's been a pleasure." He continued: "I love all the musicians here in Nashville. I never thought Nashville was going to turn into Music City, but it did. Anyway—thank you!" And he ambled off, in his last public appearance.

One month later, the indefatigable Margaret Everly reached her one hundredth birthday—as cogent in her comments about most other people, at least, as ever, but the extraordinary age had taken a toll physically. Her eyesight weakened badly, and she was less mobile negotiating the narrow stairway in her house. She had a band of neighbors she could call on to shop and run errands for her, and granddaughter Venetia Ember remained close, but a certain bitterness had set in. Martial Bekkers recalls, "The last phone calls I had with her, when she was around a hundred, she was very profound, but she would tell you stories where she was *the* one who'd created the chances for them." Visiting her, Janet Bozeman, daughter of Mack and Jeanie Sanders, old friends of the Everlys who'd been on Shenandoah radio, too, found a disgruntled Margaret saying out loud, "*I* was the real talent in the family. *I* should have been the star."

Don celebrated his eighty-first birthday out at a restaurant with Adela and Adelaida, joined by Michelle Phillips—a friend since the Hollywood days when he was with her close friend Ann Marshall. They shared some birthday cake.

It's not certain that it was the last thing mother Margaret ever said to son Donald, but he confided to multiple friends, including Del Bryant, that she'd looked him in the eye, wagged a finger, and said, "I'm goin' to outlive—*you!*"

And so it was. Don Everly died at home on August 21, 2021, after a brief hospitalization, no specific cause ever announced. He was eighty-four. Adela reportedly saw to it that his body was quickly cremated, and his immediate family apparently only got word at second hand. The public announcement came on the Everly Brothers Instagram online account space: "It is with great sadness that we regret to announce the passing of Isaac Donald Everly today. He leaves behind his wife Adela, mother Margaret, children Venetia, Stacy, Erin & Edan, grandchildren Arabella, Easan, Stirling, Eres, Lily & Esper."

The Associated Press and *Los Angeles Times* published a statement attributed to the family, via Nashville entertainment lawyer Linda Edell Howard: "Don lived by what he felt in his heart. Don expressed his appreciation for the ability to live his dreams... living in love with his soul mate and wife Adela, and sharing the music that made him an Everly Brother. Don always expressed how grateful he was for his fans."

Kyle Young, the Country Music Hall of Fame CEO, said, "As a singer, a songwriter and a guitar innovator, Don Everly was one of the most talented and impactful artists in popular music history." American papers, caught by surprise, mainly added the news flash to pre-readied Everly Brothers histories and, we can sigh, referred to him as a second musical half.

In the UK's *New Musical Express*, Mark Beaumont saluted Don in a whole new way—for "exposing the horrors" of touring with a sibling for months on end, for decades. He wrote, "Pop music has always been about the pretense of perfection.... When the Everly Brothers shattered the illusion, popular music instantly became more real and relatable. For this added layer of pop honesty and emotion, we have Don and Phil to thank."

In October, closing the "In Memoriam" segment of the annual Rock & Roll Hall of Fame inductions in Cleveland, Brandi Carlile and her twin backup singer-instrumentalists, Phil and Tim Hanseroth, marked Don's passing with a warmly received, melodic version of "All I Have to Do Is Dream." On December 6, just over fifteen weeks after Don's death, true to her word, Margaret Embry Everly died at age 102. She was interred not in Central City beside Ike, but in a mausoleum at Nashville's Woodlawn Memorial Park.

Sites celebrating the musical contributions of the Everly Brothers and the family have been established in key places they lived, utterly fitting for performers whose legacy was built on multiple regional roots.

In Central City, Kentucky, the Muhlenberg County Music Museum exhibits an extensive range of Everlys multimedia memorabilia, local family origins and Homecoming events emphasized. At the entrance to the town's Festival Square, three six-foot-tall bronze statues were unveiled in 2024 honoring Muhlenberg County heroes Phil and Don, and John Prine.

In Shenandoah, Iowa, the principal house the Everly family had lived in, relocated to a more central location near the town's general museum, serves as an Everly Brothers Childhood Family Home museum, focusing on the family's life and radio years there. Larger-than-life, well-lit cutout images of Phil and Don now greet visitors as they approach the town.

In Knoxville, Tennessee, with the efforts of some celebrated Everlys fans, an Everly Brothers Park includes signed-in-concrete walkway quotes about the Everlys from Graham Nash (who fostered and chaired the project), Simon & Garfunkel, Keith Richards, Carole King, Brian Wilson, Joan Baez, Bob Dylan, and Albert Lee. A Tennessee Music Pathways marker with the brothers' likeness forms a centerpiece.

The very name "Everly Brothers" has so come to stand for a singular level of sibling harmony in the popular imagination that there are multiple musical groups that, formally or in jest, are referred to as the Neverly Brothers, the Cleverly Brothers, the Foreverly Brothers, and even the Whateverly Brothers. That's some bottom-up cultural hold.

Both Phil and Don had expressed trepidation at times that with popular music's evanescence, what they'd been doing would only be briefly recalled and was maybe not even all that important in the scheme of things. Those were unwarranted doubts.

While the whole world seemed to be watching, and when no one was looking, those polite, photogenic brothers had had the audacity to cook up a musical combination of their own. It was steeped in knowledge of the country music and R&B that had preceded them, but it was unlike anyone else's mixture of the two. It charmed, and it became all of ours, their vocal ideas and instrumental attacks ingrained in popular music ever since. That's their lasting monument.

Phillip Everly once said, "Our music is country at heart; country in attitude . . . I guess it'll always be. . . . There's been a *lot* of pioneer rock 'n' roll. We were among the few, in our time, to do country music as a giant departure, to fuse it with rock."

And Donald Everly once said, "I guess we did our little share. It wasn't intentional, like we said, 'Let's go out and create something.' We sort of got swept up in the current. . . . We just followed our instincts. . . . You've got to do it your own way. . . . After all, you're either in the right spot at the right time or you're not."

Repeatedly, they were.

ACKNOWLEDGMENTS

MUCH OF THE EVERLY BROTHERS' STORY IS NOW HISTORY. AS I BEGAN this project, the ace Nashville guitarist Ray Edenton was the last person alive who'd taken part in the Everlys' sessions back at Cadence Records, on their original, career-making hits. I'd looked forward to discussing those sessions with him, but he passed away in September 2022, a few weeks short of ninety-six.

Pulling this story together relied heavily on scattered documentation; that makes me all the more grateful for those who shared their time, thoughts, and stories with me to add much more to the picture. The Everlys had a wide variety of knowledgeable, passionate, and very often witty collaborators and friends that have been my pleasure to get to know—face-to-face, via video or audio calls, and in a few cases, by messaging and email.

The interviewees included Pat Alger, the late Jerry "J.I." Allison, Martial Bekkers, Janet Bozeman, Del Bryant, Shawn Camp, Kathy Cole, Diane Craig, Sonny Curtis, Brenna Davenport-Leigh, Jimmy Eaton, Ron Elliott, Mark T. Greene, Bill Harlan, María Elena Holly, Silas House, Phil Kaufman, Paul Kennerley, Bernie Kukoff, Brenda Lee, Penny Campbell Loewen, Ann Marshall, Jay McDowell, Kathie McMahon-Davie, Buddy Miller, Graham Nash, Don Peake, Fiona Prine, Sam Trust, and Don Wayne. I again thank them all.

I want to acknowledge especially the multi-decade work of the Everly Brothers International fan club and their Everly.net site and EverlyNet Facebook group caretakers, who go so far beyond their expected role as promulgators of the music and memory of the Everlys they hold so dear, operating as archivists of related artifacts, reports, photos, and videos, many of which would have been lost without their dedication. I am particularly grateful for the beyond-the-call help of their officers Martial Bekkers and Bas Siewertsen, and active members Tasso Matheas, Barbara Ann Lake, Kathy Cole, Sherry Davis, Bobbie Sue Tubbs Jennings, Lynda Harpe, E. Elizabeth Beckman, and Richard Beckman.

The world of historians, journalists, and critics of American roots music is neither as broad nor as fiercely competitive as some imagine. We do tend to know each other, and sometimes rely on each other. I want to offer special thanks to my fellow scribblers who were good enough to share tips, thoughts on Everly encounters, and in the cases of Robert K. (Bob) Oermann and David Menconi, invaluable unpublished notes and drafts. And I want to acknowledge aid from Paula Bishop, Eric Brace, Patrick Doyle, Colin Escott, Lee Gardner, Peter Guralnick, Rich Kienzle, Mark Lewisohn, Marc Meyers, Betsy Phillips, Ann Powers, Jim Rooney, Andrew Sandoval, Joel Selvin, Kevin Trask, George Varga, Elijah Wald, Eric Weisbard, and Richard Wieze.

As always, the efforts of archivists and the institutions they represent have added much to what I've been able to show and report on here, including Michael Gray, Adam Iddings, Kevin Fleming, and Kathleen Campbell of the Country Music Hall of Fame and Museum, Andy Leach of the Rock & Roll Hall of Fame, Kara Molitor of the UCLA Library Film & Television Archive, Jason Lambert of Sony Pictures Entertainment, Tim Davis of the Grand Ole Opry Archives, Bill Hillman of the Everly Brothers Childhood Home, Mark Davidson of the Bob Dylan Archive, and House of Bryant Publications.

I am glad to have this opportunity to acknowledge and offer my thanks to my good friend of over twenty-five years, author and critic David Cantwell, who was kind enough to give this entire volume a once-over for comments, and astute and reliable enough that I'd asked him to make them.

This book project would almost surely not have been embarked on at all without the exceptional savvy, reliability, and keen responses of my longtime literary agent, Paul Bresnick, who noticed my involvement in an online discussion of the need for a modern, substantial Everly Brothers biography and quickly asked what turned out to be the reasonable question: "Why not write it?" That mission became real because of the faith in my ability to do the job by this book's editor, Ben Schafer of Hachette/Da Capo Press. I want to express my appreciation of the work done by him and the staff there to make this real.

Final thanks for a lifetime of ingrained, unforgettable music to the Everly Brothers themselves, and for the rewarding life I have, to my love, friend, advisor, and fellow music lover, my wife Nina Melechen.

—Barry Mazor
Nashville, Tennessee

BIBLIOGRAPHY

Amburn, Ellis. *Buddy Holly: A Biography*. New York: St. Martin's Press, 1995.

———. *Dark Star: The Tragic Story of Roy Orbison*. Secaucus, NJ: Carol Publishing, 1990.

Anderson, Bobby. *That Muhlenberg Sound*. Beechmont, KY: Muhlbut Press, 1993.

Bedford, David. *The Country of Liverpool: Nashville of the North*. Self-published, Liddypool, 2020.

Berry, Chad, ed. *The Hayloft Gang: The Story of the* National Barn Dance. Urbana and Chicago: University of Illinois Press, 2008, esp. Lisa Krissoff Boehm, "Chicago as Forgotten Country Music Mecca," 103–118.

Birkby, Robert. *KMA Radio: The First Sixty Years*. Shenandoah, IA: May Broadcasting, 1985.

Bishop, Paula Jean. "The Roots and Influences of the Everly Brothers." PhD diss., Boston University, 2011.

Brady, Erika. "Contested Origins: Arnold Shultz and the Music of Western Kentucky." In *Hidden in the Mix: The African American Presence in Country Music*, edited by Diane Pecknold, 100–118. Durham, NC: Duke University Press, 2013.

Charone, Barbara. *Keith Richards: Life as a Rolling Stone*. Garden City, NY: Dolphin/Doubleday, 1982.

Cornyn, Stan, with Paul Scanlon. *Exploding: The Highs, Hits, Hype, Heroes, and Hustlers of the Warner Music Group*. New York: HarperEntertainment, 2002.

Country Music Hall of Fame. *We Could: The Songwriting Artistry of Boudleaux and Felice Bryant*. Nashville: Country Music Foundation Press, 2019.

Delmore, Alton. *The Delmore Brothers: Truth Is Stranger Than Publicity*. Edited by Charles K. Wolfe. Nashville: Country Music Foundation Press, 1995.

Dodge, Consuelo. *The Everly Brothers: Ladies Love Outlaws*. Stark, FL: Cin-Dav, 1991.

Doggett, Peter. *Are You Ready for the Country*. New York: Penguin Books, 2000.

Egan, Sean, ed. *Keith Richards on Keith Richards: Interviews and Encounters*. Chicago: Chicago Review Press, 2013.

Escott, Colin. *Classic Everly Brothers*. Bear Family BCD 15618, 1992. Box set book.

Ewing, Tom. *Bill Monroe: The Life and Music of the Blue Grass Man*. Urbana, Chicago, and Springfield: University of Illinois Press, 2018.

Fishell, Steve. *Buddy Emmons: Steel Guitar Icon*. Urbana: University of Illinois Press, 2022.

Fogerty, John. *Fortunate Son: My Life, My Music*. New York: Little, Brown, 2015.

Fong-Torres, Ben. *Willin': The Story of Little Feat*. Boston: Da Capo, 2013.

Friedman, Douglas E. *Four Boys and a Guitar: The Story and Music of the Mills Brothers.* West Long Branch, NJ: Harmony Songs Publications, 2016.

Gerron, Peggy Sue, and Glenda Cameron. *Whatever Happened to Peggy Sue?* Tyler, TX: TogiEntertainment, 2007.

Goldrosen, John, and John Beecher. *Remembering Buddy.* New York: Penguin Books, 1987.

Gopinath, Sumanth, and Anna Schultz. "Sentimental Remembrance and the Amusements of Forgetting in Karl and Harty's 'Kentucky.'" *Journal of the American Musicological Society* 69, no. 2 (2016): 477–524.

Guarino, Mark. *Country and Midwestern: Chicago in the History of Country Music and the Folk Revival.* Chicago: University of Chicago Press, 2023.

Guralnick, Peter. *Dream Boogie: The Triumph of Sam Cooke.* New York: Little, Brown, 2005.

Hartman, Kent. *The Wrecking Crew: The Inside Story of Rock and Roll's Best-Kept Secret.* New York: Thomas Dunne Books, 2012.

Hermes, Will. *Lou Reed: The King of New York.* New York: Farrar, Straus and Giroux, 2023.

Hodge, Joshua S., ed. *Cas Walker: Stories on His Life and Legend.* Knoxville: University of Tennessee Press, 2019.

Hoskyns, Barney. *Hotel California: The True-Life Adventures of Crosby, Stills, Nash, Young, Mitchell, Taylor, Browne, Ronstadt, Geffen, the Eagles, and Their Many Friends.* Hoboken, NJ: John Wiley & Sons, 2006.

Huffman, Eddie. *John Prine: In Spite of Himself.* Austin: University of Texas Press, 2015.

Jacks, David. *Peter Asher: A Life in Music.* Lanham, MD: Backbeat, 2022.

Jarrett, Michael. *Producing Country: The Inside Story of the Great Recordings.* Middletown, CT: Wesleyan University Press, 2014.

Karpp, Phyllis. *Ike's Boys: The Story of the Everly Brothers.* Ann Arbor, MI: Pierian Press, 1988.

King, Carole. *A Natural Woman: A Memoir.* New York: Grand Central, 2012.

Kosser, Michael. *How Nashville Became Music City, USA.* Milwaukee: Hal Leonard, 2006.

Kushins, C.M. *Nothing's Bad Luck: The Lives of Warren Zevon.* New York: Da Capo, 2019.

Lewisohn, Mark. *Tune In: The Beatles: All These Years.* Vol. 1. New York: Crown, 2013.

Louvin, Charlie, with Benjamin Whitmer. *Satan Is Real: The Ballad of the Louvin Brothers.* New York: It Books/HarperCollins, 2012.

Malone, Bobbie, and Bill C. Malone. *Nashville's Songwriting Sweethearts: The Boudleaux and Felice Bryant Story.* Norman: University of Oklahoma Press, 2020.

Marks, J., and Linda Eastman. *Rock and Other Four Letter Words: Music of the Electric Generation.* New York: Bantam Books, 1968.

Mazor, Barry. *Meeting Jimmie Rodgers: How America's Original Roots Music Hero Changed the Pop Sounds of a Century.* New York: Oxford University Press, 2009.

———. *Ralph Peer and the Making of Popular Roots Music.* Chicago: Chicago Review Press, 2015.

Morrison, Simon. *Mirror in the Sky: The Life and Music of Stevie Nicks.* Oakland: University of California Press, 2022.

Murphy, James B. *Becoming the Beach Boys 1961–1963.* Jefferson, NC: McFarland, 2015.

Nadelson, Reggie. *Comrade Rockstar: The Life and Mystery of Dean Reed.* New York: Walker, 2006.

Nash, Graham. *Wild Tales: A Rock & Roll Life.* New York: Three Rivers Press, 2013.

Norman, Philip. "The Everly Brothers: Growing Apart," in *The Road Goes on Forever*, 36–41. New York: Fireside Book/Simon & Schuster, 1982.

Oberman, Michael. *Fast Forward, Play, and Rewind*. Guilford, CT: Backbeat Books, 2020.

Pecknold, Diane. *The Selling Sound: The Rise of the Country Music Industry*. Durham, NC: Duke University Press, 2007.

Pollock, Bruce. *When Rock Was Young*. New York: Holt, Rinehart and Winston, 1981.

Richards, Keith, with James Fox. *Life*. New York: Little, Brown, 2010.

Sandoval, Andrew. *The Everly Brothers: Chained to a Memory—The Recordings 1966–1972*. Bear Family BCD 16791, 2006. Box set book, with introduction by Colin Escott.

———. *The Everly Brothers: The Price of Fame—The Recordings 1960–1965*. Bear Family BCD 16511, 2005. Box set book, with introduction by Colin Escott.

Selvin, Joel. *Drums & Demons: The Tragic Journey of Jim Gordon*. New York: Diversion Books, 2024.

Sheeley, Sharon. *Summertime Blues*. Tucson, AZ: Ravenhawk Books, 2011.

Smith, RJ. *Chuck Berry: An American Life*. New York: Hachette Books, 2022.

Southall, Brian. *The Road Is Long: The Hollies Story*. Falmouth, Cornwall, UK: Red Planet Books, 2015.

Stimeling, Travis D. *Nashville Cats: Record Production in Music City*. New York: Oxford University Press, 2020.

Streissguth, Michael. *Highways and Heartaches: How Ricky Skaggs, Marty Stuart, and Children of the New South Saved the Soul of Country Music*. New York: Hachette Boks, 2023.

Travis, Merle, and Deke Dickerson. *Sixteen Tons: The Merle Travis Story*. Los Angeles: BMG Books, 2022.

Trust, Sam, with Mary Jane Fraser. *Would You Trust This Man with Your Songs? A Life in Music Business*. 2nd ed. Los Angeles: Trust Music Management, 2019.

Watts, Derek. *Country Boy: A Biography of Albert Lee*. Jefferson, NC: McFarland, 2008.

White, George R. *Bo Diddley: Living Legend*. Chessington, Surrey, UK: Castle Communications, 1998.

White, Roger. *The Everly Brothers: Walk Right Back*. Rev. ed. London: Plexus, 1998.

Wilson, Lee. *All I Have to Do Is Dream: The Boudleaux & Felice Bryant Story*. Nashville: Two Creeks Press/House of Bryant Publications, 2017.

Wolfe, Charles K. *Kentucky Country*. Lexington: University Press of Kentucky, 1982.

Zanes, Warren. *Deliver Me from Nowhere: The Making of Bruce Springsteen's* Nebraska. New York: Crown, 2023.

Zevon, Crystal. *I'll Sleep When I'm Dead: The Dirty Life and Times of Warren Zevon*. New York: HarperCollins, 2007.

NOTES

Introduction: Of Blood and Harmony

Don on "playing together": Interview with Danny Holloway, *Sounds* (UK), August 7, 1971.

Phil on "aren't yourself": Interview with Patrick Carr, *Country Music*, November 1986.

Phil on different ways of life: Interview with Tom McWilliams, *Playdate*, 1971.

Don on biography: Interview with Robert K. Oermann, September 4, 1990.

Phil on the same: Author interview with Shawn Camp.

Chapter One: South by Midwest: The Everly Family 1929–1952

Charles Wolfe on interest in Kentucky music: Wolfe, *Kentucky Country*, 5.

Ike mining and family: Interview with Jerry Bledsoe, *Greensboro (NC) Daily News*, November 29, 1971; Roger White, *Walk Right Back*, 7–8; Ike Everly in "Everly Brothers Life Story," *Country and Western Jamboree*, Summer 1955.

Ike as Rodgers fan: Margaret Everly comments in Country Music Foundation Oral History Project (hereafter cited as CMF Oral History), January 26, 1990.

E.E. Hack band: Wolfe, 40–41.

Muhlenberg County thumbpicking: Anderson, *That Muhlenberg Sound*, chapters 1–6; Travis and Dickerson, *Sixteen Tons: The Merle Travis Story*, 41–45.

Arnold Shultz's role: Anderson, 9; Brady, "Contested Origins."

Ike's books of old country song lyrics: Margaret Everly, CMF Oral History, January 22, 1990.

Ike and Margaret on marrying: Interview with Wayne Bledsoe; Birkby, *KMA Radio*; Margaret Everly, CMF Oral History, January 26, 1990; interview with Lon Goddard, *Record Mirror* (UK), October 9, 1971. And family interview with Mike Ledgerwood, *Disc and Music Echo*, September 18, 1971.

Don on not criticizing: Interview with Dutch reporter Dolf Ruesink, November 1985.

Appalachian immigration to Chicago and its music scene: Guarino, *Country and Midwestern*, chapter 2; Berry, *Southern Migrants, Northern Exiles*, 155–163, 183–192; Jesse Dukes, "Uptown's Moment as 'Hillbilly Heaven,'" WBEZ Chicago blog, April 29, 2015; Roger Guy, "Hank Williams Lives in Uptown: Appalachians and the Struggle Against Displacement in Chicago," *Journal of Appalachian Studies* 18, no. 1/2 (Spring/Fall 2012): 131–148; Whet Moser, "Chicago's Hillbilly Problem During the Great Migration," *Chicago*, January 17, 2012.

Ike on Madison Street: Ike Everly in *Country and Western Jamboree*, n.d.; Don Everly interview, *Los Angeles Times* syndicate, January 1995; *Margaret Everly on taverns and clothes:* CMF Oral History, January 22, 1990.

Ike on WJJD: Interview with Lon Goddard; *The Billboard*, October 12, 1940, 7; Margaret Everly on Red Green, CMF Oral History, January 22, 1990; author interview with Red's son Mark T. Greene.

National Barn Dance/*Midwest sensibility:* Berry, ed., *The Hayloft Gang*.

Mills Brothers and "Paper Doll": Friedman, *Four Boys and a Guitar. Phil on listening to the Ink Spots:* Interview with Nancy Anderson, *Tennessean* (Nashville), November 4, 1979.

Time in Waterloo: Margaret Everly, CMF Oral History; R. White, 9; and Margaret Everly in Birkby, *KMA Radio*, 100.

Five-year-old Don and radio: Interview with Kurt Loder, *Rolling Stone*, May 8, 1986; interview with Bill Bush, *Guitar Player*, September 1990.

Brother acts Everlys heard as kids: Don Everly interview with Gene Guerrero, *Great Speckled Bird* (Atlanta), June 12, 1972; R. White, 13; Phil and Don Everly interview in *Bringing It All Back Home*, BBC documentary, 1990. *Alton Delmore on Everlys:* Delmore, *The Delmore Brothers*, 87.

Everly Family Show *pay, local touring format:* Margaret Everly, CMF Oral History.

Learning to play right-handed: KMA Guide, October 1950, 10.

Trip to Brownie: KMA Guide, August 1949, 7; author interview with Bill Harlan.

1950 Ike Everly Family show recording: Courtesy Bill Hillman, Everly Brothers Childhood Home, Shenandoah, Iowa.

Don on radio job: Unpublished interview with Robert K. Oermann, September 4, 1990. *Folding chair incident:* Paul Davis, *Modern Screen*, October 1958.

Don and Phil in early adolescence: Margaret Everly, CMF Oral History; R. White, 14–15; *Don on career plans:* Karpp, *Ike's Boys*, 22.

Don on Hank Williams: Quote from Everly Brothers International Fan Club; *The Everly Brothers: Songs of Innocence and Experience*, BBC, 1984.

Phil on the Bell Sisters: Interview with David Simons, *Acoustic Guitar*, August 2000; interview with Joe Smith, audio recording for Smith's *Off the Record* (New York: Warner Books, 1988); interview with Tom Lanham, *Paste*, January 4, 2014; Karpp, 29. *Bell Sisters story:* Rex Strother, liner notes, *The Bell Sisters: The "Bermuda" Girls*, Jasmine Records CD, 2003.

Bishop PhD dissertation: Paula Jean Bishop, "The Roots and Influences of the Everly Brothers."

Ike on rough 1952–1953: Interview with Lon Goddard.

Chapter Two: Give Me a (Country) Future 1953–1957

Margaret on arriving in Knoxville: Interview with John Shearer, *Knoxville News Sentinel*, February 20, 2019.

Don on Knoxville years: Knoxville News-Sentinel, August 9, 1992.

Phil on WROL money: Karpp, 29; *WROL schedule:* R. White, 16.

Don and Phil on high school social life: Interviews in *Playboy*, January 1986, 194.

Phil on "back seat" dating: Interview with Julie Webb, *New Musical Express*, August 31, 1974.

Phil jacket story: Margaret Everly, CMF Oral History, January 31, 1990.

Contents of Knoxville shows: Barbara Henderson, "The Other Kids Hated Us at First," *Celebrity*, December 1958. Ike Everly in *Country Jamboree*, Summer 1958, 14. And Paul Denis, "Everly Brothers," *Teen*, 1958.

Phil on the Clovers: Interview with John Johnson, *Santa Clarita Valley (CA) Signal*, July 30, 1971.

Phil on music teachers: R. White, 18.

Phil basketball coach story: John Shearer, *Knoxville News Sentinel*; January 5, 2014; and Lee Gardner, *Metro Pulse* (Knoxville, TN), on the coach and "Cathy," Fall 1994.

Don on WLAC: Interview with Dave Booth, *Goldmine*, March 1984. *Bill Harlan on WLAC:* Author interview with Harlan.

Phil on evolving music: Songs of Innocence and Experience.

Osborne Brothers on WROL: Neil Rosenberg in *Bluegrass Unlimited*, September 1971.

Ike on buying car, backing away, moving on: Interview with Lon Goddard.

Cas Walker: Hodge, ed., *Cas Walker*.

Ike on Walker and rock and getting new jobs: Country Jamboree, n.d.

Don on firing: Interview with Wayne Bledsoe.

Buying Bo Diddley records: The Knoxville History Project, online. *Don on Bo Diddley:* Don Everly intro to G. White, *Bo Diddley: Living Legend*.

Dressing up to visit family: Margaret Everly, CMF Oral History, January 22, 1990.

Don on his teenage writing: Interview with Lee Gardner; interview with Paul Freeman, *Los Angeles Times*, January 1994. *Childhood writing:* Unpublished interview with Robert K. Oermann.

Chet Atkins on meeting Don and Phil; Don on credibility: Interviews in *The Life and Times of the Everly Brothers*, Nashville Network, 1996.

Don on "Thou Shalt Not Steal" and Chet: Unpublished portions of interview with Robert K. Oermann for BMI, 1990; and Grammy Foundation Living History video.

Letter from Mrs. Chet Atkins: Margaret Everly, CMF Oral History Project, March 9, 1990.

Leaving for Nashville: Margaret Everly interview with John Shearer; Wayne Bledsoe interview with Don Everly.

Decision to move forward as a duo: R. White, 19–20.

Troy Martin: Colin Escott, "Teenage Idyll: An Everly Brother Looks Back," *Journal of Country Music* 15, no. 2 (1993): 18–23; Mazor, *Ralph Peer and the Making of Popular Roots Music*, 238–240.

Columbia recording session: R. White; Karpp; Escott, *Classic Everly Brothers.*

Afraid they'd starve: Henderson, "The Other Kids Hated Us at First."

Took the record dub home: Country Jamboree, Summer 1958.

Don on the Ryman alley: In *Songs of Innocence and Experience.*

Felice Bryant TV show: CMF Oral History, Patricia Hall, November 19, 1975.

Everlys told to wait two years: Phil Everly recollection in Pollock, *When Rock Was Young*, 83.

"Scooter Bill" Tubb: Escott, "Teenage Idyll."

Don's marriage to Mary Sue Ingraham: R. White, 24; Dodge, *The Everly Brothers: Ladies Love Outlaws*, 115–117; Phil's recollections in *Motion Picture*, September 1959, 69.

Meeting Hal Smith, then Wesley Rose: R. White, 29; Karpp, 40–42; Wesley Rose, CMF Oral History, May 13, 1974.

Royalty rates: Sam Trust in *Would You Trust This Man?*

Archie Bleyer: John L. Clark Jr., "Archie Bleyer and the Lost Influence of Stock Arrangements in Jazz," *American Music* 27, no. 2 (Summer 2009).

"Bye Bye Love": Wilson, *All I Have to Do Is Dream*, 71; brothers interview with Kurt Loder; interview with Wayne Bledsoe.

Edenton's high-third guitar: Rich Kienzle, "Ray Edenton: Nashville Studio Rhythm Specialist," *Guitar Player*, May 1981, and author's email correspondence with Kienzle; Malone and Malone, *Nashville's Songwriting Sweethearts*; author interview with Del Bryant; Don Everly interview with Colin Escott.

Brenda Lee on Everlys: Author interview with Brenda Lee.

Phil on Monroe tour: Pollock, *When Rock Was Young*.

Letters home from Monroe/Lee tour: Margaret Everly, CMF Oral History, March 9, 1990.

Bryants on Everlys made "Bye Bye Love" giant: Transcript, Bryants' interview with Hugh Cherry, *Heroes of Country Music* radio show, July 1, 1981; Felice and Boudleaux Bryant archive at Country Music Hall of Fame.

Phil on two thousand kids singing: Interview with Joe Smith. *Don on the* Opry: interview in *The Life and Times*.

Opry debut: Ben A. Green, *Nashville Banner*, May 14, 1957. *Joining* Opry *cast:* Ben A. Green, *Nashville Banner*, May 29, 1957; and Phil comments in KHJ radio's *History of Rock & Roll*, June 8, 1971.

Country Song Roundup: October 1957, 6.

Chapter Three: The Everlys and the Bryants

Boudleaux on Ike haircut: In House of Bryant video *All I Have to Do Is Dream*.

Felice on Porter Wagoner session: CMF Oral History Project, Patricia Hall, November 19, 1975.

Boudleaux on Everlys and harmony: All I Have to Do video. *Felice on Bryants/Everly needs:* In Country Music Hall of Fame, *We Could*, 73. *Phil on Boudleaux and harmony:* In *The Everly Brothers: Harmonies from Heaven*, BBC, 2016.

Bryants' background: Wilson, *All I Have to Do*, 4–42 passim; Malone and Malone, 1–39 passim.

Felice on Everlys as "fine Swiss watch": Songs of Innocence and Experience.

Everlys first visit to Bryants' house; on Boudleaux and Don: Author interview with Del Bryant.

Felice on creating "Wake Up Little Susie": Interviews in *Harmonies from Heaven* and Nashville Network's *Life and Times*. Original lyric sheet appears in *We Could*, 63.

Peter Asher on teens and country: Interview with Dee Perry, *Ideastream*, NPR Cleveland, October 2014.

Chuck Berry on "Wake Up": RJ Smith, *Chuck Berry: An American Life*, 139.

Studio takes and Bleyer absence: Karpp, 51.

Phil on relationship with Bryants: Associated Press, "Phil Everly Remembers Bryant, Husband as More Than Songwriters," April 2003. *Don on Boudleaux:* Wilson, 77, and interview with John Tobler, *ZigZag*, May 1970.

Boudleaux on ballads: Karpp, 53.

Don on "All I Have to Do Is Dream": Interview with Andrew Sandoval, liner notes, *The Everly Brothers: Studio Outtakes*, Bear Family Records CD, 2006, 2019. *Phil on the song's impact:* Interview with Joe Smith.

Phil on "Devoted to You" and "Bird Dog": R. White, 49.

Boudleaux on writing "Bird Dog": Interview with Hugh Cherry.

"Not Fade Away" rejected: R. White, *Walk Right Back*, 50.

Felice on Everlys' harmony: In *Life and Times.*

Don on Songs Our Daddy Taught Us *project:* Escott, "Teenage Idyll."

Dane Bryant on "Take a Message to Mary": Kosser, *How Nashville Became Music City,* 92–93.

Felice on "Take a Message" writing and recording: CMF Oral History and interview in *Harmonies from Heaven.*

Boudleaux Bryant and Wesley Rose comments: Bill Maples interviews, *Tennessean,* November 24, 1957.

Paula Bishop: Bishop, "The Roots and Influences of the Everly Brothers."

Chapter Four: Watching Them Rolling 1957–1959

Don on picking up Ike: Interview with Kurt Loder.

$2,000 per appearance: Look, "The Everly Brothers: Fast Spin to Success," April 15, 1958, 32.

Phil on touring and record contract dollars: Interview with Joe Smith.

Phil's MG: "Born to Be Troupers," *Radio-TV Mirror,* August 1958. *Investments:* Paul Denis, "Everly Brothers," *Modern Screen,* October 1958.

Hank Williams memorial: Montgomery (AL) Advertiser, September 24, 1957.

Country pulp magazines on Everlys: Country Song Roundup, October 1957; *Folk and Country Songs,* January 1958; *Songs and Stars,* February 1958; *Country and Western Jamboree,* Summer 1958.

Phil on strange brand of country: In *Songs of Innocence and Experience.*

Don on treatment by the press: In Amburn, *Buddy Holly: A Biography,* 125; unpublished interview with Robert K. Oermann, 1990, and interview with Brian McTavish, *Kansas City (MO) Star,* August 7, 1986.

Richard Schickel et al.: "Revolution in Records," *Look,* April 15, 1958.

Phil: "Yes sir; no sir.": Interview with Phil Norman, *Sunday Times* (UK), 1972.

"Smoldering": Dick Kleiner syndicated column On the Record, *Tennessean,* August 28, 1957.

Don: "The acts were treated terribly.": Unpublished interview with Robert K. Oermann, 1990.

Venetia Stevenson on Ed Sullivan Show: Mike Barnes, *Hollywood Reporter,* September 27, 2022; and Dodge, 117.

"Phil's Men's Shop": Jeff Hedrick and Jon Bassett, *Movieland and TV Time,* December 1958.

Phil no teenage idol: David Griffiths and Lon Goddard interview, *Record Mirror,* May 18, 1968.

Everlys on Elvis: Interview with David Griffiths, *Record Mirror,* May 15, 1965; Don Everly interview with Colin Escott; "Those Dreamy Everlys," *16,* November 1958.

On Montreal first meeting: Don Everly in *The Real Buddy Holly Story*, Arena Films/BBC, 1986.

Phil: "like a college fraternity": Songs of Innocence and Experience.

Meeting Preston Bealle: Bealle posts to Everly Brothers International Fan Club Facebook page.

Don's clothes ripped: Dodge, 48.

Teen fan magazines: Cool and Hep Cats, December 1958, 16, November 1958; *Screen Stars*, April 1959; *Modern Screen*, February 1958 and February 1959; *Teen World*, December 1958; *TV & Screen Life*, 1958.

Sharon Sheeley and "Poor Little Fool": Sheeley, *Summertime Blues*.

Phil watching Chuck Berry writing: Matt Powell, "Chuck Berry's Promised Land," *Humor in America* (blog,) January 22, 2018.

Roy Orbison and "Claudette": Amburn, *Dark Star: The Tragic Story of Roy Orbison*, 70–73.

Phil on touring: Interview with Kurt Loder. *Hearing Cooke and McPhatter:* Guralnick, *Dream Boogie: The Triumph of Sam Cooke*, 231.

Phil on Buddy putting him to bed and Buddy "so low": Norman, *The Road Goes on Forever*, 36–34.

Studebaker scare: Billboard, December 12, 1958.

Don on Songs Our Daddy Taught Us: Quoted in Sandoval, liner notes, *The Everly Brothers: Studio Outtakes.*

Origins of "Kentucky": Gopinath and Schultz, "Sentimental Remembrance," 477–524.

Don on being from Kentucky: Interview with Tim Farmer, *Tim Farmer's Country Kitchen*, KET TV/ Muhlenberg County TV, 1997.

Silas House on being from Kentucky: Author interview with Silas House.

Bleyer on Songs Our Daddy Taught Us: Karpp, 60.

"Love's Made a Fool of You" and "Wishing": Goldrosen and Beecher, *Remembering Buddy*, 101, and Amburn, *Buddy Holly*, 170.

New York socializing: Regarding Café Madrid, Joe Nick Patoski, "The Widow's Pique," *Texas Monthly*, February 2001; regarding El Chico, Tasso Matheas on Everly Brothers International EverlyNet Facebook group (hereafter cited as EverlyNet), 2001; regarding Mama Leone's, Gerron, *Whatever Happened to Peggy Sue?*, 196–197.

Buddy and María in the Village: Author interview with María Elena Holly, 2009.

"Raining in My Heart": Boudleaux Bryant, CMF Oral History, May 12, 1983, and author interview with Del Bryant.

Don on last time he saw Buddy: Interview with John Tobler.

European tour: R. White, 49–50; tour clippings from the Everly Brothers International Fan Club scrapbook collection. Dutch Archie Bleyer Show: *The Everly Brothers: Chained to a Memory*, DVD included in box set.

Everlys and Holly funeral. Karpp, 69; interview with Kurt Loder; Goldrosen and Beecher, 147.

Jerry Allison on evolution to the self-contained rock and roll band, and playing with Everlys: Author interview with Jerry Allison, January 2009.

Sonny Curtis on meeting Everlys: Author interview with Sonny Curtis.

Phil on Buddy, altercation stories, and last meeting: Interview with Mitch Tuchman, *Time Out* (London), June 15, 1979.

"('Til) I Kissed You" outtake: Classic Everly Brothers, Bear Family Records, 1992.

Chapter Five: The Heights 1959–1961

Phil on parents, Phil and Don on each other: Motion Picture, September 1959. Don, Sue, and Phil photo: "At Home with the Everly Brothers," *New York Daily News,* October 4, 1959.

Don and Phil on love and marriage: New Musical Express, December 1958, 15.

Don on "rockabilly": Interview with Michael Aphesbero, *4 Taxis,* 1980.

Derek Johnson characterization: New Musical Express, June 6, 1958, 10.

Don on writing "('Til) I Kissed You": Interview with Kurt Loder. *Bill Porter–Archie Bleyer conflict recording it:* Bill Porter, CMF Oral History Project, February 23, 1994, and unpublished parts of David Menconi interview with Porter, August 11, 1987.

Chet Atkins on growing tensions: Karpp, 83.

"Let It Be Me" history: Bishop, 140. Don Everly interview with Colin Escott.

Phil on Paul Anka and proposed Hickory Records idea: Interview with Joe Smith.

Del Bryant on Wesley's paternalism: Author interview with Del Bryant.

Signing by Warner Bros.: Cornyn, *Exploding,* 35, and his Stay Tuned column on the Rhino Records website; *Cash Box,* February 20, 1960, 29.

Writing "Cathy's Clown": Unpublished Don Everly interview with Robert K. Oermann, 1990; Phil Everly in R. White, 58; joint interview in *Rock 'n' Roll Odyssey* film, 1995; Don Everly interview with Bill Mann, *Gazette* (Montreal), August 5, 1972; joint interview on *The David Frost Show,* May 12, 1972.

Recording "Cathy's Clown": Don Everly interview with Robert K. Oermann; Michael Fremer interview with Bill Porter for Analog Planet website, April 30, 2009; and Porter, CMF Oral History Project, June 8, 1984.

Lennon and McCartney performing "Cathy's Clown": Lewisohn, *Tune In: The Beatles: All These Years,* 333.

Writing "So Sad": Don Everly interview with Robert K. Oermann; Don Everly comment to Andrew Sandoval in *The Price of Fame.*

J.I. Allison on backing the Everlys in the UK: Interview with Keith Goodwin, *New Musical Express,* April 29, 1960. *Sonny Curtis on UK tour:* Author interview with Sonny Curtis.

Phil on Liverpool crowd reaction: Interview with Vintagerock.com at NAAM convention, 2012.

George Harrison sees show: Lewisohn, 296.

Nash and Clarke meet the Everlys: Author interview with Graham Nash; Southall, *The Road Is Long,* chapter 1.

Offstage UK activities: Spencer Leigh, "We Used to Have Good Times Together," spencerleigh.co.uk, first published in *Now Dig This,* September 2013–January 2014.

UK Everlys imitators: Alfred Rhode, liner notes, *The Brit-Everlys' Sound,* Jasmine Records CD, 2023.

Phil on recording innovations: Interviews with Joe Smith and Andrew Sandoval; R. White, 1.

Bill Porter on recording challenges: Bill Porter, CMF Oral History, February 23, 1994.

Wesley Rose response to "Temptation": Don interview with Colin Escott. *Song's history:* Sandoval, *The Price of Fame.*

Chuck Berry on listening to Everlys: Interview with Terry Roland, *No Depression* online, July 19, 2015.

Sonny Curtis on "Walk Right Back": Author interview with Sonny Curtis.

Don and Phil on acting classes: Interview with Bob Thomas, Associated Press, September 22, 1960.

Phil on leaving Opry: Pollock, 80.

Paton Price and his students: Reggie Nadelson on Dean Reed, *Comrade Rockstar.* Phil and Don interview with Martin Cohen, *TV-Radio Mirror,* July 1961.

Screen test: Karpp, 90–91.

Wesley Rose lawsuit and dismissal: Billboard, November 16, 1963. *Felice Bryant on Wesley's scheming:* Wilson, 88.

Don–Mary Sue divorce: United Press International, "Everly Brothers Named in Suit," May 23, 1961; Dodge; *Photoplay,* July 1961, 18, and September 1961, 90.

Recommendation to see Dr. Jacobson: R. White, 77–78; Karpp, 106–107.

Chapter Six: Hitting the Wall 1961–1962

One-day visit to New York: Cash Box, April 1, 1961, 35.

Max Jacobson patients and medications, including Bleyer's: David Jean d'Heur with Andrew W. Saul, *Miracle Max,* posted on DoctorYourself.com.

Methylphenidate: W. Alexander Morton and Gwendolyn G. Stockton, "Methylphenidate Abuse and Psychiatric Side Effects," *Primary Care Companion to the Journal of Clinical Psychiatry* 2, no. 5 (October 2000): 159–164.

Phil and Don on Jacobson treatments: R. White, 77–78; Don Everly interview with Kurt Loder.

Don on "Svengali-type": Interview with Steve Morse, *Boston Globe,* August 21, 1984.

Venetia Stevenson: Obituary, *Hollywood Reporter,* September 27, 2022; Hope McLean, "What Chance Does This Marriage Have?," *Photoplay,* September 1961, 90.

Calliope Records: Billboard Music Week, May 1, 1961, 1; Peter Aarts, "The Calliope," *Kentucky* (Everlys fan magazine) no. 52, 1990, 18; Roger Dopson, liner notes, *The Everly Brothers: Walk Right Back—The Singles Collection 1956–1962,* Jasmine Records CD, 2016.

Phil and Don on Both Sides of an Evening: Sandoval, *The Price of Fame,* 48.

Calliope's "Pomp": Billboard Music Week, May 22, 1961, 2; "Elgar Estate Spikes Rock Version of 'Pomp,'" July 31, 1961, 19.

Phil on looming draft question and Jack Rael: Interview with Joe Smith.

Jack Rael comments: R. White, 68–69.

Joey Paige on audition: Interview with Kevin Trask, Melbourne, Australia, radio, June 2, 2019.

Everlys in the Marine Corps Reserve: Phil interview with Joe Smith; Don and Phil interview with Derek Johnson, *New Musical Express,* September 22, 1961, and with Len Chaimowitz, *Newsday,* November 21, 1961; memories of fellow marines on the Everly Brothers International Fan Club Facebook page, March 14, 2017.

Carole King as Everlys fan: King, *A Natural Woman,* 115–116.

Don on the hectic post-marines period: Interview with *New Musical Express*, September 1963.

Phil and Ann Marshall: Author interview with Ann Marshall, and *Brooklyn Eagle*, May 9 and June 4, 1962.

Don on "Nancy's Minuet": Interview with Andrew Sandoval, *The Price of Fame*.

Del Bryant on Don visit: Author interview with Del Bryant.

Difficult 1962 sessions: Sandoval, *The Price of Fame*; author interview with Sonny Curtis; Everlys interview with Kurt Loder.

Everlys anticipate UK tour: Interview with Jonah Ruddy, *New Musical Express*, October 5, 1962, 10.

Don's breakdown in London: Author interview with Don Peake; R. White, 78–80; Fred Dellar, "The Everly Brother Tour," *Mojo* (online), July 5, 2022; Joey Paige on EverlyNet, May 29, 2021; Logan Gourlkay, *Express* (London), October 14, 1962; *Daily Telegraph*, October 15 and 16, 1962; *Evening Standard*, October 15, 1962.

Electroshock therapy: Interview with Kurt Loder.

Venetia and Ann: Author interview with Ann Marshall.

Phil goes on alone: Interview with Fred Dellar; Joey Paige EverlyNet post; Andy Gray, *New Musical Express*, October 19, 1962; "Don Everly Will Not Rejoin Phil," *New Musical Express*, October 26, 1962; "The Everly Brothers Duo Act Becomes a Solo Offering," *Stage & Television Today*, October 18, 1962.

Phil on life back home, 1963 plans: Chris Hutchins, "Don and Phil Plan 1963 Tour Here," *Disc*, December 15, 1962.

Chapter Seven: The Trying Time 1963–1967

Phil on five-year "hot period": Interview with Joe Smith.

Simon and Garfunkel Everly-like records: James Chumet, liner notes, *Paul Simon & Art Garfunkel: The Early Years*, Hoodoo Records CD, 2017.

Bob Dylan on "Highway 51": Interview with Robert Hilburn, *Los Angeles Times*, August 5, 1984.

Creedence and the Everlys: Fogerty, *Fortunate Son*; Fogerty and Don Everly in *Musician*, July 1986, 42–44.

Beach Boys beginnings and Everlys: James B. Murphy in *Becoming the Beach Boys*, 63.

Mike Love comment: Interview with Luke Winkie, *Austin Chronicle*, January 18, 2014.

John Cale, Tony Conrad, and the Everlys: Cale in Hermes, *Lou Reed*.

Ray and Dave Davies and the Everlys: *Uncut*, November 2021, 58.

Little Richard on Beatles and Everlys: Interview with L. Kent Wolgamott, *Lincoln (NE) Journal Star*, April 2, 2004.

Everlys and "Please Please Me": Karpp, 115–116.

Everlys' impact on Beatles: Lewisohn, 168 and passim; Paul McCartney interview with Callum Wells, *Daily Mail*, November 7, 2021. *BBC audition:* David Bedford in *The Country of Liverpool*, 163; interview with Jean Shepherd, *Playboy*, February 1965, 51; McCartney on Facebook reported by Kory Grow, *Rolling Stone,* January 8, 2014.

Don and Phil studio blowup: Dorothy Kilgallen column, week of June 20, 1963; Mike Connolly in *Hollywood Reporter,* June 1963.

Don on feeling better, new motto: Interview with Andy Gray in *New Musical Express,* September 1963.

European and UK tour 1963: Spencer Leigh, spencerleigh.co.uk; R. White, 84–97; 1963 Everlys tour book. *Jim Gordon:* Leigh, and Selvin, *Drums & Demons,* chapter 4.

Keith Richards on Don: Egan, ed., *Keith Richards on Keith Richards,* 190, 206.

Mick Jagger on Everlys: Interview with Alan Smith, *New Musical Express,* July 2, 1965, 8.

Don Everly on Little Richard sexual approach: BBC documentary *Rock 'n' Roll America,* 2015.

Don on song scarcity and weakness and Bryant again: Interview with J. Michael Ruddy, *New Musical Express,* April 24, 1964, 14; interview with Graham Andrews, *Record Mirror,* June 6, 1964, 10.

Bryants' lack of urgency: Malone and Malone, 108. Bryant to Layng Martine Jr. quoted in Martine's memoir *Permission to Fly* (Nashville: FieldPoint Press, 2018).

Don on carrying on: Interview with John Wells, *New Musical Express,* May 14, 1965, 13; interview with David Griffiths, *Record Mirror,* May 15, 1965.

Terry Slater on Phil's offer: In the documentary *RockHistoryUK,* 2016.

Don Wayne stays on: Author interview with Don Wayne.

Martial Bekkers on loudness: Author interview with Martial Bekkers.

Sonny Curtis on European tour: Author interview with Sonny Curtis. *Phil on same:* Interview with Joe Smith.

Don on after-effects of breakdown: Interview with John Wells. *Don and Phil comments in Wisconsin:* Interview with Alice Fulton, *Post-Crescent* (Appleton, WI), August 2, 1965.

Don on Hollywood Beat *'n Soul sessions:* Interviews with Andy Gray, *New Musical Express,* October 8, 1965, 8, and Derek Johnson, *New Musical Express,* November 5, 1965, 12.

Don and Phil Los Angeles home life: Interview with Mike Gormley, *Ottawa Journal,* November 11, 1966.

Jackie Everly report to fan club: Archive of the Everly Brothers International Fan Club, February–March 1966.

Don encounter with Robert Kennedy: Karpp, 120.

Phil on "resurgence" in money: Interview with Joe Smith.

Terry Slater on Everlys abroad: Interview with Mike Tuck, *KRLA Beat,* August 27, 1966. *On Manila:* R. White, 95.

Vietnam experience: Phil Everly in R. White; Don Everly interview with Kurt Loder.

Two Yanks project: Author interview with Graham Nash; Mike Croft interview with Tony Hicks, *Beat Instrumental,* July 1966, 10; Southall, 93.

Origins and credits in "Bowling Green": Sandoval, *Chained to a Memory.*

Chapter Eight: Relevant Again: Country Rock 1968–1970

Phil and Don on rock revival: Interview with David Griffiths and Lon Goddard, *Record Mirror,* May 18, 1968.

Everlys and Joan Baez: John Carmody, *Washington Post* and *Miami Herald,* December 17, 1967.

Everlys and Dillards: In Sandoval, *Chained to a Memory. Troubadour appearance:* Judy Sims, *Disc and Music Echo,* August 16, 1969.

Phil knocks Don down: Joe Smith in Karpp, 138.

Lenny Waronker arrival: Cronyn; Bud Scoppa 2017 interview with Mo Ostin, "Rumor Mill," *Hits* (online), 2022; Andrew Sandoval, *Come to the Sunshine* audio interview with Waronker, May 6, 2019; author interview with Ron Elliott.

Using pseudonyms for publishing: Author interview with Sam Trust.

Andy Wickham, "company freak": Jerry Hopkins, "Inside the Los Angeles Scene," *Rolling Stone,* June 22, 1968; Wickham obituary, *Times* (London), April 5, 2022.

Don on letters home, road boredom, and "beat music": Interview with Jock Veitch, *Sydney Morning Herald,* July 28, 1968.

Brothers on food preferences: Interviews with Johna Blinn, Celebrity Cookbook column, July 1968.

Latin Quarter review: Talent on Stage column, *Cash Box,* June 1968. Aaron Sternfield, *Billboard,* June 6, 1968, 15.

Joe Smith on Roots: R. White, 99. *Lenny Waronker on* Roots: Radio interview with Andrew Sandoval; Karpp, 133. *Andy Wickham on* Roots: LP back cover notes, November 1968.

Ike singing Rodgers songs: Margaret Everly, CMF Oral History January 26,1990.

Phil on "T for Texas": Interview with Barry Mazor, *Meeting Jimmie Rodgers,* 253.

Chequers show: Included on the DVD *Harmonies from Heaven,* Reelin' In the Years/ Eagle Vision, 2016; Greg Quill, *Go Set,* August 10, 1968.

Ed Ward on Roots: *Rolling Stone,* May 31, 1969. *Ed Kahn on* Roots: *Western Folklore* 29, no. 2 (April 1970).

Don on Roots: Interview with Gene Guerrero.

hungry i show: Phillip Elwood, *San Francisco Examiner,* November 8, 1968, 29.

Phil on changing audience: Interview with Dick MacDonald, *Montreal Star,* June 14, 1969. *On playing "country rock":* Interview with Michael Oberman, *Fast Forward, Play and Rewind,* January 25, 1969, 164. *Phil on folk music and Seeger:* In Marks and Eastman, *Rock and Other Four Letter Words.* Don on Seeger: Interview with John Tobler.

Bitter End show: Phil Kirby, *Billboard,* February 9, 1969; Mike Jahn, *New York Times,* February 1, 1969; *Cash Box,* February 9, 1969, 32.

Everlys and Dylan, "Lay Lady Lay": Don Everly interview with Kurt Loder; Phil Everly interview with Peter O'Brien, *Omaha Rainbow* (UK) no. 27, Summer 1981; author interview with Graham Nash.

Don teaching Gram Parsons: Karpp, 89. *Gram Parsons comments on Don:* In *Helix* 9, no. 6, September 4, 1969.

Pat Alger on Newport: Author interview with Pat Alger.

Cash approaches about TV show: Phil Everly interview with Charles Witbeck, "Everly Brothers Working for Cash!," King Features, August 12, 1970; Marilyn Beck, "Everly Brothers' Long Friendship with Johnny Cash Finally Pays Off," TV Time Service, July 5, 1970.

Robbins or Everlys for Cash replacement show: Nancy Eriksen, *Country & Western Music,* October 1970, 19.

Tommy Smothers on Everlys in Las Vegas: TV interview with Tony Sacha, *Entertainment Las Vegas,* October 24, 2019, and with Marc Maron, *WTF* podcast, January 2, 2022.

Divorces: Dodge, 117–124; author interview with Ann Marshall. *Don on marriage not working:* Interview with Mary Campbell, Associated Press, May 2, 1972, and with Blaik

Kirby, *Globe and Mail* (Toronto), March 1, 1972. *On being away from kids anyway:* Interview with Phillip Norman, *Sunday Times of London*, 1972. *On "feeling like a country boy":* Interview with Stan Sayer, *Daily Mirror*, April 23, 1977. *Phil on "bad marriage":* Interview with Mike Ledgewood, *Disc and Music Echo*, September 18, 1971, 14.

Don invites Beatles: Sandoval, *Chained to a Memory*, 120. *"Two of Us" offer:* In Jacks, *Peter Asher: A Life in Music*, 109.

Phil on TV post-divorce: Interview with Joe Smith. *First TV episode fears: TV Guide*, September 5, 1970, 25.

Phil on Don out front: Playboy interview, 1986. *Descriptions of set, and other visuals:* Screenings of *Johnny Cash Presents the Everly Brothers* episodes, courtesy of the UCLA Library Film & Television Archive and Sony Pictures.

Bernie Kukoff comments: Author interview with Bernie Kukoff.

Ike Everly appearing on campuses and at folk fests: Margaret Everly, CMF Oral History, February 23, 1990, and F. K. Plous Jr., *Chicago Sun-Times*, February 2, 1970.

Possible return of TV show: William Tusher, *Hollywood Reporter*, June 26, 1970, and author interview with Bernie Kukoff.

Chapter Nine: To the Breaking Point 1970–1973

Don Wayne on increase in bookings: Author interview with Don Wayne.

Phil on reluctance to marry again: Interview with Mike Ledgerwood, *Disc and Music Echo*, September 19, 1971.

Phil and Slater's publishing company: Phil Everly interview with Julie Webb, *New Musical Express*, 1971; Sam Trust in *Would You Trust This Man?*

Don on expected future after TV show: In interview with John Tobler.

Don on losing interest in TV and separate lives: Interview with Tom Weigel, *Cleveland Press*, December 5, 1971.

Talk of syndicated TV show with Ike: Greensboro (NC) Record, December 3, 1971.

Ann Marshall on Phil and Don and living with Don: Author interview with Ann Marshall.

Don on reasons to record solo: Interview with Danny Holloway, *Sounds*, August 7, 1971; Don Everly in R. White; Glen A. Baker, notes for the 1999 Raven Records CD of Don's 1971 and 1974 albums.

Don Everly album reviews: Billboard, Decmeber 19, 1970, 50. *Don on album in retrospect:* Unpublished portion of interview with Robert K. Oermann, September 4, 1990.

Phil on drugs: Interview with Ben Wood, *Honolulu Star-Bulletin*, November 26, 1970, and on *The Dick Cavett Show*, May 3, 1972.

Parsons and Richards playing Roots: Patrick Doyle, *Rolling Stone*, August 21, 2021, and Richards, *Life*, 310.

RCA dual and solo deals: Tom McWilliams, *Playdate* (NZ), August 1971, and Tony Vella in *Herald-Sun* (Melbourne, Australia), June 17, 1971.

Paul Rothchild house: Barney Hoskyns, *Hotel California*, 26.

Warren Zevon becomes piano player and recruits Wachtel: Zevon, *I'll Sleep When I'm Dead*, 40–42; Kushins, *Nothing's Bad Luck*, chapter 3.

Don on "Tired of Singing My Song": Phone interview with Chet Flippo, February 1, 1996; in Country Music Hall of Fame archive.

Ike and Margaret on '71 trip: Don Everly interview with VPRO radio, Eindhoven, transcribed in *Kentucky* Everlys fan magazine. Author interviews with Don Wayne and Penny Campbell Loewen.

Rotterdam show, and "Sing Me Back Home": Author interview with Martial Bekkers.

Waddy Wachtel on Don teaching him guitar part: David Simons, *Acoustic Guitar*, August 2000, 71.

Royal Albert Hall show: Author correspondence with Kathy Cole; Warren Zevon interview with Dan Forte, *Musician*, August 1982.

John Sebastian on recording with Everlys: Interview with Elliot Stephen Cohen, *Goldmine*, July 28, 2022.

Phil and Don on Stories *sessions:* R. White, 107.

Stories We Could Tell *reviews:* Bud Scoppa, *Rolling Stone*, July 6, 1972; Robert Hilburn, *Los Angeles Times*, June 1972; Julie Webb, *New Musical Express*, June 1972.

Phil on tension and his own "stupidity": Interview with Joe Smith. And interview with Mary Campbell, Associated Press, first week of May 1972.

Phil on alimony: Interview with Julie Webb, *New Musical Express*, September 18, 1971. *Don on alimony:* Interview with Blaik Kirby.

Ann Marshall on relationship with Don ending: Author interview with Ann Marshall.

Ike on missing Phil–Patricia Mickey wedding: Red O'Donnell, syndicated Nashville Sound column July 8, 1972.

Don on calling Chet Atkins: In Sandoval, *Chained to a Memory*, 153. *Phil on Atkins producing:* Interview with John Tobler, *Let It Rock*, December 1972. *Atkins on* Pass the Chicken: R. White, 108.

Don Wayne on RCA albums disappointment: Author interview with Don Wayne.

Phil on "done it all": Interview with Andrew Tyler, *Disc*, May 13, 1972. *Don on feeling nothing:* Interview with Blaik Kirby, *Toronto Star*, March 1, 1972 and with Bill Mann, *Gazette* (Montreal), August 5, 1972.

Don on solo work ahead: Interview with Danny Holloway, *New Musical Express*, September 23, 1972.

Phil on feeling betrayed: Interview with Julie Webb, *New Musical Express*, August 31, 1974.

Early 1973 reviews: John Huddy, *Miami Herald*, January 31, 1973; Edward W. Coker, *Spokane Daily Chronicle*, March 23, 1973; Peter Goddard, *Toronto Star*, March 6, 1973; Bill Musselwhite, *Calgary Herald*, March 22, 1973.

Sahara shows: Fight during Nancy Sinatra rehearsal: Ed Koch, *Las Vegas Sun*, January 4, 2014. *Gambling with Zevon:* Zevon, 57.

Karen's spinal meningitis and Don's decision to quit: Don Everly interview with Stan Sayer, *Daily Mirror*, April 23, 1977.

Phil on the split: Interviews with R. White and Joe Smith.

Advance warning to Don Wayne: Author interview with Don Wayne.

Announcement of split: Robert Hilburn, *Los Angeles Times*, morning of July 14, 1973, and other reports.

Day of split: Hilburn, July 14, 1973; R. White, 109; Zevon, 61.

Ronstadt on "Everly Sisters": Bill De Young in *Goldmine*, September 24, 1999. And in Streissguth, *Highways and Heartaches*, 95.

Chapter Ten: Don 1973–1982

Don: "debilitating" and "Country rock": Interview with Walter Carter, *Tennessean*, June 8, 1980, 10. *"Changing my name":* Interview with Patrick Anderson, *New York Times*, August 31, 1975. *"Split earlier":* Interview with Tony Byworth, *Country Music People*, April 1977.

Don: "always been solo": Interview with Alan Cackett, *Country Music People*, April 1978.

Albert Lee joins Sundance Saloon band: Watts, *Country Boy*, and Ken Sharp interview with Albert Lee, *Rock Cellar*, December 9, 2015.

Jimmy Eaton on Sundance scene: Author interview with Jimmy Eaton.

Buddy Emmons on Don's parties; Sundance stand with Don, then Phil: Steve Fishell, *Buddy Emmons: Steel Guitar Icon*, 132–134.

Albert Lee on Colton and Sunset Towers *sessions:* R. White, 115.

Don on Sunset Tower sessions: Interview with Alan Cackett, and unpublished interview with Robert K. Oermann, September 4, 1990.

Albert on tour with Joe Cocker: Watts, 131.

Lindsay Buckingham in band: In Morrison, *Mirror in the Sky*, 33; also quoted in *Rock Family Trees*, 1977, and *The Source*, 1981.

Exit/In show: Crystal Zevon and Eddie Ponder in Zevon, 79–80.

Warren Zevon on Don's guitar: In *The Life and Times of the Everly Brothers*, Nashville Network documentary, 1996.

Don on taking a break: Interview with Walter Carter. *On Los Angeles rejecting him:* Interviews with Robert K. Oermann and Patrick Anderson.

Don on performing under the radar: Interview with Stan Sayer.

Del Bryant on the "Cathy's Clown" clash start: Author interview with Del Bryant.

Don's reported 1975 letter: Brian Murphy, Frankfurt Kurnit Klein + Selz, *Advertising Law Updates*, July 6, 2020.

Ike Everly death: Obituaries, *Courier-Journal* (Lousville, KY) and UPI, *New York Times*, October 24, 1975. *Guitar on the sofa:* Margaret Everly, CMF Oral History, January 22, 1990.

Funeral grief and Ted Everly comment: Karpp, 159–160.

Phil on meeting Don: Interview with Joe Smith.

Don on "avant garde country music": Interview with Tony Byworth. *"Modern country singer":* Interview with Stan Sayer.

Don on working with Wesley Rose again: Interview with Tony Byworth. *Brother Juke-Box sessions:* Interview with Alan Cackett.

Jim Rooney meets Don: Rooney in *In It for the Long Run*, part 2.

Don at Wembley April 1977: Recording of the performance per AP reporter review/interview, *Greensboro (NC) Record*, May 12,1977; Karl Dallas, *Melody Maker*, April 16, 1977, 9; Don Everly interview with Tony Byworth.

Robbins tour's too many oldies: Alan Cackett, *Country Music People*, June 1978.

Buddy Holly Week: Reports by Trudy Anderson, posted on the Paul McCartney Project website; *New Hi-Fi Sound*, October 1985; Watts, 164; and video of event.

Don meeting Dave Edmunds: Interview with Robert K. Oermann, 1988.

Pat Alger on Brown's: Author interview with Pat Alger.

Founding of the Dead Cowboys: Author interviews with Jim Rooney, Pat Alger, and Robert K. Oermann; Jim Rooney in *In It for the Long Run*, part 2, and Robert K. Oermann, *Nashville Gazette*, July 1980.

John Prine, Brown's: His interview with Patrick Doyle, "Inside the Life of John Prine," *Rolling Stone*, January 4, 2017.

1980 European tour: Tony Byworth, *Billboard World of Country Music* supplement, October 1980, 34; video news clips of the Dead Cowboys tour and audio of the Venue show, UK (courtesy EverlyNet); John Firminger, review, *Country Song RoundUp UK*, September 1980.

Don on Polydor single: His interview with Robert K. Oermann, 1990.

Albert on Don not coming to Los Angeles: Watts, 170.

"Cathy's Clown" legal agreement and battle: Casetext, *Everly v. Everly* case summary.

Don: "miss the other person": Interview with Scott Isler, *Rolling Stone*, May 9, 1986.

Roberto Bianco: Dave Paulson, *Tennessean*, October 17, 2018, and John Nova Lomax, "Remembering Don Everly," *Ruckus*, August 23, 2021.

Diane Craig arrival: Author interview with Diane Craig.

Karen Prettyman Everly's later life: Robert K. Oermann, *Tennessean*, March 15, 1984; *Tennessean* report, June 4, 1987; Karen Prettyman obituary, *Journal Star* (Lincoln, NE), September 5, 1997.

Don: "tend to blame": Scott Isler, *Country Music*, July 1986, 44.

Chapter Eleven: Phil 1973–1982

Phil's cars: Jason Everly on the Fabulous Phil Everly Facebook page, August 18, 2023.

Phil on "watching television": Interview with Julie Webb, *New Musical Express*, August 31, 1974.

Jason Everly on his dad in the 1970s: Interview with Patrick Doyle, *Rolling Stone*, January 6, 2014.

Phil on Duane Eddy as producer: Interview with Peter O'Brien, *Omaha Rainbow* (UK), Summer 1981.

Phil nixes "Air That I Breathe" single: R. White, 124. *Hollies recording:* Southall, 152.

Bud Scoppa on Star Spangled Springer: *Rolling Stone* review, August 2, 1973.

Phil on In Session: Interview with James Brown, *Los Angeles Times*, January 3, 1974.

Everly-Sebastian-George supergroup: Fong-Torres, *Willin': The Story of Little Feat*, 81; Richie Unterberger, liner notes, Collectors Choice reissue of Sebastian's *Tarzana Kid*.

Phil suggests "Werewolves of London": Roy Marinell and Waddy Wachtel in Zevon, 69–73; Warren Zevon interview with Steve Roeser, *Goldmine*, January 8, 1995.

Phil in London: Interview with Julie Webb; interview with John Blake, *Evening News* (UK), August 28, 1974.

Solo Palomino show: R. White, 128, and Heide Ploen report on show, EverlyNet.

McCartney party: United Press International, "McCartneys Throw a Bash," March 26, 1975.

Phil on being more personally involved with songs: Interview with Peter O'Brien.

Phil: "never really were an effort": Interview with Joe Smith. *"Busy running around":* Interview with John Tobler, 1983, at Rock's Backpages (online); *"More abstract":* Interview with Nancy Anderson, Copley News Service, *Tennessean*, November 4, 1979.

Sam Trust and royalties owed: Author interview with Sam Trust, and Trust, *Would You Trust This Man with Your Songs?*

Not seeing parents: Interview with Julie Webb.

Quick Palomino return: Richard Cromelin, *Los Angeles Times*, August 1975, and Art Fein, *Los Angeles Free Press*, March 28, 1975.

Phil on divorce from Patricia and performance break: Interview with Peter O'Brien.

Phil moves to Burbank: Preston Bealle on Everly Brothers International's Facebook page, June 24, 2017.

Don call on Phil's birthday: Don Everly interview with Patrick Carr, *Country Music*, November 1986.

Dean Reed Show appearance: Nadelson; Will Roberts's documentary *American Rebel: The Dean Reed Story*, and the UK *Arena* documentary *The Incredible Case of Comrade Rockstar*.

Phil on hearing Don from Wembley and keeping "loose situation": Interview with Peter O'Brien.

Don's claim of not following Phil's records: Unpublished interview with Robert K. Oermann, 1988.

Phil on Don burdens and talent: Interview with David Wigg, *Daily Express* (UK), May 15, 1981.

Emmylou Harris, George Harrison, Bruce Springsteen using Gibson J-200: Author interview with Paul Kennerley; Zanes, *Deliver Me from Nowhere*, chapter 11.

Warren Zevon on brothers: Interview with Dan Forte, *Musician*, August 1982, and in *The Life and Times of the Everly Brothers*.

Phil suggests an Albert Hall show: Interview with Peter Holt, *Standard* (London), November 9, 1982, and with Barry Knight, BBC Radio 2, November 27, 1982.

Chapter Twelve: Reunion 1983–1984

Phil on the phone call: Billboard, June 16, 1984. *Don on the call:* Interview with Steve Morse.

Don on missed relationship: Interview with Robert Hilburn, *Los Angeles Times*, September 1984.

Phil on big hug and hanging out: Interview with Associated Press, July 1, 1983, and with Albert Watson, *Press and Journal* (Aberdeen, Scotland), September 22, 1983.

"Ike Everly model" guitar: Jim Hatlo, "On the Beat," *Frets*, April 1988; Karpp, 176–179; Jason Everly, Cleartone Strings Facebook page, April 12, 2018.

Don and Phil get together, make plans: Author interview with Diane Craig.

Sam Trust and back Warner royalties: Author interview with Sam Trust.

Before reunion show preparations: Don Everly interview with Richard Harrington, *Washington Post*, January 22, 1984, and with Ed Blanche, Associated Press, September 20, 1983.

Meeting in Nashville: Author interviews with Sam Trust and Diane Craig, and *Would You Trust This Man?*, chapter 48.

Reunion show plans: Associated Press, July 1, 1983; *Variety*, August 10, 1983; Don Everly interview with Albert Watson.

Albert Lee and Terry Slater describe London rehearsals: R. White, 137. *Dave Edmunds on after-rehearsal get-together:* Edmunds, "This Is My Story," in Yahoo online group Shakin' All Over.

Don on not worrying about his looks: Author interview with Robert K. Oermann.

Phil, pre–Albert Hall: Interview with Mike Mills, *What's On London*, November 22, 1985, and with Jim Jerome, *People*, January 24, 1984.

Royal Albert Hall concerts: As seen in *The Everly Brothers Reunion Concert* (Eagle Rock Entertainment/Delilah Films, 1983 and 2010), DVD, and video of the first show.

Don and Phil on show details: Interview with Patrick Carr, *Country Music*, November–December 1986, 43–46.

Don and Sam Trust: Author interview with Sam Trust.

Diane Craig observations after reunion show: Author interview with Diane Craig.

Margaret Everly press comments: Interview with Chuck Offenburger, *Des Moines Register* September 23, 1983, and with Associated Press, as in *Lafayette (IN) Journal and Courier*, August 4, 1983.

Concert reviews: Robin Denselow, *Guardian*, September 23, 1983; Ray Connolly, *Evening Standard*, September 23, 1983; Charles Clover, *Telegraph*, September 26, 1983.

European vacation: Author interview with Diane Craig.

Chapter Thirteen: Back at It 1984–1988

Calling Dave Edmunds: Interview with Edmunds, *New Sound*, October 1985, and Edmunds, "This Is My Story."

Don on choosing Edmunds: Unpublished portion of interview with Robert K. Oermann, 1988.

Phil on music videos: Interview with Cliff Radel, *Cincinnati Enquirer*, July 4, 1984.

Adding synthesizers: Interview with Larry Nager, *Cincinnati Post*, January 12, 1984.

Don and Diane listening to demos: Author interview with Diane Craig; Ray Connolly, liner notes, *EB 84*.

Dave Edmunds on songs received, adopted, and discarded: "This Is My Story."

Phil on "The Story of Me": Interview in Delilah Films/Cinemax *Album Flash* program on *EB 84*.

Pat Alger on "I'm Takin' My Time": Author interview with Pat Alger.

Paul Kennerley on "The First in Line": Author interview with Paul Kennerley.

Paul McCartney on "Wings of a Nightingale": Interview with Simon Potter, Music Box, European cable channel, 1984.

Don on "Wings" single: Interview with Steve Morse.

EB 84 sessions: Edmunds *New Sound* interview and "This Is My Story"; R. White, chapter 14; Albert Lee in Watts, chapter 11.

EB 84 reviews: Rich Kienzle, *Country Music*, January/February 1984, 52; Steve Simels, *Stereo Review*, December 1984.

California tour leg and Don's family: Dave Callens on EverlyNet, January 31, 2016.

Don on not taking chances, and kids: Interview with Jim Jerome.

Albert Lee on brothers touring again: Interview with Paul Freeman, Pop Culture Classics website, July 2012.

Pat Alger on becoming opening act: Author interview with Pat Alger.

1984 tour reviews: Geoffrey Himes, *Washington Post,* July 17, 1984; Robert Hilburn, *Los Angeles Times,* September 16, 1984; Mick Green, *Stage and Television Today,* November 8, 1984.

Appearance with Edan Everly, Lake Tahoe: Posts on EverlyNet, October 2019.

Don on earnings 1984: Unpublished interview segment with Robert K. Oermann, September 4, 1990.

Sailing lessons and potential boat purchase: Author interview with Diane Craig.

Phil on recording and their audiences: Interview with Dolf Ruesink, London, November 1985.

Diane and Don on "Born Yesterday" song: Author interview with Diane Craig; Don Everly interview with Patrick Carr.

Phil on "country at heart": Interview with Wayne Harada, *Honolulu Advertiser,* September 12, 1985, and with Gary Graff, *Detroit Free Press,* July 21, 1985.

Born Yesterday *reviews:* David Fricke, "Born Yesterday," *Rolling Stone,* February 27, 1986; Mikal Gilmore, *Los Angeles Herald Examiner,* February 8, 1986.

Phil unexcited by touring: Interview with Robert A. Martin, UPI, as in the *Fort Lauderdale News/Sun-Sentinel,* August 9, 1985.

Don on "strange" personal life: Interview with Kurt Loder.

Don "proud to be an Everly Brother": Interview with Scott Isler, *Rolling Stone,* May 8, 1986.

Phil on brotherhood and harmony: Interview with Jay Cocks, *Time,* March 17, 1986; comments compiled by Jean Penn, *Playboy,* January 1986; Don Everly interview with Jack Hurst, *Chicago Tribune,* August 3, 1986.

Margaret lawsuit: Associated Press, February 20, 1986; "Mother Sues Don Everly," *Tennessean,* February 19, 1986; Peter Holt, *Evening Standard,* February 1986; Susan Goldfarb, *Globe* (UK), March 18, 1986; author interview with Penny Campbell Loewen.

Pat Alger on tour buses: Author interview with Pat Alger.

Margaret in Golden Age of Radio Reunion show: Country Music Society of America member newsletter, in *Country Music,* 1986.

Don and Phil on writing memoirs and reaction to Margaret writing about them: Author interview with Martial Bekkers; Don Everly interview with Robert K. Oermann, September 4, 1990; author interview with Shawn Camp.

Shenandoah Homecoming week: Phil comments on WHO radio, transcribed in *Evening Sentinel* (Shenandoah, IA) Homecoming supplement, July 1986; columnist Chuck Offenburger, *Des Moines Register,* June 29, 1986; Associated Press report, as in *Herald* (Clinton, IA), July 7, 1986; Suzanne Muchnic, *Los Angeles Times* syndicate, July 25, 1986.

Nanci Griffith on Everlys: Interview with Bruce Honick, *National Examiner,* March 31, 1987.

Phil and Nanci: Author interview with Phil Kaufman.

Don on "many things happening": Interview with Sue Cumming, Knight-Ridder, September 29, 1986.

Tom Petty friendship with Phil: Catherine Walthall interview with Adria Petty, in "The Everly Brothers: A Family Business," *American Songwriter*, August 21, 2022.

"Selling themselves short": Don Waller, *Los Angeles Times*, October 3, 1986.

Don: "My part was self-indulgent": R. White, revised edition of *Walk Right Back*.

Goldmine review: William Robinson, *Goldmine*, March 10, 1989.

Chapter Fourteen: The Home Stretch 1988–2000

Emmons on joining band: Fishell, 175.

Tour commentary: June D. Bell, *Wilkes-Barre Times Leader*, August 13, 1987; Sandra Knipe, *Evansville Press*, August 29, 1997; Chris Lathrop, *Milwaukee Journal*, July 30, 1989; Marcy Bachman-Hartman, *Contra Costa Times*, October 2, 1986. *Apology for volume:* Steve Pick, *St. Louis Post-Dispatch*, October 10, 1988; Jill Warren, *Indianapolis Star*, July 31, 1988.

UK press and tensions: William Marshall, *Daily Mirror*, May 19, 1989; Mick Hamilton, *News of the World*, May 14, 1989.

Don on defying expectations: Interview with Stuart Coleman, BBC, 1994.

Updating well: Todd Everett, *Variety*, September 1, 1993.

Don on the band's importance: Interview with Paul Freeman, *Los Angeles Times*, January 1994.

Albert Lee on playing in the band: Interview with Ken Sharp, *Rock Cellar* online, December 9, 2015.

Central City Homecoming: Wire service reports, August–September 1988; Martha May, *Messenger* (Madisonville, KY), August 31, 1988, and report to the International Everly Brothers fan club by Chicagoan Bonnie Saltzman.

Phil on Kentucky coal mining: Interview with Martha May.

Sons' remoteness from Margaret: Author interview with Martial Bekkers.

Phil on the Everly Foundation: Interview with Thomas T. Ross, *Messenger-Inquirer* (Owensboro, KY), April 14, 1991.

Don "Important to me": Unpublished interview segment with Robert K. Oermann, October 1988. *Thumbpicking event:* Anderson, *That Muhlenberg Sound*, chapter 24.

The Session *Dublin show:* Jim Rooney, *In It for the Long Run*, and YouTube stream of the show.

David Schnaufer: Linda Paulus, *Pluck: The Extraordinary Life and Times of David Schnaufer* (n.p.: TLP LLC/Night Owl, 2021).

Don as rhythm guitar pioneer: Interview with Bill Bush, *Guitar Player*, September 1990.

Bringing It All Back Home *session:* Jim Rooney, *In It for the Long Run*; Mark O'Connor and Phillip King notes for 1991 BBC Enterprises CD set from the sessions and 1990 BBC documentary episodes.

Inviting Graham Nash to join in: Interview with *Weekend Edition*, NPR, April 9, 2016.

Phil on John Prine's The Missing Years: Author interview with Fiona Prine.

Don on Edan Everly and band: Unpublished interview segment with Robert K. Oermann, September 4, 1990.

Erin Everly and Axl Rose: Darcy in *Rocks Off*, December 2, 2022.

Jason Everly's No Ordinary Music: Polydor album notes. *Jason quoting Phil on "melody is easier":* Interview with Randy Lewis, *Los Angeles Times*, February 14, 1986.

Phil and Patti Arnold meeting: Patti Everly interview with Brad Schmitt, *Tennessean,* October 27, 2014.

Don on liking his life now: Audio interview with Chet Flippo, February 1, 1996, Country Music Hall of Fame archive.

Gang getting domesticated: Author interview with Fiona Prine.

Don on early life with Adela, and more music: Interview with Mike Boehm, *Los Angeles Times,* May 12, 1999.

Don's Kentucky inn purchase: KET-TV videos, and interview with Bob Alexander, *Tennessean,* February 14, 1999.

Everly Brothers return to the Ryman: Michael McCall, "Voices Carry," *Nashville Scene,* May 7, 1998.

Bye Bye Love *show:* Jim Patterson, Associated Press, May 9, 1998. *Margaret's reaction:* Author interview with Penny Campbell Loewen.

Phil/Patti wedding: Details from the UK fan club newsletter *The Beehive,* August 1999.

Phil's Columbia mansion: His bylined discussion in the *Wall Street Journal,* June 27, 2013.

Chapter Fifteen: Another Century 2001–2021

CMA Awards announcement: Transcript courtesy of Ken Fleming, Country Music Hall of Fame and Museum. *Del Bryant on Phil at awards:* Author interview with Del Bryant.

Everlys join, Louvins leave Opry *cast: Nashville Banner,* May 29, 1957.

Simon & Garfunkel tour: Associated Press news item, October 19, 2003; Jonathan Cohen, *Billboard,* October 26, 2004; the video *Old Friends: Live on Stage;* Paul Simon on the Everly Brothers, *Rolling Stone,* April 21, 2005.

Cleartone Strings: Phil's interview with *Guitar Player,* July 16, 2013, and with Vintage rock.com at NAAM convention, 2012; Dutch TV's *Star Children* episode on Jason and Phil, 2004, and the Cleartone Strings website.

Albert Lee on last shows and decision to call it quits: Interview with Paul Freeman, Pop Culture Classics website.

Graham Nash at Manchester: Fan audio of performance on EverlyNet and author interview with Graham Nash.

Last Albert Hall show report: Betty Clarke, *Guardian,* November 25, 2005.

Don on records, not writing: Interview with *Elmore,* November 1, 2011.

Vince Gill on Everlys: Interview with Chuck Dauphin, *Billboard,* January 17, 2014.

Phil in Columbia: Author interview with Pat Alger, and Bobby Tomberlin Facebook post. *Shawn Camp on writing and visiting with Phil:* Author interview with Shawn Camp.

Paul Kennerley on Don not playing, meeting Buddy Miller: Author interview with Paul Kennerley.

Patti Everly on COPD: Sara Malm, *Daily Mail Online,* October 28, 2014.

Phil living the "regular guy" life: Jason Everly interview with Howard Breuer, *People,* January 7, 2014; Patti Everly in Associated Press/*Daily Mail* report.

Jason Everly on late Phil and Don meetings: Interview with Patrick Doyle, *Rolling Stone,* January 6, 2014.

Duane Eddy on song written with Phil: Interview with Terry Roland, *No Depression,* July 19, 2015.

Phil in the Wall Street Journal: "Phil Everly's Tennessee Home," as told to Marc Myers, *Wall Street Journal*, June 27, 2013.

Art Garfunkel on Phil: David Browne, *Rolling Stone*, January 4, 2014.

Don on spiritual message, losing brother: Chris Talbott, Associated Press, January 5, 2014.

Memorial service: Described by Katy Nielsen, daughter of Everlys sound man Robert "Sparky" Nielsen, in her blog post "Phil Everly's Funeral."

Pre-Grammy Americana salute: Chris Willman, *Hollywood Reporter*, January 26, 2014, and Randy Lewis, *Los Angeles Times*, January 26, 2014.

Ann Marshall called by Don: Author interview with Ann Marshall.

Don statement on Rock Hall Music Masters week: Laura DeMarco, *Plain Dealer* (Cleveland), July 10, 2014.

Music Masters gala show: Chuck Yarborough, *Plain Dealer*, October 26, 2014, and video of the show finale.

Don on losing Phil: Interview with Mike Peterson, KMA Radio, January 29, 2016.

Don unrecognized at RCA Studio: Caroll Kruger, visitor, in email message to author.

Don unrecognized at supermarket and Margaret's circa 2010: Author interview with Brenna Davenport-Leigh.

Everly v. Everly *case:* Brian Murphy, Lexology, July 6, 2020, and Kathleen Lynch, McDermott Will & Emery blog, February 23, 2023.

Don appears with Paul Simon: Cindy Watts, *Tennessean*, June 21, 2018.

Adela Everly arrest: Report by WBBJ TV News (Jackson, TN), July 11, 2019, and case record.

Don spends time with Crickets: Author interview with Sonny Curtis.

Don at Musicians Hall Iconic Riff Award: Author interview with Jay McDowell and video of the event.

Margaret at one hundred: Author interviews with Martial Bekkers and Janet Bozeman.

Don eighty-first birthday dinner: Report by Stacie Griffin on EverlyNet.

Waving as they pass: Author interview with Paul Kennerley.

Don Everly's death and family statement: Kristin M. Hall, Associated Press; R.J. Smith, *Los Angeles Times*; Phillips-Robinson Funeral Home notice, Nashville, August 22, 2021, and Dave Paulson, *Tennessean*, August 24, 2021. Posts by Venetia Ember Everly and cousin Art Doss on EverlyNet, January 26, 2022.

British considerations: S. Mark Beaumont, *New Musical Express*, August 23, 2021; Alexis Petridis, *Guardian*, August 22, 2021.

Phil: "Our music is country at heart": Interview with Wayne Harada, *Honolulu Advertiser,* October 18, 1985.

Don: "We did our little share": His phone interview with Chet Flippo, February 1, 1997.

INDEX

"Abandoned Love," 306, 327

Acuff, Roy, 23, 25, 30, 48, 250, 264, 331

Acuff-Rose (music publisher)
  artists signed by, 48, 83, 116
  Everly Brothers, 48–51, 123, 133, 160,
    165–167, 172, 194, 252
  songwriters, 59, 103, 238

Adler, Lou, 137, 141, 224, 248, 251

"After I'm Gone," 343

Alger, Pat, 211, 261–265, 296, 302–304, 312,
    317, 320, 341

"All I Have to Do Is Dream"
  covers by other artists, 188, 210,
    316, 353
  influence on Beatles, 158
  live performances, 83, 109–110, 207, 338
  recordings, 63–64, 108
  reviews, 81
  TV performances, 80, 92, 111, 240, 282

Allison, Jerry "J.I."
  Crickets, 78–79, 91–93, 109, 261
  Everly Brothers friendship, 91, 117, 247,
    261, 350
  Everly Brothers recordings, 93–94,
    100–102, 165, 193
  songwriting, 93, 161

Allison, Joe, 45, 46

"All Right, Be That Way," 102

Allsup, Tommy, 92, 141, 144

"All We Really Want to Do," 229

Anka, Paul, 78, 84, 103

Armstrong, Billie Joe, xiii, 345

Arnold, Eddy, 58, 87, 98

Arnold, Patti (Phil's wife)
  meets Phil 329
  throws party for Phil, 332

marries Phil, 332–333
  life at three addresses, 341–343, 346
  Phil's CPD condition, 343

Asher, Peter, 61, 346, 347

the Association, 190, 227

Atkins, Chet
  Chet Atkins in Hollywood album, 101
  Everly Brothers Homecoming
    Festival, 325
  at Everly Brothers performances, 250, 332
  Everly Brothers recordings, 51, 52, 63,
    83, 93–94, 100, 102, 105, 107, 237–239
  Everly Brothers TV documentary, 300
  Grand Ole Opry, 38
  McCartney and, 251
  mentoring/connecting Everly Brothers,
    38–40, 42, 44, 47–48, 336, 350
  TV salute to, 323

Atkins, Leona (Mrs. Chet), 40, 42

Autry, Gene, 9, 11, 42, 43, 87

Avalon, Frank, 328

"Baby Bye-Oh," 159

"Baby What You Want Me to Do," 277

Bachman-Hartman, Marcy, 320–321

Baez, Joan, 189, 227, 252, 353

Bailes Brothers, 18, 19, 87

Baker, LaVern, 78, 84

"Ballad of a Teenage Queen," 323

Ballard, Victoria, 307–308, 314

the Band, 187, 188, 203, 206

"Barbara Allen," 11, 87, 292

Bare, Bobby, 160, 264

Barnes, Larry, 135, 276

Beach Boys, xiv, 24, 138, 156, 179,
    229, 316, 341

Bealle, Preston, 80–81
Beatles
  breakup, 215, 251
  clothing and hair, 153, 162, 165
  Everlys and, xiv, 157–159, 162, 166, 218
  girl group covers, 138
  releases, 145, 151, 179, 288
  songwriting capabilities, 166
  sound, 64, 113, 157–158, 172
  TV and radio appearances, 115, 162, 165
Beat 'n Soul (Everly Brothers album),
   172, 174–175
Beau Brummels, 193, 194, 201
"Be-Bop-a-Lula," 63, 83, 304
Bekkers, Martial, 173, 231, 232, 313,
   348–349, 351
Bell Sisters, 24
Bengston, Billy Al, 223
Bennett, Richard, 271
Bennett, Stephanie, 288, 300
Bennett, Tony, 23, 58
Berry, Chuck
  awards, 309, 331
  comeback, 186
  Everlys and, 79, 82, 90, 114, 172, 173, 326
  influence on Beach Boys, 156
  jailing of, 138
  releases, 34, 47, 61, 173
  songwriting, 93, 173
Bianco, Roberto (Robert Biles), 265–266
Biggest Show of Stars, 78–80, 84, 277
Bill Haley and the Comets, 34, 78
"Bird Dog," xv, 64–65, 111
Bishop, Paula, 25, 67–68
Black, Cilla, 175, 274
Blackhoff Boys, 14
"Black Mountain Stomp," 133
Blackwell, Chuck, 145, 147, 169
Blackwell, Ronald and Dewayne, 167
Blaine, Hal, 161, 193. *See also*
   Wrecking Crew
Blake, Peter, 303–304
Bleyer, Archie. *See also* Cadence Records
  Everly Brothers recordings, 62–63,
   65–67, 82–83, 89, 100–101, 103,
   105, 143
  Everly Brothers TV performances,
   54–55, 92
  Jacobson ("Dr. Feelgood") and, 125, 128
  LaRosa and, 74

  on musical preferences of teenagers, 72
  stepdaughter (*See* Ertel, Janet)
Blue Sky Boys, 88
"Bo Diddley," 261
Bolick, Earl and Bill, 88
Boone, Pat, 74, 82, 197
"Born Yesterday," 305
Born Yesterday (Everly Brothers album),
   304–307
Both Sides of an Evening (Everly Brothers
   album), 132, 135
"Bowling Green," 183–184, 190, 202
Boyet, Jeff, 332
Bramlett, Delaney and Bonnie, 228, 229
"Brand New Heartache," 243
Bringing It All Back Home (BBC
   documentary series), 327
The Brit-Everlys' Sound (compilation
   album), 112
Brother Jukebox (Don Everly album),
   257–259
Brown, James, 309
Browne, Jackson, 246, 273
Bryant, Boudleaux. *See also* Bryant,
   Boudleaux and Felice
  "All I Have to Do Is Dream," 63–64, 188
  "Bird Dog," 64–65
  death, 323
  "Devoted to You," 64
  "Don't Forget to Cry," 166
  drinking problem, 59, 143
  Everly (Don)'s drug use and, 143
  "Follow Me" (with Don Everly), 170
  "Honolulu," 166
  "Let's Think About *Living*," 116
  "Love Hurts," 114–115, 172
  as performer, 45, 53
  on songwriting as young-man's
   game, 166–167
Bryant, Boudleaux and Felice. *See also*
   Bryant, Boudleaux; Bryant, Felice
  "Always It's You," 115
  attending Don Everly show, 250
  background, 58–59
  "Bye Bye Love," 51, 52, 55, 58
  Everly Brothers awards ceremonies,
   277, 336
  as Everly Brothers surrogate parents, 62
  Everly Brothers TV documentary, 300
  Everlys and, 57–68

Lee (Brenda) friendship with, 54
"Like Strangers," 102, 104
"Love Hurts," 102, 172, 243
"Nashville Blues," 106
Nashville home as hub for artists, 60, 89–90
"Poor Jenny," 67
"Problems," 65
"Radio and TV," 115, 123
"Raining in My Heart," 91
"Rocky Top," 238
"Sleepless Nights," 102, 106, 243
"So How Come (No One Loves Me)," 115
songwriting credits, 254
"Take a Message to Mary," 66–67
"Wake Up Little Susie," 60–61, 351
"You're the One I Love," 166, 169
Bryant, Dane, 60, 66, 116
Bryant, Del, 51, 60, 62, 103, 116–117, 119, 143, 254, 337, 351
Bryant, Felice, 45, 64, 116. See also Bryant, Boudleaux and Felice
Buckingham, Lindsey, 250
"Burma Shave," 141
Burnette, Billy, 342
Burnette, Dorsey, 140
Burnette, Johnny, 140, 192
Burton, James, 165, 169, 181, 193, 202, 203, 240, 271
"Bye Bye Love"
　Bryants' songwriting, 51, 58
　covers by other artists, 114, 210, 251
　Don's solo career, 259, 261
　Everly Brothers recordings, 51–53, 83
　guitar riffs, 52–53, 251
　live performances, x, 55–56, 288, 338, 340, 347, 349
　Margaret Everly performing, 313
　media coverage, 71
　Phil's solo career, 280
　popularity, 55, 67, 69, 70, 74, 78, 110, 168, 336
　sound, 110, 180, 232
　TV performances, 75–76, 218, 226, 240, 323
Bye Bye Love (stage show), 332
Byrds, 170, 188, 193, 200, 209. See also Parsons, Gram

Cadence Records
　Everly Brothers contract, 46, 48–50, 100, 276–277
　Everly Brothers introduced to Great Britain, 92
　Everly Brothers recordings, 50–52, 63, 82–83, 85–89, 104, 106, 108, 219–220
　founding, 49
　LaRosa and, 74
　sales rumors, 85–86, 167
Cale, John, 157
Callender, Red, 145
Calliope Records, 131–133, 135, 145, 221, 276
Camp, Shawn, 341–343
Campbell, Archie, 293–294
Campbell, Glen. See also Wrecking Crew
　covering Everly Brothers songs, 184, 210, 221
　Everly Brothers recordings, 141, 144, 145, 161, 165, 175, 181, 193
　"Less of Me," 202
　Sundance Saloon performances, 246
　TV appearances, 169, 212, 217, 220
Cantor, Eddie, 275
Carlile, Brandi, 352–353
"Carolina in My Mind," 209
Carter, Anita, 40, 41–42, 45
Carter, June, 210, 226
Carter, Maybelle, 4, 30, 38, 42, 88, 226
Carter Family, 40, 88, 98, 217
Carter Sisters, 30, 38, 42
"Casey's Last Ride," 209
Cash, Johnny
　comeback, 98, 186
　influence of, 155
　Johnny Cash Museum, 350
　live performances, 55, 210
　peacetime army, 136
　recordings, 124, 160, 208, 297, 323
　TV shows and specials, 99, 212, 213, 215–222, 226–227, 267
Cash, Rosanne, 323, 342
Cash, Tommy, 226
"Cathy's Clown"
　covers by other artists, 308, 326
　dispute over writing credits, 106–107, 236, 254, 265, 281, 349
　Don's solo career, 259
　inspiration for, 32, 106

"Cathy's Clown" (*cont.*)
    live performances, 111, 292
    popularity, 102, 104, 106, 122, 336
    sophisticated song construction, 107–108
    US Library of Congress's National Recording Registry, 343–344
Central City, Kentucky, 323–325, 353
Chained to a Memory (Everly Brothers box set), 203
"Chains," 145
Chance, Floyd "Lightnin'," 52, 87
Chapin Sisters, 345–346
Charles, Ray
    "Bye Bye Love" cover, 114
    Everly Brothers covering songs of, 75, 83, 114, 170, 172
    hit records, 47, 76, 175
    Rock & Roll Hall of Fame, 309
    TV appearances, 187, 197
Chesnutt, Mark, 258
Chordettes (vocal pop group), 49, 92
Christmas with the Everly Brothers and the Boystown Choir (album), 146–147
Clark, Dick, 80, 107, 134–135
Clark, Guy, 260, 341–342
Clark, Roy, 227
Clarke, Allan, 110, 157, 180–181, 272. *See also* Hollies
Clarke, Michael, 190, 209
"Claudette," 83, 98
Cleartone Strings, 339
Clement, "Cowboy" Jack, 253, 262, 323, 325–326, 327, 341–342
Cline, Patsy, 54, 161, 225
Clooney, Rosemary, 131, 338
Clovers, 33, 34, 74, 83
Cobb, Walter, 4
Cochran, Eddie, 81, 82, 91, 112, 192
Coe, Catherine, 32, 106
Cohen, Leonard, 208
Cohen, Martin, 121–122
"Cold," 331
Cole, Kathy, 232–233
Coleman, Ron, 239, 246, 247
Collins, Howard, 101
Colton, Tony, 248–249, 250
Columbia Records, 4, 42–44, 154
Como, Perry, 72, 75–76, 80–81, 117

Conkling, Jim, 104–106, 119, 123
Conway, Gerry, 298
Cooder, Ry, 209, 225, 228, 346
Cooke, Sam, 84, 131, 169, 306, 309, 340
"Cornbread and Chitlings," 145
Country Music Hall of Fame, 48, 335–336
Craft, Paul, 258
Craig, Diane, 266–267, 287, 293, 294, 296, 302, 304–305, 307–308
Cramer, Floyd, 93, 230
Crandall, Eddie, 44–45
Cranham, Phil, 301, 319
Creedence Clearwater Revival, 156, 219. *See also* Fogerty, John and Tom
Crickets
    band members, 92–93, 94, 109, 247
    Buddy Holly's death, 92–93, 138
    Buddy Holly Week, 261
    Nashville's Musicians Hall of Fame, 341
    "Peggy Sue," 84, 91
    touring with Everly Brothers, 78–80, 84–85, 99, 109–111
Crosby, Bing, 11–12, 24, 113, 131, 135, 199, 331
Crosby, David, 181, 190, 228
Crosby, Stills & Nash, 181
Crosby and Nash, 228
Crowell, Rodney, 260, 346, 347
"Crying in the Rain," 138, 139, 140, 141, 147
"Cuckoo Bird," 209
Curtis, Manny, 101
Curtis, Sonny
    Buddy Holly Week, 261
    Crickets, 93, 109, 111
    on Don Everly's later life, 350
    Everly Brothers induction into Nashville Songwriters Hall of Fame, 337
    Everly Brothers recordings, 93–94, 100, 102, 146, 165, 193
    Everly Brothers tours, 171, 173
    military service, 117
    songwriting, 66, 109, 117, 161, 183, 341

Daley, Jack, 227
"Dare to Dream Again," 281–282, 284
"Darling Talk to Me," 102

A Date with the Everly Brothers (Chapin Sisters album), 345–346

A Date with the Everly Brothers (Everly Brothers album), 81, 112–116, 122

Davies, Ray and Dave, 157

Davis, Karl, 11, 88

Dead Cowboys, 262–264, 266, 325–326, 340

Dead Flowers (Edan album), 328

Dead Rock West, 346

"Deep Water," 48, 259

Delaney and Bonnie, 228, 229

Delmore Brothers, 18–19, 21, 24, *335*

DeShannon, Jackie, 82, 135, 159, 169, 203, 217

DeVito, Hank, 319–320

"Devoted to You," 64, 65, 100, 177

Dickens, Little Jimmy, 58, 59

Dickie Doo and the Don'ts, 134–135

Diddley, Bo
beat, 35, 65, 90
covers played by other bands, 114, 155
Everly Brothers Homecoming Festival, 325
influence on Don Everly, 35, 47, 52, 65, 76, 245, 251
tours and shows with Everly Brothers, 163, 326

Dillards (Rodney and Doug), 189–190, 210, 246, 259

DiMucci, Dion, 277

Dire Straits, 283, 306

Domino, Fats, 34, 78, 79, 86, 186, 309

Donnelly, Phil, 262–264, 266, 298, 301, 302, 325–326

"Don't Ask Me to Be Friends," 144, 146

"Don't Blame Me," 132, 137

"Don't Cha Know," 90

"Don't Forget to Cry," 166

"Don't Let Our Love Die," 327, 340

"Don't Say You Don't Love Me No More," 279

"Don't Worry Baby," 316, 317, 322

Douglas, Mike, 189

"Do What You Do Do Well," 226–227

"Down in the Bottom," 209

"Down in the Willow Garden," 86, 87–88, 210, 327

"Down South in New Orleans," 326

Drake, Pete, 307, 308

Drakely, Carol, 111

"Dream Baby," 282

"Dreamer," 281

"Dreaming," 262

Drifters, 33, 34, 78, 115

"The Drop Out," 165, 174

Durrill, John, 279, 316

Dylan, Bob
the Band, 187
Everly Brothers influence on, xiv, 61–62, 155, 188, 210, 221
Everly Brothers Park, Knoxville, Tennessee, 353
at Everly Brothers shows, 208
evolution of sound and image, 153–154, 188, 210, 252
Grammy Lifetime Achievement Award, 331
releases, 155, 179, 188, 207, 210
songwriting, 208, 243, 296, 306
Sundance Saloon performances, 246
Traveling Wilburys supergroup, 315

Eagles, 246, 247

Eastland, Jacqueline, 240

Eastwood, Clint, 279

Eaton, Jimmy, 247, 248

EB 84 (The Everly Brothers) (Everly Brothers reunion album), 295–299, 302

"Ebony Eyes," 116, 118, 123

Edan (band), 328

Eddy, Duane, 114, 240, 270–272, 325, 327, 341, 343

Edenton, Ray, 52, 53

Edmunds, Dave, 261, 290, 295–299, 304, 306

The Ed Sullivan Show (TV show), 74–75, 77, 80, 137, 139–140, 165, 227

E.E. Hack String Band, 4

Elgar, Sir Edward, 133

Elliott, Ron, 193, 194, 195, 201–202

Embry, Margaret Eva. *See* Everly, Margaret Eva Embry

Emmons, Buddy
Don's solo career, 246–247, 249, 257, 326
Everly Brothers albums, 228–229
Everly Brothers tours, 320, 322, 323
Everly's Lake Malone Inn, 331

Emmons, Buddy (*cont.*)
  Phil's solo career, 240, 248, 271
  Sundance Saloon house band, 246,
    247–248
"Empty Boxes," 194
Epstein, Brian, 157, 175
Ertel, Jackie
  dating Phil, 92, 104, 125, 135, 141
  divorce from Phil, 196, 213, 215–216,
    222, 271
  Everly Brothers tours, 162, 173–174
  marriage to Phil, 141, 150–151, 176–177,
    182, 196
  songwriting credits, 183–184
Ertel, Janet, 49, 92
Ethridge, Chris, 225, 228
Evans, Dale, 98–99
"Even If I Hold It in My Hand," 183
Everly, Anastasia Dawn "Stacy" (Don's
    daughter), 159–160, 162, 177, 196,
    223, 270
Everly, Charlie (Ike's brother), 3–4, 5
Everly, Christopher (Phil's son), 270, 315,
    324, 336
Everly, Don (Isaac Donald). *See also* Everly
    Brothers; *specific albums, people,
    and songs*
  acting career, 117–122
  on being "The Everly Brothers," x, 309
  birth, 8
  cars, 30, 70, 326
  childhood in Chicago, 10–14
  childhood performances, xi, 6, 12, 13,
    15–22, 24–26, 204
  childhood songwriting, 37–42
  children (*See* Everly, Anastasia Dawn
    "Stacy"; Everly, Edan Donald; Everly,
    Erin Invicta)
  on the Crickets, 79
  Dead Cowboys, 262–264, 266,
    325–326, 340
  death, 352–353
  draft concerns, 134
  drug use, 125, 128–129, 132, 140–141,
    143, 148–149, 197, 226
  Everly's Lake Malone Inn, 331
  fan frenzy, 81, 82
  fishing, 304, 331
  guitar riffs, 61–62, 65, 251, 350–351

guitars, 286–287, 291, 347–348
guitar skills, 13, 20, 255, 326–327,
  350–351
high school years, 30–42, 106
Ike's death, 255–256
Kentucky public TV appearances,
  330–331
knee operation, 342, 347
later life, 347–351
Malibu farm, 223–224, 236
Marine Corps Reserve, 136–140, 159,
  178, 190–191
marriages/girlfriends (*See* Ballard,
  Victoria; Craig, Diane; Everly, Mary
  Sue "Sue"; Garza, Adela; Marshall,
  Ann; Prettyman, Karen; Stevenson,
  Venetia; Tubb, Violet Elaine
  "Scooter Bill")
media image, 71–73, 76–77, 95–96, 97
musical influences on, 5, 18, 21, 23–24,
  33, 35, 76, 296
Nashville life, 252–267, 287, 305
philanthropy, 314, 323–325
Phil's death and, 345, 346, 347, 348
political views, 177, 189
pseudonyms, 133, 135, 138, 194
psychiatric treatment, 148–149, 150,
  159, 171
recording innovations, 113–114,
  132–133, 142, 159, 201
relationship with Margaret Everly, 46,
  54, 237, 250, 288, 301–302, 310–313,
  348–349, 351
semiretirement, 340–341, 343, 344
solo career, 41, 223–226, 228, 235, 239,
  244–268, 278, 281
suicide attempts, 147–148
Sundance Saloon house band, 246–248
on Vietnam War, 179
visiting family in Kentucky, 37
Everly, Edan Donald (Don's son), 196, 224,
  270, 301, 304, 328, 329, 341
Everly, Erin Invicta (Don's daughter), 176,
  177, 214–215, 270, 280, 328
Everly, Hattie (Ike's sister), 4, 216, 255
Everly, Isaac Milford, Jr. ("Ike") (father).
    See also Songs Our Daddy Taught Us
  Atkins (Chet) and, 38–39
  birth and childhood, 2–3

careers outside music, 3, 36, 38, 40, 47, 57–58, 70
Carolina Boys duo, 11
character traits, 96
Chicago musical career, 8–13, 88
death, 255–256, 277–278
electric guitar, 10, 13, 21
influence on Everly Brothers music, 11–14, 18, 19, 41, 205, 336
Knox County Knockabouts, 5–6
marriage, 6–8, 231–232
Nashville home, 62, 70, 311–312
National Barn Dance touring country road show, 9–10
performing with brothers, 3–4, 5
performing with Everly Brothers, 132, 210–212, 227, 230–233, 265, 287, 292
Phil's "no neck" worries, 31–32
picking fame, 128, 325, 330
Prine's grandfather and, 263
radio shows, xi, 14–17, 20–22, 26, 30, 32–33, 35–36
sons' weddings, 46, 150–151, 237
TV appearances, 189, 219, 222, 226
visiting family in Kentucky, 37
visits from Don and band, 250
Everly, Isaac Milford, Sr. (Ike's father), 3, 4
Everly, Jason. *See* Everly, Phillip Jason "Jason"
Everly, Karen. *See* Prettyman, Karen
Everly, Leonard (Ike's brother), 5, 255
Everly, Margaret Eva Embry (mother)
career as hair stylist, 36, 38, 40
character traits, 96, 301, 332
childhood, 6
death, 353
Everly Brothers fan clubs, 232–233, 256, 310–311, 348–349
at Everly Brothers performances, 73, 230–233
Everly Brothers reunion, 293–294
family radio shows, xi, 15–18, 21–22, 30, 32–33, 35–36, 189, 312–313
grandchildren, 124, 223–224, 310, 351
Holly (Buddy) funeral, 93
on Ike's career in Chicago, 10, 11
Ike's death, 255, 256
influence on Everly Brothers career, 12, 14, 18, 19, 22, 24–25, 38, 40, 205, 336

Iowa years, 14–17
later life, 348–349, 351
marriage, 6–8, 231–232
memoirs (proposed), 312–313
Nashville home, 62, 70, 288, 301–302, 311–312
relationship with Don, 46, 54, 237, 250, 288, 301–302, 310–313, 348–349, 351
relationship with Phil, 150–151, 237, 310–313
songwriting, 260
on sons' adolescent years, 24, 31–32
visiting family in Kentucky, 37
Everly, Mary (Don's daughter), 77, 214–215
Everly, Mary Sue "Sue" (Don's wife)
children, 3, 77, 97, 124
death, 124
divorce from Don, 123–124, 130, 266–267
marriage to Don, 46–47, 62, 71, 82, 92, 97, 108
marriage to Glenn Tubb, 124
media image, 73, 97
Everly, Phil. *See also* Everly Brothers; *specific albums, people, and songs*
acting career, 117–122, 279
on being "The Everly Brothers," x
birth, 10–11
BMI award, 277
cars, 30, 70, 96, 269, 326
childhood in Chicago, 10–14
childhood performances, xi, 6, 15–22, 24, 30–33, 35–36, 204
children (*See* Everly, Christopher; Everly, Phillip Jason "Jason")
Cleartone Strings, 339
death, 344–345, 348
draft concerns, 134, 136
drug use, 125, 128–129, 132, 140–141, 197
grandchildren, 342
health issues (COPD), 342–343, 344, 345
high school years, 30–37, 41, 46, 60
homes, 62, 70, 333, 341, 344
"Ike Everly model" guitars, 286–287, 291
Ike's death, 255, 277–278
Marine Corps Reserve, 136–140, 150, 159, 178, 190

Everly, Phil. (*cont.*)
marriages/girlfriends (*See* DeShannon,
Jackie; Ertel, Jackie; Everly, Patti;
Farmer, Mimsy; Griffith, Nanci;
Hebel, Virginia; Marshall, Ann;
Mickey, Patricia Louise; Taylor, Jana)
media image, 71–73, 76–78, 95–96
musical influences on, 5, 12–13, 18, 21,
23–24, 33
philanthropy, 314, 323–325
political views, 176, 271–272, 280
pseudonyms, 135, 138, 194
relationship with Margaret Everly,
150–151, 237, 310–313
semiretirement, 340–344
sixtieth birthday, 332
solo career, 41, 224, 228, 235, 240,
269–284
visiting family in Kentucky, 37
Everly, Phillip Jason "Jason" (Phil's son),
182, 214, 270, 286–287, 301, 329, 336,
339, 343
Everly, Roland (Ike's brother), 300
Everly, Stacy. *See* Everly, Anastasia
Dawn "Stacy"
Everly, Ted (cousin), 255, 300, 324
Everly, Venetia Ember (Don's daughter),
77, 97, 124, 214–215, 255, 310, 336, 351
*The Everly Brothers: Songs of Innocence and
Experience* (TV documentary), 300
The Everly Brothers (album), 82–83
Everly Brothers Childhood Home
museum, Shenandoah, Iowa, 21, 353
Everly Brothers (Don and Phil). *See also
specific albums, labels, people, and songs*
awards and honors, 308–310, 315, 331,
335–338, 346–347
breakup, 241–244
Bryants and, 57–68
clothing and hair, 74, 75, 127, 165,
177, 217–218
fan clubs, 173, 176, 231, 232
fan frenzy, 81–82
fans demanding oldies, 153–154,
170–171, 197, 206
guitars, 143–144, 286–287, 291
managers (*See* Crandall, Eddie; Daley,
Jack; Rael, Jack; Rose, Wesley)
media image, xiii, 71–73, 76–78, 95–97

memorial sites, 353–354
recording innovations, 113–114,
132–133, 142, 159, 201, 203–204
reunion, 268, 284, 285–294, 302
road managers (*See* Rose, Lester;
Wayne, Don)
tensions, 25, 146, 161–163, 191, 198,
212–214, 219, 235, 238, 241
tours and shows (1950s), 55–56, 69,
78–80, 84, 92, 99
tours and shows (1960s), 108–112,
134–136, 145–150, 162–163, 170–171,
173–175, 177–179, 182, 189–191,
195–201, 206–208, 210–212, 265
tours and shows (1970s), 212–213, 223,
227–233, 235–236, 239–243
tours and shows (1980s), 287–294,
301–304, 307, 312–315, 326
tours and shows (1988–2000), 319–323,
332, 338–340
tribute albums, 345–346
TV appearances (1950s), 73–77, 80–81,
92, 99, 140
TV appearances (1960s), 110–111,
127–128, 137, 139–140, 168–170,
186–187, 189, 196–200
TV appearances (1970s), 212, 213,
215–219, 221–222, 226–227, 236,
239–240
TV appearances (1980s), 316, 323
TV documentaries, 300, 327
The Everly Brothers (*EB 84*) (Everly
Brothers reunion album),
295–299, 302
Everly Brothers (Ike, Charlie, Leonard),
5, 25
The Everly Brothers' Original Greatest Hits
(album), 220
The Everly Brothers' Rock 'n' Roll Odyssey
(TV documentary), 300
The Everly Brothers Show (album), 213
The Everly Brothers Sing (album), 190
The Everly Brothers Sing Great Country Hits
(album), 160–161, 189
Everly Family radio show, xi, 17–18,
21–23, 30–33, 35–36, 189, 205, 340
Everly Foundation, 325
Everly's Lake Malone Inn, 331
Everly v. Everly (2017), 349

"Every Time You Leave," 260

Every Which Way but Loose (movie), 279

The Fabulous Style of the Everly Brothers
(album), 108

Farmer, Mimsy, 120, 135

"February 15th," 225

Felder, Don, 246

"The Ferris Wheel," 167–168

"The First in Line," 297, 299

Flatt and Scruggs, 98, 160

Fleetwood Mac, 236, 250, 283

Flying Burrito Brothers, 209, 225

Fogerty, John and Tom, 155–156. *See also*
Creedence Clearwater Revival

Folk Songs by the Everly Brothers
(album), 143

"Follow Me," 170

Ford, Tennessee Ernie, 30, 127–128

Ford, Whitey, 10

Foreverly (Norah Jones-Billie Joe
Armstrong album), 345

Four Tops, 182, 350

Freed, Alan, 69, 80, 83, 118, 139, 309

Frey, Glenn, 246

Frizzell, Lefty, 23, 37, 42, 257

Galbraith, Barry, 101

Garfunkel, Art, 154, 338, 344. *See also*
Simon & Garfunkel

Garland, Hank, 23, 131, 132

Garrett, Snuff, 279

Garza, Adela, 330, 340, 347, 349–350,
351, 352

Garza, Adelaida, 330, 340, 349, 351

Gavin, Peter, 247, 248–249

"Gee, but It's Lonely," 82

Gentry, Bobbie, xiii, 198, 202, 210, 221

George, Lowell, 273

Gerry and the Pacemakers, 170

Giblin, John, 298

Gibson, Don, 30, 63, 160, 161, 225, 256–259

Gibson (guitar company), 144, 282,
286–287, 291, 347

Gill, Vince, 297, 336, 341, 347

Gimble, Johnny, 237

Giordano, Lou, 90

"(Girls, Girls, Girls) Made to Love," 114

"Give Me a Future," 47, 52

"Give Peace a Chance," 213, 218, 271

Glasser, Dick, 179, 180

Godfrey, Arthur, 49

Goebel, George (George Gobel), 10, 99

Goffin, Gerry, 138, 141, 142, 144–145, 146

Golden Hits of the Everly Brothers
(album), 144

Gone, Gone, Gone (Everly Brothers
album), 172

"Gone, Gone, Gone," 168, 169–170, 174

"Good Golly, Miss Molly," 262, 326

"Good Hearted Woman," 238, 239

Gordon, Jim, 163, 164, 165, 173

Graceland (Paul Simon album), 308

"Grand Canyon Suite" (semiclassical
piece), 106, 107

Grand Ole Opry. See also Ryman
Auditorium, Nashville
Don's solo career, 259
Everly Brothers' appearances, 70, 83,
97, 118, 337
Everly Brothers childhood ambitions,
18–19, 21, 55
Everly Brothers in *Friday Night Frolics*,
55–56
Everly Brothers in tent show, 53–54
longevity, 36
Louvin Brothers, 337
National Barn Dance comparisons, 9
national broadcasts, 11

Greenfield, Howard, 138

Green River Valley Boys, 20–21

Griffith, Nanci, 314–315, 323

Griffiths, Mark, 289

Gunnels, Gene, 230, 239

Guns N' Roses, 328

Guthrie, Arlo, 210, 217

Guthrie, Woody, 218, 229

Haden, Charlie, 17, 346

Haden Triplets, 17, 346

Haggard, Merle, 202, 203, 232, 247

Haley, Bill, 34, 78

Hall, Tom T., 338

Hammond, Albert, 272

Hank Penny's Radio Cowboys, 53

Hanseroth, Phil and Tim, 353

Hardin, Glen D., 145, 169, 319

"Hard Luck Story," 183

Harlan, Bill, 20–21, 34
Harman, Buddy, 52, 107
Harris, Emmylou
    Everly Brothers and, xiii, 243, 259,
        260, 282, 347
    guitar, 282
    Hot Band, 319
    Kennerly and, 297
    Parsons and, 243, 342
    signing with Warner Bros., 195
Harrison, George, 110, 157–158, 188, 251,
        282, 286, 303, 315. *See also* Beatles
Hartford, John, 190, 198, 210, 246, 331
"Hasten Down the Wind," 230, 251
Hazelwood, Mike, 272
Heads Hands & Feet, 247, 248
Hebel, Virginia, 91
"Helpless When You're Gone," 249, 250
Hendrix, Jimi, 192, 227
"Here We Are Again," 40
"He Stopped Loving Her Today," 322
"Hey Doll Baby," 74, 83
Hiatt, John, 317
Hicks, Tony, 180–181
Higgins, Joe, 216
"Hi-Lili, Hi-Lo," 132, 135
Hill, Lamar, 262
Hillman, Bill, 313
Hillman, Chris, 190, 209
The Hit Sound of the Everly Brothers
        (album), 181–182
Hodges, Eddie, 114
Hogan, Gerry, 298
Holley family, 93. *See also* Holly, Buddy
Hollies, 157, 175, 179–181, 240, 272
Hollingshead, Bill, 242–243
Holly, Buddy
    awards and honors, 309, 343
    Biggest Show of Stars, 78–80
    Buddy Holly Week, 261
    covers played by other bands, 155, 172
    death, 92–93, 138
    friendship with Everly Brothers, 79, 85,
        89–92, 93, 131
    manager, 44
    playing with Everly Brothers, 84–85,
        89–90
    recordings, 78, 84, 91, 101–102
    songwriting, 65, 90, 91, 93, 109, 238, 239

Holly, María Elena, 91, 93, 261, 343
"Honky Tonk Man," 247
"Honolulu," 166
Hopper, Dennis, 224
"Hound Dog," 36, 43
"How Can I Meet Her?," 142
Howlin' Wolf, 34, 169, 209
Hughey, Carlyle, 183
Huskey, Junior, 43

Ian & Sylvia, 188, 252
"I Can't Recall," 82
"I Can't Say Goodbye to You," 146
"If Her Love Isn't True," 43
Ike Everly Family (KMA radio program),
        17–18, 21–23
"Ike Everly model" guitars, 286–287, 291
"I Know Love," 306
"I'm Here to Get My Baby Out of Jail,"
        88, 143
"I'm Not Angry," 138, 139
"I'm on My Way Home Again," 209
"I'm Takin' My Time," 296, 302
Ingraham, Mary Suc. *See* Everly, Mary
        Sue "Sue"
Ink Spots, 12–13
"In My Room," 341
Instant Party (Everly Brothers album), 135,
        137–138
International Submarine Band, 188
"In the Good Old Days (When Times
        Were Bad)," 209
"In the Mood," 5
"I Saw the Light," 21, 33, 189
"It's All Over," 176
"It's Been a Long Dry Spell," 168
It's Everly Time! (Dead Rock West
        album), 346
It's Everly Time (Everly Brothers
        album), 108
"It's My Time," 194
"It's So Easy," 261
"It Takes a Lot o' Heart," 45
"I Wonder If I Care as Much,"
        50, 204–205

Jackson, Papa Charlie, 3–4
Jackson, Stonewall, 264
Jackson, Wanda, 45, 264

Jacobson, Max "Dr. Feelgood," 125, 128–129, 132, 138
Jagger, Mick, 164. *See also* Rolling Stones
Jardine, Al, 156
Jarvis, Graham, 289
Jenner, Martin, 289
Jennings, Waylon, 92, 160, 238, 267, 297
John, Elton (Reg Dwight), 180–181
Johnnie & Jack, 51, 58, 326
Johnson, Betty, 99
Jones, Alice DeArmond, 4
Jones, George, 54, 78, 194, 253, 260, 322
Jones, John Paul, 180–181
Jones, Kennedy, 4, 211, 325
Jones, Norah, xiii, 345
Joplin, Janis, 200, 227, 228

Karl & Harty, 11, 88
Karstein, Jimmy, 199
"Keep A'Lovin' Me," 43
Keestone Family Singers, 145
Keillor, Garrison, 326
Keller, Jack, 141, 142, 144, 146
Kennedy, John F., 125, 136, 150, 165, 167
Kennedy, Robert F., 177, 185
Kennerley, Paul, 290, 297, 343, 347–348
"Kentucky," 11, 88–89, 205, 226
King, Carole, 138, 139, 141, 144–145, 146, 249, 250, 353
Kingston Trio, 65, 99, 156
Kinman, Chip and Tony, 305
Kirshner, Don, 137–138, 141
Kleinow, Sneaky Pete, 225
Knechtel, Larry, 169
Knigge, Bob, 230
Knobloch, Fred, 317
Knopfler, Mark, 283, 296, 305–306, 323
Knox County Knockabouts, 5–6
Knoxville, Tennessee, 29–40, 353
Krauss, Alison, xiii, 347
Kristofferson, Kris, 209, 210, 229, 252, 273
Kukoff, Bernie, 217, 218, 219

"La Divorce," 271, 278
Laine, Denny, 261
LaRosa, Julius, 49, 74
"The Last Thing on My Mind," 215–216
Law, Don, 42–43
"Lay It Down," 238, 239

"Lay Lady Lay," 208, 296
"Leave My Woman Alone," 47, 83
Led Zeppelin, 180
Lee, Albert
  Buddy Holly Week, 261
  Don's solo career, 248–250, 259–261, 264, 281, 326
  Everly Brothers band, 288–291, 294, 298–299, 301, 302, 306, 319–320, 322–323, 339–340
  Everly Brothers tributes, 347, 353
  friendship with Everly Brothers, 247, 252, 264
  Kennerley and, 297
Lee, Brenda, 51, 54, 78, 217, 296
"Legend in My Time," 257–258
Leib, Marshall, 139, 145, 147, 173
Lennon, John, 47, 107–108, 110, 157–159, 213, 215, 218. *See also* Beatles
"Let It Be Me," xiii, 100–102, 108, 210, 218, 274, 336, 341
"Let's Put Our Hearts Together," 264
"Let's Think About *Living*," 116
Lewis, Jerry Lee, 78, 84–85, 138, 186, 253, 309, 326
"The Life I Have to Live," 45
"Lightning Express," 210
"Like Strangers," 102, 104, 106, 122
Linde, Dennis, 229, 234
"Lion and the Lamb," 277
"Little Hollywood Girl," 141
Little Richard
  on Beatles, 157–158
  comeback, 186
  covers played by other bands, 155, 170
  Everly Brothers recording songs of, 113, 114, 172
  hit records, 47
  Rock & Roll Hall of Fame, 309
  sexuality, 164
  spiritual calling, 138
  tours with Everly Brothers, 163
Living Alone (Phil Everly album), 279–280
Lloyd Webber, Andrew, 331
Locke, Sondra, 279
Locklin, Hank, 23, 160, 161
Loewen, Penny Campbell, 233, 311, 348
Londin, Larrie, 301, 317, 319–320, 323
"Long Time Gone," 87, 92

"Lord of the Manor," 193–194, 207
Loudermilk, John D., 116, 168, 194
Louise (Phil Everly album), 283
Louvin Brothers (Charlie and Ira), 63, 225, 260, 281, 335, 336–337
Love, Mike, 156
"Love Hurts," 102, 114–115, 172, 243, 292, 342
"Love Is Strange," 170, 174, 177
"Love of the Common People," 186
"Lover Goodbye," 279
"Love's Made a Fool of You," 90, 109
Lovett, Lyle, 326
Lowe, Mundell, 101
"Lucille," 113, 114, 122, 128, 169, 209, 303, 326
Lymon, Frankie, 78, 84
Lynn, Loretta, 259, 338
Lynne, Jeff, 296–297, 298, 315

Malone, Kenny, 257
Mamas & the Papas, 174, 224
"Mama Tried," 203, 226, 227
Mancini, Henry, 142
"Mandolin Wind," 230
Maness, J.D., 271
Mann, Manfred, 181
Marine Corps Reserve, 136–140, 150, 159, 178, 190–191
Marks, David, 229
Marshall, Ann, 140–141, 148, 214, 223–224, 231, 236–237, 267, 351
Martha and the Vandellas, 172–173
Martin, Dean, 131, 192, 226, 275
Martin, Troy, 42–43
Martine, Layng, Jr., 166–167
"Mary Jane," 182, 190, 197
Mauldin, Joe B., 78, 92, 93, 102, 109, 247, 261
May, Earl, 15, 313
"Maybe Baby," 90, 261
"Maybellene," 34, 47, 173
"Maybe Tomorrow," 70
McCartney, Linda, 275
McCartney, Paul. *See also* Beatles
    Buddy Holly Week, 261
    at Everly Brothers concerts, 110, 164
    Everly Brothers influence on, 157–158, 159, 251

"Ike Everly model" guitar, 286
    party aboard *Queen Mary*, 275
    Phil Everly's death, 344–345
    songwriting, 107–108, 215, 298, 299, 305
McCue, Sammy, 199, 239, 277
McDevitt, Ruth, 216
McDowell, Jay, 350
McEntire, Reba, xiii, 326
McGiveney, Maura, 127
McKnelly, Kevin, 283
McPhatter, Clyde, 33, 84
McVie, Christine, 236, 283
Medley, Bill, 217, 341
"Melodrama," 145
Melton, Bob, 247
Mercer, Johnny, 187
Mercury/PolyGram label, 294, 304–306, 316–317, 322
Mickey, Patricia Louise, 226, 237, 242, 270–271, 274, 277, 278, 316
Miller, Bob, 87
Miller, Buddy, 170, 343
Miller, Glenn, 5
Miller, Roger, 141, 217, 238
Mills Brothers, 12, 338
Milo Twins (Edwin and Edward Miolen), 18, 19
The Missing Years (John Prine album), 328
Mitchell, Joni, 195, 208, 210, 228, 275
Monroe, Bill, 4, 54, 78, 98, 210, 338
Morrison, Jim, 227
Motown, 138, 179, 182, 350
"Move Over Juanita," 260
Muldaur, Geoff, 228
"Muskrat," 132, 137, 226
"My Baby," 225
Myrick, Weldon, 237
Mystic Line (Phil Everly album), 275, 276

"Nancy's Minuet," 142, 159
Nash, Graham. *See also* Hollies
    attending Everly Brothers shows, 208, 228, 327–328
    Crosby, Stills & Nash, 181
    Everly Brothers influence on, 110, 157, 180
    Everly Brothers tributes, 347, 353
    performing with Everly Brothers, 327–328, 340

Phil Everly's death, 345
  songwriting, 180–181
"Nashville Blues," 106
Nashville Sound (TV special), 186–187
National Barn Dance (radio show),
  9–10, 59
Nelson, Ricky (Rick), xi, 81–82, 86, 118,
  134, 165, 186, 217
Nelson, Willie, 238
Neuwirth, Bob, 257–258
"Never Like This," 257
The New Album (Everly Brothers
  compilation), 194
Newbury, Mickey, 238, 259
Newman, Randy, 193, 205
Newman, Tony, 262
Newport Folk Festival (1969), 210–212, 261
Newton, Matt, 332
"Nice Guy," 144
"No Expectations," 326
"No One Can Make My Sunshine Smile,"
  145–146
No Ordinary Music (Jason Everly
  album), 329
"Not Fade Away," 65, 238, 239

Ode Records, 224, 248, 249, 251
Oermann, Robert K., 22, 263
O'Flynn, Liam, 306, 327
"Oh, What a Feeling," 93–94, 99–100, 258
Oh How Love Changes (Gibson-Thompson
  album), 256
"Oh So Many Years," 19, 87, 210
Oldham, Spooner, 225, 228
"Omaha," 225
"One Too Many Women in Your
  Life," 279
"On the Wings of a Nightingale," 298, 299
Orbison, Roy, 83, 98, 114–115, 138, 170,
  250, 282, 315
"Our Song," 154, 271–272
Owens, Buck, 160, 209, 247

Page, Jimmy, 180–181
Page, Patti, 80, 134
Paige, Joey
  on "Cathy's Clown" dispute, 265
  Everly Brothers tours, 134–135, 145, 147,
    149, 162–163

Marine Corps Reserve, 138–139, 150
  Phil Everly's solo years, 165, 279,
    280, 282
Palmer, Earl, 145, 240
"Paper Doll," 12
"Paradise," 238, 325
Parsons, Gene, 209, 227
Parsons, Gram, xiii, 188, 195, 209, 243, 342
Parton, Dolly, 30, 209
Pass the Chicken & Listen (Everly Brothers
  album), 237–239, 252
Paxton, Tom, 215–216
"Pay Day," 58
Payne, Tommy, 20
Peake, Don, 147, 162–163, 165
Pearl, Minnie, 99
Peer, Rachel, 262, 264, 325–326
Peer, Ralph, 49, 192
"Peggy Sue," 84, 91
"People Get Ready," 175
Peter, Paul and Mary, 143, 163, 192, 338
Peter & Gordon, 61, 157, 170, 346
Petty, Tom, 315
Phil Everly (album), 283
Phil Everly Memorial Fund, 345
Phillips, Michelle, 224, 351
Phillips, Sam, 253, 335, 336
*Phil's Diner (There's Nothing Too Good for My
  Baby)* (Phil Everly album), 275, 276
Pierce, Webb, 55
"Please Please Me," 151, 158
"Pomp and Circumstance (The
  Graduation Song)," 133
Pomus, Doc, 175
Ponder, Eddie, 250
"Poor Jenny," 67, 98
"Poor Little Fool," 81–82, 328
"Poor Poor Pitiful Me," 274
Porter, Bill, 100, 105–106, 107, 113–114, 115
Porter, Cole, 135, 217
Porter, Mike, 317
Potter, Dale, 43
Powers, Ann, 346
A Prairie Home Companion (public
  radio show), 326
Presley, Elvis
  on Blackwood Brothers, 17
  comeback, 186
  dating, 130

Presley, Elvis (*cont.*)
    Everly Brothers on, 76
    Everly Brothers recording songs of, 172
    fan encounters, 81
    Mother Maybelle and the Carter Sisters
      touring with, 42
    movie career, 118
    music publisher, 44
    peacetime army, 136
    recordings, 43, 115
    Rock & Roll Hall of Fame, 309
    TV appearances, 36, 201
"Pretty Flamingo," 181
Prettyman, Karen
    career, 236, 252, 267
    dating/marrying Don, 236, 241, 252,
      261, 264
    death, 267
    divorce from Don, 266–267
    as Don's personal manager, 236, 252
    Everly Brothers albums and, 238
    Ike Everly's death, 255
    Nashville life, 252, 258, 263–264,
      266–267
Price, Paton, 120–121, 123, 280
Price, Ray, 42, 194
"The Price of Love," 170, 177, 291
Pride, Charley, 264
Prine, Fiona, 328, 330
Prine, John
    Dead Cowboys, 263, 325–326
    Everly Brothers Homecoming
      Festival, 325
    honors, 353
    The Missing Years (album), 328
    songwriting, 238, 253, 314, 325
    TV appearances, 273
"Problems," 65, 80
Pruett, Sammy, 43, 131
Pye Records, 274–276

"Queen of '59," 277

"Radio and TV," 115, 123
Rael, Jack, 134, 148, 227
Rager, Mose, 4, 5, 40, 204, 300, 325
"Raining in My Heart," 261
Raitt, Bonnie, 346
RCA Victor/RCA Records

Bear Family releases, 344
Bell Sisters, 24
Don's songs (Anita Carter release), 40
Everly Brothers albums, 228–230,
    234–235, 237–239
Everly Brothers contract, 228, 235, 248
Everly Brothers singles, 50, 100, 107
Nashville studio, 50, 86–88, 100, 106,
    107, 348
Phil's solo album, 240, 270
rockabilly, 48
Reed, Dean, 121, 280
Reed, Jimmy, 277
Rich, Charlie, 172, 260
Rich, Dave, 47–48
Richard, Cliff, 283, 289
Richards, Keith, 61, 164, 227, 308, 341, 353.
    See also Rolling Stones
Richardson, J. P. "the Big Bopper," 92–93
Riddle, Lesley, 4
Ritalin, 128–129, 137, 140–141
Ritchie, Jean, 202, 338
Rivers, Johnny, 102, 167–168, 280, 281
Robbins, Marty, 42, 44, 173, 213, 217,
    240, 259
Robbins, Pig, 237, 257
Robertson, Robbie, 202–203
"Rockin' Alone in an Old Rockin' Chair,"
    11, 87
Rock 'n Soul (Everly Brothers album),
    172–173
Rockpile, 261
Rock & Roll Hall of Fame, 13, 308–310,
    346–347, 352–353
Rodgers, Jimmie, xv, 3, 14, 48, 203–204
Rogers, Roy, 98–99
Rolling Stones, 154, 163–165, 169, 170, 179,
    183, 219, 326. *See also* Jagger, Mick;
    Richards, Keith
Ronstadt, Linda, xiii, 217, 219, 243, 246,
    253–254, 277, 345
Rooney, Jim, 210, 258, 261–264, 315,
    325–327
Roots (Everly Brothers album), xv,
    194–195, 201–206, 221, 227, 229
Rose, Axl, 328
Rose, Fred, 48, 117, 259. *See also*
    Acuff-Rose
Rose, Lester, 117

Rose, Wesley. *See also* Acuff-Rose;
    Cadence Records
  control issues, 100, 102–104, 112–113,
    115–117, 119, 123, 133, 165–167, 260
  Don's solo career, 250, 256–257, 260
  Everly Brothers British tour,
    108–109, 111
  Everly Brothers demo record, 50–52
  as Everly Brothers manager-publicist,
    49, 76, 105, 123, 138
  Everly Brothers publicity, 76
  Holly and, 90
  signing Everly Brothers to Cadence
    Records, 48–50
  signing Orbison, 83
"Rose Connolly," 327
Rothchild, Paul, 228, 234
Royal Albert Hall, London, 232–233, 284,
    287–288, 340
Rugg, Hal, 237
Russell, Leon, 141, 145, 161, 169, 193. *See
    also* Wrecking Crew
Ryman Auditorium, Nashville, 44, 46,
    332. *See also Grand Ole Opry*

"Safari," 225
"Sally Sunshine," 82
Sebastian, John, 228, 229, 234, 235
Seeger, Pete, 180, 210
Shafer, Darlene (Mrs. Whitey), 257
Shafer, Whitey, 257, 258
Shaffer, Paul, 350
"Shake That Thing," 3–4
Sheeley, Sharon, 81–82, 112, 135,
    159, 169
Shenandoah, Iowa
  Everly Brothers Childhood Home
    museum, 21, 353
  Everly Brothers Homecoming, 312–314
  Everly family in, 15–18, 21–26
  Everly Family radio shows, 15–18, 20,
    21–23, 26, 205
Shepard, Jean (country star), 259
Sherman, Bobby, 169, 217
Shindig! (TV show), 168–170
Shore, Dinah, 98–99, 186–187
"Should We Tell Him," 50–51
Show of Stars, 78–80, 84, 277
Shultz, Arnold, 4, 211, 325

"Silver Haired Daddy of Mine," 11, 87,
    226–227, 284, 326
Simon, Paul, 154, 308, 338, 349, 350. *See
    also* Simon & Garfunkel
Simon & Garfunkel, xiv, 179, 208, 210,
    221, 329, 338, 353. *See also* Garfunkel,
    Art; Simon, Paul
Sinatra, Frank, 131, 192
Sinatra, Nancy, 192, 240–241
"Since You Broke My Heart," 102, 258–259
"Sing Me Back Home," 202, 232
Skaggs, Ricky, 350–351
Slater, Terry
  Everly Brothers recordings, 183, 193
  Everly Brothers reunion, 287–289
  Everly Brothers tours, 163, 171, 177–178,
    199, 200
  music publishing, 222, 276–277
  Phil's sixtieth birthday party, 332
  Phil's solo career, 240, 270–271, 274,
    276, 283
  songwriting credits, 183–184, 194, 209
  songwriting with Phil, 182–184, 190,
    234, 240, 270–271, 275, 283
"Sleepless Nights," 102, 106, 209, 243
Smith, Carl, 30, 42, 43, 58
Smith, Connie, xiii, 254
Smith, Hal, 47–48
Smith, Joe, 103, 191, 192, 201
Smith, Ray, 248–249
Smith, William, 183
Smothers Brothers (Tom and Dick),
    120–121, 198, 207, 213–214
Snow, Hank, 23, 99
Snyder, Glenn, 9
"So How Come (No One Loves Me)," 115
"So It Always Will Be," 159
Some Hearts...(Everly Brothers album),
    316–317
Songs from Bikini Atoll (Edan Everly
    album), 341
Songs Our Daddy Taught Us (Everly
    Brothers album), 19, 85–89, 143, 205,
    210, 284, 327, 345
"So Sad"
  covers by other artists, 210, 254–255,
    308, 326
  Don's solo career, 250, 258, 259, 264, 326
  Everly Brothers releases, 108, 122

"So Sad" (*cont.*)
  inspiration for, 123
  live performances, 321, 328, 340
  popularity, 102, 122, 123
  TV performances, 200
Spector, Phil, 51, 113, 139
Springfields, 160–161
Springsteen, Bruce, 282
Starr, Ringo, 157–158, 164. *See also* Beatles
Star Spangled Springer (Phil Everly album), 270–272
"Stay Close to Me," 90
Steinberg, David, 206–207, 302
Steinegger, Robert, 286
Steinman, Jim, 331
"Step It Up and Go," 210, 292
Stevenson, Venetia
  background, 130
  dating Don, 130, 136
  divorce from Don, 214–215, 221, 267
  Don's daughter named after, 77, 130
  Don's suicide attempts, 148, 150
  Everly Brothers tours, 162
  friendship with Ann Marshall, 223
  marriage to Don, 139–140, 162, 176, 177, 196
  meeting Don, 75
  pregnancies and childbirth, 147, 159–160, 175, 176, 196
Stewart, Rod, 230
Stills, Stephen, 181, 190, 309
Stirling, Don, 283
"Stories We Could Tell," 234, 235, 239, 273
Stories We Could Tell (Everly Brothers album), 228–229, 230, 234–235, 237
Strange, Billy, 161. *See also* Wrecking Crew
"String Along, Sing Along," 98–99
Stuart, Marty, 325–326
Stubbs, Levi, 182
Sullivan, Ed, 74–75, 77, 137, 139–140, 165, 227
Sullivan, Niki, 78, 93
"The Sun Keeps Shining," 43
Sunset Towers (Don Everly album), 247, 248–250, 251
"Susie Q," 156, 199–200
"Sweet Dreams," 63, 161, 225, 241

Sweetheart of the Rodeo (Byrds album), 188, 193
"Sweet Little Corrina," 341
"Sweet Southern Love," 282
Sylvester, Terry, 272

"Take a Message to Mary," 66–67, 98, 99, 108, 122, 143, 209, 210
"Talking to the Flowers," 182, 190, 197
Tarzana Kid (John Sebastian album), 228
Taylor, James, xiii, 209, 210, 249
"Temptation," 113, 115–116, 118
"T for Texas," xv, 203–204, 262, 304
"That'll Be the Day," 78, 173
"That Silver Haired Daddy of Mine," 11, 87, 226–227, 284, 326
"That's Old Fashioned," 142
"That's the Life I Have to Live," 43
There's Nothing Too Good for My Baby (Phil's Diner) (Phil Everly album), 275, 276
"These Shoes," 306
"Thinking It Over," 225
"This Little Girl of Mine," 75
Thomas, Gene, 238
Thompson, Bobby, 237
Thompson, Hank, 23, 99, 259
Thompson, Linda, 210
"Thou Shalt Not Steal," 39–40, 41–42
"('Til) I Kissed You," 93–94, 97, 99–100, 111, 259, 348
Tillis, Mel, 54, 113
"Tom Dooley," 65, 98
"Too Loose," 279
Townshend, Pete, 61, 322
Traveling Wilburys supergroup, 315
Travis, Merle
  Everly Brothers performing songs by, 22, 132, 204
  Ike Everly as mentor, 38, 210, 211
  Kentucky roots, 3, 4
  Oregon's centennial exposition, 99
  picking style, 4, 38, 325
Trotman, Lloyd, 101
"True Love," 135
Trust, Sam, 276–277, 287–288, 292
Tubb, Ernest, 45, 46, 99, 247, 306
Tubb, Justin, 45
Tubb, Violet Elaine "Scooter Bill," 45–46, 48

Tucker, Tanya, 277, 279
"Tumbling Tumbleweeds," 225, 262
Turner, Jesse Lee, 102
Two Yanks in England (Everly Brothers album), 179–181, 183, 190

Valens, Ritchie, 92–93
Valentino, Sal, 193, 201–202
Van Zandt, Townes, 253, 263, 330
Velvet Underground, 157, 183
The Very Best of the Everly Brothers (album), 167
Vietnam War, 140, 178–179, 185–186, 216
Vincent, Gene, 83, 112

Wachtel, Robert "Waddy," 230, 232, 239, 250, 274, 347
Wade, Pete, 237
Wagoner, Porter, 51, 58, 247
Wainwright, Loudon, III, 232
"Wake Up Little Susie"
  Everly Brothers recordings, 61, 72, 83, 351
  guitar riffs, 61–62, 155, 251, 350–351
  live performances, x, 200, 232, 322, 338
  lyrics, 60–61, 63
  popularity, 61, 62, 70
  TV performances, 75, 80, 200, 316, 323
Walker, Cas, 29–30, 35–36
"Walk Right Back," 117, 123, 127, 128, 138, 162, 259, 291
Walk Right Back with the Everlys (20 Golden Hits) (album), 255–256
"Wanted Man," 208
Ware, John, 246
Warner, Jack, 104–105
Warner Bros. (movie studio), 117–122
Warner Bros. Records. *See also* Calliope Records
  Both Sides of an Evening (Everly Brothers album), 132, 135
  A Date with the Everly Brothers (Everly Brothers album), 81, 112–116, 122
  Everly Brothers compilations, 170
  Everly Brothers contract, 104–105, 112, 135, 191–192, 215, 221
  The Everly Brothers Show (album), 213
  The Everly Brothers Sing (album), 190

The Everly Brothers Sing Great Country Hits (album), 160–161, 189
  Everly Brothers singles, 105–108, 117, 118, 122–123, 137–138, 141–142, 145–146, 209
  Everly Brothers tours, 173
  The Fabulous Style of the Everly Brothers (album), 108
  Peter, Paul and Mary, 143, 163, 192
  Reprise label, 192, 195
  Roots (Everly Brothers album), 201–202, 205, 206
  Two Yanks in England (Everly Brothers album), 179–181
  The Very Best of the Everly Brothers (album), 167
  Walk Right Back with the Everlys (album), 255–256
Warner Bros.-Seven Arts, 192–193
Waronker, Lenny, 192–193, 195, 201, 205
Waronker, Si, 192, 193
Wayne, Don, 158, 171–172, 178, 221, 230–232, 239, 242
Wells, Kitty, 39–40, 45, 114
"Werewolves of London" (Zevon single), 273–274
"What About Me," 144
What the Brothers Sang (Dawn McCarthy and Bonnie "Prince" Billy album), 346
"When I Stop Dreaming," 63, 225, 337
"When Will I Be Loved"
  covers by other artists, 188, 210, 253–254, 277
  Everly Brothers recordings, 102, 106, 108, 122
  Everly Brothers reunion concert, 292
  influence on other artists, 155, 164
  inspiration for, 104, 108
  Phil's solo career, 276, 280
  popularity, 102, 336
White, Clarence, 209, 228
Whitley, Keith, 258
the Who, 61, 64, 174, 190, 240
"Why Worry," 296, 305–306, 323
Wickham, Andy, 195, 201, 205
"Wild Boy," 169
Williams, Andy, 49, 92, 128, 167, 219–220
Williams, Audrey, 45, 69

Williams, Hank
  Everly Brothers playing songs by,
    33, 160
  influence on Everly Brothers, 21, 23,
    37–38, 50, 133, 245, 296
  memorial weekend, 69, 71
  Rose (Fred) and, 48
Williams, Hank, Jr., 267
Williams, Terry, 298
Wills, Bob, 42, 259
Wilson, Brian, 24, 156, 341, 353
Wilson, Carl, 24, 156
Wilson, Dennis, 24, 156
Wilson, Norro, 260
Winchester, Jesse, 184, 229
Wingfield, Pete, 289, 290, 291, 298, 301,
    303, 322
"Wishing Won't Make It So," 82
"The Words in Your Eyes," 276, 277
World War II, 11–12
Wrecking Crew, 161, 175, 181, 193, 350. *See
    also* Campbell, Glen; Russell, Leon

Yankovic, Frankie, 326
"Yesterday Just Passed My Way Again,"
    257, 264, 326
York Brothers, 18, 19, 87, 327
"You Can Bet," 82
"You Made This Love a Teardrop,"
    315, 323
Young, Faron, 63, 264
Young, Neil, 243, 309
Young, Reggie, 257, 258
"Your Cheatin' Heart," 226
"You're the One I Love," 166, 169
"You Send Me," 304, 306, 340

Zevon, Warren
  Don's solo career, 250–251, 274
  Everly Brothers recordings, 230
  Everly Brothers tours, 230, 233, 240–242
  "Frank and Jesse James," 251
  Phil's solo career, 239, 240, 250,
    270–272, 275–277, 284
  "Werewolves of London," 273–274